D1572225

NEW TOWN

San Diego Comes Of Age

By

Susan Goldbeck

Disclaimer

This book is a work of fiction based on true events and real people. Most of the historical figures in the book are listed on the next page as well as the actual places, which are marked with an asterisk to show the ones that are still in existence today.

The majority of the dialogue in the book is a product of the author's imagination. Some is based on the actual court transcript in the *Tingley vs. Times-Mirror* trial. Most of the names of witnesses at the trial are real.

The actions of the lawyers for each side were attributed to one lawyer. Some dates or days of the week are manipulated in small matters for the story's sake. Mr. Otis bought his war machine after this story takes place and was included as an illustration of his character. All other historical references are accurate.

The references to the actions of the San Diego Union-Tribune and the San Francisco Chronicle are entirely fictional.

Actual Historical Figures	Actual Historical Places
Katherine Tingley	*New Town
The Horribles	*Lomaland-Nazarene College
Bum, the City dog	Isis Theater
Harrison Gray Otis	*City Park (Now Balboa Park)
Samuel Shortridge	San Diego Carnegie Library
The Honorable E.S. Torrance	The Canary Cottage
J.W. "Judge" McKinley	* San Diego Union-Tribune
Ida Baily	* Los Angeles Times-Mirror
Wyatt Earp	San Francisco Chronicle
Alonso Horton	Tropical Natorium Bathhouse
Lydia Horton	Los Banos Bathhouse
Dr. Charlotte Baker	*San Diego Children's Home
Clara Shortridge Foltz	St. James Hotel
John Spreckles	Rabbitville
Lillie Spreckles	Horton House Hotel
Albert Spaulding	The Brewster Hotel
Kate Sessions	*Old Town
Samuel Parsons Jr.	* Stingaree (The Gaslamp)
George Marston	The Cribs
	*Hotel Del Coronado
	Tent City
	La Jolla Bathhouse
	Pacific Beach Race Track
	Railroad Coffee House
	Maison Dorĕ restaurant

"I thought San Diego must be heaven on earth...

It seemed to me the best spot for building a city I ever saw."

-Alonzo Horton, about his arrival in San Diego Bay, 1877

Dedication

I dedicate this book to my long-suffering editor, coach, and very patient friend, Evelynn Kahan.

Chapter 1

(February 8, 1902)

I sat on my bed in my nightgown, motionless, numb. Mother rushed into the dark room and opened the curtains letting the sunlight stream in. She laid a dark green dress on the bed. It was one of hers. "Get dressed; it's late."

She picked up the dress and helped me put it on. It hung over my shoulders, puffed out at the bust line, and dragged on the floor. It was at least a size too big. There was no time for alterations; it would have to do. Mother took a black sash off her dress and tied it around my waist, pulling the dress up under the belt to lift it off the floor.

Mother and I look alike, with red curly hair, green eyes, and a sprinkling of freckles across the nose, but we are not sized alike. She is four inches taller than my five-foot-two height and is fuller-figured.

Catching a glimpse of myself in the mirror across from my bed, I saw a pale, seventeen-year-old girl, shrunken inside a dark green, misshapen shell with its matching hat, which Mother had screwed down on my head, doing her best to capture my unruly curls. She rubbed the dust off my boots with her handkerchief and handed them to me. I sat back down and woodenly put them on.

"Hurry, Mary Kate, Hank is here to take us."

Following my mother down the stairs, I saw my father standing stone-faced at the front door. Looking out the window, I could see Mr. Moody driving his best black carriage which we would take to the church.

1

Hank Moody is a long-time family friend. He has provided our neighborhood with livery services for as long as I can remember. The normally cordial Hank Moody didn't greet us; he simply waited while Father helped us into the carriage and then got in, the pungent smell of whiskey and sweat following behind him.

Saint Patrick's, our parish church, was just short of a half a mile away. "Just a good stretch of the legs," Father often says when we walk together on Sunday for Mass. This time Mr. Moody took us. Nobody spoke on that ride.

Soon I could see the church ahead and hear its bells ringing. It's a Spanish-style church, much smaller than the Catholic cathedral on Third Avenue. As we drove up, I noticed the familiar alcove in the front with a statue of the smiling Virgin Mary spreading her hands out to welcome passersby. Mr. Moody stopped the carriage; Father helped us down. Silence.

As we started our long walk down the center aisle of the church, Mother held Father's arm and I walked behind them. Jack Flatly was sitting in the back on the aisle next to Henry Seymour. He is Father's best friend, his boss, and the publisher of the *San Diego Union* newspaper, where Father has worked for some twenty years. Babe, Henry's wife, sat at his side, patting her eyes with her handkerchief. I recognized many others from the paper in the back rows.

Jack was Father's protégé and is now a full-fledged reporter. He has worked at the *Union* for years, starting at age twelve as a newsie, selling papers on the street. He has had nearly every job at the paper since then. My brother Tim was Father's apprentice and Jack's best friend. *Jack should be walking with us.*

He'd become like a member of our family over the past two years and was a key part of our after-dinner festivities: telling tales, singing, and dancing. As Father passed by him, Jack stood up, reached for Father, and hugged him. He didn't respond. Jack's eyes were filled with tears when Father pulled away and marched toward the empty front pew marked FAMILY.

We were a few feet from the communion rail when I saw Tim. He was in his Sunday suit; it wasn't Sunday. He was sleeping, so peaceful. I took a few steps to stand beside him, reaching out to touch his face; he didn't stir. The mournful strains of the Requiem Mass that I had heard Mother sing so many times, filled the church. She was the soloist in the choir, but not today.

Father took a position near Tim's casket like a sentry at his post, soldier-stiff, staring out, face blank. Mother had shaved him that morning, but whiskey reddened his face, and his hair was oily and unruly. He had gone missing when we lost him just a few days ago.

Mother sat in a chair next to Tim just behind the pulpit. Her lips were moving in silent prayer, a rosary hanging from her hands, and tears running down her cheeks. Somehow her freckles looked misplaced on her blotched face with her red-rimmed eyes, inflamed by too many tears. Tim had a rosary clasped in his hands too. Too late now, I thought bitterly.

The church was full and very warm. I wished someone would open a window. The exotic, spicy scent of incense from ceremonies past, remained in the air. Two large sprays of raspberry-scented roses were placed at each end of the casket. This, combined with the sweet smell of the lilies around the tabernacle, was overpowering.

Beginning to retch, I bolted towards the side door but could only manage a few steps. I plopped down in the empty pew right in front of the pulpit, sweating, trying to hold down the nausea. I expected Mother and Father to join me, but they stayed with Tim.

We have no other family in the area. The closest is Gran, and there was not enough time for her to come down from San Francisco. Some of our family still lives on the East Coast, and others remained in Ireland, at least on my father's side.

3

I sat there for a long time wanting to be anywhere but there. Nobody was around to distract me, only an empty pew behind me, waiting for a family that wasn't around to fill it. As I sat there, the memories of the day we lost Tim washed over me like a strong, unexpected wave.

Wednesday morning was the last time I saw my brother. He was still asleep as I hurried down the hall, passing his bedroom which was the one next to mine. Our dog Lucy jumped from Tim's bed where she always slept, and followed me down the stairs, the tapping of her claws announcing her presence behind me. Mother told me at breakfast that Tim was staying home; he had a headache again today. This was not like him; he was never sick.

I made a little spending money taking care of those fractious Olsen twins on Wednesdays. Mrs. Olsen was an hour late that day. She may have missed the trolley, or it may have been full as it often was at that time of day. It was near suppertime when I started home and just about dark.

Not far from the Olsen's house, there is a large Chinese community, Chinatown, we call it. It extends from First Street to Fourth, between K and Market. It borders our neighborhood on its western end on First; Rabbitville, it's called by folks here.

My mouth watered as I walked a few blocks down First, the smell of Chinese cooking filled the air. Just ahead, I saw the familiar sight of a Chinese angler coming down the dusty, dry street with a pole balanced on his shoulders with a bucket of fish on each side. It must be about five-thirty; he was returning home from his daily fish sales. He looked down as I passed; the strong smell of fish was his only greeting.

Almost home, turning the corner on G Street, I saw our house in the distance. It's a two-story white saltbox trimmed in black, with a red door and mother's roses growing in the front yard, not yet in bloom. As I reached the porch steps, a cool gust of wind from the bay hit my face. It felt good. I sucked in the air with pleasure. It had the familiar smell of the sea, salty and a bit fishy. As I skipped up the steps, as usual, the top one creaked.

Pulling the door open, I was surprised that there was no music. Hmm... That's funny; Mother always has the gramophone playing while she fixes dinner. As I opened the door, I saw my mother and father sitting in the front room with Dr. Haskell. The looks on their faces and the rosary in Mother's hand told me something terrible had happened.

"Sit down with us, Mary Kate," Father said grimly. "It's Tim, darlin,' he's very sick."

Father's Irish brogue always thickens when he is under stress, even though he has lived in this country most of his life. Dr. Haskell explained that Tim had some kind of brain infection.

"It's serious. He has developed both a high fever and chills. He's asleep now; not much I can do. We'll just have to wait and see."

Dr. Haskell, who delivered Tim and me in our house less than two years apart, sat vigil at Tim's bedside most of that night. At about four o'clock in the morning, Tim slipped away.

We were in the front room when Dr. Haskell came in. "He's gone. I'm so sorry."

None of us moved. None of us spoke. I didn't even notice the doctor leaving. We just sat there frozen, dumbstruck.

"We can't know why God calls the people we love home" Father Hackett boomed from his pulpit. I jumped; his voice startled me and brought me back into the church. He continued booming. "Tim's death was God's will; we don't always understand the ways of God." Just stop, I thought, putting my hands over my ears.

5

Chapter 2

I don't remember much about the days after Tim's funeral; they were very dark days. Father was drinking heavily. My parents fought every night, always about "the drink." Father ate very little and rarely came out of my parent's bedroom. The smell of whiskey, sweat, and grief was what came out of that room.

Father refused to go to church. He never was much for "churchin', as he calls it, but he goes to Mass with us every Sunday to please Mother. Now there is a resentment of God growing in him. He is angry at the heavens for what he saw as the needless loss of his only son. I harbor some of those feelings myself.

Prayer is Mother's refuge; it always has been. She prays the rosary and cries in the darkness of their bed at night, trying to be the good soldier and keep the rest of us from falling apart. I heard Father shout at her one night, slurring his words, "Stop with the mumbo-jumbo, Maggie. It isn't going to bring our Tim back, is it?"

Me, I find some comfort in my journal. I had been writing in it daily since I was a young girl. After a few days of trying to come to terms with my loss, I began to read about the times I shared with my brother. Randomly opening up to an entry some ten years ago, I sat back in my chair, sighed, and remembered the day as if it were yesterday.

It was a Saturday. Tim was always flirting with the forbidden, and I was always game for one of his "ventures," as he liked to call them. One day he had a notion that we should go up to the Stingaree and have a look-see. He had suggested it many times before, but we always chickened out.

"Mother and Dad are off to the bathhouse today. This will give us plenty of time," he told me in a conspiratorial whisper on the porch.

The Stingaree was about three-quarters of a mile up a steep hill from our house. It is a long strip of brothels and gambling halls, mainly on the far end of Fifth Avenue, dead-ending at the wharf. It's the red-light district of the city, a place we were never to go. Its status as strictly *verboten* made the prospect of a trip there even more enticing.

The Stingaree got its handle from visiting sailors who named it after the unique species of stingray, equipped with an especially powerful sting, plentiful in San Diego Bay. "The sailors are going to get stung one way or the other," my father liked to joke.

Of course, respectable people in town had nothing to do with this neighborhood, which gave it particular appeal to kids looking for a bit of mischief. The Stingaree had the usual lure of forbidden fruit and was just a few long blocks up the hill. We knew that a trip there would be a notch on our guns with the rest of the kids; none of them had ever been there. We knew, of course, that we would never live to tell the tale if Father, or worse, Mother, found out that we had gone there.

A few months before, Eddie, one of the kids in our gang, told Tim and me that some of the Chinese ran opium dens in the Stingaree and had what they called "cribs." Part of Chinatown was on the border of the Stingaree. Eddie explained that the "China Dolls" sat outside near the cribs waiting to be selected. "Kinda like a display of fish at the market."

I turned to Tim. "I really want to see that."

"Me too," he replied.

Of course, I didn't know what this meant, but I wasn't going to sound dumb by asking Tim or Eddie. It sounded interesting, that was for sure.

All the kids knew that Wyatt Earp, the famous Tombstone, Arizona sheriff and gunslinger, now lives in San Diego and runs four gambling halls in the Stingaree. Father would tell us tales of Wyatt Earp's escapades whenever he ran across him around town. He was the town's biggest celebrity.

We had Tombstone-style shoot-outs in our own O.K. Corral, right here in Rabbitville, using the empty corral at Moody's. We took turns playing Wyatt Earp, Doc Holiday, and the other gunslingers that shot it out at the O.K. Corral that infamous day. We made wooden guns and slung them around our waists on gun belts made of strips of ripped-up old sheets. Needless to say, we were not too quick on the draw with this arrangement.

Every time the subject of going to the Stingaree came up, Tim would say, "Wouldn't it be fun to see Wyatt Earp through the window of one of his places?"

"But we don't know which ones are his or what he looks like," I told him.

"We can recognize him, I'm sure," Tim replied, although we had never seen Wyatt Earp, even in pictures. I figured Tim knew a way to identify him. He pretty much knew about everything that mattered to me.

At about noon, Father and Mother packed a picnic lunch in a basket and took off for the bathhouse. We watched them walk away and waited until they got down the street.

"Time to make our getaway," Tim said.

It was a little after one and quiet on Fifth Avenue when we got there, just the tinkling of someone playing the piano somewhere. It was nothing like we expected. It was hot that day, and we were dripping with sweat, our faces flushed from the walk up the hill. The heat appeared in ripples on the dusty street. A few horses were tied up in front of one of the gambling halls. I smelled the sweet scent of horse droppings, hot and baking in the sun. We were disappointed. Where was the wild, rowdy place we heard so much about, a gunfight in the street, a brawl maybe?

Tim looked through the large front window of the first gambling hall we came to. It was hung with dirty white curtains on the bottom half. I couldn't see anything. Tim was tall enough to see just fine. I picked up a brick that was helping to hold up a sign next to the window advertising the games played there: Keno, Poker, and Faro. I stood on it so I could see.

There were round tables with men playing cards, sitting with a few pretty ladies, all dolled up like they were at a party. A man was listlessly playing the piano on the right side of the room. A long wooden bar in front of a winding staircase was on the other side of the room, where the bartender was drying some glasses. A red-haired lady sat near him, playing solitaire. A painting of a naked woman resting on a bearskin rug hung over the bar.

"Never saw anything like that," Tim said.

A cowboy danced with one of the ladies in the space in front of the piano. She was blonde and dressed in red satin; she looked very pretty. He was very drunk, and he hung all over her. Before long, she squealed as the couple crumbled in a heap on the floor. This prompted the men at the card tables to roar with laughter and give a hearty cheer of approval.

The next thing I heard was the loud crash of the swinging half-doors hitting the wall next to us, flung open by a tall woman who stepped out on the wooden walkway where we were standing. It was the red-haired lady from the bar. We jumped back from the window, causing me to fall on my behind. I quickly recovered and stood at attention, without the brick, standing slightly behind Tim, my eyes wide.

I looked up at the lady. The strong scent of her perfume filled the air. She looked mad. Her hair was pulled back from her face and was crowned with two large black ostrich feathers. She wore a ruffled yellow satin dress that fell just below her knees; her legs were covered with black fishnet stockings, and one had a rip in the knee. Her cheeks and lips were rosy red; her ears sparkled with shiny black earrings.

"What are you kids doing here?" she shouted. "Git, go home! "

Before we could answer, let alone move, she yelled a lot louder, "Git, now, and don't come back!"

We took off and ran as fast as we could down the hill looking behind us from time to time to see if we were being followed. Tim told the story to Eddie and the gang over and over again for as long as I could remember, adding a few embellishments as time went on. I looked down at the last page I read, which ended with, "Shucks, we never even got to see Wyatt Earp."

I sat back in my chair and remembered that some years back, Mother and Babe went to see Henry and Father off at the train station. They were going to the long-awaited Hundred Round Fight on the border near Tijuana. Wyatt Earp was going to be the referee. Folks thought he was trustworthy because he was a former sheriff. Father had heard that he was going to take the train.

It seemed like the entire male population of San Diego had been siphoned off and boarded the train that day to attend the match. The rest of the citizenry was at the station to give them a proper send-off. We didn't see Wyatt Earp that day, either. He must have snuck onto the train because he didn't make an appearance before it left for Tijuana.

Father and Henry loved the horse races. They often saw Wyatt Earp at the racetrack in Pacific Beach. He won a racehorse named Otto Rex in a poker game. He was always at the track on Sundays when the large-purse races were run.

"Wyatt Earp is a funny fella'," Henry told us one day. "He never has any expression on his face when he drives his horse around that track in his little buggy. His face looks the same whether he is winning or losing."

Tim and I never did set eyeballs on Wyatt Earp. He left town a few years back after losing his stake speculating on San Diego real estate. Sighing and looking up from my journal, I felt a lump in my throat, tears running down my cheeks, thinking about what a wonderful brother I had lost.

As Tim's sidekick, I was always included in his "ventures," even though I'm a girl. The rest of the gang at first wanted no part of Tim's kid sister, but they tolerated me because of him. Of course, I did everything I could to act like anything but a girl, and mostly held my own, but my puny size didn't help much in that effort.

Over the past year, Tim's friends from the paper, Jack and Charlie, both a bit older, with their keen interest in young ladies and other pursuits that young men have, took Tim into a world that didn't include me, where I couldn't follow him, at least not yet. I missed him, but I understood.

Chapter 3

I had never seen my father drink. Mother told us that he quit drinking entirely after Tim was born some twenty years ago. Before that, he was a regular at Patrick's bar, just around the corner from the paper. He would go there every day after work with his cronies from the *Union*. Mother never said so, but apparently, his drinking got out of control.

One day Father stopped going to Patrick's. He never again drank in the house. I suspected that my mother had laid down the law after Tim was born. They never spoke of it, but we never saw either of our parents drink, nor did they serve alcoholic drinks to guests. My grandfather on my father's side "died of the drink," as my mother described it. Father never spoke about him. He died when they still lived in Ireland when Father was a boy.

There was a parade of people dropping by the house after Tim's death. Friends often came by when Mother was at church. Most left casseroles and other food. Even Mother's dressmaking customers had come by to pay their respects. She created dresses for some of the most prominent women in the city. They all left flowers that filled the front room with a sickening sweet fragrance. The flowers did not cheer. They were but a bitter reminder of why they were brought.

My father got used to eating Chinese cooking when he lived in San Francisco when he was a reporter for the *San Francisco Chronicle.* Chinese chow-chow houses, as they are called there, were some of the most popular eateries in the city. Chow-chow is a mixture of fresh vegetables and meat fried at high temperatures with exotic spices. The dish is a holdover from the gold rush days when there were often Chinese cooks at the mining camps. Some of those cooks made their way to San Francisco and now cook in the kitchens of some of the wealthiest families in the city.

There are no Chinese restaurants in San Diego. So, when my parents moved to Rabbitville, Father made friends with Li Wang, a cook in Chinatown. The Chinese fishermen often went to him for a hot meal after a long day on their fishing boats. Father went up there one day and asked him to prepare a Chinese dinner for us every Tuesday night. Li Wang could barely speak English, but somehow this was worked out.

Father would pick up the metal pails of food every Tuesday at five-thirty. Li Wang would cook what he had that day. Before long, he got to know our favorites and would make them for us. Eventually, when Tim and I got old enough, picking up the chow-chow became our job. Sometimes Father had the food delivered.

The Tuesday after Tim's death, Li Wang knocked on the door. Tim and I hadn't shown up as he expected to pick up Tuesday's dinner. I burst into tears when I opened the door and saw him there. He looked around and knew that something very wrong had happened. He didn't look at me, he put the pails of food on the doorstep and hurried away, not waiting to be paid. Standing there for a moment, I wondered if anything would ever be the same.

My best friend, Theodora, who lives down the street, helps out by cleaning our house every morning before she goes to her father's office where she works. She doesn't try to console me or talk to me. She knows that is not what I want, at least not yet.

Theodora felt the loss of Tim acutely. We all played together as children. Father built us a playhouse out back and furnished it with a little wooden kitchen that Mother painted. We had our meals on an old trunk with a stained tablecloth, using chipped dishes that Mother gave us. We often played house there. I was always the mother of our little family with a baby in my arms. Tim was the father;

Theodora was the horse. She loves horses. She was a horse that went inside our little house. That didn't seem at all unusual at the time, I thought with a smile.

Lately, Mother and I saw that the relationship between Theodora and Tim had gone beyond father and horse. We both felt that she and Tim would marry someday. Theodora is a kind, bright, beautiful young woman who is also very funny. She has big brown eyes and long, golden blond hair that she ties up in a ponytail, "like a palomino," she says. She has a beautiful smile complimented by deep dimples on each side.

She's much more of a girly girl than I am. She has become very interested in boys, always pointing out the pluses and minuses of one particular lad or another. Theodora had eyes for Tim very early on, I knew. Lately, he seemed to be looking back at her with those same eyes.

Father didn't come out of the bedroom to greet any visitor. The only friend he wanted to see was a bottle of whiskey. He didn't wash, shave, or even change his clothes. He started to stink.

After returning from church on Wednesday afternoon, one week after Tim's death, Mother checked in on Father, then peeked into my room where I was reading my journal.

"I'm going to do some hand-sewing on the porch; can I make you a cup of coffee?"

"No thank you, Mother."

There are four rockers on the porch. Would we remove one now? The rocking chairs were given to us by Gran when she came down from San Francisco to help Mother with Tim when he was born. He was her first grandchild. She wanted somewhere to rock him.

Gran didn't approve of my mother marrying my father. "She didn't think I was good enough for her. Just might have had something there," he'd often say with a chuckle and a squeeze of his bride's shoulders.

Mother is a marvelous singer who trained to sing at the San Francisco Opera and had good prospects of becoming an opera star. She abandoned that dream to become Father's wife and our mother. Gran naturally blamed Father for this. He told us that this stung Gran even more because she is also an excellent singer who had the same dream derailed by her own decision to marry and have children.

My father has a wonderful personality. He's smart, kind, generous, and good-natured. He is a big, burly Irishman— handsome, too, in a rough-and-tumble kind of way. Mother says he always had a way with the ladies. His disinterest in his clothing is apparent. Mother tries to spruce him up, but so far, with little success.

"I have enough clothes, Maggie." This includes two shirts and two pairs of pants that Mother keeps clean and in good repair. He has one Sunday suit that is a bit worse for wear and a bit too short. Father is tall and muscular. He has beautiful reddish brown hair, is clean-shaven, with big brown eyes and a touch of mischief in his smile.

He's a great storyteller. "It's in the blood," he says.

He is also an excellent singer, an Irish tenor. I love to hear my mother harmonize with him. He loves to dance and is the best dancer I know. He has a temper, but we don't see it often. Father is a lot of fun. He has taken us on many "ventures" himself over the years.

"He has a smile that could melt any heart," my Gran remarked one day after she got to know him . . . and love him too, I thought.

15

Gran stayed for a few months after Tim was born, and they got pretty close. Now she comes for a month-long visit every spring.

Father stumbled into journalism, working part-time at the *Chronicle* as a printer. He is a self-educated man who loves to read and loves to write. He worked his way up at the paper to lead reporter. He tells of being mentored by Joe Bryant, the best reporter there. He taught him how to mold his storytelling ability into being a newsman.

Most everyone likes my father. My brother looked just like him, but Tim took after Mother in temperament: quiet, steady, and sensitive. Me, I'm more like my father. Hot-tempered and sometimes moody; I talk too much and laugh too loud. I can tell a good tale and 'loves to write and read. I'm a fine Irish dancer, even if I do say so myself.

Mother's family is Irish on her father's side, so she can jig with the best of us. We often kick up our heels together after supper, although usually, Mother provides the piano accompaniment.

Our front porch was constructed before Tim was born by my father and Hank Moody. It is a great place to relax, with the wind blowing off the bay most afternoons and early evenings. We often sit out there after dinner on warm nights, and there are many in San Diego. Mother plays the gramophone, often her favorite operas, while we rock quietly and share stories from our day.

On warm days we keep our front door open to allow the breeze from the bay to cool the front room while the strains of famous operas stream out into the neighborhood. Our neighbors identify our house to passersby as "the white one with the opera."

Later Wednesday afternoon, Mother came to my room and asked if I wanted to walk to the old wharf with her. This is something we usually do as a family after Sunday dinner.

"The fresh air will make you feel a little better. I want you to come with me—it's a beautiful day."

And so we went. She didn't ask Father.

"Your father doesn't feel well."

I knew what that meant; he was drunk. We got up to leave, and there was a knock at the door. Mother opened it, and there stood Jack. She didn't greet him. She looked down at the bottle of whiskey he had in his hand, then looked up at him, worry and grief marring her otherwise beautiful face. She said nothing about the whiskey; she simply sighed.

"Mike's in the bedroom. We're taking a walk to the old wharf."

This wharf was built at the end of Market Street by William Davis, an early developer of our neighborhood. He envisioned it being the start of a grand downtown living area adjacent to the new heart of downtown by the bay rather than miles out of town. He called this settlement New San Diego.

He even brought ten prefabricated saltbox houses around the Horn to encourage people to move there. Financial reverses stymied his plans and caused the project to be abandoned by all but a few rabbits. This is how our neighborhood got its name: Rabbitville. A few years later, a freighter rammed into the wharf and severely damaged it. It was never repaired. One unusually cold winter, the soldiers stationed at the nearby army barracks used some of what remained of the wharf for firewood; now it was in pretty sad shape.

As long as I can remember, the old wharf hosted several boats that were abandoned there. It's a boat graveyard. Twenty or so years ago, a new wharf was built by Alonso Horton at the foot of the Stingaree. Upper Fifth Avenue is the financial center of the city, and the seedy red-light district, The Stingaree, is down the hill on its southern section at land's end.

All but three of the saltbox houses brought by Davis were destroyed over the years. My parents bought one of the remaining ones many years later when they moved to San Diego. Father said there wasn't a single tree in the neighborhood then. Now, Rabbitville is thriving; houses have been built all around ours, and trees grace every street.

Alonso Horton, considered to be the founder of modern San Diego, saw from the day he arrived the potential that lay right before his eyes. Everyone knew the story of his first day here. He stepped off the rowboat, which took him to land from the ferry he had taken from San Francisco. He saw the train station and the busy activities at the harbor, looked around, and wondered where the town was.

"Why it's a few miles from here, sir, right below those hills," his boatman told him, pointing to the foothills overlooking the bay, "we'll get you a carriage to take you there."

"Why that doesn't make any sense at all," Horton replied.

Waiting for his carriage, he admired the natural harbor, the wonderful climate, and the stunning beauty of the place. He later recalled his thoughts at that time: "I thought San Diego must be heaven on earth. It seemed to be the best spot for building a city I ever saw."

He watched goods loaded onto wagons from ferries arriving from ports all over the state and, indeed, all over the world. He knew that the city's future was moving its operations from what we now call Old Town to the area bordering the waterfront and the train station, the heart of commerce. From that day forward, he set about to build that modern city and what soon became known as New Town.

Horton knew what he was talking about. He was a very successful mid-west developer of small towns and cities; one of them, Hortonville, bore his name. He came to San Diego from San

Francisco because he had heard about the area's potential for development. He wanted to see it firsthand.

As Mother and I approached the old wharf, I remembered playing there often with Tim. We commandeered a rusty old fishing boat there and turned it into a pirate's ship. Mother made us a flag with leftover black material with a white skull and crossbones she painted on it. We hung it on the boat's mast, awaiting epic sword battles with other local pirates we knew would come. They did, of course. Tim had a scar to prove it over his right eye from a sword fight gone awry.

Mother and I walked in silence, looking out at the bay before us. The sun traveled for just a moment behind a group of feathery clouds, causing a shadow, then bright sun, with spires of light reaching like spindly fingers down to the water.

"Maybe that's God's grace coming down to us, Mary Kate."

I wasn't so sure. We watched the sunset, and before the shade of darkness was pulled down over our neighborhood, we headed home. Jack was still in the bedroom with my father when we got back. I sat and read in the front room. Mother was sitting in Father's chair, sewing.

Jack came down the stairs, flushed with drink. He opened the front door, paused, and looked back at us, a cloud of grief shrouding his eyes. "Good night to the two of ya. We're going to get through this, you'll see." He turned and was gone.

Chapter 4

The next night Jack came for supper, this time without the whiskey. Fiona Riggs, one of Mother's dressmaking customers, was coming over for a fitting at six, so we ate very early. I could smell the chicken casserole that our next-door neighbor Mrs. Burley had dropped by earlier that day that was heating in the oven. I was setting the table when I heard a knock at the door.

"I'll get it, Mother."

"Come in," I called. Jack opened the door, his form backlit in the doorway.

"Hello, Mary Kate."

He came toward me dressed as he always is, in a white-and-brown-striped collarless shirt and brown pants topped with his tattered brown vest with its missing button, his pockets full of pencils and pieces of paper, just in case a story or something came up, I suppose. He wore his signature newsie cap with his long brown hair, desperate to escape from under it and mostly succeeding. Jack always needed a haircut.

"He's no Beau Brummel," Father said at dinner a while back. I shot a glance at Mother at the time; Father had no room to talk. Jack has dark auburn hair, which he keeps corralled under his newsie cap, which he wears most of the time. He has big brown eyes with more than a hint of mischief in them most days. Those eyes can turn black in a minute, as he's quick on the trigger when it comes to getting mad.

Mother says he has as a charming, full-of-the-devil smile. "This is what makes him irresistible to the ladies. He also has a vulnerability about him that makes women want to protect him, to change him, but that's not likely going to happen,"

"He loves our ma," Tim said a while back; it's because he has no mother of his own."

Jack drinks too much and is not opposed to mixing it up bar fighting. He sometimes comes over with a black eye or a cut on his face or on his knuckles. "Just a little disagreement, just a wee communication problem," he'll say, or something like that. Father always wants details, and Jack is more than obliging, exaggerating, I suspect, more than just a bit for the good of the tellin'.

Jack immediately headed for the kitchen. "How's the prettiest lady in San Diego?" he said, grabbing Mother and kissing her on the cheek. She huffed, pushing him away but loving every minute of his attention. He flirts with her shamelessly.

"Let's eat," she said.

Jack gobbled the chicken casserole and took a hefty second portion.

"Mike's asleep," Mother told me.

We all knew better. Jack surprised me when we were clearing the dishes by asking if I wanted to take a walk to the old wharf with him.

"Sure," I said, following him out the front door. "I'm going for a walk, Mother," I called to her.

"Take your sweater, Mary Kate; it's chilly out there," she called.

I reached for my old blue sweater, which was hanging by the door. We walked for a while in silence. When we got there, Jack nudged my elbow to the right.

"Let's go this way,—I want to show you something."

21

We walked down a bit and then came upon a scruffy-looking red and white sailboat, moored not far from where our pirate ship used to be. It had the name *"Seren"* written on its stern; the *"ity"* had peeled off.

"Welcome aboard," Jack said, offering his hand to help me up.

The boat was fairly good-size, about thirty feet. You could see that it had once been trimmed on the top half in red, which mostly had peeled off, showing gray, rough wood, weathered by the action of the salt and the sea. As I stood on the deck, I could see down the hatch; the door was open. It had a commodious sleeping area warmed by smooth, varnished light-brown wood.

"The hatch is normally locked, so the sleeping area downstairs is still pretty nice. I was here earlier today, so I left it open."

He planned this walk with me, and I was anxious to hear why.

"I've stacked some trunks in the bow where we can sit," he said, motioning for me to sit down.

"I come here when I need to do a bit of thinking. Nobody has used this boat in years. My father told me that sometimes people buy pleasure boats thinking they will use them all the time, not realizing how much work it is to maintain a boat. Dad jokes that you need to have a friend with a boat, not own one yourself."

"He says that many of these folks lose interest in doing the upkeep on their boats—don't want to pay to have someone else do it or even pay to have the boat taken away. They leave them here and just walk away. Dad says this is one of those boats. He has wanted to fix it up with me for a long time, but so far, he hasn't had the time. He works so much, such long hours. He has to, even with my salary."

Jack comes from a family of five children and they hardly saw their father. Tim said that Jack's father had a fondness for the drink

22

and that almost every day he spent time drinking with his pals from the docks after a long slog at work. Jack's mother died giving birth to his youngest brother; Jack was only ten at the time. After that, most of the mothering was done by his older sister Francine— Franny, as he calls her. She's married now and lives with her family on a sheep ranch in Mission Valley.

As we sat in silence, my thoughts were about Jack. I wondered about his loss of not only Tim but of the only home life he had. He has been close with our family since my brother started at the paper two years ago and with my father before that.

Jack is self-educated but had the best teachers: Henry Seymour and Father. They feel a special kinship with Jack, both having come from poor families and both made their way up from the bottom of the news business.

Before Tim's death, Jack would come for dinner a couple of nights a week. He has a wonderful singing voice and has my father beat as a skilled storyteller. Outrageous, humorous tales that he insists are "God's truth" are his specialty. He sometimes strays to the bawdy side, but his charm and good humor keep my parents from holding him back—that is, if they even could, once he gets wound up into a tale.

Mother, Father, and Jack would regale Tim and me night after night with their beautiful harmonies. Jack is an Irish tenor like Father. Mother sings and plays the piano. We all like to dance, especially Father. We push the furniture aside in our large front room and watch him go. Mother has many lively pieces she plays on the gramophone, especially for dancing. She squeals with delight as my father whirls her around the room when they take to the floor. Father told us that everyone in his family could dance, especially his grandmother, who taught him.

He taught Tim and me to dance, and we made a pretty good team on the dance floor. Jack joins in, but he's no dancer, to be sure.

Two left feet, maybe more, but his lack of grace he sure makes up for in enthusiasm. The musical gene missed Tim and I—we were both terrible singers, but we enthusiastically joined in the singing nonetheless. Jack often teased us by suggesting we would sound better singing "a wee bit more softly."

He got me out of my reverie when he stood and turned my way. "I'm going to see if I can get your father to help me work on this boat. One thing he doesn't need right now is too much free time. Did ya know he used to own a sailboat himself in San Francisco?"

I nodded.

"But first, we need to get him back to the paper. Henry's coming over tomorrow morning to convince him that we need him to come back to work. If he won't, maybe he will in a few days, maybe a week. I've been covering your father's stories with Henry's help, but your father is hard to replace, and we are getting jammed up."

"Henry is a darn good newspaper reporter, ya know. Years ago, he and your father were comrades in arms at the *Union*. Your dad was new to the paper, and Henry was a top-dog reporter. Years later, Henry bought the paper."

His boat repair plan was a way, and a good one too, that he and Father could spend time together, and it was a reason for Jack to rejoin the family. He knew he was welcome to come over anytime, but after we lost Tim, he didn't have a reason to. He and Father working on this boat was that reason.

Jack went on to tell me how he could help Father once he got back to the paper. He said he would take Father to Patrick's if he wanted to go there and let him cry in his beer for a bit. "He has to stop drinking, and this may take a while. Don't ya worry now; I will see him home safe.

Jack looked at me with such sadness in his eyes. Ya know, Mary Kate, someone blasted a hole in his heart, and it needs time to mend. We all miss Tim terrible."

I looked back at the sunset, which was blurred by the tears welling up in my eyes. Jack put his arm around me and gave me a squeeze.

"Terrible is right," I said. We sat in silence for a few minutes.

"We better shove off, Mary Kate—it's nearly dark." We didn't say much walking home. I thought about the plan Jack and Henry had worked out. I was sure Mother was in on this too. It was surely worth a try. It had to work; it just had to.

Chapter 5

Mother and I were eating breakfast the next morning: Irish soda bread with currants and Mother's strong coffee. Father still was not coming to the table for meals. Molly Moody had brought the soda bread yesterday afternoon along with our laundry, which she had been doing since Tim's death. I looked across the table. Mother seemed prettier, brighter, and, yes, more hopeful. She got up to reheat the coffee; she was singing. I hadn't heard her sing since we lost Tim.

Thunk—I heard the familiar sound of the morning paper hitting the house. It landed, no doubt, on the pool of papers that had accumulated there. It had been eight days since Tim's death; the papers were beginning to pile up. There was a sharp knock at the door. I wondered if it was the paperboy curious about the stack of papers, and then I remembered . . . Henry.

"I'll get it," Mother said, opening the door to a familiar male voice.

"Good morning, Maggie."

"Good morning, Henry; come in. Mike's in the bedroom."

Father fell into a well of despair when we lost Tim. It was a well with such steep, slippery sides that it seemed like we could do nothing to help him out. I hoped that Henry could turn things around. He is such a good friend, not only to my father but to our whole family.

He nodded to me as he went up the stairs to attend to what I knew was the difficult task at hand. About half an hour after he arrived, I heard a knock on my bedroom door; I'd retreated there to read my journal.

"Come in," I said, thinking it was Mother. "Mr. Seymour." My eyes widened in surprise.

"Mind if I sit down?"

He smiled and sat on the bed across from me. He told me about the plan he, Jack, and Mother had hatched to get Father back to work. He said that Father agreed to give things a try the next day.

"I told him we'd take it slow and for him to take whatever time he needed." He paused and was silent for a minute.

"I had an idea. Why not come to work as your father's apprentice Mary Kate? You're a good writer; remember those three short stories you showed me last year? They were pretty good. And how about your journaling?" he said, looking at the collection of my journals standing on top of my bookcase, each with the year on its spine in felt numbers.

I wrote in my journal every night before getting into bed. I hadn't been able to do that since we lost Tim. I always wanted to be a writer, to write novels like Jane Austin or Louisa May Alcott, who are two of my favorites.

"You've been a writer for a long time, Mary Kate. Tim was about your age when he took the job as your father's apprentice. He did just fine, and he didn't have much experience writing."

"You know, journalism is a different kind of writing, but it's still writing. It's storytelling too. Your father is self-educated like I am, and he's one of the best reporters I know."

"If you come and work with him, at least until you start teacher's college in May, you and your father can get to know each other better. This could fill a hole in both of your lives right now. Your father and Jack taught Tim to be a pretty good reporter. You will have the two of them in your camp and me to boot. I'll always be there for you if you need a hand."

"Your father can be a bit prickly, but if anyone can handle him, it's you. If he gives you a hard time, you can always come to me and I'll help you out. You seem to be a little at loose ends right now. I think this would be good for you *and* your father. Besides, I'd like to see a pretty face at the paper again," he said, smiling.

Henry stood up to leave. "We used to have a pretty little redhead just like you working for the paper. Ruby's her name. She's married now; she quit to have babies. She's a bit rough around the edges, and you know what, I believe she lives right here in Rabbitville. She's a great gal and a talented reporter. We had a lot of fun together. She's great pals with your father too. Maybe your father and I will take you to meet her when things settle down, and they will, Mary Kate, they will."

He paused for a few seconds, looked at me intently, and put his hand on my shoulder. "So, what do you think of the idea; would you like to give it a try?"

"Yes, yes I would," I said and looked into his eyes and smiled.

"Now let me go and speak to your father. I'll see what he thinks of the idea. Cross your fingers." He opened the door, closed it after him, then reopened it and peeked in. "By the way, let's not let your Father knows this was my idea."

After he left, I sat back and thought about how much I cared for Henry. He and his wife, Babe, are family to us. They are close friends of my parents—they come over for dinner and card playing often, love chow-chow nights, and are always at our house on holidays. They have no children and treat us like a benevolent aunt and uncle.

Henry loves to share his books with Tim and me. We often have lively discussions about them, as well as about the serialized stories of the West found in popular magazines that he often brings over. He would sometimes read them to us after dinner.

Henry should have been an actor; he's that good. When Henry reads a tale, he puts you right into the story. Even my mother and father love to listen to him read. Bret Harte and Mark Twain are our favorites. Tim and I loved Edgar Allan Poe's stories and poems and we are particularly fond of Mary Shelley's *Frankenstein.*

Henry loved *The Wizard of Oz,* which I lent him last month. Gran sent it to me for Christmas. I noticed one day when I was visiting Father at the paper, Henry had a quote of the Wizard talking to the Scarecrow pasted to his office wall: It was something about the Wizard telling the Scarecrow that he did not need a brain, but that what he did need was a diploma. Mother said that Henry was self-educated and resented the notion that the only people who had any sense had a college degree.

One particular tale Henry told us many times, and we never got tired of hearing it. He calls it "The night I 'bout peed my pants at the finest restaurant in San Diego."

After finishing our pie, he sat back in his chair to tell his tale. He said that he had taken Babe for her fortieth birthday to the Maison Doré, the finest restaurant in the city. It was ice cream night which was the first Saturday of the month. Each Wednesday before, the restaurant ferried a large block of ice wrapped in burlap from Lake Tahoe to make ice cream on Saturday night.

It was the only place in town that served ice cream, which was the favorite dessert of Wyatt Earp. The night we went, the restaurant was full of folks wanting ice cream and a look at our local celebrity, who was known to always be there on ice cream nights.

"Sure enough, Henry told us, Babe and I passed by Wyatt Earp and his wife when we were taken to a small table off the beaten path near where they sat. We kept an eye on them all through dinner. Nobody approached them. I was the lead reporter at *The Union* then, and I resolved to ask the man a question or two on my way out of the place."

Henry said that it was well known that Wyatt Earp hated to talk to anybody, especially reporters, about the famous shootout at the OK Corral, an event that made him an overnight hero across the country.

"I told Babe that I was going to try to get a quote for a feature story I planned to write. I had quite a bit of skill in getting even reluctant people to talk to me, so I wasn't nervous—Babe was."

"We paid the bill after finishing our ice cream, and on our way out the door, we came upon the Earp table. He had finished his ice cream, and a large empty bowl sat in front of him. He looked down as we approached, avoiding making eye contact with either of us. I stopped about two feet from his table for just a second, and he looked up."

"'Marshal Earp, I am a reporter from *The San Diego Union.* I'm writing a story about you. I'd like to ask you about that day at the OK Corral and I. . .uh… I stopped in midsentence when he looked up at me and gave me a steely, cold stare that not only said no, but hell no. He said nothing."

Henry leaned back in his chair for a few seconds, nodding, no doubt remembering that night.

"Wyatt Earp is known to be an exceedingly taciturn gentleman. Instead of a response to my question, he looked down at the floor. Then, to my horror, I watched as his right hand slowly reached down toward his boot where it was well known that he kept a small pistol."

I froze…'Is he going to shoot me?"

I couldn't move. Babe reached for my arm and pulled me toward the exit. When we reached the door, she looked back. She saw Earp bring his hand up with a napkin he had picked up from the floor. He placed it on the table in front of him. He didn't look up. Babe pushed me out the door."

Henry paused and looked at Babe. "My wife has delighted in telling the story ever since."

Henry told us that he never wrote the story about the shoot-out at the OK Corral but that he did do some research about Wyatt Earp after that night. After doing some digging, he found out why he didn't want to talk about that infamous day and his actual role in it.

"You see, the legend that soon grew legs after the shootout far outdistanced the truth of what really happened. Rather than a hero, many people in Tombstone thought Wyatt Earp was a cold-blooded killer."

"As it turns out, he was not the marshal on that day but rather a pick-up volunteer of his brother Virgil, who was the marshal. Wyatt was deputized the day of the shoot-out, as was his younger brother Morgan and Doc Holiday.

The shoot-out didn't involve out-of-town marauders, but rather some disreputable cowboys that lived in Tombstone, who many said had a private dispute with the Earp family."

Henry paused for dramatic effect. "The battle didn't even occur in the OK Corral but up the street in a back alley. Virgil Earp was wounded, as was Doc Holiday. Morgan was killed.

Wyatt Earp killed two of the bad guys, but there was considerable dispute afterward as to just who *were* the bad guys that day. There was a long court proceeding about the whole thing. Earp was eventually cleared, but many folks in Tombstone felt that he

31

should have been tried for murder. Even today, nobody really can agree as to just what happened on that infamous day."

Henry sighed and continued, "Still, Wyatt Earp became the hero of the day as the tale was told and retold in the press; he was the man who cleaned up Tombstone and saved it from the forces of evil. This was far from the truth, but most folks in San Diego believed the legend, and Earp didn't correct them."

"I think he became the hero of that famous shoot-out because he looked like most folks would like a hero to look. He was the most comely of the men there that day. He's a tall, handsome, rather thin man with a chiseled face, steely blue eyes, and light brown hair. One reporter described his prominent mustache as resembling the horns of a steer curling down around his chin. I'd say that's pretty accurate."

Henry said that Wyatt Earp came to San Diego not too long after the shootout in Tombstone, to invest in real estate and get rich. Virgil, who had already moved here, had made some good money, so he encouraged his brother to join him.

The Earp brothers didn't want any part of Tombstone because they knew they had a target on their back. This was from the allies of the slain cowboys as well as up-and-coming gunslingers from all over, who wanted to challenge them to enhance their reputation, their own legends.

"Wyatt Earp ran four gambling halls in the Stingaree, Henry told us. It was said that he made a thousand dollars a night in profit. During the last boom, he used his money to buy San Diego real estate. Like so many others, he made a lot of money right away. But being a gambler, he stayed too long at the table. Eventually, he lost his investment in the last real estate bust. He left town a few years back, nearly broke, and moved north to try his luck elsewhere. He took his wife and his racehorse with him."

"He never used his gun in San Diego. He got a challenge or two from up-and-coming gunslingers from time to time, but he never engaged them in a fight. I was sure glad he didn't make an exception for me," Henry chuckled.

He looked at my father, "You know, Mike, Wyatt Earp wanted two things more than anything: to get rich and have sons. He never got either. He had many women, more than one wife, and he thought it was his bad luck that all the women he tried to impregnate were barren. After many years of trying for a son, he discovered that none of his five brothers could father a child either. As it turns out, the pistol-packing he-men, the Earp brothers, were shooting blanks."

Mother and Father laughed at this, but I didn't understand what this meant. Tim didn't either.

I sighed and thought about the many good times Tim and I had with Babe and Henry, and about his suggestion that I take Tim's place as father's apprentice. I opened my 1902 journal and wrote the first entry I had made since we lost Tim. I wrote about the prospect of working for my father, and then sat back and thought for a minute. What would these pages reveal in the rest of this year? A year when everything had changed.

I wondered how things went between Henry and Father. He didn't report back, so I guess things went as planned. I'll just have to wait and see. About an hour later, there was another knock at my door.

"Mary Kate, may I come in? Mother called.

"Yes, come in, Mother."

She opened the door and sat down on my bed. "Henry has persuaded your father to come back to work tomorrow for a few hours. He told him that the work was becoming overwhelming and that he and Jack couldn't handle things without him much longer.

Henry has filled in as much as possible, but your father is the grease that makes the wheels turn at the *Union*."

"There won't be many people there on a Saturday. Jack will be at the paper in the morning. He can bring your father up to date and give him some space to get up to speed and on track again. He'll have Sunday off and hopefully, he'll be ready to go full-speed on Monday."

Mother said that she and Henry agreed that work might be the only thing to get Father out of his misery, at least for a few hours a day. He would be too busy to do much thinking. She stressed that the real problem was that Father would have to stop drinking, which might take some time. Henry said he could help with that if need be—Jack too.

"He quit drinking before, and he can do it again, Mary Kate. He's been dry for more than twenty years."

She was quiet for a moment. She said nothing about my working with Father. Mother took a deep breath and began to sob. "I'm sorry, dear," she said, then turned and rushed out the door.

The next morning when I came to the breakfast table, I saw the empty coffee cup with the pot sitting next to it at Father's place at the table. I touched the pot. It was cold. Father must have left for the paper before the sun came up. Mother was at the stove frying some eggs. She brought them to the table in the skillet and put them on my plate. I took some freshly made bread from the plate already on the table.

She picked up the coffee pot. "Let me heat the coffee for you."

"Thank you, Mother; that sounds good. Father must have left really early," I said.

"He did, and that's promising."

After breakfast, I got up and went out to the porch. Ten days of papers had spilled on the floor in a hapless little puddle, lying there to the left of the front door where they had been kicked out of the way. I picked up the one on top of the pile and went back inside. Sitting in Father's chair, I opened up the paper and looked at the front page where his stories usually dominate. Mulling over the prospect of Father back at the paper, and letting out a deep sigh; I wasn't sure he was ready.

Jumping up, I went back out to the porch and picked up the rest of the pile of unread papers. Opening the door with one hand, I brought the stack inside, and a couple of them dropped to the floor. Tossing them into the fireplace, railing against them, I said out loud to nobody in particular. "Let's be done with these tokens of our misery; I'm going to make a fire tonight after dinner. We need some warmth in this house."

Filled with hope as the warm orange glow of the sunrise bathed our front room, I wasn't sure yet that Father wanted me to become his apprentice, but I was pretty sure Henry would convince him. I sat in Father's chair and thought of the life I was embarking on—excited, yes, but fearful too. This time, I had no sidekick.

Chapter 6

My heart sank when I heard the creak of the top step and saw Father come through the front door at lunchtime. He never came home for lunch. He must have decided he was not ready to return to work and quit early. Mother was at the sewing machine working on a dress for one of her clients.

"Hello, gals," he said, not cheerfully really, but it was at least a greeting.

Mother looked up from her sewing. "Hello, Mike, I've got some chicken casserole from last night's dinner. Are you hungry?"

He didn't answer; he just sat down at the table. Mother brought him a bowl of casserole and a piece of apple pie, got the coffee pot off the stove, and poured him a cup. He didn't eat much, but he ate. I got my coffee and sat down at the table. Father stirred the cream in his coffee and then turned to me.

"Mary Kate, would you come back to the paper with me after lunch? I need to show you something."

I nodded.

"OK then," he said with a faint smile.

We walked in silence the few short blocks to the paper on Fourth Street at C. Pretty soon, I saw the *San Diego Union* plant, as Father calls it. I've been there many times. It is an attractive, fairly new wood building with two stories and large arched windows in the front on both floors.

It has gingerbread trim on the roof eaves designed to take a bit of the chill off the prefabricated-box architecture seen in buildings all over town. Lumber was hard to come by and bricks were expensive, so prefabricated building materials brought from the East Coast around the Horn are often used here.

This relatively new building has a big, somewhat shabby-looking sign, *San Diego Union*, fastened on the roof. The paint is peeling a bit; it is much older than the structure. Father told me Henry insisted that the original sign from the Old Town office be used.

"It's history," Henry said, "the *Union* is the most important and longest-running newspaper in San Diego."

Father used his key to open the front door. "Nobody home," he said, making way for me and pulling the door shut behind him. The newsroom was empty, hot, stuffy, and smelled of ink, tobacco, and sweat. "Jack will be back later. He is out on a fire story in the valley. Charlie went with him to get a picture."

A vacant newsroom was not unusual on a Saturday afternoon. Father told me that most of the reporting, advertising, and other material was submitted to the printers by Saturday so that they could be ready for the Sunday and Monday editions. This gave most of the staff the day off on Sunday.

As soon as we got into the newsroom, Father turned to me. "Let's go upstairs for a minute, 'Little Bit.' We can use Henry's office. It's more private; I'd like to have a chat with you."

He headed toward the stairs. I was surprised to hear Father call me "Little Bit." It was his pet name for me when I was a child. I hated it. I've always been small, and I resent being short-changed. I didn't like being just a little bit of anything. Father meant it as a term of affection. He hadn't used it in many years. It was clear that he used it now to lighten the mood between us. It did.

I followed him up the stairs to the second floor. The one large office at the left side of the room has glass on the top half with black letters trimmed in gold:

HENRY SEYMOUR
PUBLISHER

The door was ajar, and Father ushered me in. I looked out the large window facing the bay; there were many ships in the busy harbor. I felt the warmth on my face from the afternoon sun streaming through the glass. The desk was covered with old editions of the *Union* and all manner of paperwork in no particular order. It was a mess. There was a shiny new telephone on a side table beside a brand-new Remington typewriter.

"Is this the only telephone here?"

"There are four: this one, mine, Jack's, and Cheesy Wilke's."

I had met Cheesy; he's the paper's advertising salesman. He is a tall, beanpole-skinny, middle-aged man, a fastidious bachelor, with dyed black hair and a spiky mustache pomaded to his face. He's called Cheesy, Father told me, because he has eaten cheese sandwiches for lunch without fail every day of his life. No exceptions. He doesn't mind the handle. I remembered my meeting with Cheesy a few months back, and I couldn't picture him as a salesman. Still, Father said he was a good one.

There was a bookcase in the corner of Henry's office that was full to the limit, with books facing in all directions and a wooden chair in front of the desk, also stacked with paperwork. If you came to see Henry, you apparently had to stand. Father told me that Henry said that he didn't like what he called "an unhealthy state of order" in his office. He certainly got his wish. There was a worn, wine-colored leather rolling chair that Henry held forth behind his desk. Father saw me looking at it.

"Ya know, Henry's kinda funny. He's sentimental and loves tradition, yet he's crazy about any new invention. He always buys the latest gadget, the latest model. I betcha' any day now we'll see him pull in front of the paper in a shiny new automobile."

Father picked up the paperwork on the chair in front of the desk, put it carefully on the floor, and motioned to me to sit down. He pulled over Henry's chair and sat facing me. I knew what was coming; I planned to act surprised.

"Sit down, Mary Kate. He paused and looked down." I want you to come to work with me as my apprentice, he said in a slow, measured tone, "I need you near me."

The unsaid sentiment that hung in the air was plain: I'm lost without Tim. He paused for what seemed to be a very long time, his eyes still downcast. Looking at me at last, he went on.

"You can work with me on my stories, write copy, and do research on the people and places involved in the news. Soon you'll do the women's stories. Nobody wants to do them, so we don't. Henry said that this stuff sells papers, and we need to get these stories covered."

"He's right. We call them who was there and wud' they wear stories. engagement parties, weddings, society teas, charity balls, and women's stuff. When we can get someone to do these stories, they always appear in the Sunday morning edition. The paper has a special section on Sundays just for women. Have you seen it?" I nodded.

He stood for a moment and looked out the window and then leaned against the sill facing me. "We put the women's advertising in this section along with paid announcements like engagements, weddings, births, deaths, obituaries, and the like. You would write them or edit the copy provided by customers and then run them over for their approval."

"It's a perfect beat for a woman. You're a smart girl. You like to write and love to read. You can even have your mother whip up a few nice dresses for you to go to these frou-frou society affairs."

He sighed, gathered his thoughts for a few seconds, and then looked at me with such sadness in his eyes. "You may not have thought about working with me, but it would mean so much to me, darlin'," his voice cracking, he looked down again.

"All I ask is for you to try it out for a few months. If you still want to start teacher's college in May like you planned, fine. But for now, you're kinda' at loose ends."

He sighed. He looked so tired, but he went on.

"I had to teach Tim to write news copy, but you can hit the ground running, being a writer and all. I think it will be good for you too. Who knows, maybe you will end up with printer's ink in your veins just like your old man."

He stood and walked to the window, turned to face me, sitting on the sill, wincing when he did. His back must be ailing him again.

"Jack will help you along the way. He was always there for Tim, and he taught him a lot. Henry will help too; he's so fond of you. The gang here at the paper are great people, especially Henry. He's the boss yes, but he is also a talented newspaperman."

Father stood up and rubbed his lower back. "I'm sorry," he said, my back is acting up a bit today, and I didn't sleep well last night because of it."

He looked at me with a look of uncertainty on his face. I knew how he felt; it seemed like nothing was certain anymore.

"All I ask is that you give it a try, and if you don't like it, you won't be letting me down if you don't want to stay. What do you say?"

"When do I start?" I said with a smile.

He smiled and sighed. *Relief? I thought so.*

"How about Monday?" he said, returning my smile.

"Sounds good."

"All right, then, Monday it is. I have already cleared this with Henry. Oh, and Mary Kate, he offered to pay you for doing odd jobs, mostly deliveries and pickups. It will be piecework. This will be for Cheesy and me, mostly".

"Ad copy needs customer approval before printing, so you will be the runner for those, and the announcements and obits you'll be editing need customer approval. Oh, and the *Union* does outside printing work, which also needs approval before it goes to print. Most of the errands can be done taking the trolley; for all others, you will have to walk or rely on Moody's. The paper has an account there."

This came as a surprise; Tim wasn't paid at all. I suspected this was Henry's idea. Father led me downstairs to show me the operation there. He pointed to a small table right inside the front door where a large box sat with a sign on it, Hot Box.

"This is where the wire service news bulletins we get from the Associated Press are put along with press releases, customer-written obituaries, other announcements, ad copy, and the police blotter. You need to check the box frequently; we all do.

Pointing to the closed door near the Hot Box, he told me, "The photography development room is Charlie Wilson's domain. You've met Charlie, haven't you?"

A telephone rang on the table behind the desk. Father turned and picked up the receiver. "The *Union*," he said brusquely, not appreciating the interruption.

41

Hmm…*Charlie Wilson.* I smiled, remembering the day we met.

Jack and Charlie were numbers one and two of the *Three Musketeers*, as these good friends were known at the paper; number three was my brother Tim. One Saturday, Charlie picked up Tim and Jack in his parent's old buggy to go ostrich riding—that's right, ostrich riding. This was done at an ostrich ranch in Mission Valley, where young men would show up on Saturdays to have some rather lively rides on the big birds.

I remember Father telling us while we were in our rocking chairs on the porch that day, that raising ostriches was a lucrative business. "The big birds are from Africa, and they like the climate here. The feathers are in high demand for use in women's fashions and are shipped all over the world. There is a ranch on Coronado Island too, but they don't give rides."

He leaned back in his rocker, and after a few seconds of wool-gathering, he added, "I went ostrich riding with Hank Moody a few years back and fell off a couple of times that day. Ostrich don't take much to being ridden. This unfortunate attitude results in many an intrepid young man landing on his keister after being bucked off by the big birds."

"Is this one of your tall tales, Michael Riley?" Mother asked, looking rather dubious.

"No, Ma'am, it's a fact."

Mother looked at me and rolled her eyes. The boys returned that day laughing up a storm with a bit of beer in them. Charlie and Jack were pleased to join us for dinner. Jack told us, as only he could, and with no exaggeration, mind you, of the pride and perils involved in their ostrich riding that day, singling out each of them for special mention. All three had fallen off the birds at least once, but they all had more than one great ride.

"Those birds got to like us," Jack claimed.

"I'll just bet they did," Mother replied.

My thoughts were brought back to the newsroom when I heard Father end his call by saying, "Sure, Jack, I'll pick it up on the way home."

Father finished up his tour of the paper, letting me know where everyone worked and what went on there. "We need to stop at the police station to get up the police blotter. Jack will pick it up at our house on his way back to the paper. It needs to be picked up every day. We sort of take turns; whoever can do it does it. If it is really important news, the sergeant at the front desk will call me."

As he locked the door of the paper, he turned to me, "Oh, and Mary Kate, I'll get you a spot to work on Monday, maybe tomorrow."

Father and I didn't talk much on the way home. We all walked to the wharf before dinner that night to watch the sunset. This was the first time we had done this as a family since Tim's death. Father filled Mother in on his plans for me to become his apprentice. There was a light sprinkling of rain. A couple of minutes later, the clouds parted, and the sun came out, fingers of light reaching through the clouds to the bay. Mother's words about God's grace came to mind.

Lying in bed that night, thinking about working in Tim's place as Father's apprentice, I thought about how hard it would be to fill Tim's shoes. I could do the work, but could I fill the hole in Father's heart from the loss of his only son? It was a tall order. Still, Father was right; my working with him could be good for both of us. Me, a newspaper reporter? It was an exciting proposition.

Chapter 7

Monday morning, I walked to the paper at eight o'clock, anxious but excited. I wore my uniform brown, as Mother calls it, a dress I wear most every day. Glancing in my bedroom mirror, it looked fine to me. My unruly red curls were jammed into a clip at my neck, nothing fancy. I dusted off my black boots, which Mother pointed out at breakfast, had seen better days.

The newsroom was abuzz with busy people when I arrived. Father, Jack, and Cheesy were hard at work at their desks. Where would I be working? Charlie walked in the door right behind me and greeted me warmly.

Father smiled when he saw me. "Hello, daughter."

He had left for the paper before first light. This was not unusual. He always got there early. He gestured to the chair next to his desk for me to sit. My behind had barely landed when he started to rattle off the jobs I'd be doing for him. Mid-sentence, Henry approached Father's desk.

"Mike, I just got a call from Fred at the courthouse. Judge McKinley has just filed a $50,000 libel lawsuit on behalf of Kate Tingley against none other than the *Los Angeles Times* and its publisher Harrison Gray Otis."

Father whistled. "I'm on it, Henry."

Henry looked at me and smiled. "Welcome aboard."

Father yelled to Jack across the room, waving him over to his desk and then turning his attention to me.

44

"OK, Mary Kate, this is big news. Go to the courthouse right now, as quickly as you can. See Fred in Court Records, second floor. Ask him to see the *Tingley* lawsuit. He gave us a head start. There will probably be other reporters asking for the lawsuit real soon. Copy it and bring your notes right back. We've got to get this story ready for tomorrow morning's edition."

Jack came over and stood by Father's desk, waiting for his orders. He nodded to me with a smile.

"Jack, Katherine Tingley has filed a $50,000 libel suit against the *L.A. Times* and its publisher Harrison Otis early this morning. Get the background from the archives and get me information about Tingley and Lomaland from the *Union* and the *Times*, and, uh . . . check the *Chronicle* too."

"I will have Mary Kate help you with this when she gets back from copying the lawsuit at the courthouse. Check for background on Harrison Otis as well. He owns the *Times,* and I hear he's quite a character. The *Chronicle* will have some material about him. He's very active in Republican politics in the state; he's tangled with the governor a few times as I recall."

Jack nodded and replied, "I have a friend who just started working for the *San Diego Sun.* He used to work at the *Los Angeles Herald.* I'll call him and get the skinny on Otis. I'm sure there is no love lost there."

"Great . . . and check to see if you can find out either from your friend or in the archives whether the *Times* has been sued before for libelous material it printed. If so, what happened? And ask Charlie to dig up pictures—Lomaland, Tingley, Otis."

"I'll try to get in touch with Judge McKinley, Kate Tingley's lawyer; I know him well. He's a Los Angeles lawyer who does a good deal of work down here. He used to be a judge in the Los Angeles Superior Court, 'didn't like it, and went back to law practice. This is why folks call him Judge. I've covered a number of the trials he was involved in. He's a straight shooter. He'll give me a quote and let me know who will be representing the *Times.*"

I watched Father's face as he talked to Jack; a remarkable change had come over him. It was as if a curtain had lifted. He was a newspaperman once again, orders to his troops tumbling out of him, energized by that printer's ink which had started to flow when he heard tell of this big news story on his favorite beat: the courthouse. Father's demeanor told me he was indeed "on it." He is back with us, I thought, for just a second too long.

"Git, Mary Kate," he barked, now!"

I jumped up and headed for the door, then stopped and turned to him. "Where do I get a pencil and notepad?"

Father ignored me. Cheesy, who had the desk next to Father's, jumped up and shoved a pencil and notepad at me. I suspected that he knew a volcanic eruption had been narrowly avoided.

Rushing out the door, heading down the few blocks to the courthouse, and walking down C Street from the paper, a dry, dusty, cocoa-colored street, I shivered. It was cool but sunny. Turning left on Third, I walked the short block to Broadway.

It is a wide boulevard ending at the bay. It is a paved street bordered by recently-installed bright, white cement sidewalks, similarly appointed to the rest of the major streets in the business districts of the city. I smiled at a few shop owners sweeping in front of their businesses. It was early; there wasn't much traffic. Usually, you can see an automobile here and there downtown, but not today.

I passed the large three-story Horton House, which was the first luxury hotel built in New Town about twenty years ago by Alonso Horton. Three blocks beyond it, the courthouse loomed. It is one of the more impressive buildings in the downtown area; the land for the building was donated by Alonso Horton. As I approached, I looked

46

up at the four-story structure, cement over brick, built in a classical style and graced with a tower crowned with a gold statue of the blind Lady Justice, with her scales in hand, sparkling in the morning sun.

I had been to the courthouse several times with Father and Tim. It has three courtrooms on the first floor connected by a long hallway, with offices, jury rooms, and judge's chambers in the back. The building has many large windows kept open on warm days to allow a breeze to come in from the bay.

I rushed past a bailiff standing just outside the front door, a cigarette dangling from his mouth. "Good morning, Miss," he said. Nodding, I rushed by him. Taking the stairs to the second floor and looking left, there was a sign over the counter in the first office stairway, COURT RECORDS. I approached the man standing at the counter, which was probably Fred. Stacks of light-blue files were lined up behind him, resting on their side.

Fred is a man of about fifty, bald, with bright blue eyes and a welcoming smile which he greeted me with when I approached him. He wore a white shirt and a perky blue-spotted bow tie. A little out of breath and no doubt flushed from my run over there, I greeted him with my best smile. "You must be Fred." He nodded.

"Mary Kate Riley, reporter for the *Union*. I need—"

He interrupted, "Daughter of my man Mike Riley, I suppose?"

"Yes, I'm his apprentice."

"And a lucky apprentice you are. Mike is a great reporter. He'll teach you a lot. What happened to your brother Tim who used to come up here for Mike?"

A shadow fell over my face; tears welled in my eyes. I looked down and felt a warm tear hit my hand resting on the counter. I took a deep breath. "He died," I said without looking up.

Fred paused for a moment, and then he said softly, "I'm so sorry, Miss."

I wiped my eyes, took a deep breath, and looked at Fred. He turned and picked up a blue file with paperwork attached from the desk behind him.

"Imagine you came to take a gander at the *Tingley* lawsuit."

"That's right. My father asked me to copy it."

"All right then, here it is, he said, handing it to me. "I expected somebody would be right over to check it out. Mr. McKinley filed it first thing at 8:10 this morning." He pointed to where he had checked in the lawsuit with the time, date, and his initials on the top of the first page. He nodded to his left. "You can use that table right over there."

The loud ticking of the clock above the counter distracted me. It was 8:55. The lawsuit which would soon be the talk of the town, the state, and even the country, was but forty-five minutes old.

Sitting at the table, I began reading the paperwork, copying the most important parts. Katherine Tingley had sued the *Los Angeles Times* claiming that its owner, Harrison Gray Otis, libeled her in numerous articles it printed over the past two years. He did so with malice, she claimed, in that he knew the statements were false when he printed them and published these outrageous materials simply to sell more papers.

I was anxious to know just what the heck had been said about Mrs. Tingley and her Lomaland, the fantastic utopian community she founded on the Point Loma peninsula, which bordered the northern part of the San Diego Bay.

Moving quickly through the introduction and a few pages of legal blather, there it was: the articles published by the *Times* were identified by date of publication and attached to the lawsuit. They

48

were set out in general terms and were all introduced by inflammatory headlines. They included references to Katherine Tingley doing outrageous things as the "Head Spook of Lomaland," which was mostly referred to in the *Times* as "The Spookery in Point Loma."

There was more as I read on, much more. Mrs. Tingley was described as a dictator who starved and mistreated the children under her care. Her followers at Lomaland were treated like convicts and worked like slaves. She was a homewrecker who separated husbands and wives and was a threat to the sanctity of the family. Katherine Tingley was a hypnotist, a sorceress, and a fake medium who claimed she talked to the dead. Even her dog Spots, Mrs.Tingley told her followers, was the incarnation of a prominent long-deceased Theosophist.

I already knew that the Theosophists were the group Mrs. Tingley led at Lomaland. They had cut quite a swath through the cultural and artistic life in fledgling San Diego. Everyone knew about them.

The Theosophists provided many cultural offerings in town: plays, musical and dance productions, as well as lectures about Theosophy at their Isis Theater in New Town. They had remodeled the Fisher Opera House and restored it to its former glory. Tim and I went there with our parents for the grand opening.

I already knew quite a bit about Mrs. Tingley and Lomaland. Father talked about what was going on there when he would write a story about it in the paper. Tim had helped with Father's articles on the place and did most of his research. He always shared with me the stories he was working on and often asked me to look at his work and make suggestions.

Father had been promising to take us there one Sunday, but so far, it hadn't happened. Father works very hard six days a week, and it is hard to get him to do much of anything on the one day he has off. And, he often takes side jobs in the neighborhood to make a little extra money for the family coffers.

As I continued to read the lawsuit, the one word which was pounded home over and over again in the *Times'* articles was that Mrs. Tingley was, above all else, a fraud—a grifter, taking other people's money under false pretenses, which it was claimed, she put to her own use.

Mrs. Tingley said that she had done none of those things. She said that as the worldwide leader of the Theosophists, she has met with presidents, kings, queens, and maharajas, and brought Theosophy's message of brotherhood and peace.

She went on to say that Lomaland, founded by the Universal Brotherhood and Theosophical Society under Mrs. Tingley's leadership, is supported entirely by the goodwill and donations of the followers of Theosophy to support its mission to better mankind. Lomaland, as well as other Theosophist centers, have been established throughout the United States, Europe, and Asia.

Mrs. Tingley claimed that she suffered damages when her credibility was sullied by the *Times'* articles because her good name was essential for raising money for the cause. She said that the articles got worse and more inflammatory as time passed. She said that she asked Harrison Otis to stop publishing the articles, but he ignored her. Mrs. Tingley wound up her lawsuit, asking for compensation of $50,000 for the damage to her reputation and her physical and emotional injuries.

Done.

I sighed, took a deep breath, put my hands behind my neck, twisting my head from side to side, and heard my neck crack. I could almost hear Mother whispering in my ear, "That is far from ladylike." I cracked my neck again.

Leaning back and thinking for a moment, it was clear that Mrs. Tingley filed the lawsuit for a public airing of the truth. I wondered how many of the stories that The *Times* printed were true.

Surely he hadn't just made them up . . . the Los Angeles Times? If I read them in the Times, I would think they were true, or they wouldn't print them. Folks trust what they read in the paper. I thought of the responsibility a reporter has to tell the truth. It seems obvious, but I never had any reason until now to doubt that this is what all reporters try to do.

All I knew about Otis was what I read in the lawsuit. He owns the largest newspaper in Los Angeles and is second only to the *Union* in circulation in San Diego. Did he deliberately print articles that were not true? At ten minutes to twelve, I returned the file to Fred.

"Nice to meet you, Miss Riley."

I thanked him, hurried back to the paper, and put my notes in Father's inbox.

"Good job, Mary Kate," he said, leaning back in his chair. This is an important case and an important story. Henry wants us to give it our full attention. There will be press from all over the state, even the country, covering the story of these two very large personalities. They are both leading citizens of their communities: one from San Diego, one from Los Angeles, its older and wealthier cousin up the coast, which by the way, is a bit of a bully. It's their story, Tingley and Otis, but it's also about the bitter rivalry between the communities they represent."

He thought for a second or two and turned back to me. "Katherine Tingley and her Lomaland are seen in these parts as a curiosity. It's true that San Diegans have never seen anything quite like Lomaland, but we do know it has been good for our town."

Father's phone rang. "Hey, Judge, he said, I see you've been a little busy."

They spoke briefly. Chuckling softly, Father put the phone back on the hook and turned to me. "That was Judge McKinley; I got a good quote."

"OK, Mary Kate, go upstairs and help Jack with his research."

When I went upstairs to the archive room, Jack had his head down, buried in his research, his smudged reading glasses held together with a piece of blue string on one side. He looked up and smiled when I came in. "Hey Jack, Father sent me up here to see if you need any help with the research."

"Yup, I'm just about done with Otis and have done a little work on Kate Tingley and Lomaland; you can finish it up and write something for the story."

Jack stood and knitted his fingers together, cracking his knuckles; stretched a bit, took a deep breath, and sighed.

"Here are my notes so far. It's pretty impressive what Kate Tingley's done out there. I've been meanin' to get out there to have a look-see, but so far, I haven't had the chance. Handing me the notes, he added, "You can use Henry's typewriter in his office; he's gone for the day."

I did about an hour of additional research and wrote a draft in my best printing. After several revisions, I thought the end product was pretty darn good and went to Henry's office to try typing it on his brand-new Remington. 'Problem is, I can't type. Struggling, using only two fingers, it was slow going. I didn't notice that Jack had come into the office as my back was facing the door, my head down, trying to type.

"Oh for heaven's sake, Mary Kate, why didn't you tell me you couldn't type? Git, I'll type it; at the rate you're going, it wouldn't be done until next week," he said with a deep sigh, irritated

Picking up my notes, he turned and must have noticed the stricken look on my face. He realized he had been too rough on me; this was my first day, after all.

"The good news is that your printing is clear; I can finish this in no time. Meantime, go round up Charlie and get the pictures he found of Tingley and Otis and bring them up to me."

I returned about a half hour later with the pictures Charlie gave me. Jack was still working on his part of the story. My contribution had been typed and was sitting next to the typewriter.

"I'm done here Jack; I'm starving. 'Gonna run home to get some lunch. Can I bring you anything?"

"No thanks, I had lunch a while back. I'm almost done here myself. Go ahead. Ah…Mary Kate," he said, picking up my part of the story and handing it to me, "Drop this in your father's box on your way out."

"Sure," I said. "Oh, and thanks for typing it for me."

Sitting at Cheesy's desk next to Father's, I read over my work one more time. I was proud of it:

Katherine Tingley is the worldwide leader of the Universal Brotherhood and Theosophical Society. The Theosophists claim to be an organization dedicated to the betterment of humanity through education at its centers around the world. This includes Europe and the Far East. It has its headquarters and the Raja School at Lomaland, a five-hundred-acre Utopian community built on the hills of the Point Loma Peninsula, which is an arm of land wrapping itself around the northern edge of San Diego Bay.

The once-barren desert has been transformed in less than ten years into a garden-like setting with hundreds of trees, flowers, and agricultural fields and orchards where fruits and vegetables, many of exotic varieties, are grown for consumption by the residents. Lomaland sports the only Greek theater in the country where musical and dramatic performances by students are offered to the public. The Theosophists have provided important cultural contributions to San Diego of musical and stage productions at the Isis Theater in New Town.

The school has the nation's first high school band and orchestra, a school of photography, and a school of forestry. It also has a first-rate weather station which is used throughout the entire San Diego region.

Lomaland's stately, exotic temples, two of them reaching four stories high, are crowned by purple and sea-green glass domes, which were recently lighted. They are quite a sight at night when they are visible far out to sea. Lomaland is well thought of in San Diego. It is second only to the Hotel Del Coronado as the area's most popular tourist destination.

Chapter 8

The walk home felt good; it turned out to be a very nice day with just a bit of a chill in the air that often blew off the bay at this time of day. Mother wasn't home. I took an apple and some cheese and sat down in Father's chair for a minute to clear my head. The door opened and Mother came in with food she'd bought.

"Can I get you a 'cuppa?" she offered.

I smiled and nodded, that expression reminding me of Gran. She's a confirmed tea drinker.

"Do you want some cookies with your tea?"

"Yes, please, that sounds good. Oh, Father said we would be about an hour late tonight. Katherine Tingley filed a lawsuit against the *Los Angeles Times*. We need to get the story in the next edition."

I sat in the front room and had a quick cup of tea and two crinkly Snickerdoodle cookies topped with cinnamon. It was nice to relax for a minute. Before long, I heard the sizzling sound of the lamb that Mother was braising; it smelled wonderful. She was making stew for dinner. I sipped the rest of my tea and then took the teacup and my plate into the kitchen.

"May I have two more cookies to give to Father and Jack; drop one in for Cheesy, too, please."

Mother nodded, smiled, wrapped the cookies in a tea towel, and handed them to me. I shoved them into my satchel and was out the door. "See you later, Mother."

It was cool, so I hurried to warm up. *Here I am, Mary Kate Riley, returning to her job at the San Diego Union, my first day... and what a day it has been.*

Father was still working on the story when I got back to the paper. He hadn't had a chance to look at my work. Jack came downstairs and put his part of the story with the photographs Charlie had pulled for him from the archives in Father's box. Reaching into my bag, I handed him a cookie.

"Hmm . . . my favorite, Snickerdoodles," he said, smelling the cookie and then taking a big bite. I left a cookie on Father's desk and one on Cheesy's desk. It was nearly quitting time, and Father was finishing up on the *Tingley* story. I looked at the clock. It was nearly five o'clock.

Expecting to walk home with Father, I had some time to kill. Pawing through the papers in the Hot-Box, there were some obituaries and engagement announcements which I took a stab at editing up in the archives. Before I did, I pulled out some old editions and followed the format used for this type of thing.

Cheesy had returned from his sales calls when I came downstairs. He thanked me for the cookie and surprised me when he asked me to follow him to the storage shed out back.

"Your Pa wants me to set you up with a workspace, Mary Kate. Come with me; let's go upstairs first," he said.

I followed him upstairs, where he showed me the supply cupboard. He took out a bell jar, sharpened some pencils and put them in the jar, picked up a few tablets, and grabbed a few of what he called paper clips, which he sprinkled on his desk downstairs on the way to the backyard shed.

Responding to my curious look, he told me, "Henry is crazy for anything new, and paper clips are his latest thing. It's a simple idea, but they are *so* useful. I brought a few so you can try them. " He

56

picked up two sheets of paper and attached them with the paper clips, giving me a satisfied smile.

"Now, let's go and find you some office furniture."

"Where will I be working?" I asked.

"You'll see," he said.

I was less than dazzled by my choices in the storage shed. Cheesy pulled out a small brass lamp with a green glass shade that was chipped on one side, a dirty but fairly nice oak writing table, a very worn but serviceable rolling desk chair with a dirty wine-colored leather seat, and a dark green bookcase badly in need of some paint.

He carried the table and I rolled the chair into the newsroom with the lamp balanced on its seat. He stopped at a small, doorless, windowless coat closet across from Charlie's darkroom. He wiped them off and then arranged the table and chair facing the opening of the closet. Both pieces cleaned up nicely.

We went back to the storage shed, got the office supplies, and then arranged them on the desk. Looking quite pleased, Cheesy turned to me. "We need to find a little bowl for the paper clips."

Catching his enthusiasm, I said, "I have just the thing at home. I'll bring it tomorrow."

"I'll paint the bookcase for you on Saturday. Now give it a try."

I squeezed in behind the table and sat down. It was a small space where only a "little bit" of a woman would fit. "How do I look?"

"Perfect, just perfect," he said with a satisfied grin.

It wasn't perfect, but I appreciated that I had my own space to work. Thanks, Cheesy."

Pretty soon, Father came over. "Ya got your own office already, have ya?" he said with a wide grin I hadn't seen in a long time.

"I don't think anyone else could fit in here," I said.

"You look good there, girl. The story is in, so let's get on home."

Father didn't ask me any questions about my contribution to the story before we left. He told me he would use what he needed. I was proud of it. He would add Jack's Otis research and finish up the story for page one above the fold.

We walked the few blocks home pretty much in silence. It was six-thirty and just getting dark. Father looked exhausted. I was pretty tired too. He surprised me by hopping up the stairs of our house, skipping the creaky step, and greeting my mother inside with a squeeze and the brief pinched smile of a very weary man.

"Hello, wife, smells mighty good around here. Let me get washed up, and let's give that stew a taste."

Mother was playing Mozart on the gramophone. We sat down at the table as she put down a tureen of lamb stew and a basket of hot biscuits laced with sharp cheddar cheese, Father's favorite. He ate like it was his last meal. I smiled at Mother, just watching him. He was healing. It was a grand moment.

I barely touched my dinner and instead filled the air with excited blathering about my first day at the paper. Father said little but smiled and nodded from time to time. Mother seemed delighted to see my excitement about the story and our team effort in getting it in the next edition.

I needed no rockin' to fall asleep that night I was tired, but anxious as a kid on Christmas Eve to see the *Tingley* story in the morning edition. I put my head on my pillow and thought about my first day at the paper. Before too long, my day caught up with me, and I dropped off to sleep.

My alarm clock went off at six, but for once, I was glad to hear it. I jumped out of bed, got washed up, dressed quickly, and went down for breakfast wearing my uniform brown.

Mother was at the stove.

"Mornin' Mother."

"Hello, dear, let's get you into that dark blue dress I fixed for you yesterday," she said and poured me a cup of coffee. Annoyed, I looked down at my dress. "This is fine, Mother."

"No, you have to look presentable."

"All right, I said, irritated. I'll change after breakfast."

I looked outside as Mother dished up my breakfast. Father had already left for the paper. Frowning at Mother, very disappointed; I was so anxious to hear his comments on my work.

He left the paper folded at my place at the table with the story facing up. "TINGLEY SUES THE TIMES" was the headline. Next to it, Father wrote, "Good job. M. R." My heart was racing with excitement; my first news story, at least a part of it. Briefly glancing at the picture of Lomaland next to the headline, I got right to the story. My smile soon evaporated; so much of my work about Mrs. Tingley had been cut. Father added this to the story.

> Katherine Tingley has plenty of admirers but she is from being universally loved. Critics say she is an autocratic, inflexible woman. She makes no bones about her place as the final word as to what happens at Lomaland and with the Universal Brotherhood organization itself, over which she is its supreme leader.
>
> Mother Purple, as she is called by some of her followers, traipses around in flamboyant purple costumes and is often seen holding court in a colorfully painted wagon with a carved, throne-like chair attached to the back.

> She has run afoul with the local clergy for what they claim is not giving enough credence to the Christian faith in her version of Theosophy, which is non-denominational. It embraces religious dogma from many faiths: Buddhism, Hinduism, Islam, and Christianity, as well as the works of great philosophers and thinkers.

After reading Jack's contribution, I recognized what a good writer he is. His Harrison Otis was perfect:

> Harrison Gray Otis has been an outsized personality in Los Angeles since he bought the Los Angeles Times some ten years ago. It has a current circulation of 29,000. He is a large man who sports a walrus moustache and a goatee. He was wounded two times in the Civil War. He was made a general at the end of his military service over thirty years ago, but still wears his dress uniform, ribbons and all, whenever he can, and insists on being called General.
>
> Otis was key in the development of the City of Los Angeles. He founded the Chamber of Commerce and was a leader in bringing a reliable water source to the city. He had an important role in bringing the transcontinental railroad terminus to Los Angeles rather than San Diego. Otis reportedly did whatever it took to make sure Los Angeles won the prize and reportedly engaged in many underhanded practices. He is not well regarded by anyone in this area.
>
> He is a controversial figure and is by some accounts a bully, who unashamedly makes it known that his way is the only way. He is in a constant state of battle readiness and refers to his home as *The Bivouac* and the *Times'* offices as *The Bunker.* He drives an outlandish automobile he calls his War Machine which is equipped with long horns in front that look like elephant guns ready to fire at whatever enemies may come his way. He runs the *Times with an iron hand with this motto: "Everybody likes to see somebody else kicked,* preferably below the belt."
>
> Cartoons depicting the antics of Otis often appear in rival papers in Los Angeles and as far away as San Francisco. He proudly displays them on the walls of his office. He is the current vice president of the Associated Press, the newly formed national wire service that shares the news with member newspapers all over the country. He is active in Republican circles and has run for state-wide office three times and lost. All his campaigns have been characterized by his dirty campaign tactics.
>
> Otis keeps a highly- publicized enemies list, which contains the name of the current Democratic governor Hiram Johnson, who recently said of Otis,"...(he) sits in senile dementia with gangrene heart and rotting brain, grimacing at every reform, going down to his grave in snarling infamy."

> The attorney for Katherine Tingley, Los Angeles attorney J.W. McKinley, an active Democrat, tops the list. He had this to say about Otis: "Harrison Otis likes to call himself The General. 'More like a pen and ink assassin. Nothing he has written about Katherine Tingley is true. He did it to sell papers, plain and simple."
>
> Father wound up the story by saying that the Times is represented in the matter by San Francisco lawyer Samuel Shortridge one of the finest trial lawyers in the state.

Reading the story again, I realized that Father was right; my part of the story was not balanced. I had put in only the positives about Katherine Tingley. Father's story presented the woman as she is, warts and all, which resulted in a presentation that not only was more accurate but had far more depth and interest.

When I got to the paper that morning, Father took the time to emphasize how important it is to give as much balance and texture to a story as possible. "You do that by getting to know the people you're writing about. Everyone has some critics, some flaws, and some good points. You did fine. It was your first day —this will take some time."

He asked me to keep track in the future of what the *Times* wrote about the *Tingley* lawsuit and how other papers presented the case. He told me to take notes of what I saw as the strong points in how the story was handled, what the paper's slant was, along with new facts that might come up. He said that I'd be getting news releases from other member papers of the Associated Press, so I should watch for them.

"It's my job to retrieve these missives and put these in the Hot Box. Otis is a board member for the Associated Press, so look for him to pass around to members very slanted materials about the case. You will find that some articles from out-of-state papers simply mimic what Otis has printed in the *Times.* "

Father stood up, walked over to the Hot Box, dropped something in, and then returned to his desk.

"And Mary Kate, write me a note from time to time about what you find in other publications or about the case in general or the players in it. I'll read them when I get the chance and then put them on your desk. I don't want to miss some of the good information you pick up along the way that we can find a place for in one of our stories. You can put them in a *Tingley vs. Times* folder you can put in the archives."

"If you write rather than tell me, I can consider it when I am not busy, and it won't get lost in the shuffle or forgotten. If I hear anything, or Jack does, we will put a note in the Hot Box for you to put in the folder."

A couple of weeks later, Fred called Father and told him that the *Times* had filed a response to the *Tingley* lawsuit. He sent me over to the courthouse to copy it. I gave the notes to him and I summed it up this way: Yes, the *Times* printed the articles about Katherine Tingley, but they are all true. And, in any event, a newspaper has a first amendment right to print anything they want as part of the constitutional protection of a free press.

Chapter 9

It was eight o'clock when I got to work, it was Monday of my third week at the paper. Father and Jack were working hard at their desks. Squeezing into my little office, there was a stack of papers on my desk. I flipped through them, finding obituaries, wedding and birth announcements, and other materials for my Sunday edition. On the bottom of the pile came a surprise. It was a flyer advertising a production of Shakespeare's *A Midsummer Night's Dream* at Lomaland; handwritten on the bottom was "See me, M.R." Excited, I trotted right over to Father's desk. I thought he planned to take Mother and me to see Lomaland and the play.

"Good morning," he said.

Glancing at the flyer, he got right to business.

"Get Charlie to take you to Lomaland to see this play—it's Saturday. He can get a horse and buggy from his father or Moody's. Check the place out; do a story for the front page. Include a few lines about the play and the theatrical and musical offerings that Kate Tingley offers there and at the Isis, she and her gang make quite a cultural contribution to this city. Henry thinks we need to write about it more. And …

"But Father," I interrupted; I thought we were going to make this trip together, as a family."

Yes, yes, that's what I said, and we'll still do that. "I'm too busy to do it now." You go with Charlie. Hmm…" he paused to think for a minute. "And watch the Isis Theater's offerings for the next few months; it's on upper Fifth Avenue. Take your mother to a play, a musical production, or a lecture by Katherine Tingley; take

Theodora too. Your mother would like it, and it will deepen your knowledge of what Mrs. Tingley and her crew are all about. Henry will buy the tickets."

"Oh, and you might want to write reviews of the productions you see for your women's section; these should be stand-alone articles. We might even get some advertising out of it. I'll mention to Cheesy that he should check with Mrs. Tingley's people about putting ads for these productions in the *Union*.

Father leaned back in his chair and thought for a moment. "Remember, Kate Tingley is the San Diegan in this dogfight, so we need to give her plenty of ink. Besides, Otis runs his own inkpot, and you can be sure he will give his side plenty of coverage."

"Could *you* ask Charlie to take me to Lomaland?"

"No, I can't," he said gruffly, work it out."

Later that morning, after first taking a swig of breath for courage, I knocked on the darkroom door.

"Come in," Charlie called.

I passed through the curtains inside the door that kept outside light from coming in and stepped into the darkroom. It smelled of chemicals and was glowing with an eerie red light. Charlie was bent over the chemical bath where he was developing photographs. A few were drying on a clothesline contraption he had hung near the processing trays.

"Oh, hello, Mary Kate," he said, distracted.

I told him about the trip to Lomaland and his role in it. He looked up at me, visibly irritated.

"I have plans for Saturday," he said tersely.

Saying nothing in response, I turned on my heel and left the darkroom. Walking home later that day, Father said that Charlie would get a horse and buggy and pick me up at home on Saturday at nine in the morning. "You can wait for him on the porch."

There was no mention of any dispute, although there was mighty chilly weather between Charlie and me that week. This was pretty much what I expected would happen. Jack and Charlie had not exactly welcomed me with open arms at the paper.

"Women don't belong in the newsroom," Jack had announced my first week, quickly adding, "Nothing personal, Mary Kate."

I resented the high-handed way Jack and Charlie treated me, not as the third musketeer like Tim was, but as an interloper, an outsider who was not welcome. This surprised me about Jack because he is like family to me. I couldn't quite account for his standoffish and sometimes rude behavior. And he set the tone and took the lead for Charlie to treat me the same way. I wondered what to expect when we took the trip to Lomaland. It could be a very long day.

Saturday came, and Charlie was late. It was cool that morning, overcast, with no sun in sight, but I knew the sun would soon push through. Sitting on the porch waiting for him, I was scheming how to wheedle myself into any photo opportunity he might get with Katherine Tingley so I could ask her a few questions. Father had told me that Mrs. Tingley was forbidden by her lawyer to give interviews until after the trial, but it was worth a try.

I was excited about the prospect of visiting Lomaland and seeing *A Midsummer Night's Dream.* This would be my first play, Shakespeare, no less. The night before, Mother surveyed my clothing choices for a cool morning ride in an open buggy and later seated in an outdoor theater. She lent me her amethyst brooch to wear on her heavy white wool shawl, which I would wear over my purple velvet church dress. Gran had given the broach to her as a remembrance of Tim's birth. It was March, so it could be a bit chilly, especially on the coast, so the shawl would come in handy. Mother found a black, wide-brimmed felt hat of hers to protect me from the sun and avoid garnering even more of those noxious freckles.

I decided to wear my old black boots because they had a particularly high heel. This added a couple of inches to my height and are comfortable and broken in, to say the least. I wanted to be more than a "little bit" of a reporter for the *Union* on my first trip to Lomaland. Charlie is tall, six-foot-three, so standing next to him would be less than impressive, even with the heels.

Father was sitting in his rocker on the porch waiting with me. "You look pretty, Mary Kate," he commented.

"Thank you." I was surprised and pleased; Father isn't much for compliments.

Charlie had told me it was well known that Katherine Tingley rarely turned down a chance to be photographed. She was also known to be a genius at self-promotion and that of her cause. This was an essential element of her fundraising efforts. She also knew that the grand social experiment that was Lomaland was a remarkable event in San Diego's history, and she wanted it to be recorded for posterity. While researching this past week, I read that Lomaland itself had a first-class photography department.

At about 9:20, Charlie drove up. I was alone on the porch; Father had returned to the house. I could see that the contraption that passed for a buggy was dilapidated, to say the least. The leather on the seat was cracked, and the stuffing was partially exposed. The brown sway-back mare was in a similar shape.

"Good morning, Charlie said, obviously irritated; get in," he ordered.

"Good morning," I said, a lilt in my voice, hurrying off the porch. There was a stirrup-type contraption used to hoist a passenger into the seat. Charlie made no effort to assist me, and I was determined not to ask him for help. *Could I make it up there by myself?*

Pulling my skirts together and putting my boot in the stirrup, I started to swing myself up. I tilted backward and started to fall; Charlie grabbed my arm and roughly pulled me up into the seat, laughing while he did so. I was not amused.

"Thanks a lot," I said, really irritated; my face was beginning to get red and hot.

"Off we go," he said, clicking the horse forward. She didn't move. Taffy, let's go," he said and clicked again, this time snapping the whip, which didn't touch the horse, but it got her attention, and she began to move forward.

It turned into a beautiful day, the sun had come out, and the mostly dirt roads were dry and in pretty good shape. We made the nine-mile journey in a little over three hours, including occasional rest stops for Taffy along the way. It didn't take long for me to tell that despite his professed irritation about the trip, Charlie was just as excited about the prospect of his first visit to Lomaland as I was.

We left Rabbitville, crossed Broadway, and before long, we were in the country. There is nothing there but small sheep and cattle ranches. We passed the large sparkling white home of Alonso and Lydia Horton high on the hill above us. We continued for miles and saw nothing but dry, wheat-colored grasses, chaparral, and an occasional oak tree, their dark green shapes dotting the golden landscape.

There were very few trees in arid San Diego and almost none in Rabbitville when my parents settled there. There were many now. Father planted two fruit trees in the backyard, but we had to help nature out by bringing water in, especially during dry spells. We had a shared well that served our neighborhood. There was not much water for development or farming in San Diego. I wondered where Mrs.Tingley got the water for her Lomaland.

It took only a short while for the ice to melt between Charlie and me. We were not far out of New Town when he began to whistle *Bicycle built for two,* a very popular little ditty we often sang at home. "Come on, join in, Mary Kate."

'Problem is when I tried to whistle, nothing came out but dry air; it was like air escaping from a bicycle tire. Charlie started to laugh, and I abruptly stopped whistling. He said nothing; he just chuckled again to himself, shaking his head in mock disgust. 'Couldn't fault him; I am a pretty pitiful whistler.

Charlie and I shared a love of adventure, and this trip to exotic Lomaland was just that. Neither of us had been there. I found myself laughing at Charlie's stories which were mostly about things that happened at the paper. I especially enjoyed hearing about various outings that he and Jack had had with Tim. We also talked about our personal lives, our interests, and how he came to be a news photographer.

He told me, as we drove along, that his parents' families both lived in New York. His grandfather Wilson was a successful banker in upstate New York, and his father followed him in that business. He added that he was expected to do the same.

"They were unhappy that I wanted to make my life as a news photographer. It certainly doesn't pay much. But they couldn't dissuade me. Eventually, my mother let them know that photography was my calling, "my gift," and that they should leave me alone. They did, but it does come up occasionally; my father always hopes I'll change my mind. After all, I'm their only son."

Charlie drove a ways further when we took a break to give Taffy a drink. The sound of her slurping the water told us she was mighty thirsty. I took out a canteen of lemonade I had brought and poured two glasses. It was tart, but it tasted good.

We got back on the road, and Charlie resumed his story. Warming to the task, he enthusiastically spoke about this time in his life. The more he talked, I began to understand and respect him as someone who had a vision of what news photography should be.

He said that his grandfather Hal on his mother's side is a professor of English literature at New York University, N-Y-U, as Charlie called it. He said that he stayed with his grandfather in New York City every summer, and he often took him to the museums there.

"We went to museums of all kinds, all of them of great interest to my grandfather. His enthusiasm for these places and what they had to teach us was contagious. One of those museums was the New York Metropolitan Museum of Art."

"He would tell me about paintings and other types of artwork and about the artists themselves. He is what I call an *interested* human being. He is interested in just about anything in his world and its people. I learned that quality from him. It is important as a photographer, especially a news photographer."

Charlie said that one day they chanced upon an exhibition of an early photojournalist—Alfred Waud. He told me that he was an artist and a photographer assigned by *Harper's Weekly* to cover the great battles of the Civil War. The exhibition covered the Battle of the Wilderness. Waud made phenomenal sketches of battle scenes and took hundreds of photographs. "Most battles in the Civil War were fought near big cities, and people often came out to watch them. Waud went out to the battlefields with his heavy equipment, his large camera and glass plates and captured what he saw—and, more important, what he felt when he saw it."

Charlie paused, he seemed to be remembering those days at the museum.

"There were sketches and photographs of seriously wounded, panicked soldiers on the ground, the ambulance corps beside them trying their best to care for them while fires ignited by guns and canons burned around them. Waud captured those moments and recorded them for posterity, for history, in a way that the printed word alone just could not do. This was something new, something exciting; I was mesmerized by it."

"I was seventeen that summer and often returned to look at the Waud photographs a number of times. They spoke to me. I knew then that photojournalism was what I wanted to do with my life. "

"My grandfather was more than happy to oblige. He set me up with photographic equipment and made a darkroom in a shed in his backyard. He also got me an apprenticeship with the portrait photographer Peter Morley who was in the NYU neighborhood."

Charlie had been talking so much that he got thirsty again. He pulled the reins and stopped the carriage. "Got any more of that lemonade?"

I nodded and poured him another glass and one for myself. He clicked the horse forward and continued his tale.

"I was pretty much Mr. Morley's pack-mule that summer, but I learned to take photographs. He was no great artist. He did not, and could not, teach me what makes a great photograph; just mechanically how to take a photograph and how to print them.

He also helped me make the acquaintance of well-known photographers in town who took event photographs. These, by their very nature, must be aimed at capturing a moment, the event that was taking place before the camera. It was, in a sense, news photography."

"Hanging around with event photographers, they shared techniques with me about equipment use and photography in the field. This was invaluable. They taught me that taking a great news photograph was a combination of study and accident. I developed an eye for what makes a good photograph. By the time I got to San Diego, I was a trained news photographer."

He said that a few months later, his father was sent to San Diego to look over the prospects for establishing a bank there.

"He took my mother with him. Things looked very promising. The lure of this place, with its spectacular weather, the beauty of the bay, not to mention the intoxicating idea of moving West, was so great that my parents packed up and moved to San Diego just a few months after they returned home from their visit."

"Still in school, my parents left for the West Coast without me. I finished college and moved to San Diego a month later. I had just turned eighteen. I was young, but even then, I had developed a pretty extensive portfolio of photographs."

"I applied for a job at the *Union* first thing. Henry looked at my photographs and hired me on the spot. The *Union* had a photographer at the time who Henry said was a drunk. He said he planned to give him his walking papers, and he did."

We passed Fort Rosecrans, the military presence on this side of the bay at a small harbor called La Playa. It wasn't impressive; just some wood barracks and one brick building with a large canon sitting in front of it. A lighthouse and a small military presence were at the other end of the peninsula, which guided ships into San Diego Bay when its light was not obscured by fog and it often was.

This was where Cabrillo landed and claimed San Diego for Spain. Eventually, the tall, lighted temples at Lomaland, further down the peninsula, were used to guide ships coming into the bay where the fog was not as much of an issue.

Soon we arrived at the dirt road that would take us to Lomaland, which had the same arid, treeless grassland that we had seen all along the way. I thought about what Katherine Tingley once said about this peninsula, that it was the place she would build what she called her "White City on the hill, facing east, overlooking the Pacific." Remarkably, she bought the property for Lomaland, nearly five hundred acres, sight unseen. "White City? Maybe someday, but so far, I couldn't see it.

'Word was that Mrs. Tingley met John Fremont, one of the West's greatest explorers, at a social function on the East Coast. He recommended Point Loma to her as a perfect location for the utopian community she planned. She believed him, and years later, after sending agents out to scout it, she bought the property without ever having seen it. On a cloudy day in July 1885, witnessed by thousands of curious San Diego citizens, she laid the cornerstone for what is now Lomaland.

As we drove further, the landscape began to bloom on one side of the road. We had arrived—Lomaland, the intriguing, mysterious social experiment in this most unlikely place.

Chapter 10

I was sure that Charlie could sense my excitement as we drove along. He seemed to have a can't-wait attitude too. We passed the lower section of the property, which was bordered by a wooden fence with a large stone gate fashioned to look like the original found somewhere in ancient Rome. We could see that it was locked. "The main gate must be ahead," Charlie said.

He gave a click or two in a futile effort to urge Taffy to speed up. She had one speed, slow. Soon we arrived at an even more impressive stone gate at the crest of a hill, styled after the original somewhere in ancient Egypt.

I knew from my research that Mrs. Tingley was always on about the study of what she called "antiquities." Finding reproductions of them here was no surprise. They were reproductions, yes, but they were well done.

The Egyptian gate, which welcomed visitors to Lomaland, is impressive indeed. It is about thirty-five feet high in what was made to look like ocher-colored stone. It has two slender columns on each side. There are two identical gates, much smaller, on each side of the main gate, with interior wooden gates to secure the property with locks when it is closed to visitors. On the far side of the gate, there was a group of horses, buggies, and carts tied up to a wooden rail.

"Whoa, Taffy," Charlie said as he guided her to a place at the rail, positioning her so she could reach the watering can when tied up. He jumped off the buggy and reached up to help me down, a pleasant surprise. He pulled himself back onto the buggy, unfastened his camera bag tied to the back of the seat, and handed it to me.

Charlie had told me on the way that the invention by George Eastman of the very portable Kodak Brownie camera last year, revolutionized news photography. He said the old box and glass plate cameras were so big and cumbersome and that the development of pictures produced with them was such a long process. "This made contemporaneous shots essential to the newspaper business, difficult if not impossible."

"The Brownie has changed all that. It allows us to take news photographs for use in the next edition. It also has made photography accessible to everyone; it's easy to use and affordable. "You ought to get one; they're cheap, only a dollar."

"Now everyday people can take candid pictures of their family and friends, capturing their memories, the times of their lives. The next thing we need is a better way to provide lighting for night and inside use. They've got something now, but it doesn't work well; the best photographs from the Brownie are taken outside."

Then I spotted it, the "Tingley Wagon" that Father talked about when the lawsuit was filed. It was a wagon at the head of the line of carriages and buggies. It was painted with a great flourish on both sides with the sun, the moon, flowers, vines, birds, and even monkeys, all circling the name "LOMALAND," which was written in large purple letters. An elaborately carved wooden chair with an overstuffed purple velvet seat was mounted on the back.

"Madam Tingley's throne, no doubt," Charlie remarked.

We walked to the small archway where several beautiful young women checked in visitors. They were dressed like fairies or nymphs and wore pretty flowered wreaths around their heads laced with white satin ribbons which blew in the wind.

They wore white calf-length dresses made of some type of gauzy material. This was layered with uneven pointy hems showing quite a bit of leg, which Charlie pointed out with a grin. They wore sandals, the likes of which I had never seen. They were white, flat-soled fabric shoes with laces that tied up the nymph's bare calves. Some might call their attire a bit revealing, racy even, but I assumed they were costumes for their roles in *A Midsummer Night's Dream.* Charlie handed the tickets to the prettiest of the nymphs, who seemed to be in charge.

"We are here to see *A Midsummer Night's Dream.* I'm a photographer for the *Union*. I would like to take a few pictures for the paper."

She took the tickets and gave him a dazzling, flirtatious smile. "Of course, sir," she cooed, let me know when you want to pause during our tour to photograph something and we'll stop."

She left for a minute and briefly chatted with the covey of nymphs standing a few feet away. When she returned, she told us that since we would be stopping more than the regular tour, being press and all, it would be just the three of us in her group.

"My name is Pamela," she said, again flashing that dazzling smile apparently reserved for Charlie alone. "Let's get going."

The Universal Brotherhood at Lomaland employs many forward-thinking ideas of universal peace, a better, kinder way of living, and progressive ideas about nutrition, education, and prisoner issues like capital punishment. But when it comes to matters between the sexes, it is straight out of the Victorian age, as is Katherine Tingley herself.

No interpersonal contact between young people is allowed at Lomaland; nothing even close to a one-on-one relationship between young girls and young men is permitted. I guess their hosting operations at events like this one give the nymphs a chance to hone their flirtation skills, which, as I observed, were quite well-honed already.

75

Jack told me yesterday that young men coming of age sexually at Lomaland have to be restrained by what they call "sleep jackets" at nighttime to guard against what he called "self-abuse." He was laughing a little when he told me this. I nodded and laughed with him but had no idea what he was talking about.

Babe came over for dinner last night and I asked her about it privately; I could ask her about anything. She gave out a raucous laugh at the question. After she explained things, I was relieved that I hadn't asked Jack to explain it, and just pretended I knew what he was talking about.

As we walked up to the Egyptian gate, you could see that it was positioned to frame the large temples of Lomaland in the distance with their exotic glass domes of purple and sea green. The click, click, click of his Brownie told me that Charlie recognized this as a great shot, perfect for page one, above the fold.

As we began our tour, I learned from our guide that Mrs. Tingley had her hand in everything at Lomaland, she even designed the attachments to one of the smaller temples. Pamela pointed to the brightly colored yellow and red glass flames on the corners of the building as she imparted this information. I suspected that the flames give a rather garish effect to the otherwise beautiful buildings when lit at night. She explained, in a most serious and respectful tone, that the flames represent wisdom. Charlie raised his eyebrows and smiled at me.

"Most of the structures here are topped with purple glass domes, even many of the small circular "Lotus Pods" which house the children of the community, who we call Lotus Buds. They sleep away from their parents, who live elsewhere on the property. This is part of the revolutionary child-rearing philosophy put into practice at Lomaland."

"Theosophists believe that children should be taught in the life-affirming ways of Theosophy at an early age so that the baggage often brought by way of instruction and discipline by their parents, doesn't interfere with their spiritual development."

She stopped and looked at us and then spoke in a very solemn tone. "No physical discipline is ever used at Lomaland. There was a recent inspection of the school at Lomaland by State officials. They were impressed with how advanced the children were in their studies and how quiet and well-behaved they were."

We walked to the crest of the hill where you could see the agricultural fields and other trees, plants, and flowers that were thriving, with the blue Pacific shimmering in the distance. Most of the structures at Lomaland are surrounded by exotic trees and flowers. It was spring. There were sprawling wisteria vines with their purple flowers in full bloom everywhere the eye could see. It was impressive, magical, fantastic. A white city on a hill? Pretty darn close.

Before long, our nymph guide proudly showed us the most impressive structure: the magnificent Greek theater. It is just stunning, beautiful. The large, elegant structure was placed on the cliff with its perfect pillars sparkling white in the sun, its fan-shaped white amphitheater facing the Pacific below. Our nymph breathlessly told us this was a replica of the one in Greece, and that it is the only one in the United States.

Pamela and Charlie talked for a few minutes, and then we found seats in the last row of the amphitheater. The sounds of a small musical ensemble tuning up behind us filled the air. "Stay here," Charlie told me, "I need to find seats up front where I can get up easily to take my shots."

With minimal effort and a great deal of charm, Charlie got us two seats in the first row on the aisle, not far from a small portable wooden staircase leading to the stage. Two older women he had spoken to whose seats he wanted, beamed with approval at this handsome young man. They happily moved over so he could be near where Mrs.Tingley would take the stage and make welcoming remarks. He waved me to come down and take my seat next to him. He got up so I could take the inside seat; the ladies didn't beam at me.

Soon, our nymph came down to the left side of the stage area and walked up the steps. She faced the stage as if watching the play, then turned to look at Charlie. He gave the pose a thumbs-up and a wide grin. She returned his smile and went back into position with her dress and the ribbons in her hair blowing in the breeze. He stood up, aimed his camera, and took a few shots.

"Perfect," he said.

He took a small piece of paper and a pencil from his pocket, went to the stage area, and handed it to our nymph. She wrote something on it and returned it to him. He told me when he came back to his seat that he had asked her for her last name and address so he could send a copy of the picture to her and, I suspected, ask to see her again. He handed me the note. She had printed "Pamela Spaulding, Lomaland." I was surprised at feeling jealous at the attention Charlie was showering on this very pretty girl.

I recognized the name. Her father, baseball legend Albert Spaulding, lived at Lomaland in the most prominent residence there. He had even built a golf course not far from his home. Spaulding and his wife were the most important supporters of Katherine Tingley and the Point Loma Theosophists, financially and otherwise. His daughter, Pamela, is beautiful, charming, *and* rich. Naturally, Charlie got her address.

Jack and Charlie are quite skilled with the ladies. Father sometimes regaled us at dinner with stories about the bevy of beauties that would stop by at the paper, dropping off lunch, cookies, and all manner of goodies for them.. Charlie was awfully handsome, so tall, and with that dark hair and those beautiful blue eyes.

Jack was handsome, too, but in a different way. Charlie was the kind of young man every mother welcomed her daughter to bring home for supper. Jack, not so much. He had a rough-and-tumble appearance, with that mischievous bad-little-boy look found so often in his big brown eyes. And Jack could *be* a bad boy. He likes to tease, likes to fight, and has a quick temper.

Tim had been timid with the fairer sex and proudly told me that Charlie and Jack were showing him the ropes. He had shared a few stories of young ladies they had introduced him to, although he never took one out.

The theater was nearly full. People were twittering with anticipation. The stage was set with a hand-painted background of a magical forest. It had a large weeping willow tree about fifteen feet tall with a rough-hewn bark and drooping branches with silvery leaves and purple flowers.

The show was about to begin. The nymphs that greeted us at the front gate, including our Pamela, took to the stage, followed by a great round of applause. They carried tall poles festooned with purple satin streamers, which blew in the cool breeze coming up the cliffs from the ocean. Then, as if heralding the arrival of a queen, the trumpets sounded, and the queen of Lomaland, Katherine Tingley, took to the stage.

She was decked out in a long purple dress with a three-foot train that pooled at her feet. She had white scarves circling her neck and off her shoulders that streamed behind her as she walked. She had a shock of thick black hair tied into a bun laced with pearls at the nape of her neck. Her hair was streaked with white around her face, giving her an otherworldly look. There was no doubt about it: even before she spoke, the woman had presence.

I had never seen Katherine Tingley in person. Still, like everyone else in San Diego, I had heard a great deal about her and had seen pictures of her in the paper and in my research for the trial.

She was smaller than I expected, plump, and on the plain side. None of these demerits affected the charisma and power of this woman and the simple message she conveyed.

San Diego's potential was being unlocked by visionaries who could see what it was destined to become, and yes, one of those visionaries was Katherine Tingley. She recognized the potential here from the first and built her dreams around it. It was not so much what she said that day; it was how she said it.

She only made brief remarks, welcoming the guests to Lomaland and giving a little pitch about what a remarkable social experiment it is. She told us that Theosophy had no less a goal than changing humankind for the better: "If people could learn the tools of good living, they could be happier and healthier, and we could all live together in peace."

It was not the power of her words but the power of her belief in those words, in her mission, that was so compelling. It was her life's work, which she fully believed in and wanted to share with humankind worldwide. She told the crowd, "Things can be better, so much better, and we can start right here, right now, at Lomaland."

I could hear the click, click of Charlie's camera and the scraping sound of his advancing his film about a dozen times as he took photographs of Mrs. Tingley during her remarks. Charlie told me that taking several photographs is a good way to get one or two really good ones in the bunch.

Both Charlie and I enjoyed the play. We hurried to leave Lomaland in time to get home before dark. We stopped along the way. There is a small harbor with a Chinese fishing village, and behind it, there is a small Indian community.

The Chinese were putting away their fishing equipment for the day. We sat on a bench by the dock and finished our picnic lunch. I shivered and pulled my shawl closer. It was getting cooler, with a slight breeze coming our way. Charlie excused himself and stepped away to answer nature's call behind a stand of trees up the hill.

"We'd better take off," he said when he returned, handing me a small beaded change purse that he had bought from the Indians.

"Why thank you, sir," I said, very pleased. He smiled rather shyly in response.

We didn't talk much on our way home; we both were tired. Charlie dropped me off at home. I thanked him for taking me and told him how much I had enjoyed the day. "I did too, he replied.

"See you Monday."

Chapter 11

The next day I slept in a bit. It was Sunday. After church, I wrote the first draft of my story wanting the events of the day before to be fresh in my mind.

I worked all week on the story and a separate piece about the play that was to go into my women's section. Henry helped me with the play review after dinner. He and Babe often came for dinner on Sundays.

This was the first Sunday my announcements and articles would appear in the women's pages. Father gave me until Friday to get the Lomaland story and *Midsummer Night's Dream* piece ready for the printers. He wanted them both in Sunday's edition with the Lomaland story on page one above-the-fold.

He gave me high marks for the story after only three rewrites, which isn't many for him. Jack told me in my first week that Father's teaching method is pretty basic. "He reviews what a reporter writes and either keeps it without comment or sends it back with the notation, "No, M. R." leaving them to figure out what he wanted. Before long, they did."

Charlie's photograph of the temples at Lomaland, as framed by the Egyptian gate, which made the front page, was perfect. The shot of Mrs. Tingley watching *A Midsummer Night's Dream* from the sidelines of the Greek Theater appeared next to the story's jump, the continuation of the story on page two. He captured her perfectly. Her head was thrown back; she was laughing at something from the play. Candid, it revealed another side of the grand Madam Purple: playful, funny.

Father was right; seeing Lomaland and Mrs. Tingley in her habitat gave me a better insight into what she was all about. The best part of the trip for me was getting to know Charlie better and becoming friends with him.

My relationship with him improved dramatically after the Lomaland trip. He was friendly and helpful and even took to sharing his most recent jokes with me. He doesn't have Jack's skill as a storyteller, but I sure enjoyed his attention.

I talked about my feelings about Charlie with Theodora. She is man-crazy, and I planned to go to her on all things romance when I had any. She mostly talked about her experiences. I was very interested in those stories, and she was very funny in the tellin'.' We often sat on the porch, rocking in our chairs, laughing about her experiences, especially when she talked about the young men she called "clunkers."

"Are you attracted to Charlie?" she asked me. Theodora was attracted to just about any young man she met, so she wasn't any stranger to the idea. She always seemed to be in love with one lad or the other.

"Yes, I think I am," I replied.

"How does he feel about you?"

"No sign of that. He treats me like a work friend, but now a friend he likes a little better." She said she thought his giving me the Indian-beaded purse was a clear sign of romantic interest. Try as I might, it didn't seem that way to me.

On Thursday of that next week, Charlie surprised me by inviting me to his parent's home on Saturday night for their twenty-fifth wedding anniversary dinner. "It will be just a few friends and family. It's a little bit formal, though, nothing too fancy, just not a work dress.

"I'd be delighted," I said, flabbergasted at the invitation.

Was he courting me? I asked myself and, later, Theodora.

"Of course he is, you ninny," Theodora replied.

As amiable and even helpful as Charlie had become, Jack was quite the opposite. He made a point to let me know he was most unhappy that I was given the Lomaland assignment by myself. I was an apprentice, after all. It was an actual news story in the field, scheduled for the front- page, his turf.

Jack had a sit-down with Father about his giving me what he considered his story; after all, it was planned for page one, above-the fold. Father didn't mention it to me, but Cheesy told me about it and said that the discussion got pretty heated. *Great, my interactions with Jack are going to get even worse.*

He let Charlie know, without saying it, that he was annoyed that we had a good time on the trip. After all, Charlie was always Jack's number-one ally. He was miffed that *his* friend didn't back him up and punish me for grabbing *his* turf and elbowing into *his* territory. I'm sure he thought my family connection with the boss was how this happened, and I was sure he was worried about it happening in the future.

Jack's nose was clearly out of joint about this, and his gruff manner towards me became even more so. He has always treated me as an annoying kid sister when he came to the house before Tim died. Now I sensed that he felt somewhat threatened by me and even jealous. He seemed to feel I intended to take his place with my Father at home and at the paper.

I looked forward to Saturday night. Mother altered her cream-colored, lace wedding dress for me to wear to the party. She had made it herself and beaded it with seed pearls in the front. It had a high neck and long lace sleeves. It hugged my slight figure, and I looked pretty good in it.

84

Mother was excited about my night out with what she called "My young man." The night of the dinner, after quite a bit of squirming on my part, she fixed my hair on top of my head with a string of pearls woven through my red curls, a few tendrils at my neck and ears. "Hold still," she kept saying, irritated.

She finished her handiwork by putting her pearl drop earrings on my ears. Mother clucked over me like a mother hen, and when I came downstairs, I could tell that Father was pleased not only with how I looked, but that I was on my first outing with a young man. "You look darn near as pretty as your mother did in that dress."

"Charlie is an awfully handsome young man; you will make a lovely couple," Mother chimed in. I suspected she had already put him on her list of eligible young men.

"He is just a friend, Mother," I told her, but I wasn't so sure.

Things were changing. First Father complimented me on my appearance when I went to Lomaland, and just a week later, he did it again. I liked it, this new side of my father; I was changing too.

Charlie arrived to pick me up dressed in a black tuxedo, looking, as my mother said later, "criminally handsome." *Yes indeed.* He didn't compliment me on my appearance, but I could tell by how he looked at me that he approved.

"Let's get going, he said, and we walked towards the door.

"Have a good time," Mother said. Father piped in… "And Mary Kate, I paused and turned to look at him. "Happy Birthday."

"It's your birthday? Charlie said, surprised.

Returning his smile, "Yes, I am eighteen years old today."

"Well, happy birthday Mary-Kate-Riley," emphasizing each part of my name as he said it.

Charlie helped me into the beautiful black carriage and his driver, Ben, made his way up to Banker's Hill. The carriage stopped in front of his parent's house, and what a house it is. It is a three-story tan-colored beauty trimmed in dark green, burgundy, and white. It has a large round turret on the third floor that looks out to the city and the bay. The sun sets in that direction; it must be a spectacular sight from that window.

As we walked up the front steps, the door was of carved wood with a clear, leaded-glass insert with an intricate design. The house is situated among several houses equally as grand. It is set off by a large Carolina pine in the front yard, its dramatic spires reaching for the sky.

Charlie opened the door, and his father, Thomas, who Charlie strongly resembles, and his mother, Maisie, were waiting in the foyer. They greeted me warmly and introduced themselves. Mr. Wilson is tall and handsome, with striking blue eyes like Charlie's. He is silver-haired and greeted me with a charming smile.

Charlie's mother is a beautiful woman who was dressed in an elegant dark-green low-cut dress that accented her sparkling green eyes and lovely figure. She had a wild mop of red hair that she let loose to cavort around her head in a riot of curls. No freckles, I noticed; where _did_ she hide them?

"So nice to meet you, dear," his mother said, extending her hand. "Charlie has told us so much about you. So glad you could come."

Mrs. Wilson was not only beautiful but charming and very funny. She was the hit of the party and couldn't have been more gracious. She loves to tell stories and is her own best audience, giving out a raucous laugh at the punch line, causing everyone to laugh whether the joke is funny or not. She clearly dotes on Charlie, her only child. Mr. Wilson was quiet and a bit stiff. I guess that was right; after all, he is a banker.

There was a short period after we arrived when guests chatted a bit and drank cocktails in the large front room of the house. Charlie got me a cherry brandy, my first; I liked it. Before long, he gave me his arm and took me to the dining room.

The silver service and fine china were set on a long mahogany dining table on a cream-colored tablecloth. There were off-white, glowing candles and two lovely bouquets of cream-colored roses in low crystal vases. The scene was understated and elegant.

About twenty people were sitting around the table. Still, everyone was so cordial that it seemed like a small family affair. I sat next to Charlie's mother at dinner, and we chatted as if we were long-lost friends. We ate roast beef and potatoes, with a starter of what tasted like mushroom soup. It even had a special spoon. It was topped with a dash of cream; delicious. We all talked, laughed, drank champagne, another first for me, and toasted the Wilsons for their twenty-five years together.

At one point, Charlie told everyone of our recent trip to Lomaland and what a fantastic place it is. I added my two cents and said I was especially impressed with Mrs. Tingley. "She has done many wonderful things out there."

A couple of the other guests chimed in with their impressions of Lomaland, all were positive.

"The whole thing is a bit different, to be sure," Mrs. Wilson said. "Kate Tingley has undoubtedly ruffled the feathers of our local clergy, but I think most people believe the work she has done at Lomaland has been good for San Diego."

"I can say this: the musical productions I have seen at her Isis Theater here in town are first-rate. The restoration the Theosophists did of the old Fisher Opera House is exceptional. The place has been brought back to its former grandeur. And Lomaland has produced excellent musicians, singers, dancers, and dramatic performers."

"Did you know that all students at Lomaland must learn a musical instrument regardless of talent? The Theosophists think it is an essential discipline in any child's education. It sounds like a good idea. I tried to get Charlie to learn the piano, but he refused to practice."

She shot a disapproving look at her son, who simply smiled back at her. She turned to me, "Have you met Katherine Tingley, Mary Kate?

"Not yet, but I look forward to it.

"Are you covering her case for the paper?

"Yes Ma'am, as my father's apprentice."

"Have you met Mrs. Tingley?" I asked her.

"I have not; she is not much for mingling in San Diego society. I would like to meet her; she's an interesting woman."

There was much conversation at the table—mostly family stories from the guests who all had known the Wilsons for a long time. Everyone was relaxed and having a good time; a gathering of old friends celebrating a lovely couple. It wasn't the stiff, formal affair I had expected. I was very comfortable with these people.

After we finished the dessert, more champagne was delivered to each guest, the glasses were already poured. Mr. Wilson, who was seated at the head of the table, stood up. "Please, everyone, join me in a toast. He raised his glass and looked at me,

"To the lovely Mary Kate Riley…Happy Birthday. She is eighteen years old today. We are so pleased to have you here tonight to celebrate your birthday with you." He raised his glass and saluted me with it.

My face burned with blush while everyone else looked my way and raised their glasses. I felt Charlie touch my left hand to reassure me. *Was this a romantic gesture?* He then raised his glass and toasted me with his other hand with a wide smile. It was a grand moment and one I would never forget.

When Charlie took me home I wondered whether he would make any romantic overtures, a kiss goodnight maybe. He had not done anything like that during the party. Maybe I was just there as a female friend, a buddy from the paper.

Still, he was charming, gracious, and very funny, very much like his mother. His jokes, which it seemed this group of family friends was used to, were met with groans at the punch lines, but that didn't slow him down in his efforts to make them laugh.

Charlie and I had a good time together. At the end of the evening, Ben drove us to my house. We talked about the various people at the party and what a nice occasion it was. Ben pulled the carriage up in front of my house and stopped. Charlie jumped out, helped me down, and followed me up the porch and to the door. Nervous; I had never kissed a man, or a boy, either.

Theodora and I had practiced what she was sure would be my first kiss. We didn't actually kiss, but she told me how to prepare and what to do to respond. She used a hand mirror on my desk for the last part, giving the mirror what looked to be a passionate kiss. This prompted a cackle of laughter from both of us.

When Charlie and I got to the door, I stopped, got on my tiptoes, turned my face toward his, and waited for him to kiss me. I had practiced this move with Theodora. But he didn't kiss me. Instead, he simply ignored my state of humiliating readiness to be kissed and simply said, "Good night, and thanks for going with me. And Happy Birthday."

"Thank you for a wonderful evening, Charlie. I liked your parents very much." He smiled and opened the door for me to go in, the tips of my ears burning with humiliation. I was disappointed and was glad it was dark because it hid my blush.

Lying in bed waiting for sleep, I thought about Charlie kissing me, putting his arms around me, disappointed that he didn't see me that way, the way I was starting to see him. Didn't he find me attractive at all?

I re-hashed the evening with my parents at breakfast, omitting the kiss or no kiss issue. Theodora came over at about noon. She planned to stay for lunch as she often did on Sunday visits; we rarely went to her house. Her father was always working, and her mother was in feeble health.

We sat on the porch and reviewed every detail of my night with Charlie. We kept our voices to a conspiratorial whisper because my father was in the front yard pruning the rose bushes. She was surprised that this was simply a party I was invited to as a friend who just happened to be a female. She was even more shocked that he didn't kiss me. "It was your birthday, for heaven's sake."

I told Theodora before the day came, that my parents and I had decided we wouldn't make a big fuss about my birthday this year. We all agreed that it was too painful for all of us without Tim. His loss was still so new, so raw. So, I was not surprised that Theodora didn't mention my birthday on Sunday.

"Be careful what you wish for," my Gran often says. I admit being disappointed that my eighteenth birthday was utterly uneventful at the Riley house, even though that is what we planned. After about an hour of talking about the night at Charles's parents' while rocking in our chairs on the porch, I heard Mother's voice, "Lunch is ready, everybody, come in and eat."

I looked in the front yard to see if Father had heard her; he must have gone in the back way; he wasn't there. Theodora opened the door, and we went in. I was greeted with a hearty "Happy Birthday" from my mother, father, and Theodora. Presents wrapped in colorful paper were piled on the table. Streamers were strung across the front room. Theodora had made the banner that hung over the table, which proclaimed, in big blue letters, EIGHTEEN!

Mother had made a beautiful birthday cake and placed it next to the presents. A plate of sandwiches was next to that, along with a bowl of fruit salad, my favorite, and a pitcher of lemonade. A brand new blue women's bicycle was parked in front of everything. I could see this was the newest model with a skirt- guard designed to keep women's dresses from catching in the spokes. Having fallen twice off Tim's bicycle and suffering a few scrapes and bruises, my parents wouldn't allow me to ride his bicycle again. My parents would not relent.

Being left behind stuck me in my craw as the gang liked to ride around quite a bit on their bicycles. Theodora received a women's bicycle for Christmas, and now I had one so we could ride together. "Gosh, thanks," I said, looking at my parents. They were all smiles too.

"Let's take a ride after lunch; you can ride your bike down to my house; I'll get mine, and off we'll go," Theodora suggested. She seemed as excited as I was about the bicycle.

Without further ado, Father urged us to get to the eatin' part of the celebration. "Let's eat," he said; I'm hungry, and it's an hour past my lunchtime." He sat down at his usual spot at the head of the table. Father was a very regimented kind of man when it came to his feeding schedule: breakfast at seven, lunch at noon, dinner at six.

Mother and Theodora put the presents on the kitchen counter with the cake while I put the plates, silverware, and napkins at the places at the table. We sat down, chatted away, ate lunch, and then I opened my presents.

Theodora raced our bicycles all over New Town, riding mainly in the flat parts bordering the bay. Did I miss my brother? I did, but only fleetingly. I knew somehow he was there with us, wishing me Happy Birthday as he always did, and that gave me a good feeling.

Chapter 12

I was busy my first two months at the paper, learning and doing, meeting people all over town, and enjoying the process. It was nice making a little money too. Father was still drinking but had cut down a great deal. His drinking caused him to be irritable at work, very irritable. Added to this, he was having some back problems, having hurt it moving some furniture for a neighbor last summer. This left him more impatient than ever, his temper at a hair trigger during his morning hangovers.

Everyone in the press room tried to avoid him if he overdid his drinking the night before. He did not spare me and snarled at me as he did to everyone else when he was in one of these dark moods. One time I left crying, as much as I tried to hold back my tears. Cheesy followed me outside and assured me that it was nothing personal. "Just give him a little more time to work things out."

This was hard because I had never experienced this treatment from my father at home, ever. But, he was drinking less and less. Mostly, when he was in these moods, like everyone else at the paper, I tried to figure things out on my own or ask for help from Jack or Henry.

I was excited about being part of Father's coverage of next Saturday's opening of the Carnegie Library, the first library to be built in San Diego. Lydia Horton would be the guest of honor. It was mainly through her efforts that the Carnegie Foundation was persuaded to fund the library construction. Carnegie had built libraries nationwide, and this was the first one it funded in California.

The whole town was expected for the celebration. People were talking about it everywhere I went. And by the way, we know how to celebrate in San Diego. I already knew from attending community celebrations with my family over the years, that people come out at the drop of a hat for one event or the other. Bands are always present, as are various singers and quartets we have come to recognize and expect at town celebrations.

We used to have a town dog, *Bum,* a stray adopted by the City, and he would always be an honored guest, but he died a few years back. *The Horribles* would be there for sure. This is a passel of citizen-clowns that show up at town celebrations in the most outrageous homemade costumes and perform silly, often bawdy, routines, mostly in bad taste. They are much beloved here.

Mother said that the ladies in town would be baking up a storm: cakes, fruit pies, cookies, brownies, strudels, meat pies-the works. Mother made six dozen Snickerdoodles that she placed in a large basket sitting on a beautiful red-checked lace-trimmed cloth spilling over the sides which made for a beautiful display on the food table.

She told us at dinner the night before that the celebration would have lemonade, iced tea, and beer. Joe in County Records told me yesterday that the gambling-hall owners from the Stingaree were arm-wrestled into providing free beer. On Thursday morning, there was a change in plans. Father told me that he had decided to give Jack the library story.

"This way, he said, I can focus on my bride. I'm takin' her to the celebration, then out to dinner."

My parents' twenty-second anniversary had just passed with little fanfare and no recognition from Father. Mother didn't say anything, but I could tell she was very disappointed.

The surprise was that Father asked me to interview Lydia Horton after the event for my Sunday women's section.

"Have Charlie get a shot of her to go with your story. Check up in the archives and see what you can find out about our Lydia," he said. Write out a few questions and run them by me. Better yet, run them by Jack. Ask Henry how to contact Mrs. Horton to set up the interview. They're good friends."

Henry was in his office and was pleased to be of help. He picked up his telephone. "Connect me with Mrs. Lydia Horton, please."

No other information was needed for this connection. Alonso and Lydia Horton were the most well-known people in the city. Everyone knew she worked as the librarian at the new Carnegie Library, which had already been open for a few months.

"Lydia, Henry Seymour here. How are you? Fine, fine," he said. "I'd like to have you interviewed after the doings on Saturday for our Sunday edition. I'm sending over one of my most promising young reporters, Mary Kate Riley. That is, of course, if you can find a few minutes of your time to speak to her. . . great, great, Lydia. Now don't be too rough on her."

There was a pause in the conversation on Henry's end. "I suppose you're right about that," he said with a chuckle.

"Mary Kate will be at the library right after the festivities conclude, at least those involving you. Thank you, Lydia ... and Lydia, congratulations. You did us all a great service in getting that library funded. I'm looking forward to seeing you honored on Saturday; the whole town is. Goodbye now."

He put the phone on the receiver and looked up. "She's quite a gal," he said.

It was on. Sucking in my breath, I wondered if I was up to it, my first solo interview. Henry picked up on my nervousness. "Don't worry, Mary Kate, you'll do fine. Your interview is with one of the nicest women in town. She is perfect for your first shot."

"Write out your question, and make sure you listen to her answers. 'Sounds obvious, I know, but new reporters are often so anxious to get their next question asked that they don't listen to the person they are trying to get to know. Listening is an essential tool of a good reporter. You can do this, girl; I know you can."

Turning and heading for the archives across from his office, I looked back. "Thanks, Mr. Seymour." He nodded and smiled.

I researched Lydia Horton for the rest of the day and wrote out my questions for her and some background materials for my article. Reading this over, it seemed like a pretty good start. The next day, I put the article aside to finish other work.

Friday was already a busy day for me as I had to get my women's-page submissions edited and approved by the customers. I had to pick up the real estate sales records and had a few other deliveries for Cheesy. The little extra money I earned at the paper felt good. I was a *paid* newspaper reporter.

Jack was out on a story. He came in about twelve. I approached his desk; he was scribbling away on a sheet of paper, working on the story of the brawl he covered that morning at a bar by the docks. 'Word was that extensive damage had been done by the pugilists, both to each other and to the establishment. He didn't look happy when I interrupted him.

"Jack, would you mind looking over my questions for Lydia Horton for tomorrow? When you get a minute?" I added nervously.

"I guess," he snarled and continued working.

Irritated, I tossed the questions into his box. The entire afternoon went by and he didn't get back to me. Charlie, on the other hand, happily agreed to take a memorable shot of Lydia Horton to go with my article while he was at the celebration.

Later that afternoon, I was at the courthouse in County Records on the second floor. "Hey Joe, how do?" I said with a lilt in my voice.

"Mighty fine, he replied. "You goin'' to the big doins' tomorrow? "

"Sure am."

He smiled and handed me his book of recent property sales. Luckily there were not many that week, so I could make quick work of it. This was my column, and it appeared in the women's section every Sunday. No writing was involved, nor editing, just a listing of the sales that week; who bought and sold what property and for how much. Father said this column was the most popular regular feature in the Sunday edition.

He told me that there was great interest by almost everybody here in land sales. This was by both actual players as well as armchair speculators. What is my property worth? How much will I need to buy a piece of property? And of course, Father told me, many San Diegans read the real estate column because they are just plain nosy and, he added, "that's not a bad thing in our business."

"It's what gives us readership; people want to know what is happening in the city and other places too. And now, with the telephone and the Associated Press wire service, they can not only read local news but be informed on a timely basis on national and world news."

There had been three major real estate booms and busts in San Diego. These fluctuations had a significant impact on most all businesses in the area in terms of employment possibilities. Many people left town. The city had a major loss in population when it lost its bid for the terminus of the transcontinental railroad to Los Angeles. This affected the entire economy of the area. Speculators lost their investments in real estate, and many had to move out of

97

town because they couldn't find jobs that they expected the railroad to bring.

The construction of Lomaland and the Hotel Del Coronado provided much-needed assistance to the economic well-being of the area; both involved major construction which created jobs. These significant projects were a real economic shot in the arm the City of San Diego so dearly needed at the time.

It was near quitting time. No word from Jack. I went to his desk and asked him if he had a chance to look at my questions for the Lydia Horton interview the next day. Again, he was not pleased, an attitude that was starting to get my dander up. He picked the questions out of his box and read them without his reading glasses in less than a minute. "They're fine," he said, shoving them back at me.

Jack has very poor eyesight. He told us that he read a great deal as a boy in the poor light of a gas lamp in his bedroom. He needed to wear glasses to read now, and he always carried them in his vest pocket.

"Please, Jack, can you look at them? It's my first interview." No smile from me; I resented having to beg him.

He huffed impatiently, then grabbed the questions from my hand, put on his glasses, and read them through this time. "They're fine, Mary Kate, really," a hint of apology in his tone. "How 'bout putting one in about living in the shadow of a living legend?"

"By the way, your dad wants me to review your interview story before it goes to the printers tomorrow tonight. I'll be at the paper doing my story after the celebration so that I can look it over then. Meet me here. Oh, he said, time will be short to get the interview story in, so if you need help with the article, let me know."

"Okay, thanks, Jack." He didn't reply; his head went down, and he returned to typing his story.

Chapter 13

On Saturday morning, I put on the emerald green dress and matching hat with the interesting speckled feathers tucked into the band. I got them both from one of my mother's dressmaking customers, Fiona Riggs.

The two women became friends over the years and naturally, Mother spoke about her family during fittings and the like. I was sure that Mrs. Riggs knew all about me. She knew I was about her size. So, when I started at the paper, Mother recognized that my uniform brown would not do for the society functions I would be covering, so she decided to speak to Mrs. Riggs.

She told her that I was about her size, had a new job, and could use better clothes. She suggested to her that she might give me her cast-offs. "I just don't have the time to make her all the dresses she needs, or the money for them for that matter. She needs to look nice.

Mrs. Riggs replied, "I'd be delighted to give her my dresses."

The next time Mrs. Riggs came over for a fitting, she brought a large trunk filled with dresses. Mother altered them at the bust line, as I had none, and they served me well. At first, I wasn't much interested in clothes, but I soon realized that Mother was right, looking my best was important in my line of work.

I checked myself in my bedroom mirror as I left that morning, and felt good about my appearance for my interview with Lydia Horton. There were no women in the news business in San Diego that I had met or even seen, so I didn't know how a serious-looking newswoman dressed.

My hair was in a clip in the back of my neck, and my curls were already beginning to become unruly in the damp air. Curls peeked out from under my hat by my ears. Mother wanted me to put my hair up, but she didn't push it.

I stopped at Moody's to catch a ride up the hill to the library celebration. It was quite a hike, and I had a long day ahead. Frank Moody, Hank's oldest son, drove me there, and on the way, he complimented me on my dress.

"It matches your pretty green eyes, Mary Kate."

"Thank you, Frank."

Frank has flirted with me for years. I pretended not to notice that his actions were meant to be flirting, and he never pressured me for a real response. He finally figured out that I wasn't interested. *And he _be_ correct.*

It was a beautiful sunny day, as we reached the top of the hill, a crowd was already gathering in front of the new library. I couldn't wait to see it. Soon it came into full view, a grand new building sparkling bright white in the morning sun.

It's a Roman-style Beaux Arts building with an ornately decorated arched entry, crowned with a beautiful leaded-glass window. Two matching but less grand windows are on each side, set back on the wings of the building. The words SAN DIEGO'S FREE PUBLIC LIBRARY are etched on a cement banner across the front of the building. The library's benefactor, Andrew Carnegie, has his name presiding high at the top section of the building. It was impressive. Pride welled up in me just seeing it.

Tim and I used to go to the poor excuse for a library that we had before this one was built. It was in an office building where two rooms were reserved as the library. The book selection was pitiful, and what they did have was old and in bad shape.

The worst part was that the rooms were segregated by gender. I never understood why. Tim and I hardly ever went there. We mainly went to see if there were any new books or magazines. The Carnegie was the first actual library in the city, and it was a significant contribution to bringing the city into the modern age.

Frank pulled the buggy over to the right side of the street. Jack and Charlie were sitting on bleachers near the stage, draped with red, white, and blue bunting. Charlie waved and made way for me to sit with them to watch the proceedings. It was early, but the area was rapidly filling with people. He came early to save the seats; he needed a good vantage point for his pictures. There was a buzz of excitement in the air. It promised to be a fun afternoon.

After I joined them in the bleachers, Jack brought each of us a beer, my first. It tasted nasty, and I drank only a few sips. Jack told me, "'Careful now, you don't want to be a booze-bag for your interview with Mrs. Horton."

Charlie laughed. I didn't. Sometimes I don't know when Jack was serious or just teasing. Before the program started, Charlie said, "Hey, Mary Kate, look who's here."

He pointed off to the area near the far side of the stage. It was the Tingley Wagon, and there sat none other than Mother Purple herself. She was alone except for her driver. She was dressed in purple, but this time it was a toned-down, dark purple dress with a simple wide-brimmed black hat. She obviously wanted to draw as little attention as possible.

Mrs. Tingley is a known teetotaler, so it did not surprise me that she left right after the program and before the heavy celebrating got going. She obviously wanted to miss this part of the proceedings, which, if true to form, would get pretty rowdy. She came to celebrate this landmark event in the city and to honor Lydia Horton for making it happen. I wondered if she knew Lydia Horton, who used to live with her former husband at the foot of the Point Loma peninsula.

The program began with a few comments by our mayor, honoring the work of Mrs. Horton in connection with the library's funding. Then the band stuck up with *"Darling Lydia,"* and the crowd enthusiastically sang along. Mrs. Horton, all smiles, sat in a chair on the stage next to her husband Alonso, looking very pleased, as he listened to the crowd serenade his wife.

She's really beautiful, I thought, and so young.

There were a few other speeches, and then the mayor introduced Mrs. Horton, which triggered a huge roar of approval from the citizens of San Diego.

"I appreciate being honored here today, but it would not have happened without the inspiration and support of many others, especially my husband, Alonso." She turned to him; he smiled and nodded.

"The people of San Diego have much to be proud of. The completion of our beautiful library is just another major step on our young city's path toward taking its place as a modern city on the world stage."

She left the stage accompanied by hearty applause; the band struck up with another round of *Darling Lydia,* and the crowd enthusiastically continued their serenade.

After the program, I went into the library which was filled with new books in beautiful oak bookcases. There were large, colorful, watercolor landscapes on the few walls without bookcases. I paused to look at them and noticed that they had the initials L.K.H. on the bottom. *Lydia Knapp Horton.*

They were beautiful. I knew from my research that Mrs. Horton was an accomplished painter. The rooms in the library were paneled in oak that matched the bookcases. All this warmth was quite a contrast to the buildings elegant but cold white exterior.

I had walked only a few steps into the library when I spotted Lydia Horton sipping a cup of tea, sitting at a desk with a gold sign in front of it, LIBRARIAN. She was a bit flushed from the excitement of her day, which was a warm one. I was surprised by how beautiful she was when I saw her on the stage, but she was even prettier close-up, even at sixty years old. She was over thirty years younger than her husband Alonso and his third wife; the other two had died.

Her dark brown hair, laced with only a few strands of gray, was rolled up on top of her head, with soft curls framing her face. She has a lovely, swanlike neck and a porcelain complexion. Her striking, intelligent, and at times playful blue eyes and her charming smile completed the picture. She wore a simple blue velvet dress. Her matching bowler, with one purple feather and a few purple and blue ribbons, was retired to the chair beside her desk. She had worn it for the ceremony, and it looked splendid on her. I extended my hand to her.

"Hello, Mrs. Horton, Mary Kate Riley, reporter from the San Diego *Union*."

She took my hand. "Hello," she said, "Lydia, please. Sit down, dear. How lovely you look in your green."

My heart was pounding, but I tried to act like interviewing her was nothing out of the ordinary. I needn't have worried. We chatted briefly to break the ice before we got started. She offered me some tea from a beautiful white teapot with a Blue Willow pattern; it was just like one my mother had. She poured the hot tea, moving the small pitcher of cream my way. "Cream?"

I nodded, and she handed me the cream. I went through one question after the other, following up on some, and listening to her answers as Henry had schooled me to do. After talking for a few minutes about my family and my work at the paper, it seemed like I was chatting with an old friend.

Finishing up, carefully writing down her answers to my questions, I knew this interview was special. I wanted the public to get to know this fine woman and have my interview capture the best of her. It did.

Q. What do you admire most in a friend?

A. Loyalty.

Q. What trait do you dislike the most in your fellow human beings?

A. People who put on airs. Your value as a human being is in what you do for others, not how much money or status you have.

Q. What do you like best about yourself?

A. My sense of humor.

Q. What do you dislike most about yourself?

A. I hate to admit it, but I haven't been able to break the habit of gossiping. I call it commenting. I'm not mean, but I do like to pass on news. It's a hard habit to break; it's my New Year's resolution every year, for gosh sake.

I am told that I am a determined woman, which is usually not said as a compliment. They mean that if I think something is right, I'm like a dog with a bone. It's true, but I like that about myself. I could be more flexible to be sure. On the other hand, the Carnegie folks kept saying no to the funding of our new library, the one we are sitting in right now. I just wouldn't take no for an answer.

Q. What is your greatest achievement?

A. Well, I still have a lot to do in this life, but I would have to say my two sons. They are wonderful young men, both of them. I'm very proud of them.

Q. You are married to Alonso Horton, recognized by most people here as the founder of modern San Diego. Do you resent living in such a large shadow?

A. No. I'm proud of Alonso and all he has accomplished for this city. He is kind, generous, and, most of all, a happy man. I don't see myself in his shadow. He always has encouraged me to be the woman I wanted to be. He has never held me back.

Q. What would you most like to be remembered for?

A. I've always tried to be a kind, generous, happy woman who serves her family, her community, and her fellow man, she paused, and *woman*, whenever I can.

Q. What is the most important issue you are working on at this time in your life?

A. I'm an avid supporter of women's rights, including the right to vote. The slaves were freed nearly forty years ago and given the right to vote. Women should be freed from their bondage and recognized as full citizens of this country. This includes the right to vote, to be on juries, and to have all the rights men enjoy.

It's coming; I can feel it, and soon. I'm especially concerned with how women are disadvantaged in the area of family relations. Women should have an equal say and equal opportunities in those matters. They are half the marital equation, but not under our current laws. As it is, a woman with an abusive husband must stay with him or leave her children with nothing but the clothes on her back. She has no rights. This is just wrong.

I've never forgotten the words of Susan B. Anthony when she spoke to us on the courthouse steps when she visited San Diego some fifteen years ago. She told us that our government robs women in a marriage of custody of their possessions, their wages, and even their children—and thus, half of the married people are left wholly at the mercy of the other half. Fixing this situation is a high priority for me and many other women in this city.

Q. What is your greatest hope for the new century?

A. That women will come into their own, to be free to make decisions about their own lives, not what is decided for them by their husbands or parents or anyone else. I'd like to see a woman working outside the home be accepted because she wants to be there, not just because economic circumstances require her to be. I went to work at the library to help support my family. Now, even if we didn't need the money, I still would work here. I love it.

Queen Victoria has died. The Victorian era has died with her. It is a new century; we need to look to the future for new ideas and new ways of doing things. It's such an exciting time. There is so much that's new: electric lights, telephones, automobiles, and even paper clips. She picked an errant one off her desk and tossed it in a small crystal bowl with some others. We need to have new thinking, too, especially about the role of women.

Q. Mrs. Horton, you are known as a great philanthropist in the city. Will you tell our readers what you have observed in your work with the poor in our city?

A. As you may know, I founded, with the help of many others, the Wednesday Club, which has as its principal charitable work funding the San Diego Children's Home. The Home serves disadvantaged children but also women who have been left unable to support themselves for one reason or another. If a woman has always worked in the home or has small children and her husband gets sick, dies, or leaves her, what is she to do?

I cannot emphasize enough to your readers how much the basic needs of the poor are served at the Children's Home. Once a year, we have an open house; it's at the end of this month on the twenty-third. I urge all your readers to come to see for themselves all the good work done there. Hopefully, they will want to volunteer or contribute in some way. There will be free refreshments too.

Q. One more question: have gender-segregated reading rooms been eliminated in this new library?

A.   I am happy to say yes; no more reading rooms separated by gender. This is a new century, a new library, and we are committed to doing things in a new way.

Did you know that our new library is one of the few open-stack libraries in the country? This policy allows patrons to browse for materials in the stacks without the librarian accompanying them. This is revolutionary; you will soon see all public libraries provide this vital service to their patrons.

Concluding the interview, I shook the lady's hand and thanked her. Leaving the library that afternoon, I thought of Henry's description of Lydia Horton the other day: "She's quite a gal."

It was four o'clock when I decided to walk back to the paper, needing some fresh air to clear my head. The town celebration was still in full swing, so I would have difficulty getting a carriage to take me there. It had cooled down a bit, and the breeze felt good. Walking down the hill, I decided there was no way I could write and edit a story about my interview that afternoon, let alone get it typed. Next Sunday's edition, maybe? No, it had to go with the library story that Jack was writing.

Stepping up my pace, I got the notion to use the most important questions and Lydia's answers, edited down a bit, and leave the interview in a question-and-answer format. The printers had planned to stay late for Jack's story and Charlie's photographs anyway. A question-and-answer format? I'd never seen it done in the *Union* or any other paper, for that matter. This would surely cause a volcanic eruption from Jack.

He was not back at the paper when I arrived. I went upstairs to the archives where he would not disturb me before my article was finished. I didn't have time to type it, so printing would have to do. I chose a Q&A format as a time-saver initially. Still, the more I worked on it, the more I was convinced that this was a unique way to let the reader get to know this impressive woman in her own words. Reading it over again, it looked good.

I went downstairs. Jack had returned and was at his typewriter working on his front-page story about the day's festivities. I took the interview, edited and neatly printed it, and placed it in his box. He looked up but said nothing. He stopped typing, put on his glasses, picked up the article, and began reading it as I stood by his desk. He scoffed and looked at me with aggravation written all over his face.

"This isn't how we do it at all; it's... it's ... I don't know; it's something else," he said curtly.

Angry, I was tired, my fuse was short, and I had just about enough from Jack Flatly.

"It's the women's section, Jack; it's not news, something you constantly remind me of. My voice was raised in anger. "My job here is to help the reader get to know this fascinating woman a little better. What better way to do that than using her own words?"

"Whoa," he said, surprised by my outburst. He'd never seen me get mad. He sat back in his chair and thought for a minute. He finished reading the interview. It was a mighty long minute.

He turned to me and, with no smile, mind you, put his two thumbs up in the air.

"Great job. It's different, but it's damned good. It's so good I'm not going to cut it. I'll get it to the printers with my front-page story and the library picture. Bill said they could set the type without me typing your interview because your printing is clear," he said pleasantly. *O.K. then, I thought.*

As I started to walk away, he added. "Oh, and Mary Kate, you'll love Charlie's picture of Lydia Horton. She's sitting on the stage, a close-up, a headshot, her head tilted with interest and a big smile on her face, a burst of confetti in the air, and a sliver of the new library behind her. It's magic, it surely is".

"Go home now, Mary Kate, ya must be pretty tired," he added with a smile. He looked tired, too; it had been a long day for both of us.

"Good night, Jack," I said jauntily, heading towards the door.

"Wait, Mary Kate, I heard him call. It's dark. You can't go home alone; let me just get this stuff to the printers and I'll walk ya."

Just then, Father came through the door. "I've come to walk ya home, Mary Kate." Turning back to look at Jack, he called, "Good night."

"'Night," he said and returned to his typing.

Father and I walked home, and this time I asked him about his day and Mother's. He told me they enjoyed the library celebration, as everyone else seemed to. They had schnitzel in an early dinner at the Hofbrau, a German restaurant a few blocks from the new library. "You'd be surprised at the number of German immigrants living in San Diego," he told me.

"There was an oompah band at the Hofbrau; the place was lively and crowded. Many people had come from the celebration with a few toots of beer under their belts. There was dancing, mostly polkas, which I took to mighty well, mind ya. We both enjoyed it . . . 'need to get the girl out more often, I suppose."

The next day, a Sunday, I came downstairs after sleeping a little later than usual. Father was at the breakfast table reading the paper. I could see he was reading Jack's story. The headline on page one was "SAN DIEGO OPENS CARNEGIE LIBRARY," with Charlie's picture of the library on the page next to it. Beside it was a picture of San Diegans celebrating this landmark day in the young city's history, a couple of the *Horribles* cavorting in the foreground.

After finishing the story, he turned the page and read my interview with Lydia Horton. Without looking up, he handed the paper over to Mother with the page still turned to my interview. I sighed, impatient to read it myself.

A few minutes later, she finished reading it. She jumped up and clapped her hands, "Brava, Brava!" she said with gusto, recalling her opera days. Father had a broad smile of approval on his face. "I have never seen an interview done like this in a newspaper, but it works, Mary Kate, it works well. It's personal, Lydia Horton in her own words, and it's good, very good. This took guts, Mary Kate—did Jack approve?"

"Well . . . there was a bit of pushback at first, but then I got his best compliment: two thumbs up."

"That's about as good as you're gonna' get from *our* Jack," Father said.

Mother handed the paper to me, and as I read Jack's story on the front page, Mother served me eggs and baked beans, my favorite, along with currant scones from the day before. We usually had Special Breakfast on Sundays, but I suspected she was taking it easy, the big doins' yesterday and all. Mother filled me in on her evening with Father, which she thoroughly enjoyed.

"And I got an anniversary present too," she said, obviously pleased, opening the collar of her blouse. She was wearing a small cross hung from a delicate gold chain.

"It was my mother's," Father said. "I thought I lost it, but in cleaning out underneath the house last month, there it was in an old wooden box."

"It's beautiful, Mother."

I returned to the paper and quickly finished Jack's story which, as usual, was very well done. He took the time to interview a couple of citizens about their feelings about the new library. Their comments were touching and captured the pride in this accomplishment we all felt that day. This personal touch added something special. Jack knew that this was the story about the new library, yes, but it was about our city too. This was a milestone of which all San Diegans could be proud.

Jack's story was a great setup for my interview. And then, turning the page, there it was with Lydia Horton's picture. Jack was right; I loved the shot of Lydia.

He changed my headline from "An Interview with Lydia Horton" to "A Conversation with Lydia Horton." It was far better; it personalized it. And there was more. There was no introduction to the interview when I gave it to Jack. He added it under the headline: (*Union reporter Mary Kate Riley sat down with Lydia Horton after being honored at yesterday's library opening.*)

"Woo-hoo!" I squealed with delight. I put the paper down and turned to my Father. "My name—it's—in there," I stammered, "Jack put it in. I sure wasn't expecting that."

Chapter 14

Mother and I were doing the breakfast dishes the next morning, and we were talking about Lydia Horton. "Would you like to go with me to the open house next weekend at San Diego Children's Home and you can meet her? She was delighted.

I had been spending much more of my free time with Mother since Tim was not there. She taught me to can fruit and make a pie crust this past week. My apple pie sure didn't look like anything Mother had ever made, but it was pretty tasty. I've enjoyed spending this time with Mother, just the two of us. These mother–daughter moments brought me much closer to her.

The open house was on a Saturday. Father usually went to work, but only a half day. He told us that he had decided that he wasn't going in because his back had been acting up. "I'm gonna take it easy, and with my two girls gone today it will be quiet."

He looked up from his paper when we were standing at the door about to leave. "You sure got all dressed up to meet Lydia, Maggie; you look very nice."

She was wearing a dress I hadn't seen before. It was a pale sea-green silk with a high neck and beautiful tucks in the bodice and matching rosebuds around the neckline. She wore the simple gold cross Father had given her. The dress was one of her creations. She wore no hat but did her beautiful dark red hair in the very popular Gibson- girl style, which was complimented by her simple pearl earrings. She looked prettier than I had ever seen her.

I wore my emerald green dress which was becoming my new uniform, but skipped the matching hat and corralled my hair in a clip instead.

Father had arranged for Frank Moody to take us to the Children's Home. I hadn't thought about how we were getting there. He must have walked up to Moody's early this morning; it was only a few blocks away. I could see that Frank Moody had pulled up in front of the house. "We can't have the two most beautiful women in San Diego traipsing through these dusty streets, now can we?"

We arrived at the Children's Home early and were surprised to see Babe Seymour. She was standing on the far side of the room under a sign that read TOURS. The room was large, with yellow-striped wallpaper, lace curtains on the windows, and lovely watercolor paintings of San Diego landscapes on the walls. I didn't need to ask; I recognized the artist's style; Lydia Horton painted them.

There were other artists' works as well, all with prices on them. They were being sold to benefit the Children's Home. The beautifully upholstered chairs, settees, and card tables were pushed against the walls. I was sure that all the furnishings were donations from the well-heeled Wednesday Club members, the primary funding source for the Home.

Lydia Horton approached us looking pleased to see us there. She wore the blue velvet dress she had worn for the library opening. "Hello, Miss Riley," she said. "I am so glad you could make it. I suspect this beautiful woman is your mother?"

"Mother, this is Lydia Horton." She responded with a smile and extended her hand.

"Maggie Riley—it's such a pleasure to meet you. My daughter has told me so much about you, Mrs. Horton."

"Lydia, please," she said, clasping Mother's hand. "I'd love to stay and chat, but I am the official greeter. Please call me Mary Kate and we'll all meet for tea, "Soon, I hope," she said, looking at Mother.

"I'd like that very much," Mother replied, beaming with pleasure.

We caught up with Babe, who greeted us warmly and told us that she was on the board of directors at the Children's Home. "I am anxious to show you around so you can see what good work is done here. First, I want you to meet someone; come this way."

We followed her into a large kitchen where a woman was putting a coffee pot on the stove. She turned to us when we came in. She was a plain, plump, middle-aged lady with curly gray hair and bright blue eyes. She had on a floral apron over her plain, gray silk dress. Her face was flushed from working in the warm kitchen.

Babe nodded to her. "Dr. Baker, I want you to meet two of my dearest friends, Maggie Riley and her daughter Mary Kate. She is a reporter for the *Union* and will be doing a story on the Children's Home. Dr. Baker is one of the founders, and she is still the heart and soul of the place."

She smiled, wiped her wet hands on her apron, and gave one to my mother to shake her hand. "So pleased to meet you, ladies. I wish I could spare the time to talk right now, but I have been given some jobs to do in the kitchen. Our cook is ill today. Babe will show you the place, and I hope you will come back before you leave so we can have a chat. Right now, I am awfully busy doing last-minute things for the party."

"Of course," Mother said. May we be of some help?

"No, no, no, she said. I'm fine here".

"It was so nice to meet you," Mother said.

Babe told us when we left the room that Charlotte Baker is a specialist in obstetrics and gynecology, and she is the first woman doctor in San Diego.

"She's a gynecologist and is married to Fred Baker, who is an obstetrician. They have their office in New Town up on Fourth and C, very near the paper. They live in Point Loma and believe it or not, weather permitting; they usually take their sailboat to work."

"They are a remarkable couple," Babe told us. "She has four children, runs a busy medical practice, and in her *spare* time, Babe laughed, she's the leader of the women's suffrage movement in San Diego. She is incredibly generous and is known for never refusing a patient because of need. I can tell you this: she is a force of nature, and if anyone can get us the vote, it's Charlotte Baker."

After Babe took us around and filled us in on the specifics of the excellent work done at the Children's Home, Mother put her hand on her arm.

"What can I do to help, Babe?"

She thought for a moment. "Maggie, I know just the thing. We get so many donated women's dresses and children's clothes, many quite nice, but they often don't fit right. It would be wonderful if you could help with the alterations so these children and their mothers can look their best. Looking good does wonders for your attitude, your confidence, especially when so many things have gone wrong in your life."

"I'd be pleased to help," Mother said. "Why don't you pick a day, and I'll come over and fit the children and the women, take the clothes home to alter them, and bring them back the next week or so.

"That would work fine, Maggie. How about being on our board, Maggie?"

"No, no, I wouldn't fit in, Babe."

"Oh, don't be silly, Maggie. "Promise me you will think about it?" Mother nodded.

"So Maggie," Babe continued, "when can we come over again for chow-chow? I so love that spicy food."

"Whenever you can make the time—you know that, Babe. Just let me know when you are free. Mike and I are almost always free," she said with a bit of a smirk and a roll of the eyes. "We did have an awfully good time at the library party Saturday. Mike even took me to the Hofbrau for dinner and some polka to celebrate our anniversary."

Babe nodded. "It was a great day, all right. I was so glad to see Lydia get her due; she's just the best. And Mary Kate, great job on the interview."

As we continued on the tour, Babe introduced us to some of the women residents. Babe told us a little bit about how women ended up at the Home. We sat down and talked to a couple of them. I never knew about such things. Babe said that women sometimes left their families in the East to start a family and a new life in the West with their husbands. Most had no marketable skills. Their husbands died by accident or disease, and some of the women were abandoned.

"Why didn't they just get married?" I asked her.

"Getting a husband isn't too difficult with the shortage of marriageable women in the West, but few men want to take on a woman with children. Most people feel that a family should take care of *their own* in times of trouble. 'Problem is many women who had come west as wives and mothers no longer had *their own*, the support of their families they had left so far away. Some just don't have families."

We walked into the reception room where there were trays of beautiful *petit fours* and a variety of tea sandwiches. The table was graced with a beautiful vase with yellow roses in the center of the table. Babe stopped for a moment and continued.

"These women have no way of supporting their children, or themselves for that matter. Some turn to prostitution or working in a saloon. Some women stay here with their children until they can get on their feet, learn a skill, get married, or make some acceptable plans for their families. But, there are very few jobs available to women that would pay even enough to support one person let alone children."

Babe walked us to the buffet table, where we helped ourselves to some of the food and sat down at one of the tables. She joined us. "I can't stay long, but we can chat for a few more minutes." As we sipped our punch, she told us about the prostitutes that ended up at the Children's Home.

"Some of the women come here to die or stay a long time because their health is too poor for them to do much of anything in terms of making a living. This includes both prostitutes and saloon women from the Stingaree, which pretty much uses these women up and throws them away. These are prostitutes, who get sick from syphilis, gonorrhea, tuberculosis, botched abortions, hepatitis, as well as diseases suffered by the general public, simply have nowhere to go."

"I have put a great deal of pressure on some of the brothel owners, many of them former prostitutes, and I am pleased to say that they are now big supporters of the Children's Home. I finally got them to recognize the need for them to help some of their own. Charlotte is leading the effort to get rid of or at least curtail prostitution in this town, but so far, she hasn't had much luck."

A small group of women came into the room. Babe stood, "I have to go; people are starting to arrive and will want to have tours. Take a look around; we are doing such good work here for so many."

Mother and I talked about what we had seen that day as Sean Moody drove us home. Mother said she was excited about the idea of getting involved in helping at the Children's Home, working with women like Lydia Horton, Babe Seymour, and of course, Dr. Baker.

This surprised me, as the mother I knew was nothing like these women. Maybe I didn't know her as well as I thought. Mother dismissed the idea that she could ever fit in on the board of directors. She would fit in just fine.

I asked her why there was so much prostitution in San Diego. She said that with the shortage of women in the city and added to that the large transient male population coming off the ships docking in the harbor, it is seen by most as a necessary evil.

"It's tolerated, but it is looked down upon by polite society. Let me say it differently; *the women* are looked down upon." She stopped, turned, and gave me a determined look. "It's against the law, but these laws are ignored. Prostitution is the exploitation of women, plain and simple. But women are not held in high regard in our world. Why we can't even be trusted to vote."

After that day, dinner conversation at our house between my mother and Babe was often about the work they were doing at the Children's Home. Mother very much warmed to the task and was extremely active in helping in any way she could. Eventually, she took a seat on the board of directors.

I was proud of her and surprised too. It was a side of my mother I didn't know, but I loved her even more now that I did. Father was not surprised. "Your mother has lots of spirit, Mary Kate; she just doesn't advertise it like some do."

After writing about the Children's Home for the paper, I asked Father if I could do a feature in my Sunday women's section on particular unfortunate women of San Diego, the "*Soiled Doves*," as some men called prostitutes. He gave it no thought whatsoever.

"No, absolutely not. Nobody wants to read about prostitutes."

Mother privately agreed with me. I wasn't going to give up, but it might take some time. These women were an important part of life in our young city, and they had a story to tell.

I usually went to the Children's Home with my Mother and helped her with her work. I made friends with a young woman who left her life as a prostitute in the Stingaree because she became too ill to do the job. Her name was Hattie, and I visited her whenever we went there. We were always able to have long visits because Mother took some time to measure the women and children so that she could do her alterations.

Hattie and I had many things in common, and we soon became good friends. We shared a love of books and music. I brought her books to read but her skills were poor, so that before long, I read the books to her. This was enjoyable for both of us. We could share the stories, laugh at the funny parts and cry at the sad ones.

The Children's Home had a gramophone, and Mother let me take some recordings she had to play for Hattie. I even taught her to waltz. We would go into the main room and waltz around it together. She particularly loved these visits.

"I always loved music and wanted to learn to play the violin," Hattie told me. "My father played the violin, but when he died, supporting the family was all that was important. Mother soon followed him to God's rest, and learning to play the violin was out of the question. It was all about survival. The violin was one of the first things we sold to buy food and supplies."

Disappointed that Father was so dead-set against writing about women like Hattie, I resolved that one day I'd tell the story of the woman of the Stingaree. I'd give it to Father, and perhaps I could change his mind.

Father did approve of my doing a story about Dr. Charlotte Baker and the suffrage movement in San Diego. He approved of my story, not of women trying to get the vote. He seemed to think all the fuss about women voting was silly. This irritated me; Mother too.

I called Dr. Baker and set up an interview for the very next week. I did it in the Q&A style that was so successful in my interview with Lydia Horton. I was glad that I did, as it turned out well. Dr. Charlotte Baker is a woman with a great deal to say.

Charlie made a point to tell me that his mother loved the article about Dr. Baker." My mother is active in women's suffrage," he said, with a tone of less-than-full-throated approval.

Chapter 15

It was Sunday; it felt good to sleep late on my day off. Looking out my bedroom window, the early morning coastal fog had already burned off. It was going to be hot. I picked out a light muslin dress for Sunday Mass with Mother. She made it for me for Easter Sunday services last year. Father left early to help Jack work on the *Serenity*. I remembered the name partially remaining on its stern when I visited the boat with Jack right after Tim's death.

He had asked Father to help him restore it, and this was the first day they had a chance to work on it together. Jack wanted to get the boat seaworthy for summer sailing. Mother got up early to make breakfast for Father, and she made a picnic lunch for him to take to the boat. The basket was still sitting in the front room on his chair when we left for church.

"I'll run it down there when we get home," I said. "Why don't you just take a day just for you, Mother?"

"That sounds nice dear; maybe I will."

Father had made great progress since I last visited the *Serenity* in March, but he hadn't had time to work with Jack on his boat project. Now he was ready to help him put the *Serenity* back into service. He was excited about the idea.

Father had refurbished a sailboat when he lived in San Francisco and spent quite a bit of time sailing on the bay there, weather permitting. The climate in San Diego was far more hospitable; sailors took to the bay most of the year.

"What happened to that boat, Father?" I asked him at dinner the night before.

"Your mother was just about to have Tim, and I had a new job down here, so I sold it very cheap to a friend at the *Chronicle*. "*Mickey's Fin,* I called her, after myself; she was a real beauty."

Father and Jack were removing the hardware from the boat when I got there. Next came the sanding, then the painting. Jack said it would require multiple coats of paint and varnish. It would be white on the lower half and red on the top. I couldn't wait to go out on it. I'd never been sailing.

Father said he looked forward to sailing again. Mother, no. She can't swim and doesn't like the idea of being out on a small boat. I can't swim either, but I'm a risk-taker like my father, a lover of most fun that comes my way. Mother is afraid of the water; I'm not, but I know I should learn to swim. *Tim had planned to teach me.*

Jack told me that Charlie had no interest in sailing. "He can't swim, and he's afraid of the water. He got into some trouble while swimming in a lake as a boy and almost drowned. He won't go near the water since then."

Another young man was helping on the boat that day, Izzy Taylor, a good friend of Jack's. He had just refurbished his own abandoned sailboat with Jack's help. Izzy is a little older than Jack, tall and skinny, a "beanpole," Father says. He's boyishly handsome, with sun-streaked light brown curly hair, blue eyes, and tanned, honey-colored skin without a single freckle.

Mother had made lunch for the three men, and they were glad to have it. I sat with them for a while as they ate lunch on the deck. Jack was the source of a few laughs as he told us of his experience with the young woman he had gone out with the night before. Apparently, things didn't go well.

"Jack Flatly, don't you kiss and tell." I chided him.

"There was no kissin' Mary Kate—that was the problem."

122

I shook my head, smiled, and went below while they finished their lunch. I measured the pillows and curtains in the hold as Mother had asked me to. She planned to make new curtains with some leftover navy blue and white striped material and some red pillows to match the soon-to-be shiny bright red and white hull.

The red had lost much of its luster from the action of salt as well as the weather beating it took over the years since its former owners had left the boat for dead. There were large sections where there was no red paint left at all, just dry, gray wood.

"A lot of sanding and some paint and varnish are all she needs," Father said.

As I measured for the curtains, I thought about how Henry, Jack, and Mother's plan to get Father back to work to distract him from his grief did the trick; and of course, the passage of time helped with the healing too. He had a few stops and starts, but he wasn't drinking now. I'd like to think that my working with him helped us both heal the deep hurt and loneliness we felt when we lost Tim. Our relationship is growing stronger every day, as friends even. Father is a great boss and a great teacher.

Mother is constantly on the lookout for a "Mr. Right" for me. She often brought up possible suitors at dinner, usually the sons or other relatives of her dressmaking customers. I invariably would roll my eyes at my father.

Tim teased me mercilessly about these "fish, "as he called them, who needed to be hooked and reeled in. "Ya just need to get your hook in them, Mary Kate," he would say, laughing, with Father often joining in. Jack often chimed in with the teasing, too, often suggesting to Tim that young men, all potential prey, needed to stick together and "ought to be darn careful."

Mother had been conducting this search for a suitable husband for me before Tim died, but finding a man, let alone a husband was the last thing on my mind. I didn't want to be a teacher either. Mother encouraged me to enroll in a teacher's college at The Normal School, the only college in the area, as simply as a stop-gap measure until I could find a suitable husband.

I had agreed to go to college in May, but reluctantly. So it wasn't hard to give up the idea after starting at the paper. I'm a writer; it's what I've always wanted to do.

I'm not even sure how to get there, but what I'm doing now is observing and meeting people and writing about them. If someone interesting comes my way, and this happens often, I jot a few notes in my journal with the idea that this man or woman might find their way into one of my books. This is good practice for writing novels where creating unique characters is so important.

Writing about people is what news reporting is, to a large extent, about. It is a skill I'm honing at in the paper. It feels right, and teaching never really did. Henry told me recently that Mark Twain started as a newspaperman, and now he's the most popular writer in the country. His stories are good, yes, but his characters are even better.

When I came up from the hold after finishing my measuring, the men were discussing the details of the work ahead. Father turned my way, "Tell your mother that Jack and Izzy will be joining us for dinner."

"OK, will do." I smiled and turned to get off the boat. Izzy offered his hand to help me step down onto the dock.

"Thank you, Izzy, I said with a smile."

"You are quite welcome," he replied.

I was happy that Jack and Izzy would be at dinner. This meant singing and tale-telling afterward, maybe some dancing. It had been a long time. I smiled just thinking about how far we'd come, looking back at the name on the boat. Soon she too would be back to her former glory, the "*i-t-y*" completing her name: *Serenity.*

I told Jack that night that we missed seeing him at the house. He was pleased. After he and Izzy left that night, Father told me that Izzy had asked if he could call on me. I was surprised but told him it was fine with me.

"Good," he said, "Because I already gave him the go-ahead as long as he brings a reliable chaperone. Izzy told me that he and his older sister Marlene were close and would have her and her fiancée Tom with him every time he took me out. He said that they are great fun and that he was sure that you'd like them. Izzy said that Jack and his gal-of-the-week could chaperone too, adding that he and Jack had been friends for a long time."

Chapter 16

Izzy and I spent the summer going to all sorts of places together, sometimes with Theodora and her current beau, sometimes with Jack and Mary, but mostly with his sister Marlene and her beau Thomas. Izzy was right; I liked them both.

One weekend, Jack and Mary went on Izzy's sailboat with us to a concert at the gazebo in Tent City. It was my first time on Coronado Island. Izzy's boat is a striking, polished natural wood sailboat with dark blue, white, and gray trim.

"You should have seen her before Jack and I started to work on her; it was a pitiful-looking old wreck," he told me when he first showed me the boat.

Izzy had given me a few sailing lessons, and he got me a life vest because I couldn't swim. He told me he would teach me in the next week or so. Jack and Mary were impressed as I sailed the boat, "*De Ja Vu*," across the bay.

It was a warm July day, and Tent City was great fun. It is a fabulous village of two hundred or so mostly red and white striped tents, running down the narrow strip called The Strand which. borders the beach going south starting at the Hotel Del Coronado. You could rent a tent very cheaply and stay the night or just enjoy the fun during the day. Tent City is run by the hotel and has its own trolley.

The owners of the hotel built this remarkable city of tents for the *hoi polloi* like us to have a chance to enjoy Coronado even though we couldn't afford the hotel. It was so much fun that even the wealthy guests at the hotel spent considerable time there. Street vendors sell lemonade, beer, hot dogs, cotton candy, and saltwater taffy. Entertainers hold forth up and down the Strand: jugglers, magicians, even an organ grinder with a monkey.

There is also the endless delight of people-watching as they stroll down the boardwalk. There are also free concerts in the gazebo on weekend nights and holidays, courtesy of the Hotel Del, as we locals call it.

Izzy docked in Glorietta Bay. We took one of the small boats sent out to help arriving visitors get to shore operated by young men who lived in Coronado. It was a good way to get to and fro and they made a bit of money for their trouble. When we arrived on shore, we walked across the street and around the magnificent Hotel Del, which was situated just across from Glorietta Bay, It was the most famous place in San Diego. Mary and I had never been in Coronado and we wanted to go inside. Jack and Izzy were not interested. "Maybe we'll go on the way back," Jack told us. *Fat chance, I thought, irritated at Jack.*

We soon arrived on the boardwalk which ran through the heart of Tent City. I looked back at the impressive white structure of the hotel with its signature red roofs. A bright yellow trolley that ran down the Strand honked and stopped for us but we waved it on its way. There was so much more to see walking.

We stopped to hear the barbershop quartet that sang at the gazebo that afternoon. It was the first large structure when you left the hotel grounds. It was beautiful, painted a bright white. The quartet knew all the popular songs and sang many standards as well. We had a great deal of fun singing along. Jack loved the singing, and to my surprise, Izzy kept up with him with his fine voice. Mary joined in and could sing well too.

Mouthing the words but keeping my voice out of the mix, I was sure everyone would be grateful for this consideration. I couldn't help but think of Theodora, my singing buddy. She couldn't sing either. We would hide in my room and sing together to our heart's content when nobody was upstairs or sometimes on our front porch when Father and Mother were inside.

Later that day, we went to the beach. I waded in the surf, getting the lower part of my dress wet. I had pulled it up and tied it at my waist, but this arrangement didn't work well. Mary stayed on shore, "I'll just watch," she said.

Jack and Izzy removed their boots and their shirts, pushed up their pants legs, and waded pretty far in. We were surprised by a big wave crashing in, and we all got much wetter than we'd planned. I squealed and tried to avoid the roiling surf which had bubbled up nearly to my waist. The water churning around us was warm, and the beautiful white foam shone brightly in the sun.

We laughed as we made our way out of the surf against a strong current pulling us back in. We laughed as Izzy helped me walk in the water which was pulling me down, what with my petticoats and long dress. But as we got to shore, being all wet was of no never-mind because it was warm in the sun. We stretched out our legs sitting in the sand and our clothes dried pretty quickly.

I looked over at Mary. She was one of those girls that not only was beautiful but seemed to remain that way no matter what she was doing. I might resent this if she wasn't so darn nice; she's funny too. Her hair stayed in place and she never dribbled mustard from her hot dog on the front of her dress or anywhere else. She kept her broad straw hat on so she didn't sunburn. She is dark-haired and blue-eyed and had lovely porcelain skin which would burn easily. "She's black Irish," Jack told me, which I knew was Irish with the black hair-blue eyes combination. I liked Mary. She was quiet at first but was great fun once she warmed up to us.

Mary didn't swim or play in the sand; she just wanted to enjoy the view. I went in the water, played in the sand, and sat in the sun without a hat. By day's end, I was a sunburned, wrinkled, disheveled mess. I didn't care; it was fun. Izzy didn't seem to mind. He didn't get sunburned; his already browned skin just got browner. Jack got a bit of a burn, but not too much. He had been outside on the weekends working on the *Serenity* and already had a bit of color.

Later that day, while we sat in the sand waiting for the sunset, Jack entertained us with not one but two stories that he told us had been passed down from his namesake, his Uncle Jack Flatly, who lived with his family in Los Angeles. He told us that Uncle Jack was a dockworker like his father, and worked and lived at the port in San Pedro.

His first story was about "The Great Hunger," the potato famine in Ireland in 1845 which drove Jack's family, along with tens of thousands of other Irish people, to leave whatever they had to board ships to America or face certain starvation. Many had already been lost to famine. Jack came over on one of these ships as a small boy.

The ships were dirty, crowded, and filled with disease. Many of the passengers died on the voyage. The heart of the story was his grandmother's actions on one of these ships. She nursed the sick, delivered a baby, and gave most of her food rations to others.

"They'd be needin' it more than me," Jack said, mimicking her voice and brogue. He has a rich, deep voice that he uses with great effect to draw you into his stories. He said that his grandfather Sean played the fiddle on the ship.

"This provided many moments of joy and respite on a dismal voyage. People sang, danced, and told stories as well as poems and limericks, which were sometimes humorous but were often very sad. "After all, grief and loss went with us all to America," he told us. "Leaving Ireland was leaving all I had left of my ma' except in my heart."

He paused and thought for a moment. "I tried very hard to remember my mother, but eventually her face disappeared from my memory. My sister Franny has a picture of her in a locket, but it is so unclear it is hard to see what she looked like," he said with sadness and loss in his voice.

Mary was moved to tears during Jack's tale as her grandmother died on the voyage to America, also a refugee from the potato famine. I asked Izzy, who had known Jack for a long time, if he was getting serious about Mary. He replied, "Is Jack Flatly serious about any gal?"

The second story he told us was about his parent's wedding day. He always took the roles of different characters in his tales with great dramatic effect. He had the Irish brogue down pat, as well as the unusual laughs, unique figures of speech, or other funny attributes of one character or another. We all shared a lot of laughs that afternoon.

Jack finished the second story, then picked up my boots from the sand, brushed them off, and handed them to me. "Put these on Mary Kate," he said rather gruffly.

Sometimes, too many times for my liking, he talks to me like he is my father or his kid sister, who most of the time, annoys him. He likes to order me about. It's irritating. Jack looked up at Izzy. He was watching the swimmers in the rough surf; the foam had taken on a beautiful peach glow in the early evening. The sun had not set but was moving in that direction.

"We need to get going, Izzy; Mary Kate's father will tan our hides if we get her home too late. Mary's pa will too. What time is it?"

Izzy took out his gold pocket watch which he had told me was a gift from his father. "It's seven-thirty. There is plenty of time to get back to town by eight-thirty. It's too late to walk back; we need to get the trolley to Glorietta Bay, and then it's only a short sail home.

If we leave now, we have plenty of time to make it to town before it gets dark."

Mary had not taken off her boots, so she was ready to go. I was lacing mine as fast as I could. Jack sighed loudly and asked me, clearly irritated. "Ya ready, Mary Kate?"

"Yes, I'm just getting this last boot laced."

We saw the trolley arriving in front of us. "Run!" Jack called, and as we ran to catch it, he called out to the driver, "Wait for us!". Leaving one boot partially untied, I tucked in the laces, and taking Izzy's hand, we ran to get on board.

Most of the day visitors had left, so the trolley was almost empty. I squealed, hopped on, and held on tight as the wind tossed my hair around as we headed back to Glorietta Bay. I was sure I looked like a wild, red-headed madwoman; my hair had gone haywire in the damp air, and my face felt hot from too much sun. I probably hatched a thousand freckles, but I didn't care, it felt great.

After we had been courting for about a month, Izzy took me to the wedding of his cousin Emily at the Unitarian Church. I was surprised to see Lydia and Alonso Horton there. Izzy told me they were good friends of his parents who helped get the Unitarian Church started in San Diego.

"Mr. Horton does not align closely with any faith, but he was very generous in giving money to any church that wanted to get started in the city. The Unitarian Church was one of those churches. He became a member at the urging of his second wife who was a Unitarian. After she died, he met Lydia there."

I hoped to meet Mr. Horton after the ceremony, but he and Lydia snuck out right after the nuptials. This wasn't a surprise; Alonso Horton is ninety-five years old and probably didn't socialize much these days.

Izzy and I had a good time at the reception in the church hall. I liked his parents very much. They had an excellent musical ensemble that knew all the modern tunes. Izzy is an excellent dancer, and so is his father, who squired me around the dance floor several times.

The more I saw Izzy, the more I liked him, and he was *so handsome*. Theodora thought he was my prince and urged me to snap him right up." He's just *dee-licious,"* she said after meeting him at our house one Sunday.

"You sound like my mother," I told her.

Izzy had a lovely family and a great group of friends. We had many good times, and he's very romantic. I got my first kiss— a number of them, that wonderful summer.

My parents, particularly my mother, liked Izzy and thought that he was "*the* one," *the* man for me. He was rich, handsome, had a successful career, and she found him most amiable. Check and double-check the list of qualifications Mother kept in her head Father liked him too, but he didn't join in Mother's opinion that he was *the* one for me, but he didn't shoot the idea down either.

Jack, Izzy, and Father finished work on the *Serenity* in late June. Jack and Father took her out every Sunday and sometimes after work during the week for a sunset sail. Jack was right; Father enjoyed fixing the boat and he loved sailing her with him. It did bring Jack back into the family fold, as he was always over for dinner and a sing-along after a sail. We all missed him.

One day in late July, Father surprised me as we finished up at the paper. "Jack and I are going for a sunset sail, why not come along?"

I clapped my hands in delight. And so, Father and Jack took me out on the *Serenity* for the first time. It looked beautiful, brand-new. Father was a very skilled sailor tacking back and forth over the dark waters of San Diego Bay. A warm summer wind propelled her across the water. Father gave me a sailing lesson, and I surprised him with my skill; I hadn't told him that Izzy had already taught me a bit about sailing.

When it was my turn to take the boat across the bay, I squealed when the boat leaned over more than I had planned; it was scary. I thought we were going over. I looked up at Father for help, but he and Jack just laughed. Soon the boat righted itself. When it was Jack's turn, he bent the boat way over, leaning back in the opposite direction, then he smoothly brought her around and tacked the other direction.

I practiced my sailing skills with Izzy for most of the summer. We sailed the *Déjà vu* about once a week, sometimes with Marlene and Tom and occasionally alone. We didn't share the details of the alone time with my parents or anyone. These times were very romantic. We docked at the edge of the bay near the old wharf and spent a good deal of time talking and getting to know each other better as we sat on the deck enjoying the beauty of the bay. And yes, there was some kissing and snuggling too.

Chapter 17

Babe, Henry, and I were walking toward the front entrance of the Hotel Del when Henry stopped us and pointed to the sky. "Look, ladies,"

A massive orange globe of a moon rose over the central tower of the "Wedding Cake," San Diego's now world-famous hotel. We were there to attend the Wednesday Ball.

Despite the name, the ball wasn't held on a Wednesday but on the second Saturday in August. It was named after the Wednesday Club which hosted the event annually to raise money for the Children's Home. The Wednesday Ball was its primary funding source. It was the social event of the year, and it was something that should be part of my Sunday women's section coverage. I was thrilled to be going.

Babe and Henry were pleased to escort me. They attended the ball as the owners of the city's most influential newspaper and as one of the event's sponsors. I was dressed in Mother's cream-colored wedding dress and matching slippers. My normal pasty-white, freckled face had turned a golden brown over the summer; my green eyes looked even greener, and my hair was sun-streaked.

Babe looked lovely in her blue brocade gown, which matched her beautiful eyes. Henry looked, well, like Henry. He wore a plain, ill-fitting dark suit. He's not one to dress up much for anything. I loved him for it. He is comfortable just the way he was.

Lillie Spreckles, who chairs the event this year, is the wife of sugar heir John Spreckles, who is a leading developer of the City of Coronado as well as its crowning glory, the Hotel Del. He is one of the wealthiest men in the San Diego area and a key player in moving the city into the new century.

In its fifth year, the ball is attended not only by San Diego's upper crust but also by wealthy visitors from the east, who, Father jokes, treat the word *winter* as a verb. They "wintered at the Del" with their families, servants, and tutors in tow.

Father said it didn't take these East Coast visitors long to realize what a spectacular place San Diego is, and all year round, mind you. This little secret is no secret anymore. The Del has become one of the top resort destination hotels in the world in only a few years, really putting San Diego on the map. The development of the hotel as a world-class tourist destination made folks here suddenly realize that the most important product San Diego had to sell was its spectacular natural beauty and its wonderful year-round climate.

Wealthy refugees from the cold winters in the East come to the Del for extended stays every year. Now some come there for summer as well. They look forward to going to the Wednesday Ball as the highlight of the summer season. They are most welcome as they can be counted on for big contributions to the cause.

The hotel had opened just fifteen years before. A couple of rich hunting buddies, Elisha Babcock and Hampton Story, regularly rowed to Coronado to hunt rabbits on what was then a desert island. After a few trips there, no doubt taking in the beauty of the bay around them, they decided that it might be nice to build an upscale hunting and fishing lodge on the island. They were willing to rough it, but not in the extreme, don't ya know. Before long, they decided that a world-class resort would be an even better idea.

First they bought the entire island peninsula of Coronado, a dry, dusty, chaparral-covered rabbit habitat. There was a small ostrich ranch on the island but not much else. They announced at groundbreaking that their goal was to build a hotel that would be the talk of the Western world.

Almost immediately, they subdivided the land and quickly sold the lots. They used the profits to finance the hotel, along with contributions from other investors. Purchasers built houses on the lots, and some of them moved to Coronado. Others rented the houses to the tradespeople working on the hotel. Businesses serving these residents soon sprung up, and the city of Coronado was born.

It took only eleven months to complete the hotel. This was remarkable because most of the materials needed to construct it had to be brought to the area by train or shipped in, often around the Horn. Skilled artisans were required, and for the most part, had to be imported as well. The project provided employment for many in the area, which resulted in a much-needed boost in the local economy.

The Del is modern in every way. It has electric lighting, and Thomas Edison himself supervised their installation as well as the all-electric elevators. The rooms have private baths, and some even have telephones. Not only did the hotel draw visitors, but it promoted investment in San Diego real estate and other businesses.

The Wednesday Ball is sold out every year and always provides a large haul for the Children's Home. The Del is not only the finest venue in the area for such an event, but it also has the only ballroom large enough to accommodate it.

We walked into the lobby; it was quite a sight. It has a beautiful open-beamed redwood ceiling under which there were groupings of intricate wicker chairs with embroidered cushions that matched the beautiful designs of the Persian carpets.

Well-heeled guests dressed in formal attire were sipping cocktails and sitting on velvet settees bordered by palms and ferns, which were placed in ornate Chinese pots. There is a large, intricately designed, stained-glass window on one side of the room.

I left Henry and Babe in the line to get their table assignment. I spotted a young man dressed in a gold and red hotel uniform with a silly-looking little round hat on his head, sitting at a table checking in attendees. I approached him and held out my hand.

"Mary Kate Riley, special event reporter for *The San Diego Union.* Would you mind if I grabbed a chair and sat next to you? I need to get the names of the notables as they check in."

He shook my hand. "Theodore Martin, glad to meet you. Sure, you can sit here, but no furniture moving when you are dressed for a ball, Missy," he said, flashing his most flirtatious grin and exposing some regrettably bad teeth."

"Let me just pull a chair over for you." He ignored the guests waiting in line, walked across the room, and pulled over a chair. "I know most everybody, but if I don't, their names are on their tickets."

Along with lending me her lace wedding dress, Mother had done up my hair in a Gibson-girl hairstyle, and I felt pretty good among the elaborately attired women in this crowd. I looked around the spectacular room that Theodore called The Gallery. The ceiling is hung with cut-crystal chandeliers equipped with the latest in electric lighting; everything at the Del is state-of-the-art. Above the gallery, there is a second-floor balcony. Several hotel guests and even a few children watched the busy scene below. Theodore suggested that after everyone was checked in, I take an elevator up to the second-floor balcony because it gave a great perspective on the scene below.

He told me that Mrs. Spreckles, "Lillie," he added with familiarity, had arrived very early to the ball. "She's in charge of the whole shebang this year. They live across the street in a mansion on Glorietta Bay, so I expect her mister will be along later. She's in the ballroom seeing to last-minute details."

I jumped up and went to the ballroom to see if I could get a quick quote from the mistress of ceremonies before things got going and she was too busy. It was located beneath the hotel's signature red turret, which, when lighted, could be seen for miles.

The roof members of the ballroom were left uncovered and were of polished redwood. I was enchanted by the scene that Mrs. Spreckles had created. This year's ball had an Arabian Nights theme which made an already-elegant ballroom even more so. Life-sized palm trees made of colored silk were placed throughout the room. They were back-lit from below with some type of lighting arrangement to give the impression of a sunset behind them.

Dramatic, exotic flower arrangements were placed throughout the room. Gold and cream-colored striped sultan's tents were put up where the buffet dinner was to be served. I peeked into one tent, which had silverware set out in it alongside the hotel's elegant crown-embossed china, so fitting as the icon of the Del Coronado, "the Crown" hotel. The other tents were for the food. That reminded me that I was hungry. Excited and nervous, I had forgotten to eat dinner.

The large ballroom is circular, bordered by windows and doors leading to the outside, with the dance floor and bandstand in the center. The toots and moans of the instruments filled the room as the members of the orchestra, dressed in black tuxedos, tuned their instruments.

The doors were left open for ventilation by the breeze from the sea. It was a warm summer night. I walked out one of the doors on the ocean side and looked up. The night sky was stunning—star-filled and moon-lit. The small outdoor patio was strung with lighted paper lanterns, their colors glowing, swaying together in their moonlight dance in the soft summer breeze. I could hear the pounding of the surf nearby and could see its iridescent fringe slapping the shoreline. It was magical. I wished for a moment, that I wasn't there as a reporter. This was a new world for me and was such a long way from Rabbitville.

After getting a quick quote from Mrs. Spreckles, I complimented her on the staging she had done for the ball. She was pleased. Returning to my seat next to Theodore, I saw that there was now quite a line. Henry and Babe, now at the front of the line, picked up their seating assignments and headed toward the ballroom.

Theodore huffed, "Tell your boss that black tie doesn't mean black suit."

Meow. Theodore was in no position to be a fashion arbiter.

An unescorted woman, avoiding the line, approached Theodore's check-in desk. It was Lydia Horton. "I beg your pardon," she said to the man at the front of the line. "May I interrupt for but a moment?" Theodore looked up.

"Please young man, ask your manager for someone to help check people in. We don't want people waiting."

"Right away, Mrs. Horton." I wasn't surprised that he knew her; everyone knew who she was.

As she turned away from the check-in desk, she paused. "Hello, Miss Riley, so nice to see you," she said, then returned to her friends.

"You know her?" Theodore asked, impressed.

"Yes, I do. Lydia Horton was my first interview. It was at the opening of the Carnegie Library in April. She couldn't have been more gracious."

"She's the president of the Wednesday Club—for life," Theodore said.

I knew Lydia Horton founded the Wednesday Club shortly after marrying Alonso Horton. He was at the top of his game then, flush with the money he made in the development of New Town. This group of wealthy women met for lunch weekly to discuss charitable work. They came up with the idea of an annual ball at the Del as a benefit for the San Diego Children's Home. It helped that one of the hotel's owners, John Speckles' wife, Lillie, is a club member and endorsed the idea.

Theodore mentioned that Lydia Horton was no longer the actual club president because, he explained, she had to work during the day. "She was appointed as the club's honorary president in perpetuity, he said, and she always attends the Wednesday Ball."

Theodore confided in a loud whisper that she always wore the same gown. "Nobody minds," he assured me.

This irritated me; I thought she looked lovely. Next in line was a middle-aged man, a bit on the plump side, not blessed with particularly good looks, wearing a plain black suit. Theodore said nothing about this fashion *faux pas.* He was accompanied by his wife, who was walking behind him. She was dressed in a rather plain, blue silk dress. As the couple stepped forward, I recognized Dr. Charlotte Baker right away.

"Hello, Dr. Baker," I said, standing and putting out my hand to shake hers. "Mary Kate Riley, reporter for the *Union.*"

"Of course. How are you, dear? 'Very nice article you did about the Home, and of course, I loved the article about me," she said with a chuckle.

"You know her too?" Theodore asked me. He had so much respect for this pair that he spoke of them only with admiration. "They may not dress like swells, but they are two of the most respected people in San Diego."

A strikingly beautiful Mexican woman, Theodore said was Señora Maria Estudillo, approached the table with her husband. She was so stunning that she commanded the attention of both men and women; everyone stared at her. She could have worn a gunnysack and looked beautiful with her mocha skin, black hair, and unusual green eyes. Her entourage, consisting of twelve guests who I presumed were the cream of Mexican society in San Diego, remained to the side of the counter.

She wore a white gown with a black lace overlay at the hem and bodice. Her beautiful black hair flowed down her back, held in place with a crown-like black comb. She wore simple pearl earrings and no other jewelry.

The Estudillos and their entourage were holdovers from Mexican rule of the area less than fifty years before Baja California became part of the United States. Most of the powerful families left when Mexico withdrew, but some remained. They are still considered part of the elite class in San Diego society. There is no rancor or bias against these wealthy Mexican families. After all, they are old rich, a rarity here.

I was surprised when Charlie turned up at the check-in table. He was dressed in a black tuxedo and tails and looked dashing indeed. My heart fluttered a bit when I saw him. A beautiful blond woman dressed in pink silk chiffon graced his arm. I recognized her right away. "You look so handsome, Charlie," I said, smiling.

"Thanks," he said. "Pamela, this is Mary Kate Riley—she's a reporter for the *Union*."

I smiled and put out my hand to greet her, "You were our nymph guide for *A Midsummer Night's Dream*, right?"

"Yes, that's right," she said with a smile, pleased that I remembered her.

Charlie told me as he waited for his seat assignment that his mother was on the board for the Wednesday Ball. "She wants more young people to come to the ball, so she urged me to attend and paid for the tickets."

Charlie and Pamela were the only young guests. This was an older, people-with-money-enough-to-donate type of crowd. Charlie turned to leave the table, taking the lovely Pamela's arm and escorting her to the ballroom.

Later, when I was checking out the proceedings there, I saw Charlie waltzing her around the dance floor while the orchestra played *The Blue Danube.* They made a beautiful couple. I felt a pang of jealousy or maybe disappointment that I was not in his arms.

Charlie didn't ask me anywhere again after his parent's anniversary party. He treated me as a friend, and to be fair, he never promised or even hinted at anything else when he invited me to the party. But I was seeing Izzy now and enjoying the summer with him, so it was fine. *Still...*

I knew Charlie was courting somebody special over the summer, but I didn't realize it was our nymph guide. I bet he'd be kissing her goodnight. I knew, of course, that Pamela Spaulding fit much more into Charlie's world than I ever could.

Hmm, her prominent name is certainly one I should drop in my story as part of the who's-who at this spectacular gathering of the glitterati of San Diego society.

We left the ball at about nine-thirty as we had planned. I was glad to be tucking out early. Theodore was moving in for the kill. I could tell he planned to ask me to go out with him. I didn't like him much, even if he had better teeth.

Henry had arranged for the printers to stay late that night to hold the women's pages for my story. I had written it during the dinner service, sitting in the elegant gallery area, which at the time was deserted. All I had to do was edit and print it neatly enough so the printers could understand it well enough to set the type. I was getting quite skilled, as any good news reporter must be, in writing a story on the fly on a short deadline. We took the ferry home and

Henry and Babe dropped me off at the paper. They told me they were going out for a drink at the Brewster Hotel and would return in an hour. *One hour?*

I just made it. The story, no picture this time, turned out well. Henry even complimented me on it. Mrs. Spreckles called me at the paper the following week, thanking me for the wonderful description of *"our* Arabian Nights-themed ball. I worked so hard. It was a beautiful night. Even the moon cooperated," she said softly.

I bought my own typewriter with my earnings from the paper and a contribution for my birthday from Babe and Henry. Theodora knows how to type, and she's teaching me. Lydia Horton helped me find a how-to-type book from the library. She said it was one of the most popular new books.

Mrs. Horton remembered that I wanted to become a novelist and told me that not so very long ago, Mark Twain was the first novelist to submit a type-written manuscript to a publisher. "And he's doing quite well," she added with a smile.

Practicing my typing every night, I was grateful to have Theodora to coach me on weekends. Her father is an accountant; she types for him when he needs her. She works in his office several days a week and is pretty skilled. I'm getting better all the time and type most of my stories now if there's time.

Mother surprised me one night by asking me to teach her to type. I was delighted. It was a task we worked on together at the kitchen table after dinner. Father could type but in an awkward, nobody-really-taught-me kind of way. He sat in his chair and read; he seemed to enjoy the alone time our typing sessions gave him.

Chapter 18

At the end of the summer, Izzy and I parted. He wanted a wife and had made that very clear early in our relationship. I told him then that I wasn't ready to settle down, but I think he thought he could convince me as the summer went on. He offered me his grandmother's diamond and ruby ring and asked me to marry him. I turned him down. There was so much to love about Izzy, but I didn't *love* him. I wasn't interested in getting married and was not even close to being ready to settle down.

Izzy may have loved me; he said he did, but I suspected he was just in a hurry to have a wife and family. He was ready; I wasn't. He was already set up in his father's successful real estate business, and his father had already bought him a beautiful home on First Street.

This suspicion was confirmed when only six weeks after we stopped seeing each other, Jack told me that Izzy was getting married to a girl he had courted before me. I already knew this having put his engagement notice in the paper the previous Sunday. I wondered then what my life would have been as Mrs. Isadore Taylor.

"Ya missed your chance, Mary Kate, and *that guy* has money," Jack quipped.

I rolled my eyes, but I wondered, and just for a moment mind you, if I had made the mistake of not taking the proposal more seriously.

Missing Izzy and not having anyone else to fill the gap in my dance card, I filled my days with my work at the paper. Charlie had lost his lady love, Pamela. He told me she was off to college in the

East. He didn't appear to be grieving, to say the least, based on the parade of beauties dropping by to see him at the paper.

It gets pretty hot in October in San Diego, and there was a feeling in the air that the seasons were changing and that fall was on its way. It was a Friday, and I had just returned from my deliveries, pick-ups, and my usual trip to the courthouse to get the real estate statistics. Jack and Charlie met me at the door to the paper, and they, Jack really, asked me to a barbecue the next day at his sister Franny's ranch in Mission Valley. She lived there with her husband, Jim, and their three children. He made it clear that it wasn't a date, that he was taking Mary, and that I would be *with* Charlie.

"I've got a buggy to take us."

"Sure," I said with a wide grin," happy I was asked.

"Charlie and I will pick you up about noon."

"Great, I'll wait on the porch."

Things had improved over the past months between Charlie, Jack, and me, just as Father told me they would. This was especially between Jack and me. Jack and Mary often went to various "ventures" with Izzy and me over the summer. We always had a grand time.

But going somewhere with Jack and Charlie outside the paper meant a lot. Was I now one of the musketeers? Well, not really, but I was moving in that direction, or at least it seemed so. *The musketeers were men, so maybe I'd never get there.*

I was looking forward to going to the barbecue because my social life pretty much came to a standstill after I stopped seeing Izzy in August. It returned to its pre-Izzy status, dull as dirt. Mother said she had some other young gentlemen who she wanted me to meet; I declined. I missed Izzy.

145

Pleased with the invitation to the barbecue, I sat at my desk and decided to celebrate by doing the unthinkable, the unimaginable, at least to almost everyone at the paper— I would take my father to lunch. I had quite a reputation as being frugal; Jack called me a cheap- skate. He liked to tease me about this and often claimed that I probably still had my first communion money.

When I went over to my father's desk, he looked up from his typing. "Waterfront for lunch, Father? It's on me," I said, putting a silver dollar on his desk as proof of solvency.

"OK then," he said, smiling broadly and jumping up, "let's go."

We walked to the Waterfront, and both had the blue-plate special. As we waited for our food, it occurred to me that I had never been anywhere alone with my father. This was a first. I told him how pleased I was to be included in the plans for the barbecue Saturday. He smiled. "I told you those boys would come around; you are getting to be darn good friends."

After we finished our soup and sandwiches, Father, who loved his pie, looked at me and asked, "Do you want me to buy dessert?"

"No sir, I do not. This is on me," I said defensively. Father just looked at me, and a rather dubious look it was.

"Big spender, are ya?"

I smiled back at him while the waitress put our apple pie in front of us. It is the only dessert served at the Waterfront. As we walked back to the paper, I thought about how far Father and I had come in the past six months. Henry told me that my Sunday women's section had become very popular and that this had increased the advertising revenue as well as selling more papers.

I was expanding my range of topics in that section. Father was even giving me some hard news stories to cover for the daily editions without intruding into Jack's stories, his front-page turf. I knew Father was proud of me, and he told Henry one day in my earshot, "She's a natural in the job."

Henry shook his head in agreement. "I never doubted it."

Come Saturday after lunch, I was sitting on the porch with my parents, waiting to be picked up for the barbecue. Jack pulled up in an open buggy he'd borrowed from a friend. Mary sat next to him in the front seat. Charlie was seated in the back. The buggy was a surprisingly nice one. The horse pulling it seemed long overdue for a trip to the glue factory. She reminded me of Taffy.

The last time I rode in an open buggy with Charlie was on our trip to Lomaland in the spring, and I almost fell off trying to get in. This time Charlie jumped up and helped me in. Father handed him a basket of cheddar cheese rolls that Mother had made for us to contribute to the dinner. He handed them to me. Charlie had on a gambler's hat and looked quite the rake as he got in the buggy and sat down next to me. Mary and I held on to our seats as Jack suddenly moved the buggy forward, nearly knocking Mary off the seat.

"Good afternoon Miss Riley!" Jack bellowed; he was obviously in high spirits and ready for a good time. He looked rather dashing in *his* wide-brimmed gambler's hat, leaving his signature newsie cap behind for a day. Sitting beside him, Mary looked exceptionally pretty in her yellow dress and wide-brimmed straw hat. They made a handsome pair.

I figured that when the boys asked me to the barbeque, Charlie didn't have anyone to bring, and at the last minute, they invited me; someone probably canceled. I didn't care—it was nice to be asked.

I wore my light blue muslin short-sleeved dress and my mother's wide-brimmed straw hat. I didn't need a shawl; it was already really hot. It was expected to be well over a hundred degrees that afternoon. October is one of our hottest months in San Diego. We were sweltering at the paper all of last week. The building is facing the wrong way to get any breeze from the bay. Jack waited for me to take my seat next to Charlie. "We're off!

Along the way, Jack and Charlie competed with each other telling jokes and stories nearly the entire hour it took us to get to the ranch. Charlie, at one point, started whistling *"Bicycle Built for Two,"* as he had on our Point Loma trip. Jack joined in. He suddenly turned back to me with a lilt in his voice, "Aren't you gonna whistle, Mary Kate?"

I suspected a trap. "Sure," I replied. Charlie had probably told Jack about my whistling on the trip to Lomaland, but I had been practicing and gave it a try anyway.

"Oh no," Jack said, "That is so wrong, so very wrong." Both he and Charlie laughed.

I smacked Charlie hard on the leg. "You told him," I said.

"Me? Well, I might have mentioned it."

Jack's sister, Franny, and her husband, Jim, were standing on the porch when we pulled up in front of the house. It is an attractive adobe with an enormous, bright pink bougainvillea climbing over the roof of the porch. These plants thrived in an arid climate like San Diego and graced many houses throughout the city.

I liked Franny and Jim immediately; they were so friendly and made us feel right at home. I looked around after Charlie helped me out of the wagon. About twenty people sat under the large oak tree at picnic tables topped with red and white checked tablecloths, drinking beer or lemonade. Jim said they were neighbors and people that worked with them on the ranch.

"These are the early arrivals, he told us; we expect quite a crowd. Franny's been cooking and baking for two days,"

148

We arrived there a bit early so that we could give Jim and Franny a hand. The party was a celebration of her thirtieth birthday. Mary and I helped with last-minute food preparations: a fruit salad and spicy baked beans, Franny's specialty. She was pleased with the contribution of the cheese rolls as she said they were perfect with her menu. Jack and Charlie helped Jim set up the bar-b-que pit and began to season the large pig for roasting. Jim lit the fire, and it didn't take long for the smell of fire-roasted pork to fill the air.

After getting the pig started, Charlie and Jack, along with Jim, played ball with the kids, Jack's nieces, and nephews. Franny, Mary, and I sat on the porch for a few minutes after we gave the finishing touches to the food preparation and spent a little time getting acquainted. It didn't take us long.

Franny is one of those people that even when you first meet her, it is as though you have known her all your life. Later everyone sat on two long plank tables to eat the delicious spit-roasted pork, beans, fruit salad, cheese rolls, and lemon pies Franny had made from the lemons in their yard. The pungent smell of the lemons on the tree filled the warm air.

After dinner just about sunset, Jim announced that it was time for the dancing. A planked dance floor was set up for the party with torches surrounding it, providing a soft light aided by the nearly full moon. There was a hot, dry wind that evening, so typical at this time of year; Santana or Satan's breath, as the Mexicans called them. These dry winds brought high temperatures and fanned fires throughout the San Diego region every fall.

The sound of the two fiddlers tuning up filled the air. They were excellent and played popular modern songs, lively dance numbers, and some classics when they switched gears from fiddlers to violinists.

At Charlie's request, one of the fiddlers played a beautiful waltz; I recognized it, *The Waltz of the Flowers,* which mother often played on her gramophone. He danced with Franny, who seemed to enjoy it immensely. They were the only couple on the dance floor. I don't think her husband Jim could dance as they didn't dance together at all. He didn't seem to mind a bit.

After that, Charlie and I danced several waltzes, and he complimented me again on what a good dancer I was. "My father is quite the twinkle toes," I said; he loves to dance, he's really good, and he taught me."

He held me pretty tight while we were dancing, in a romantic sort of way, putting his hand on my lower back and pulling me close to him. After our fifth waltz of the evening, he took my hand and walked me off the dance floor, then released it. *Hmm, was that a romantic gesture? 'Sure seemed so. I'm not putting my mug out for a kiss this time, though.*

Charlie asked Mary to dance, but she said she wasn't much of a dancer and didn't know the waltz. Jack did dance with Mary once or twice, but never a waltz. I wasn't sure if Jack could waltz.

The fiddlers played a couple of lively circle dance numbers where the four of us, as well as Jim and Franny, took the floor. After a while, Jack and I, along with Franny and Jim, danced an Irish jig together, moving faster and faster as the fiddlers picked up the pace.

We were dripping with sweat, and our faces were bright red when we finished. We switched partners and did it all again to the next tune, much to the delight of the crowd, who stood on the sidelines clapping to the music. For the third jig, brother and sister, Jack and Franny, took to the floor alone to show us all how it was done, moving faster and faster to keep up with the fiddler, both collapsing in laughter on the floor, out of breath, at the last strum of the fiddle. I asked Charlie to jig, and he politely declined. "I don't jig."

I resolved to teach him the Irish jig one day; it's so much fun. Mary didn't join in the jig either, but she and Charlie seemed to enjoy watching us dance, laughing and clapping vigorously to the music.

We all talked and laughed all the way home. The moon was nearly full, and Jack had brought a lantern for the wagon to help light our way. Some of the main streets in New Town were lighted, but off the beaten path in the neighborhoods, it was pretty dark.

We all had a bit of beer that day, even me; I was getting used to the taste. We did a bit of singing too. Jack, Charlie, and Mary knew all the popular songs. Charlie, I discovered, has a fine voice.. I knew the songs too and joined in, but very timidly. After I started singing, Jack announced sarcastically, "Mary Kate, I think maybe your singing has improved." I responded to that comment with a smack on *his* back.

"Ow," he said. Mary smiled at me.

Jack pulled up in front of the house at about ten o'clock. The porch light was on. Charlie helped me get out but did not walk me to the door. Father and Mother were sitting on the porch. I wasn't surprised; it was so hot that night that they had come outside for a little respite from the stuffy, hot house. Father had the porch light on. I walked up two stairs and then turned back. "Goodnight, Charlie, Goodnight, everyone," I said, looking up at Mary and Jack, "it was sure fun."

"Good night," Charlie said and hopped into the wagon's back seat. "Goodnight, Mary Kate, and to the two of ya as well," Jack called, then he clicked the horse forward.

Chapter 19

Tim's birthday, October twenty-ninth, was a somber, sad day. He would have been twenty-one. Mother and I had gone to mass that morning to pray, not for Tim; we knew he was in a good place. We prayed for us, the Rileys, who still hadn't filled the space Tim left behind. It was as if part of me was gone forever.

We had no friends at the cemetery with us that day, just Mother, Father, and me, standing at Tim's grave, still in shock that he should be lying there, underneath the earth. It just felt so wrong. His name, etched into the headstone, had a look of unreality to it. It couldn't mean Tim, not our Tim. Mother visited his grave from time to time, but Father and I couldn't face it.

It all happened so fast. It was hard to imagine that less than a year ago, he was healthy and happy, and then, a few days later, he was gone, and he was never coming back. There was so much to tell him, so much to do together. He left us so suddenly we didn't even have a chance to say goodbye.

Would the pain of his loss ever go away?

Looking over at my father, standing over Tim's grave, his face took on the vacant, nobody-home look that day, the one he had for so long after Tim's death. It scared me. He hadn't said a word all day. Mother simply held his arm with her left hand and offered her support. She had a bouquet of flowers for Tim's grave in her other hand, which hid the rosary beneath it.

Father did not resort to drinking on that day, but he relapsed the next. I went to see Henry and told him Father had slipped back into his well of grief and drink. He just shook his head. "That's too bad,

Mary Kate, but he'll come around, I promise. To tell you the truth, I am not surprised. Tim's death really laid him low."

Father didn't go to work and remained drunk. He didn't come out of his room for nearly a week. Mother and I didn't talk about it, but I could see the fear and pain in her eyes. Jack came to see Father once after work, but he didn't speak to anyone but Father. He looked so downtrodden and sad when he walked silently out of the house that day. He didn't come back.

But, Father's dark return to this terrible time of excruciating pain, of bottomless loss, did pass. A few days after Jack's visit, Father came down to breakfast and was off to the paper early as usual. *How did things turn around?*

Mother said it was the Blessed Mother. "She answered my prayers."

Maybe, I thought, but whatever it was, we were mighty glad.

Chapter 20

A few weeks later, Henry surprised me by asking me to cover the wedding of Grace Spreckles, the daughter of John and Lillian Spreckles. "It's at the Catholic cathedral on Third; the reception will be at the Del. It will be quite a do, no expense spared. It is the talk of the town, and we should give it some front-page ink. Bring Charlie for some photos."

I researched the article before the event; I wouldn't have much time to get the story to the printers after the wedding. Henry said it would be a front pager with what he called "A Charlie Special."

Father of the bride, John Spreckles, was second only to Alonso Horton in helping nascent San Diego rise from obscurity into a modern metropolis. He is the wealthiest man in San Diego.

He was especially enamored with Coronado and pretty much built it, including the town itself. He was instrumental in the completion of the Hotel Del, which was in some financial distress at the time. He loved the idea of a world-class resort in Coronado and jumped at the chance to be involved in its development. He now reigns over the place in his mansion overlooking Glorietta Bay on one side and his glorious hotel on the other. John Spreckles, the king of Coronado? This is something nobody would dispute.

Spreckles, who hails from San Francisco, and still keeps a home there, had sailed his yacht *Lurline* into San Diego Bay in 1887 to pick up provisions. He immediately recognized its potential. He, like Alonso Horton before him, was smitten with the place.

Perhaps his most important contributions to the area are the significant transportation improvements in San Diego, including a trolley system and the installation of a local railroad that joined communities in the far reaches of the county. He converted most of the horse-drawn trolleys to electricity-powered ones. He brought a reliable water supply to the area and worked with Elisha Babcock to bring a dependable water source to Coronado.

The Spreckles family was also significant in the city's cultural development and are major philanthropists. Spreckles is a name that appears on the list of major donors to every worthy cause.

Henry was right; everyone knew the importance of the Spreckles family in San Diego and would want to read about this special event in their lives: the marriage of their daughter Grace. I went to ask Charlie about the wedding, and to my dismay, he hadn't heard he was going with me on Saturday. He was very irritated with me. "Come on, Charlie," I said. Henry wants you to take pictures and to go with me to this wedding. It was not my call."

When he acted like this, it took away any fantasy I had that he might have romantic feelings toward me. Ben drove us in his father's best carriage to the Catholic cathedral on Third Street late Saturday afternoon. The wedding was at six. Charlie wore a dark suit and had his camera bag in his hand.

I wore one of Fiona Riggs's castoffs that Mother had designed for her. It was a calf-length, dark blue silk tea dress. The matching hat had a wave of blue netting in the front that just fell just over my eyes. It was a French design mother had copied; not quite dressy enough for the occasion, but appropriate for us worker bees.

Looking into my bedroom mirror after she finished, I nodded approvingly at that pretty, grown-up woman looking back at me. Clothes were becoming important to me. They were my work uniform in a sense. Dressing well was necessary to make a good impression when going out to cover fancy social functions for my women's pages. My recent social experience with Izzy required me to spruce up my appearance as well. I liked it.

155

Izzy came from a wealthy family, and Mrs. Riggs's dresses came in handy on those occasions that called for me to dress a bit nicer. She had excellent taste, and then there was her fortuitous habit of never wanting to wear anything twice. Of course, it didn't hurt that my mother was a seamstress who could make alterations to the gowns Mrs. Riggs gave me. Mother stressed from the time I started at the paper how important dressing well was for my success. I know now she was right.

Charlie was all smiles when he picked me up to take me to the wedding. He apparently had forgotten about his anger about being given the last-minute assignment, and he was perfectly charming. The church where Grace Spreckles was to be married is a large structure in the Moorish style. We got there early so that I could note who among San Diego's elite were guests and so that Charlie could take pictures.

Guests had already started to arrive, and many were seated in the church when we went in. Despite the family's connection to Coronado, there was no church there large enough to accommodate the crowd that was expected for the wedding.

"I'm going to wait until after the bride and groom leave the church to take some candid shots. There won't be enough light inside to use the Brownie," Charlie said.

We took seats in the far corner of the church in the back to be as unobtrusive as possible. The church was bedecked with cream-colored flowers nestled in ferns at every pew and at the altar. Colored prisms of light shone through the large, stained glass windows. The entire presentation was stunning.

The church was full when John Spreckles stood at the back of the church with the bride, his daughter Grace, beside him. He is an attractive, rather distinguished-looking older man. The groom and his attendants stood at the altar waiting for the bride, looking very elegant in their long-tailed tuxedos.

A small orchestra in the choir loft played a lovely piece I didn't recognize. My mother gave me an excellent education in music appreciation, but I wasn't familiar with this one.

This instrumental musical offering was followed by a soloist's enchanting voice echoing through the church to celebrate the bride's arrival and then came the opening strains of the wedding march. Everyone stood, turning with a collective lean to get a gander at her when she began her walk down the aisle. She looked beautiful and happy. Her father looked proud as a peacock, and he teared up a bit walking the down the long aisle of the cathedral with his eldest daughter on his arm.

I wrote in my notebook. "The bride wore an exquisite but unadorned, cream-colored silk-satin gown with a long train. Its lines were simple but very modern, right out of Paris courtier." This was an expression I picked up from Fiona Riggs and used from time to time in my women's articles where fashion was involved. It certainly was involved today. This was a very fine–feathered crowd.

Grace Spreckles topped her elegant ensemble with an unusual headpiece: a cream-colored satin turban that surrounded her beautiful face, with a long veil streaming behind her. She carried lilies with sprays of baby's breath. Her bridal attendants were all dressed in light peach silk, as were her two young nieces, who looked about five, who walked just behind the bride's train sprinkling rose petals on their way down the aisle.

This performance was highlighted by a bit of humor when one of the petal- sprinklers tripped and fell flat on her face. The basket and the petals went flying, and the sweet young girl burst into tears. This was met with soft, affectionate laughter from the onlookers. I included this little antidote in my story; it gave a funny, human touch to what seemed to be an infallible presentation at this wedding.

After the ceremony, Charlie worked his magic. I saw him take a lovely shot of the bride and groom as they came out of the church, ducking their heads and laughing, avoiding the rice flying around them. A few minutes later, he got a candid shot of John Spreckles, who was somewhat flushed, giving his daughter an affectionate squeeze. Another was of Lillie Spreckles, who he caught dabbing her eyes while friends congratulated the newlyweds.

The Spreckles' had their own photographer, but Mrs. Spreckles wanted to see all the photographs taken that day. She asked Charlie for copies of his pictures and made a point to ask us to the reception at the Del. "Thank you, Ma'am, but we aren't dressed for that."

"Pshaw, don't worry; we would love you to join us. You might get some good pictures there too." She looked at me. "Hello, Miss Riley." She remembered me from the Wednesday Ball. "Please, do come; it will be quite a party. A special ferry will leave for Coronado at seven."

After she left us, Charlie asked me if I wanted to go. Ben waited for us out back and could take us to the ferry.

"Sure, I'd love to," I replied. "But we must get home before ten to get this in the Sunday edition. The printers will be waiting for the photos and the story.

"OK, but it's still early. Let's just stay for an hour or so," he said.

Mrs. Spreckles had outdone herself in her decorations in the hotel's ballroom. The color scheme was cream and white, with cream-colored flowers in dramatic arrangements throughout the room, bright green ferns, and other tropical-looking plants. There was a fine orchestra, and lobster was served for the main course at dinner. It was just about the best food I ever ate.

Charlie left me at the table from time to time to take his pictures. As I sat there, I thought of my envying him and Pamela Spaulding at

158

the Wednesday Ball. Now I was here in that same ballroom, Charlie holding *me* tight as we danced every waltz. He surprised me by holding my hand on the short ferry trip home, the lights of New Town sparkling in the distance. The wind on the bay was a bit chilly. Charlie put his arm around me.

This time I knew Charlie saw me as a woman, not just a friend from work. Ben met us at the harbor and took us to the paper and waited to take us home. After we got the story to the printers, Charlie took me home and kissed me goodnight. This time he took the lead and I wasn't the lady in waiting. It was a sweet kiss, and I did not hesitate to return it.

Charlie and I started going out together pretty regularly after that. I liked that very much, and my parents approved. Mother was soon ready to reel this fish in, convinced that Charlie was *the* one for me. "He's so handsome and such gentleman."

Jack and Mary often acted as chaperones for us which worked out fine because we all got along well. Sometimes Charlie's older cousin Harry and his wife Molly went with us. It was a happy time. Was I getting serious about him? Maybe. I wasn't ready to marry Izzy or anyone else just a few months before, but now, I wasn't so sure.

How did he feel about me? After the Spreckles' wedding, Charlie took me out often, but not exclusively. This was disappointing. Charlie made a point to let me know that I was not the only woman he was escorting around town. He didn't hesitate to tell me that he took some other gal to a party or an event as if I was, once again, just a friend, someone he worked with who he kissed quite a bit. This bothered me. Was I just one out of a string of pretty ponies?

But, I didn't have much time to think about it. The *Tingley* trial was coming up soon, and Charlie and we would be together a great deal, most every day in court and late nights at the paper. I was sure things would get sorted then. I smiled and thought of Tim. Charlie and I being together so much would give me time to reel this fish in, that is, *if* I really wanted this particular catch.

Chapter 21

Public opinion in San Diego grew in support of Katherine Tingley in the months since the *Tingley v. Times-Mirror* lawsuit was filed. Harrison Otis knew he had to get the trial moved, preferably to Los Angeles; otherwise, Mrs. Tingley would battle him on her home turf. She had already chosen the field of battle when she filed her lawsuit in San Diego, and Otis knew that was a significant advantage. The jurors deciding the case would be San Diegans.

Otis' first effort to move the case to Los Angeles was just a month after the case was filed. He was rebuffed. A month before the trial started on December 18th, he renewed his efforts to get the case moved out of San Diego... *to anywhere but here, I thought.*

Father was covering a murder trial at the courthouse the day of Harrison Otis' second bid to transfer the Tingley case out of San Diego. Father sent Jack with me to cover the hearing. I was never sent alone as an apprentice to cover an important story.

It was just a few minutes before ten. Jack being Jack, arrived at the paper late, and we had to almost run to the courthouse to be on time for the ten o'clock hearing. Mrs. Tingley's lawyer, J.W. "Judge" McKinley, followed behind us as we entered the courtroom.

"Where's Sam?" he asked the clerk, who shrugged in response. "Oh, that's right, he always likes to make an entrance." The clerk smiled but said nothing.

J. W. McKinley is a pleasant-appearing, rather ordinary-looking man. He is middle-aged and balding and must have gained a few pounds recently because his suit coat buttons strained around his ample belly. He's a rather short man; his pants were too long and pooled around his feet; the sleeves of his coat fell to the middle of his hands.

"*Tingley v. Times-Mirror Company,*" the clerk called.

Mr. McKinley took his place at the counsel table, standing before the judge. Right on cue, the courtroom doors opened and Sam Shortridge, the attorney for the *Times*, walked in and stood before the judge.

He's not a particularly handsome man of about forty-five, who presents a far more elegant picture than his counterpart. His hair is graying and sparse, but he seems to have arranged it on his head to give what he does full effect. He is clean-shaven and impeccably dressed. His clothes fit him perfectly; he wore an expensive custom-tailored suit. He's a tall, slender man with swarthy, sun-browned skin and piercing green eyes. His appearance spoke of old money, sophistication, and success. He was quite a contrast to the rather frumpy-looking. McKinley, who looked far more at home in this San Diego courtroom.

Judge E. S. Torrance, who was already on the bench, and who would be the trial judge in the Tingley case, nodded to Sam Shortridge.

"This is your motion, Shortridge," he said, dispensing with the *Mr.* "This is the second time you have brought this to me, and I don't appreciate it," he said gruffly. "You have the laboring oar. I have read your voluminous papers and all the two hundred sworn affidavits you have submitted. No need to rehash anything that is in them here."

"He's a little grumpy today," I whispered to Jack.

As Mr. Shortridge began his argument, I was surprised by his deep, rich voice. "May it please the court," he began,

"My argument is the same as it was last spring, but this time I have significant evidence to support it. The simple fact is that the vast majority of the men in the jury pool we canvassed, well over two hundred, have stated under oath that they could give an even-handed decision to Harrison Otis or his paper in this case. I submit that there is an overwhelming bias here against my client, who simply cannot get a fair trial in this community."

Judge Torrance listened intently, and for a second I thought he was buying what Mr. Shortridge was selling. He nodded to Mr. McKinley.

"I have put everything I wanted to say in my opposition papers, Your Honor, and I won't rehash them now."

"I appreciate that, Mr. McKinley. Anything further, Mr. Shortridge?"

"No, Your Honor."

"Motion denied. The defendant has fouled the jury pool with his repeated downing of San Diego and its citizens. This, Mr. Shortridge, is not disputed by you, but ironically is the very basis for your motion and is supported by the statements you have offered in evidence."

Judge Torrance leaned back in his chair and leveled a piercing look at Mr. Shortridge. "I think the folks down here can be as fair as folks anywhere else. This bias about which you take issue has nothing to do with Mrs. Tingley or the articles printed about her in the *Times*. The case will be heard in San Diego. See you both on the 18th of December in this courtroom. Now let's go get some lunch."

Neither lawyer looked surprised.

This was my first experience with the judge presiding over the *Tingley* trial. He is a man of about sixty, with bright blue eyes and a ruddy complexion. He has white hair but not much of it and a beard and mustache stained a bit by the tobacco he chews most of the time. Father told me that although he is a bit rough around the edges, Judge Torrance is a no-nonsense judge who abhors unnecessary histrionics from the lawyers before him.

"He hates to waste time, both his and the jury. Still, he is respectful and gives the lawyers before him a great deal of leeway as long as they don't abuse his largesse," Father said. "He's no fool. He's been on the bench for a long time, and lawyers don't get much by him."

"Oh," he added. He chews tobacco and occasionally spits into the spittoon nearby, usually hitting his target with remarkable aim. He's quite a character, it's true, but he's a fair, intelligent judge who knows the law and how to control his courtroom."

"There will be no circus acts by anyone at this trial, despite the notoriety and public interest about the case. And, by the way, he is a drinking buddy of Judge McKinley down at the Harbor Bar —it's the courthouse hangout."

Father warned me that Judge Torrance ran a tight ship and set the time of opening, closing, and breaks, and expected everyone to keep to that timetable.

"Don't be late, Mary Kate. Judge Torrance doesn't tolerate stragglers, late arrivals, or people traipsing in and out during the proceedings."

One night at dinner a week or so ago, Father pulled out from his repertoire of tales one about Judge Torrance. He did this with the usual voice modulation and a wee touch of an Irish brogue.

"Over the years covering trials before Judge Torrance," he told us, I observed that he has a variety of ways of silently expressing his disapproval of what he sees as misconduct of one kind or another in his courtroom".

"One method he uses frequently," Father said, lowering his already deep voice, "I call the horse-eye. This is where the good judge leans over his bench, raises one eyebrow, and gives a one-eyed stare at the offender, like a horse eyeing a pesky fly. If that doesn't do the trick, he does the same with both eyes and a stern set of his jaw. Raising his voice an octave, Father went on, "And what does he do if that doesn't work, you might ask? That's right, the kick."

"He warns the offender that if the offense happens again, they will be sorry. He forecasts what penalty will be in store for them depending on the gravity of the sin: contempt of court, a fine, jail time, or exclusion from his courtroom. I've found that the kick stymies any further misbehavior."

He added, "Good lawyers generally know how far they can push this judge. Skilled lawyers push that boundary whenever they can. Most of them have experienced the kick once or twice, and they want to avoid it if possible."

Walking out of the courthouse after the judge ruled, Jack turned to me. "Do ya want to go to the Waterfront for lunch,? I'm starving."

"Sure, but Jack," I said sheepishly," I don't have much money with me… I don't have any."

He laughed. "When I ask a lady for lunch, I take care of the tab, especially at the Waterfront."

I knew the Waterfront Café well. I had just taken Father there just a month or so ago. It was a favorite for reporters covering the courthouse and for court employees. It had a good, cheap lunch. Best of all, it was fast.

"OK, then," I said, let's go."

Before we left the courthouse, I tugged Jack's sleeve. "Hold on a minute, Jack, let me run upstairs and get my real estate statistics. It will save me a trip back here today."

"Sure," he said, I'll just get some air out front."

I picked up that week's sales records. I found Jack waiting outside the courthouse, talking to a bailiff who was smoking a cigarette. Jack likes to talk to almost anyone he meets. He is like my father in that way; that's what makes them good storytellers and good reporters. They like people and love to tell stories about them. I nodded hello to the bailiff; I'd seen him many times. He smiled and nodded back, taking a drag of his cigarette.

Jack and I walked down Broadway towards the bay which had gone missing that morning, obscured by a layer of fog. The sun was just about to break through. We saw in the distance at land's end, right on the bay, the Tropical Natatorium Bathhouse, a large, ornate structure.

Jack paused. "I love to go to that place. They've got steam-heated hot-water baths, a Turkish steam room, and a large warm saltwater pool with slides, swings, and diving boards. It's fed by seawater through gates that open and close automatically with the tides. It's great fun, all for a quarter, and they even throw in a free towel." He added, "I'm a darn good swimmer, ya know. I like to dive too. You still don't know how to swim, do ya? Izzy said he was going to teach you."

"No, he never got around to it. So, for now, I love to go into the water, but I just paddle around. Tim was gonna...."

"I'll teach ya to swim, Mary Kate... be glad to," he interrupted, looking away.

I'm sure he thought that since Tim was gone he felt he had to step into the breach. *He's right*, I thought, as the familiar sadness overtook me once again.

Pretty soon, after we turned the corner, we walked past another, even fancier, bathhouse; its name, Los Baños, was etched in the front as part of the ornate trim. It was a beautiful building that was considered to be an architectural showcase in the Moorish-Spanish style. It was of much more recent vintage than the Tropical Natatorium. It was an exclusive, members-only bathhouse. There were big doings a few years back when it opened. Father wrote a story about it for the paper—front page. Tim and I had walked down that day to check things out.

"Have you been here?" I asked Jack as we walked by.

"Nope, too rich for my blood. They never got around to asking me to be a member."

"The first time I ever swam in a pool—well, not swam really, was, believe it or not, at the Del. It was on the annual Newsie Day, put on by the hotel and the *Union*. I was fourteen. They did it for the newsies every year and still do. We always looked forward to it. We got to use the pool for two hours; they even gave us bathing suits."

"They made us a great lunch too, but not in the fancy dining room. They pitched us a big white tent on the grounds and we ate there. Probably didn't want us oiling up the finery inside," he said with a huff.

We walked to the next block and saw the Waterfront Café sign sticking out over the walkway. As usual, the place was busy and noisy. We sat at the counter and had a nice lunch of ham sandwiches and chicken soup, the special.

Jack entertained me with some tales of his adventures as a swimmer and diver at locations around the county. "They have a great bathhouse at La Jolla Cove, too," he said. You can take a train there and make a day of it."

After we finished eating, Jack asked me what I thought of Sam Shortridge.

167

"Smooth as silk," I said.

Jack shook his head in agreement. "That's for sure, but smooth talkin' didn't do him any good today. It was pretty much over before Mr. McKinley even opened his mouth."

"And he hardly did," I said.

"Judge Torrance clearly wants to hear the case, Jack said." He all but argued the matter for McKinley."

"I think if anything turns the tide against the *Times* and Harrison Otis, it is the very thing Shortridge complained of today. San Diegans, for the most part, hate Los Angeles, the *Times-Mirror* newspaper, and its publisher, Harrison Gray Otis. Why? Because, as the judge pointed out, they are always downing San Diego and not to mention the shenanigans they pulled to get awarded the railroad terminus."

"So even though the jury might not go along with what they see as all the strange doings at Lomaland, Katherine Tingley is one of their own, a San Diegan. They know that she and her followers have been good for San Diego. They have brought a good deal of money into the city, not to mention music, theater, and other cultural contributions. And don't forget that the building of Lomaland provided much-needed jobs in this area. Kate Tingley employed a lot of men to build that place."

Nodding, "I agree, Jack, and developing cultural resources for an emerging city like ours is very important. Mrs. Tingley has certainly pushed San Diego forward in that way. She has brought music, dance, and theater to the city. Lomaland has some fine resident writers, poets, and artists; some are world-renowned."

"That may be true, but it often comes down to who the jury likes or dislikes," Jack replied. "I can't imagine the General would win in that contest either; from what I hear, he is a real jackass."

"I have heard that too. But maybe he'll behave himself at the trial. I know you haven't been to Lomaland, but have you met Katherine Tingley?" I asked him.

"I can't say that I have. I saw her for the first time at the library opening. Like almost everybody else, I have heard a lot about her and read about her. I'm hoping to meet her during the trial. I'll definitely want to see both Otis and Tingley on the witness stand. It should be quite a showdown."

"I glanced at my watch; it was getting late. "I've got to get going, Jack—it's Friday, and I have most of my pickups and deliveries today."

"I'll do the story on the hearing, Mary Kate. I'll show it to you, and you can make additions if you have any. If you don't have time, I'll just do it."

Chapter 22

The alarm clock screeched in my ear, waking me to a morning I had looked forward to for months: the first day of the *Tingley v. Times-Mirror* trial. I donned one of Mother's long-sleeved dresses that she'd cut down to fit me, a dark brown number with a white collar trimmed in black. Wore my new, two-inch-heeled black boots hoping to add a little height. As I pinned up my unruly mess of curls, a few stragglers still peeked out at my neck and around my face; Mother's black bowler would cover most of it. Glancing in the mirror as I passed it, "Best I can do," I said out loud and hurried down the stairs.

"Good morning, Mother. Where's Father?"

She didn't answer. She set down a plate of fresh soda bread, thick bacon, and scrambled eggs. Special breakfast on a Thursday? It looked and smelled delicious; I was hungry. Mother turned and went for the coffeepot and poured me a cup. After I took a few bites of food and a sip of coffee, she sat beside me. "Your father wants to talk to you. His back is worse today."

I rushed up the stairs and sat down on the side of his bed and could see right away that he was in pain.

"I can't make it down there today, Mary Kate; you'll have to go alone."

A cold fear gripped me. "No, I can't, not alone; I won't know what to do."

"You don't have to *do* anything. It will be a slow day in court. All that's going to happen is the attorneys will start to pick a jury. That will take at least a day, maybe two. I should be back with you tomorrow, and then I'll have the weekend to nurse my back. Jack is out on a story this morning but he should be there before lunch."

"Now go eat your breakfast; you'll be fine."

"I've lost my appetite," I said, heading towards the door.

"Oh, and make sure Charlie gets pictures of Harrison Otis and Katherine Tingley for tomorrow's edition. I'm sure he will, but remind him. He will have to wait for a break because they must be taken outside, maybe at the lunch break."

"I'd like to set our readers up for the battle between these two important leaders of these rival cities. A picture of them for tomorrow's front page would be great. There won't be much interest in the jury selection, so it's a good time to introduce these gladiators to our readers before the real battle begins. Charlie will be down at the courthouse when you get there, so you'll see at least one friendly face this morning."

He had come over for dinner the night before, and we all talked about how excited we were to cover the trial. Father didn't seem like he was in much pain then, so I didn't worry about it. But as it turns out, I would be going it alone for the morning session of the first day of this important trial. I was glad Charlie was going to be there for support.

"Your mother will let Henry know I need some cover for the first day or so of the trial. He'll have to double up on Jack's work, and he will have to cover most of the trial days until I get back, with your help, of course."

He didn't look at all concerned about me going it alone.

"Don't worry, there are only two days left before the weekend break; I'm sure to be fit by Monday and hopefully tomorrow. As I said, not much is going on in the first two days, just jury selection and maybe opening statements."

171

"And Mary Kate, he added, you'll want to get there early and get the best seat possible—first row, aisle of the press section. You can do this, my girl; I know you can."

Giving my father a rueful smile, I leaned over and kissed him. "Get some good rest. You look like you are hurting."

"That I am, now git."

I took a deep breath and, with a sigh, blew it out as I went to my room, a deflated balloon coming to mind. Grabbing my Press badge and fastening it to my waist, I checked my satchel: a handkerchief, two pencils, a tablet, a mirror, a small lunch Mother had packed for me last night, and a flask of water. All set. Swallowing hard, hurrying downstairs, and giving Mother a tentative look, I headed for the door.

Mother reached out and gave me a squeeze. "Good luck, dear, you'll be fine."

"I hope so," I said, a bit of wobble in my voice.

My first trial. "I'm a reporter for *The San Diego Union*," I said proudly to nobody in particular as I started the short walk to the courthouse. I have Press credentials to prove it, touching the large badge at my waist. Now I had to prove myself.

It was a bit chilly, but the sun was shining. As I hurried down Broadway, I knew there would be excitement everywhere I went. Everybody in town was talking about this trial. There would be press at the courthouse from all over the country. But *this* morning, I would be the only reporter for *The San Diego Union*, the city's most important and longest-running paper. *Scared? Darn right.*

You could see three horses tied up at the hitching post in front of the courthouse, a few buggies, and a hansom cab dropping off passengers. There were numerous bicycles beside them in a rack but no automobiles. The city had installed a bright white sidewalk a while back, putting a nice frame around the building and highlighting the newly-landscaped grounds. Looking up, the blind Lady Justice holding her golden scales shone in the sun at the top of the building. As I walked up the path to the front door of the courthouse, I saw the words "Hall of Justice" etched above the impressive archway that extended to the second floor.

Would she bring justice to Katherine Tingley?

There was a long line outside the front door. Father told me that the parties to the *Tingley* case, their attorneys, and the press would be allowed in before any spectators. "Pardon me, Press, pardon me, Press," I repeated, going to the front of the line. I took my Press pass off my waist and held it high, showing it to the bailiff monitoring the front door. He ignored me. "Press," I said a bit louder.

The dress I wore was conservative and may have made me look older, but my five-foot-two height, my red curls peeking out from under my hat, and my freckled face belied any impression of maturity that the costume might have otherwise conveyed. But, I sallied forth and started to walk past the bailiff and into the building when he put his arm down in my path.

"Young lady, you need to go to the end of the line. You have no business up here in front."

I had been to the courthouse almost twice a week for nine months to cover hearings with Father, research court records, or pick up my real estate sales statistics. This particular bailiff was often smoking a cigarette out in front. I couldn't believe he didn't recognize me. Puffing up my five-foot-two self and flashing my Press pass, I tried again.

"You remember me. I'm Press. I'm Mike Riley's apprentice at the *Union*. I'm covering the *Tingley* trial."

He took the Press pass and looked it over carefully. "So, where's Mike?"

"His back went out. I'm here to cover for him for a day or two," I said, feeling the heat rising on my face.

"All righty then, Miss," he said, suddenly waving me through.

A passel of reporters, a few photographers, and a few spectators were waiting in the hall outside of Department One where the trial was to take place. Charlie was standing in the back of the pack, a camera slung around his neck. He smiled and waved. I returned his greeting and called, "Father wanted me to remind you to be sure to get a shot of Tingley and Otis for tomorrow's page one." He nodded and smiled. I didn't stop to chat, wanting to be first in line at the door of the courtroom.

Charlie and I were seeing each other regularly now. We were both very excited about the trial we were about to witness. After all, our city hosted what was considered by many to be the trial of the century. It was big news. There was press from all over the country, about twenty reporters in all. Nothing quite like this had ever happened in San Diego.

Before long, the hall was a beehive of activity, with people milling around outside Department One. Everyone was talking about the case, wondering when the leading players would arrive. A bailiff was monitoring the courtroom door. It was eight-thirty, and the trial started at nine.

There was an excited twitter from the crowd;. I turned to see why. Harrison Otis, the owner, and publisher of the *Los Angeles Times,* was walking down the hall with his lawyer, Samuel Shortridge.

Pigeon-chested, standing straight as if at attention, Mr. Otis walked toward the door to the courtroom. The General, as he likes to call himself, is a tall, heavy-set man in his sixties, who carries an air of power. He's handsome in an older-gent kind of way. He's white-

174

haired and balding, with a ruddy face adorned with somewhat out-of-date bushy side-whiskers, a large walrus mustache, and a goatee.

His steely blue eyes stared straight ahead, acknowledging no one as he walked past. He's not a cordial man, and he made no effort to connect with anyone in the crowd, some of whom were ogling him as if a celebrity had just arrived.

The guard opened the courtroom door for him, and as he walked by me, I was consumed by a waft of the smell of stale cigars drowning in the heavy-handed use of men's cologne. He seemed to have bathed in *Jockey Club*, the wildly popular men's fragrance favored by upper-class men.

He wore a conservative gray-pinstriped suit. He topped this off with a red silk cravat held in place by an ostentatious diamond stickpin. These dandified additions, ensconced in a cloud of cologne, added a rather feminine touch to his efforts to present himself as the manliest of men.

Samuel Shortridge followed him through the door. Once again, the man was impeccably dressed, this time in a custom-tailored navy blue suit and a gray silk tie. As he passed me, he paused, "Hello, Miss Riley, so nice to see you again." He kept walking, not waiting for a reply. I was shocked; I had never met the man.

A few minutes before nine, the guard nodded to me to come in. I took my seat on the front-row aisle of the press section on the left side of the wood-paneled courtroom, which was the largest one in the building. It had a large window on the left side, and the witness stand and the jury box were on the right. There was a short wooden barrier between the spectator seating and the counsel tables where the lawyers and their clients sat. It had a gate that opened in the middle like the doors of a saloon, which was used to get to the area before the judge, who sat in the middle of the room. The witness stand was adjacent to the judge's bench and near the jury box. The press sat on the left-hand side of the spectator section.

A few minutes later, three rather irritated reporters stumbled over me to fill up the first row of the church pew-like benches. Mr. Otis was seated at the counsel table next to his lawyer just a few feet in front of me. Judge McKinley was sitting alone at the plaintiff's counsel table, on the right side of the courtroom, the one closest to the jury box and the witness stand.

He must have arrived through another entrance; he didn't pass by me coming in. He had lost a bit of weight; he had a fresh haircut and a new brown suit, which this time had been tailored to fit him. He topped this off with an attractive red silk paisley tie. He's not particularly handsome, but he looked his best for his first appearance in this celebrated trial.

Where is Katherine Tingley?

"All rise," the clerk called in a loud voice, "Department One of the San Diego Superior Court is now in session, the Honorable E.S. Torrance presiding in the case now before the court, *Tingley vs. Los Angeles Times Mirror.*"

I heard the clock on the wall clicked forward; it was nine o'clock. The judge took the bench and looked at the spectators who were still standing. "Good morning. Before we get started, there is a matter that I need to take up with the lawyers. Spectators, please step outside; Press may remain."

The spectators headed out the door. The press gang was still on their feet waiting for the judge to order them to sit. Before he did, he looked at me.

"Out," he said firmly pointing to the door.

I looked around, wondering who he was talking to. Both lawyers and Harrison Otis, all still standing, turned and stared at me, and once again, I could feel the heat rising in my face. I took a deep breath for courage and stared back at the judge.

176

"Out," the judge repeated with a dismissive wave and a stern look. Putting my head down and taking a last look at him, I left the courtroom, humiliated. The hallway was full of spectators, but Charlie wasn't around. Hurrying to the small coatroom at the end of the hall and closing the door, I sat down on a lonely-looking little chair and the tears poured out of me.

After a few minutes of feeling very sorry for myself, I needed to pull myself together and fast; the courtroom door would be open any minute now. I was a member of the press and had a right to be in that courtroom and would have to go back there and sort this out. But how?

Taking the mirror out of my satchel, what I saw there was a sorry mess. My eyes were red, my face a map of red blotches. I took a deep breath, wiped the tear tracks from my face, blew my nose, straightened my hat, and charged forth, summoning as much courage as I could muster, but plenty scared.

There was a line of spectators waiting at the courtroom door. Stepping to the front and in my most determined voice, I said to the bailiff monitoring the door, "May I speak to you privately?"

Annoyed, he signaled me to step away. We walked toward the opposite side of the hallway, but before we got there, he stopped and looked down at me. "What can I do for you, Miss?"

Taking a deep breath, I looked up at his six-foot-three self and replied, "Will you ask the judge when we go back in if I can have a minute of his time?"

"No, Miss, he won't do that, and I won't ask him."

Not knowing what else to say, I just turned and walked away, going to the end of the line drawing curious stares from all of the spectators that waited there.

After a few minutes, the courtroom door opened and the clerk told the bailiff to bring in the spectators. Following them in, the spectators took their places in the gallery. I turned to the left and went to my seat in the press section, front-row aisle, but remained standing. The rest of the press was already seated. The judge was on the bench, and with a wave of his hand and a firm voice, he said to the spectators standing before him on the right side of the gallery, "Please be seated."

They all sat down. I stood alone in the front row. My mouth was dry, and my legs were shaking. The judge glared at me. "Sit down, Miss," he said firmly.

I held my ground, trying to get the words out, but nothing came.

"Is there a problem?" he said, clearly irritated.

"Yes, Your Honor," I said, in a too-loud voice that sounded like it came from someone else. I swallowed hard, trying to force more words out, which, when they did come, poured forth in a wobbly, too-rapid stream.

"My name is Mary Kate Riley. I'm a reporter for *The San Diego Union* and am a member of the Press Corps. I. . . I, you, uh, probably didn't know this when you ordered me to leave with the spectators while allowing the rest of the press to remain."

I looked up at Judge Torrance with determination on my face. Somehow my fear evaporated. He sat silently for what seemed like a long time, and after taking a couple of chews on his tobacco, he looked at me and said, "No . . . no, I didn't." He paused. "Now sit down," he said gruffly.

After I sat down, Judge Torrance, with a remarkable aim, spit a stream of juice from the tobacco he was chewing into a nearby spittoon. I didn't know if this was a reflection of his attitude about our little dust-up or just time for a spit-out.

Sam Shortridge, Harrison Otis, and Mr. McKinley all were twisted around in their chairs, looking at me. The two lawyers smiled; even Mr. Otis nodded his approval. The judge turned to the lawyers. "Let's get started with jury selection, gentlemen. Bailiff, bring in the jury pool."

One by one, the men from the jury pool took seats in the box. It occurred to me that there would be no women on the jury. Mrs.Tingley could definitely use a woman's perspective, but only voters could serve. *That was just so irritating.*

Women had made great strides in San Diego in the effort to secure the vote, and the issue was gaining momentum, but the vote for women was still a ways off. I remembered Jack's and Charlie's comments about the large parade promoting women's suffrage that ran down Broadway last summer. Jack covered the story for the paper, and Charlie took an interesting picture of four women riding on an extravagant float. The parade was front-page news and was led by the leader of the suffrage movement in San Diego, none other than Dr. Charlotte Baker.

"It was just plain stupid," Charlie commented to me at the time.

"Those women looked ridiculous on those crazy floats," Jack chimed in. These sentiments pretty much summed up the attitudes of even the most modern men on the subject, at least in San Diego, my father included.

When the jury box was full of potential jurors, Judge Torrance looked at the lawyers. "All right, gentlemen, let's get started with your questions. Mr. McKinley, you're up first."

Mr. Shortridge stood to address the judge. "Your Honor, may I inquire where the plaintiff, Katherine Tingley, is this morning?"

"Mrs. Tingley, unfortunately, has been injured in an accident; she's broken her foot. She will be at the Brewster Hotel recuperating until at least next Tuesday."

179

There was a murmuring heard from the gallery. Mr. Shortridge sat down; Harrison Otis leaned over to him and, in a loud whisper, said, "We're finished—our goose is cooked."

Looking around, wondering if anyone else had heard him, it didn't seem like they had. At the ten o'clock break, I introduced myself to some of the other reporters who waited in the hall. They were very cordial. All of them I met that morning were from out of town; most were staying at the Horton House.

They complimented me on standing up to the judge. They laughed about his marking the occasion with his remarkable spit into the cuspidor. None mentioned hearing the comment Mr. Otis made about Mrs. Tingley.

I was looking forward to getting to know the members of the press pack covering this trial. At least so far, the ones I met were very accepting of me, the only woman among them. They even invited me to go to lunch with them. Jack hadn't arrived by the lunch break.

I turned down Charlie's invitation to join him and some other reporters for lunch at the Waterfront, deciding instead to do some research about other lawsuits involving Mrs. Tingley. Father says that a background like that gives depth to a story. I headed upstairs.

"Hello Fred, please give me any cases in which Mrs. Tingley is a party."

He smiled and nodded. A few minutes later, he handed me three files. I was reviewing them at a table next to the counter when the bailiff from our courtroom came in to jawbone with Fred about the trial. I got a kick out of his descriptions of the players, he being a seasoned trial watcher and all.

Half-listened to the bailiff's palaver, something he said caught my attention: "Everybody was surprised that Mrs. Tingley wasn't there today. Judge Torrance announced first thing that she had an accident, had broken her foot, and would be recuperating at the Brewster Hotel until Tuesday. And ya know what, Fred? That just ain't so. I have it on good authority that she's not at the Brewster. That's where she planned to stay, but she is staying with the Hortons on the hill."

"I guess the judge wasn't informed of the change of plans. Reporters will be buzzing around at the Brewster," he said with a chuckle, "but they won't find her there. No sir, they won't find her there."

I made quick work of my file review and went downstairs to wait for Jack. He didn't arrive, so I sat in the courtroom half-listening when the trial resumed after lunch. At the same time the lawyers took turns questioning potential jurors, I made notes about what I had observed that morning in court and hatched a plan to try to interview Mrs. Tingley using my inside knowledge of her whereabouts. I also wrote a note to my father telling him where I was going knowing full well that he would never have approved. Always late, Jack was outside in the hall talking to some reporters at the three o'clock break.

"Hello, Jack," I said with a smile.

"What did I miss? I got hung up in National City."

"Nothing much—jury selection is all; they should finish tomorrow. Oh, and Jack, Katherine Tingley won't be at the trial until Tuesday; she broke her foot. I'm going to slip out to try to get an interview with her. She—"

He interrupted, "She's not giving interviews."

"Well, I'm gonna try," I countered. "Here are my notes from the morning session and a note to my father—be sure he gets it."

"OK, but you're wasting your time. McKinley has forbidden her from speaking to the press before she testifies, and so far, she hasn't.

181

But we don't need two reporters here for jury selection, so give it a try—no harm in that."

He left it at that and turned and walked toward the pack of reporters. He was buddies with most of the local guys. I knew Jack thought Mrs. Horton was staying at the Brewster. What I had in mind was a far different story: I would be trying to get the interview up on Horton Hill by myself. He would never have okayed this but he didn't ever have to know. It was still early: I probably wouldn't be let in to see Mrs. Tingley, let alone interview her, and would have time to walk to Broadway, take a trolley down the hill, and be home before dark.

Chapter 23

Picking up my satchel from the bench where I had been sitting, and turning toward the front of the courthouse, I rushed out the door onto Broadway, where I could catch a trolley.

I knew where to find the Horton home; everybody did. It shone like a white elephant on top of the hills. Alonso Horton built the State Street house, his fifth mansion since he came to San Diego, to entice home buyers to invest in the large development he had plotted below at the foot of the hills near the bay.

His house is now the only structure in the area after the real estate market went bust yet again. He couldn't sell the land below which is now inhabited only by a few rabbits, another Rabbitville. He recovered from the previous two economic busts, but he was too old at ninety-five to reinvent himself again. Rushing out of the courthouse, I saw the eastbound trolley pulling away, traveling up the hill on Broadway toward Fifth.

Darn, it. It would be at least a half hour before the next one, and even then it might be full at this time of day. There was a trolley going north on First and I hurried to catch it. Hopping on and grabbing a seat; a trolley going south passed us jammed with people, mine was almost empty. I was the last remaining passenger at the end of the line on Cedar Street. The only way to get up to the Horton's house from there was to hoof it.

It was a warm afternoon; the trolley ride left me dusty, covered with sweat, and already thirsty. I looked up Horton Hill, as it's called, to the large white house sitting on the top of the ridge. It has a cupola, a widow's walk on the roof, a bit of gingerbread trim to take the chill off its boxy prefabricated shape, and large windows facing the bay, wrapped by a large porch. Horton said he had always wanted a house with a magnificent view of the city, the harbor, Coronado Island, and Point Loma. This house certainly fits the bill.

He designed the house to be cooled in hot weather by air circulation through the front windows by the wind blowing up the hill from the bay. Horton positioned the house so that he could mount the widow's walk on the roof and see the ships arrive in the harbor. He is known to spend his time in his rocking chair on the porch, admiring the beautiful sunsets and looking over the young, dynamic city—New Town, that he founded and, in many ways, built.

He is known to spot ships arriving in the bay from the widow's walk on the roof and make his way to the harbor as the city's unofficial greeter. He has rosy cheeks, a jolly disposition, and a long white beard. Children often asked, is that Santa Claus?

Alonso Horton may have lost his fortune, but he still enjoys being the city's goodwill ambassador, welcoming visitors to the town he loves. He is a rare bird, a legend in his own time. Even rarer, he is known to be a happy and satisfied man. Perhaps I would meet him at the Hortons *if* I was invited in, which was not very likely.

I looked around for a place to clean myself up and saw a small run-down store with a CLOSED sign on its door and two tiny ramshackle houses next to it; both looked deserted. Nobody was around so I went behind one of the houses, pulled up my long sleeves, and loosened my collar. Taking out the napkin in my lunch kit, I wet it to wipe down my face, neck, and sweaty armpits. A cool breeze hit my still-wet face. I wanted to be as fresh as possible when I got to the house. Looking around; nobody saw my little *toilette.*

I crouched down and relieved myself, wetting my skirts quite a bit. Taking a swig of water, I looked at the hill I was about to climb to get there. There was nothing but patches of dirt, straw-colored grasses, chaparral, and the skeleton of one dark oak, long ago felled by lightning.

The Horton home, shining in the golden light of the late afternoon sun, didn't look too far away. Gaining entrance would be quite another matter. I drank another gulp of water, took a deep breath, and started up the hill. After climbing two long blocks, my feet were beginning to hurt. My new boots, which I had saved to wear to the trial, needed more breaking in.

Pausing for a moment, I could see to my north in the distance, a cowboy rounding up a small herd of cattle. He surprised me by taking off his hat and waving at me in greeting. I waved back and continued my trek up the hill, glancing at the cowboy from time to time, hoping he would ride over to talk to me. Maybe I needed some company— some encouragement, really.

After another brief respite at the halfway point, the idea of trying to get up this hill and interview Mrs. Tingley seemed foolish.

This is crazy; Mrs. Tingley will not see me, let alone let me interview her.

Turning back down the hill, after walking about fifty feet, I changed my mind again and headed back toward the house. Father had shared with us often how he had gone out on a limb to get a story. This seemed doable.

As I proceeded up the hill, it appeared that the large garden just below the porch was secured by a retaining wall. I planned to get up that wall and onto the bank and see if I could go in the back door. It was probably open, as it was an unseasonably warm day, and the bay breeze would come in handy to cool the room.

Mrs. Tingley was likely to be sitting just inside that door. She needed to be off her feet, and she wouldn't want to be stuck in a back room all day when she could appreciate the breeze and the

185

view from the front of the house. If I got up to the back door, I would simply call to her.

She might, just might, out of curiosity, hearing a woman's voice where you wouldn't expect to, let me in; she'd probably at least call to me so she could see who it was. She would surely wonder how a woman got out there. Katherine Tingley wasn't a woman to sit all day and do nothing. She was probably bored and might even want some company.

How was I going to persuade her to talk to me? I'd think about that when I got there. If the back door was open and nobody answered my call, would I just go in? The large front windows were open. Was Katherine Tingley sitting right inside them?

The house loomed larger and larger as I neared it, walking up the hill. You could see what was an elaborate garden, complete with statuary, was secured by a failing, poorly-reinforced retaining wall. The garden was overgrown and neglected. There were a couple of peach trees badly in need of pruning.

The house needed a great deal of work. There was plenty of peeling white paint, a broken porch railing, and a decrepit roof with evidence of poorly done spot repairs. It looked elegant from below, but it didn't pass muster close-up. This, the last of the Horton mansions, was a shadow of its former self.

From my research earlier in the year, I knew that the Hortons had no money to repair the house. The fact is, Alonso Horton is broke. He lives in the State Street house with his wife, Lydia. They have no paid household help and rent out its many bedrooms to what they call friends, boarders really, that they have taken in to keep afloat; some of them exchange services for room and board. Maybe one of them might let me in? Maybe Alonso Horton was at home; at his age, he probably didn't get out much. He was known as a kind man and might allow me to at least *see* Mrs. Tingley.

Lydia Horton wouldn't be home from work. Mother and I have become quite friendly with her over the past year working at the Children's Home. She is the primary financial support of her household, working as a librarian five days a week. This is quite extraordinary for a woman still at the top of the social ladder, the upper crust of San Diego society. The Hortons are, after all, San Diego royalty. They have the title, respect, and affection of the people of San Diego, but their castle is falling down around them.

About twenty feet from the retaining wall I saw two big rocks; one had a flat top—well, somewhat flat. Dripping with sweat, dusty and dirty, I considered another wipe-down. No, that could wait until I got to the top of the bank.

Taking a rather uncomfortable, very short sit-down on one of the rocks, looking at the wall more carefully, I could see that somebody had tried to reinforce it with some very weathered pieces of wood that were set in both directions. The wall was failing, cracked from top to bottom in several places. The good news was that the wood boards gave me a ladder-like mechanism to climb to the top of the wall.

How was I going to get up on the bank from there? Sighing, I'd figure that out if I got up there. If the statue near the wall was sturdy, maybe I could grab it and pull myself up on the bank.

Stepping about two feet up to the first rung of my ladder with my satchel on my arm, and pulling up my dress with the other hand, I decided to throw the satchel onto the bank; it was cumbersome. It didn't make it, fell to the ground, and I had to start over.

Reaching the first level again, I easily pulled myself up to the next wood beam. I heard *r-r-r-r-rip* and looked down. The hem of my dress had torn on a piece of drainage pipe protruding from the wall; a long, jagged piece of the dress hung down below the hemline. '*Can't do anything about it now.*

Giving my satchel another hard toss, it made it onto the bank where it would be waiting for me if I got up there. I repeated the step-up a third time and saw that the base of the statue was just within reach. This would be the hardest part, getting up onto the bank. The top of the wall was about chest level as I stepped on the final rung of my ladder.

Hmmm. . . . my dress needed to be out of my way when I swung my leg over the bank. Should I take the dress off, throw it on the bank with my satchel, and put it back on outside the porch area? Who would see me? Somebody in the house might, even Mrs. Tingley herself. If they did, they would surely think there was a crazy woman out back with no dress on.

Nixing the no-dress idea, I pulled it up and tied it in a makeshift knot near my waist, keeping it out of my way as much as possible. My once-white undergarments were filthy, covered with dirt from my walk up the hill.

Standing on the last rung of my ladder, I had a full view of the house, the porch, and the five-foot marble likeness of some goddess that had stood for many years in the garden near the edge of the retaining wall.

The four large windows inside the wrap-around porch and the back door were all wide open, the curtains blowing up and down in the wind, waving to me, just waiting for me to arrive. Tall enough to put my hands around the base of the statue and pull myself onto the bank, I pulled first gently, then as hard as I could. It held firm; it was sturdy enough to hold me. Taking a deep breath and gathering my resolve, embracing the statue's base, and using every ounce of strength, I pulled myself up the wall. As I swung my leg over the top of the wall, the statue began to wobble.

Chapter 24

The next thing I remember is waking up with the pin from my Press- pass, pricking me in my side. I abruptly sat up, opened my eyes, refastened the badge, and felt the softness of the velvet of the fainting couch where I had been sleeping. Reaching up to touch the painful knot that was growing on my head, I realized that my hat was gone.

As I looked around, disoriented at first, my eyes met the powerful gaze of none other than Katherine Tingley. She sat across from me with her casted left foot propped up on an overstuffed stool. I stared for a moment and blinked in surprise, not quite believing she was seated right in front of me.

"Hello, Miss; how are you feeling?"

"I'm fine . . . I . . . guess."

"What brings you here, young lady? Press?" she asked without warmth.

I took a breath, pushed my wild curls out of my face, wondering for a second what happened to Mother's hat, and for once, thought about what I would say. Not much came out.

"Yes . . . Ma'am," I croaked.

"Well, Miss ... she looked at my Press badge, "*Mary-Kate-Riley*," saying my name deliberately, "my lawyer will not allow any interviews, even for intrepid young women reporters like you. Until he gets here, you can tell me a little bit about yourself and your day and how you happened to come up here."

Thinking for a moment, I sighed, smiled, and turned to Mrs. Tingley. "I just happened to overhear the bailiff at the lunch break saying you were recuperating here. I knew no other reporters would find you, so I decided to see if I could get an interview."

"I left the courthouse at the afternoon break but missed the eastbound trolley, so I decided to hike up here after taking the northbound trolley to Cedar Street. I made it—almost.

After getting to the bottom of the retaining wall supporting the garden area, I climbed the wall. I tried to pull myself up with my arms around a statue near the top of the wall, it seemed secure. It wasn't."

"I pulled the statue down with me, and it must have fallen beside me. Thank goodness it wasn't a very long fall. I must have hit my head on a rock or something, which knocked me out. The next thing I knew, I woke up on this couch."

"This certainly was a way to avoid my dilemma of how to get you to see me—probably not the best idea," I said wryly.

"Why didn't you simply knock on the front door?"

"Well, I considered doing that, but I figured nobody would let me in."

"You were right about that," she said. Mrs. Tingley picked up the tale. "A cowboy riding nearby saw you fall, rode over here, picked you up "like she was a feather," he said and brought you to the house. He was a sweet man, quite handsome. He only stayed long enough to make sure you were all right; then he insisted he had to leave to get back to his chores. He wouldn't even take any reward."

"So you were at the trial today?" she asked.

"Yes…Oh, you'll be interested in hearing the comment Harrison Otis made to his lawyer after he heard you had broken your foot. He said this in a very loud whisper: 'We're finished—our goose is cooked.'"

She surprised me by letting out a loud, raucous laugh, clapping her hands with delight. "I hope they *are* finished. Go on, dear." She gave me a mischievous smile. "My lawyer didn't say I couldn't listen, only that I had to keep my mouth shut. I'm very anxious to hear what happened today, as well as your take on the players in this little drama. A trial is a bit like a stage play, isn't it?"

I nodded, thinking how much Mrs.Tingley herself is involved in stage productions, including writing and acting in many of them. She loves drama. She's quite the performer, and that talent would serve her well at the trial.

"By the way, Miss Riley, she said, I hope you'll join us for dinner."

Very pleased, I replied, "That would be nice—I haven't eaten all day. I'm starving."

"Young people are always hungry," she said with a smile, shaking her head.

"You know, Miss Riley, I haven't heard of a woman reporter, at least around here."

Mrs. Tingley leaned back in her chair, adjusting her broken foot on the stool. She looked relaxed and seemed to be poised to hear a most amusing tale. I resolved to do my best not to disappoint.

Father is a great Irish storyteller, but I can spin a tale pretty darn well myself. I suspected she was glad to have some company after being stuck all day in this big house, and so, I continued, leaning forward in her direction.

"My father is the editor and lead reporter for *The San Diego Union*; the courthouse is his beat. He asked me to be his apprentice when my brother Tim, who was in that job, died very suddenly in February"

"It was horrible. My father and I were so devastated that my mother and his boss, Henry Seymour, thought my working at the paper would be good for us both. It has been."

"My first day at the paper was the day you filed your lawsuit," I continued. "It was big news; it still is. There were twenty reporters down at the courthouse today from all over the country."

"I have worked on your case this past year with my father and have done a great deal of research about you, Lomaland, Theosophy, and Mr. McKinley. I have also researched your nemesis, Harrison Otis, as well as his lawyer, Sam Shortridge."

Mrs. Tingley gave me a little smile; she was all ears.

"I never thought about becoming a newspaper reporter—my parents suggested becoming a teacher. I was set to go to teachers' college in May. My mother thought it was a good fallback job until I married. But really I want to be a writer, to write novels. I will someday, but now the printer's ink has gotten into my veins. I love writing for the paper and am good at it."

"I saw your interview with Mrs. Horton. Well done," Mrs. Tingley piped in.

Gratified, I murmured, "Thank you."

She went on, "Lydia is a wonderful woman. We became friends when I first came to Point Loma; she used to live there, you know."

"Have you been to Lomaland, Miss Riley?"

"Yes, I was there to see *A Midsummer Night's Dream* in March," I replied.

"You may recall that Charlie, our photographer, took a nice picture of you watching the play. It was in the paper along with a front-page story I wrote about Lomaland."

"Yes, I do remember seeing that. Your Charlie has quite an eye for a good photograph."

"Did I meet you that day, dear?"

"No, I was too scared to approach you," I admitted.

"I assure you I don't bite," she said with amusement. She leaned back in her chair, and we both took a break. Filling up my empty glass with water, I raised the pitcher to her.

"May I pour you some water Ma 'me?"

"No, thank you, dear; I have my pitcher over here," she said, pointing to a small glass pitcher beside her chair.

So tell me, Miss Riley, what did you think of Mr. Shortridge?"

"Smart and smooth. He appears to live up to his reputation as a very good trial lawyer. He has a deep voice and a measured way of speaking. He certainly commands your attention."

"Hmm," replied Mrs. Tingley. "What is his background?"

I thought a moment. "Looking at the two lawyers, you'd never know that Sam Shortridge doesn't have nearly as sterling a pedigree as does your lawyer, Harvard-educated J. W. McKinley. Sam Shortridge hails from a small college and law school in the Midwest. His family was not poor but was certainly not well-heeled.

He honed his rhetorical skills at the foot of his father, a lawyer-turned-fiery Methodist minister. Sam Shortridge sports the persona of a man born with a silver spoon in his mouth, but it's an image he created for himself."

"Well, that's interesting," she replied. "Where is your father—was he at the trial today?"

"No, I was looking forward to covering the trial with him, but his back went out on Monday. He nursed it along and thought he could make it today. He couldn't and had to send me alone. As an apprentice, you are never sent alone. It was pretty scary."

I told her about having to insist I be let into the courthouse as press and about my dust-up with the judge. She smiled and shook her head.

"You are short in stature and a woman, a very young woman," she said. "You have to stand up for yourself, or you might as well do something other than what most see as a man's job. You need to be forthright and determined, but I caution you that is not seen as feminine. Believe me, I know," she said rather sadly.

I looked out the front windows; it was just getting dark. My parents would worry. I must have slept for at least an hour.

"How were you planning on getting home?" she asked as if she had read my mind.

"I didn't think that far ahead. This was my chance to set myself apart from the rest of the press, to get a scoop, to prove myself to them and especially to my father. I so want to make him proud of me."

"I'm sure he already is, dear," she said warmly. "I will have Mr. McKinley drop you off at home."

As if he heard his name called, there was a knock on the front door.

Chapter 25

Mr. McKinley opened the door and stepped in. "I thought I told you no interviews," he barked, glaring at Mrs. Tingley.

She was not dismayed and quickly smoothed over his ruffled feathers. She assured him that we hadn't talked about her at all but rather about my accident and what happened at the trial that day. He accepted this explanation, and we had a very pleasant dinner. He was keen to hear my opinion of the various players in court that day, especially Mr. Otis and Mr. Shortridge.

Mr. McKinley gave me a scoop about the trial. He said he intended to ask Judge Torrance on Monday for a jury viewing of Lomaland. It was likely to be denied, and it would surely get the judge aggravated with him, he told us.

He said that he was hoping that Otis' objection to them seeing the place would somehow get to the jury. "They'll ask themselves, what are they hiding? They will also resent that they didn't get to see the place. I'm sure they're curious about it." He added, "But I 'm afraid the judge will take the jury out before he hears this."

It was apparent that Mr. McKinley was hoping I'd put this maneuver in the paper. At least one juror might read about it in the *Union* even if the jury didn't hear about it in court.

"So, tell me, Miss Riley, how you planned to get home when you decided to come up here? Mr. McKinley asked me. Before I could answer, Mrs. Tingley answered for me.

"Young people are not planners, Judge. They always have a "the Lord will provide" kind of attitude. Shaking her head, she continued,

"Miss Riley had no idea how she would get down the hill and back home, alone, on foot, and in the dark."

Mr. McKinley smiled at me and said he knew my father well from other trials of his that my father had covered, and that he liked and respected him. "Mike Riley is a darned good reporter. We've become friends over the years. I'll be pleased to see you home; my driver will pick me up here in two hours." I looked at the large wooden clock on the wall; it was seven ten and already dark.

Hmm… That would make it after nine when I got home; Father would be angry, but at this point, this was my only option. Besides, this would give me a chance to ask Mr. McKinley more questions about the trial and the case. Of course, bringing a scoop home with me might smooth things over.

Mr. McKinley helped me into his carriage just after nine o'clock. It didn't take us long at all to get to my house. The porch light was on, providing the only light in the otherwise pitch-dark neighborhood. It was about nine-thirty. Mr. McKinley jumped down and reached for my hand to help me out.

"Let's get you inside, Miss Riley; your father is probably worried."

As I started up the steps, Father came through the front door. Mr. McKinley turned to get into the cab and then greeted him through the window.

"Hello, Mike, got your girl home for ya. She's going to make a fine reporter. She's got a lot of gumption."

I winced; Father didn't reply. The look on his face told me he was plenty mad. Mr. McKinley caught that too, uttered a quick "Good night, all," and made his getaway.

Saying nothing, nodding for me to go ahead, Father walked slowly toward the front door behind me, still favoring his back. I opened the door, and he followed me inside, calling out to Mother at the foot of the stairs.

"She's home, Maggie; she's home safe." He gestured to the chair near the window across from his chair. "Sit," he ordered, wincing as he sat down. "Where in the hell have you been?" He asked me in a loud, harsh tone.

All of a sudden, I felt drained. My hair was a mess, my dress was dirty and torn, and my face was bound to be pretty dirty as well. I took a deep breath, and my tale tumbled out of me. I got to the part where I learned that Mrs. Tingley was at the Hortons' rather than at the Brewster Hotel when Father interrupted me.

"So, you lied to Jack, did ya?"

"Well, not really. I told him that I was going to leave early to see if I could get an interview with Katherine Tingley. I just didn't mention that she was not at the Brewster as everyone thought and that I intended to go to the Hortons.' If I had told him the whole story, he would have said no."

"You're darn right he would have; anybody would. So you went alone, a young woman, knowing you would be coming home on foot in the dark."

The volume of his voice rose, his Irish brogue now very much evident. He was yelling now. "That house is in the middle of nowhere! There's nothin' out there! What were ya, thinkin' girl?"

"There wasn't a lot of thinking involved," I admitted, wincing when I said this. "It seemed possible when I started up the hill. I didn't think about how I'd get home. It was unlikely that I would get the interview with Mrs. Tingley, and I thought I'd have time to walk home while it was still light."

"Go on," he said, leaning back in his rocker, leveling a malevolent stare in my direction. For a second, I thought he might fire me from the paper. I'd never seen him so mad. I got to the part about climbing up the retaining wall with the statue coming loose, tossing me off the wall and falling next to me when he interrupted me.

"You could have been killed, and who would have found you out in that godforsaken place? How did you get to the house if you were knocked out in the fall?"

I told him about my rescue by the cowboy, and his face softened a bit. Rushing to give him some good news, I told him about my scoop.

"Father, I got some good material for the paper for my efforts and have really opened communication in the future with the Tingley side of the case."

"I talked to Mrs. Tingley for about an hour before Mr. McKinley arrived. He spotted my Press pass attached to my dress right away. At first, he was angry, thinking I was interviewing her, but after she told him I wasn't, all was well. We had dinner, and we talked about what happened in court that day. It was the best roast chicken dinner I ever had."

"I need a drink of water," I told him and went to the kitchen. I poured a full glass of water from the pitcher on the counter, gulped it down, then returned to the chair across from my father. Suddenly the stress of my day sunk in. I have never been so tired.

Father was still fuming mad. He sat there glaring at me, shaking his head in what looked like disgust, sighing from time to time. I continued, hoping to cool him down, telling him about the rest of the chit-chat at dinner.

"Mr. McKinley asked me about my impressions of the trial and the various players in it: Judge Torrance, Sam Shortridge, the General, and of course, his own performance. He was especially interested the Harrison Otis's comment: 'We're finished, our goose is cooked,' which I heard him say to Sam Shortridge when the judge told us that Mrs. Tingley had broken her foot. That gave Mr. McKinley a big laugh."

Father interrupted, "McKinley is a good enough lawyer to know the trial would never be about anything but Katherine Tingley—what she has done and not done at Lomaland. Otis was right to be concerned; even a lawyer the caliber of Sam Shortridge can't be too rough on a wounded bird."

"Mr. McKinley told me that Sam Shortridge, who knows he has no case, tried to get his client to settle the matter, but he wouldn't. His comment to Mr. McKinley was, "Harrison Otis won't settle any case, especially this one, which would involve his admitting he was wrong, and to a woman no less."

"That quote is not for publication, Mr. McKinley said, because it was just a chat between two lawyers."

"Oh, and Father, he told me that he intended to ask Judge Torrance on Monday for a jury visit to Lomaland, so they could see what was going on out there with their own eyes."

"That's brilliant," Father said. "If the jury finds that there is nothing even close to the 'Spookery' described in the *Times* articles—and they won't—case over."

"Mr. Mc Kinley said he wanted to meet with me from time to time during the trial to get my take on the proceedings, my impressions of the witnesses, and the like."

"Sure, Father replied, I'll meet with him and Shortridge too—we want to be even-handed."

Yawning, , thinking I was off the hook, but then it came:

"You need to get to bed. You can sleep later tomorrow because I'm taking you off the *Tingley* trial. I should fire you for the stunt

199

you pulled today, but I'll give you another chance; you can stay as my apprentice."

The look on his face and the firm set of his jaw told me it would do me no good to argue.

"Don't ever do something like that again, or I *will* fire you. We were pretty worried; your mother was frantic. Jack is very upset too—after all, he was responsible for you. You let him down, Mary Kate. . . you let us all down."

Chapter 26

Early the next morning, Mother woke me to let me know that I had to go to the courthouse after all; Father still wasn't feeling well enough to be there. "He can't even stand up straight. He didn't sleep at all last night." She looked pretty tired. She sat down on the foot of my bed and sighed. "Get up, get dressed, and hurry, or you'll be late. Your father said that Jack is out on a story, but he should be there before lunch to take over. You are to return to the paper when he does."

I got up and looked in the mirror, my black eyes had fully emerged, as had the angry red bump on my noggin. Mother had hung my filthy, tattered dress on the armoire's open door, no doubt as a reminder of my escapade the day before. It was covered with dirt, and the ripped fabric hung lifelessly from the hemline. She had hung a dark blue dress she had selected for me on the other door of the armoire. Dark blue was a poor choice. It matched the color of my bruised eyes, making them look even worse.

Mother handed me her black bowler I wore the day before. The cowboy had retrieved it when he came to my rescue. I put my hair under it, jammed it on my head, and checked it out in the mirror. It was a bit crunched—very much showing the effects of my having fallen on it. The crunched hat with my crunched face seemed fitting.

I turned and looked at Mother. "Just a wee disagreement with a six-foot statue,' I'll tell Jack, hoping to joke him out of being mad at me." She was not amused. Mother would never have let me wear a hat in this condition. She was punishing me.

I rushed down to breakfast. It was decidedly chilly at the table. She was lying in wait for me to have her say about my little trip up to the Hortons,' but the time of reckoning would have to wait.

I quickly looked at the paper and checked out the day- one story about the trial Jack had written. The "two gladiators" shot that Father wanted was beside Jack's story. Charlie couldn't get a picture of Mrs. Tingley at the courthouse; she wouldn't be there until Tuesday. He pulled a shot of her from the archives. He did get a picture of Mr. Otis as he left the courtroom. He looked rather deflated; maybe he was just tired.

"Mary Kate, there is no time for that; you'll be late." Gobbling down my eggs and biscuits and gulping the rest of my coffee, I kissed her on the cheek, picked up my satchel, and rushed out the door.

"Thanks for breakfast, Mother," I called to her. She didn't say anything in reply. *Ouch.*

I took my front-row aisle seat in the courtroom and put my satchel beside me, saving a seat for Jack. Charlie hadn't arrived either. I took some notes about the jury selection, but the process was pretty dull. It was nearly noon and no Jack. Sometimes he would get caught up on a story in the field, and there was no telling when he would show up. After Mr. McKinley took his turn questioning potential jurors, Judge Torrance nodded at Sam Shortridge to begin his questioning.

During the morning break, I asked another photographer if he had seen Charlie. He said that he told him that he had another assignment. "He'll be back before the afternoon break."

The jury was impaneled and sworn in before lunch. It was made up of sun-weathered ranchers and farmers, all sporting a wealth of whiskers. Modern, sophisticated men were clean-shaven, a style that arrived here shortly after Gillette invented the safety razor a year or so before. Overnight, wearing a crop of whiskers became *passé.*

The appearance of these jurors told me one thing: these men were conservative, old-fashioned, and not the least likely to be impressed by the progressive ideas of Katherine Tingley. Score one for Otis.

After lunch, there was still no sign of Jack. The judge took the bench, brought in the jury, and looked at Mr. McKinley. "Are you prepared to give your opening statement, sir?"

"Yes, Your Honor."

He approached the podium, which had been placed in front of the jury box waiting for his arrival. "Good morning, gentlemen," he said, taking the time to look at each of them. As he continued, he adopted the subtle twang of a country lawyer rather than the tone of the Harvard-educated lawyer and former judge that he was.

He was one of them, don't ya know.

"I get to speak to you first because my client, Katherine Tingley, is the plaintiff in this case. She is the one who was damaged by the actions of the defendant, Harrison Gray Otis—the General, as he likes to call himself," he said derisively. The General is the owner and publisher of the Los Angeles *Times*. After that, when the words the General came out of his mouth, the moniker was dripping with sarcasm.

"Katherine Tingley brings this matter to court asking you to compensate her for the damages she suffered when the libelous articles about her appeared for nearly two years in the *Los Angeles Times.* " He paused, "None of them were true."

Mr. McKinley walked over to the open window as if he needed some air. He turned to the jury when he got there. "At the end of the trial, Mrs. Tingley will ask you, by your verdict, to compensate her for the substantial damages she suffered due to the *Times* printing of these lies, and to discourage the printing of articles of similar stripe in the future."

"Mrs. Tingley didn't want to have to bring this lawsuit, no gentlemen, she did not. She begged him to stop printing these lies. The General refused. Why?" He paused. "Money," he said in what sounded like a low growl.

"Printing this outrageous material was good for his paper's circulation and made the General money. It's just that simple."

Mr. Shortridge jumped to his feet. "Your Honor, I object to Mr. McKinley referring to my client as the General in this trial. He is entitled to be called by his given name, Harrison Gray Otis."

Judge Torrance thought about this for a moment and turned to Mr. Otis. "Do you mind being referred to as the General in this trial?

"Certainly not," he replied.

"Then the General it will be. Mr. McKinley, you may proceed."

Mr. Shortridge sat down, his face expressionless. Was he angry that his client undercut him? No doubt, but he didn't want the jury to know he had lost the skirmish.

Mr. McKinley told the jury that the defense would simply be a smokescreen of second and third-hand unfounded gossip, crazy theories, and beliefs of people with an ax to grind against Katherine Tingley and her followers.

"These tall tales not only strain belief; they date back years ago, well before Katherine Tingley even came to California."

Raising his voice at each point, Mr. McKinley charged forth. "By the way, gentleman, the General here has never met Katherine Tingley."

There was a long pause while Mr. McKinley once again surveyed the jury. "Did he or any of his minions ever ask her if the things he was told about her were true before he printed them? No… he did not."

"Did *he* take the time to visit Lomaland to see if the horrible things he printed about what was being done out there were true? No… he did not."

"Did the General ever even send his troops out to verify if the information he planned to print about Mrs. Tingley was true?" A bit louder, "No, gentlemen…he did not. The evidence will show that neither the General nor his troops were at Lomaland—not ever."

Even louder, with plenty of outrage in his voice, "Will the General bring out his big cannons now, by way of evidence in this trial, that the libelous articles printed in the *Times* are true? No…because he *can*-not. The fact is, gentlemen, he just didn't care. His only concern was whether the articles were still making him money."

Mr. Otis squirmed in his chair and loudly cleared his throat, making a sound similar to artillery firing in rapid succession. He did this each time he heard the incoming blasts that Mr. McKinley leveled against his character. This had the desired effect of disrupting Mr. McKinley's delivery and distracting the jury from the point he was making.

Judge Torrance flashed Mr. Otis a warning glare the first time he did this. He paid the judge no mind. The second time Judge Torrance gave him another warning glare, this one far more ominous. The General glared right back at him.

Judge Torrance looked at Mr. McKinley. "Give me a minute, please," and turned to the General. *Here it comes, the kick.*

"Mr. Otis, the General, or whatever you call yourself, you're not foolin' anybody. Your behavior is disruptive, and I won't stand for it, If you clear your throat or do anything else to disrupt these proceedings, you will be removed from this courtroom. Am I clear?"

At first, Mr. Otis didn't answer; he simply stared defiantly at the judge. It was a standoff, but soon the General went into full retreat. He lowered himself into his seat, seeming to shrink in size, his face flushed. "Yes sir," he squeaked, his response barely audible. There were no more interruptions.

"You may continue, Mr. McKinley."

"Thank you, Your Honor." Mr. McKinley turned his attention back to the jury. "As you heard yesterday, Katherine Tingley has been injured—she has a broken foot. God willing, she will be well enough by Tuesday to take the stand and speak to you."

"You will get to know this fine woman and hear about all her good work at Lomaland. You will learn that this work is entirely supported by donations to the cause, a cause she will tell you has but one goal: to serve and improve the lot of humankind. You will not hear a shred of evidence that she took any money for her own use, as Mr. Otis has repeatedly claimed."

Mr. McKinley left the podium, approached the jury box, and put his hands on the rail. "Mrs. Tingley will tell you the articles the General so callously published in the *Times* damaged her in that if she is believed to be a fraud, a humbug, a sorceress, an abuser of children, how many people will donate to her cause in the future? Not many. No gentlemen, not many."

"If her credibility and reputation are allowed to be besmirched, it will seriously affect her ability to continue to fund her good works and those of her followers. This is why the General's lies could not simply be ignored. They threatened the very lifeblood of Lomaland, the charitable donations it relies on for its sole support."

"Gentlemen, Katherine Tingley will tell you that the printing of these *terrible* lies about her personally and about Lomaland, the culmination of her life's work, caused her great physical and mental distress. And another thing, he said, pausing for a moment, the lies printed in the *Times* were becoming more frequent and getting worse as time went on. She could see everything she had worked so hard for being destroyed. It was unbearable."

Mr. McKinley returned to the podium and took the time to look at each juror as if he sought their agreement with what he was telling them. "Mrs. Tingley will call Harrison Gray Otis, the General himself, to the stand."

"I tell you, gentlemen, he will be his own worst enemy. He will testify that he is the owner and publisher of the *Los Angeles Times* newspaper. He will boast that he has the ultimate say over this mighty voice which reaches readers not only in Los Angeles, but here in San Diego, all over the state, and indeed, all across the country."

He walked over to the jury box and again put his hands on the rail, leaning forward towards them. "You see, he said this rather softly as if he was sharing a confidence with these men, "he can't hide who he is; he can't help himself. He is no hero, wartime or otherwise, but rather a tin soldier, puffed up with his own self-importance—in a word, a bully."

Mr. Shortridge started to rise and object but was stymied by the judge's warning glare. Father told me that interruptions of opposing counsel's opening statements are not favored by any judge and are usually denied. He said that they usually backfire anyway because bringing a point up by objection only draws attention to it.

Mr. McKinley continued, "The General won't deny printing the articles in question; he will admit that Mrs. Tingley told him to stop, he refused, and his circulation went up. Chuh-ching," he said, making the sound of a cash register. He will admit to you that he had no information that these outrageous lies were true—not before he printed them or even now."

207

He took his place back behind the podium. "Mr. Shortridge here," he said, turning and waving his glasses with one hand at his opposing counsel, "will avoid any mention of the defendant's misconduct, but instead, he will put Katherine Tingley on trial."

"You will hear a barrage of unmitigated and unsubstantiated attacks on her character. You will learn that these claims are untrue and will be some of the most unreliable evidence I've come across in all my years of lawin'. "

Mr. McKinley left the podium and walked towards his counsel table, but then he turned suddenly and looked back at the jury. "And, by the way, Harrison Otis has a habit of printing lies about our citizens and our city, always poking at San Diego to get his way in the ongoing rivalry between the two towns. This is nothing new gentlemen, nothing new at all."

"I object, Your Honor." Sam Shortridge jumped to his feet in feigned outrage. "There will be no evidence of this claimed rivalry in this trial."

Judge Torrance looked askance at Mr. McKinley. "Move on, Mr. McKinley."

"Yes, Your Honor," he replied, turning his attention to the jury once again, leaving them with a promise to ponder over the weekend and to remember as the evidence came before them: "I promise you that what I have said today about what the evidence will be in this trial is the evidence you will have before you. At the end of this trial, I ask you to hold me to this promise."

He paused and began to walk from the podium, but then he turned and looked back at the jury, pointing in the direction of Sam Shortridge. "And by the way, gentlemen, I ask you to listen to the promises that Mr. Shortridge makes about what the defense evidence will be, and hold *him* accountable for *those* promises.."

208

Mr. McKinley sat down, and the judge gaveled the proceedings closed for the day. Jack had arrived just after the afternoon break. He sat in the back of the press section and rushed out of the courtroom ahead of the crowd. I had a front-row seat to the proceedings, but I was one of the last to leave the courtroom.

The protocol set by the judge on the first day was that the judge and jury left first, then the litigants and their lawyers, then the spectators and the press. This was a problem only when Father and I wanted to get a quote from one of the lawyers or a witness leaving the courtroom.

Mr. McKinley looked my way when he left the courtroom, "Good afternoon, Miss Riley." Sam Shortridge and a disgruntled-looking Harrison Otis followed him out the door, looking face-front.

Jack had arrived in the courtroom after the three o'clock break and sat in the back row of the press section. He was nowhere to be found when I left the courtroom. He was probably back at the paper. I wasn't looking forward to confronting him; I had some fences to mend.

Chapter 27

I chatted with one of the other reporters as I left the courthouse. We both agreed that Mr. McKinley did a fine job in his opening statement. Stepping through the front door, I was greeted by a breeze coming off the bay. It felt good after being in that stuffy courtroom all day.

Some of the press boys were outside smoking and going over the day's events. Smiling at them, a couple of reporters waved. Stopping at the bottom of the stairs to take a breather, I was surprised to see Charlie photographing the General and Sam Shortridge standing by a bench near the sidewalk in front of the courthouse.

As I approached them, Mr. Shortridge was calmly smoking a cigarette while the General gave him a piece of his mind. You could see that the conversation was intense, at least on the General's part. The General was clearly wounded by the artillery lobbed at him by Mr. McKinley. As I passed, Mr. Otis gave a dismissive wave of his hand in response to something his lawyer said. After passing Mr. Otis and Mr. Shortridge, Charlie caught up with me.

"What the heck happened to you?"

"I fell trying to get an interview with Mrs. Tingley yesterday. It's a long story. I'll tell you about it when we get to the paper."

"That must have been quite a fall; did you get the interview?"

"I did, but things didn't quite work out as planned. Let's talk at the paper." He smiled, and we continued our walk up Broadway. We had only gone a few steps when I heard a voice behind me:

"Miss Riley?"

We stopped and I turned to see who had called my name. "Hello," I said, surprised to see Sam Shortridge standing there.

"I'd be interested in your thoughts about the trial so far," he began.

"Mrs. Tingley is local; she is well known to people of this area. I'd like you to help them get to know my client better. I didn't eat today; may I ask you to join me for an early dinner?"

It took me a minute to respond, feeling a bit uncomfortable and a lot flustered. "Yes, uh, it . . . it might be interesting for us both."

"Fine," he said, "I'm staying at the St. James. They have a wonderful restaurant, The Savoy. Shall we make it at five-thirty in the dining room?"

"Yes, but I might be a few minutes past. And I'll need a ride home; Father doesn't like me to walk home after dark."

He gave me a curious look. "I certainly wasn't planning on letting you walk home, Miss Riley, no matter what time it is."

He turned to the General, "Harrison, I will see you at the hotel at eight."

"I'll be there," Mr. Otis replied rather gruffly.

Mr. Shortridge put his hand out to Charlie. "Sam Shortridge."

"Charlie Wilson—I'm the photographer for the *Union*," he said and shook his hand.

Mr. Shortridge surprised me again by joining us on our walk to the paper. Charlie and I headed up the hill. Mr. Shortridge tagged along, not saying much until we got to Second Street, where Charlie and I would turn to go to my house. We stopped to make the turn; Mr. Shortridge stopped with us. "See you at The Savoy, Miss Riley," and he continued his walk up the hill. Charlie and I headed

211

across Broadway after waiting for the trolley to pass. It was loaded with passengers heading home from work.

"The Savoy, hmm… he said with a sly grin.

"It's business Charlie," Father will probably go with me."

Watching Sam Shortridge head toward the St. James on Sixth Street, I wondered whether he and his client had planned to take a handsome cab back to the hotel from the courthouse. He didn't strike me as a man who would walk three-quarters of a mile or so to his hotel, uphill. I recalled seeing the hansom cab waiting at the rail in front of the courthouse, not far from the bench where Harrison Otis and Sam Shortridge were talking. He saw me walking up the hill and decided to walk; I was sure of it. He admitted to wanting to curry some favorable press coverage for his client.

When it came time to turn off on G Street to go to my house, Charlie said, "Make sure there is no funny business from Mr. Shortridge at this *business* dinner."

"Oh, don't be silly, Charlie. It's not like that at all. He just wants some good local press for his client. And like I said, Father will probably be there with me." *He probably wouldn't.*

"You just mind yourself, Mary Kate, that guy is a smooth operator if I ever saw one." He turned with me to walk me home.

"You don't need to walk me all the way home today, Charlie; it's not far. You need to get back to the paper and get your photos done for the printers. But would you call Moody's when you get there and ask them to take us to the St. James at five thirty?"

"Sure, I'll see you tomorrow."

As I got to my house, walked up the front stairs, and heard the familiar creak of the top step, I wondered if I should change. *I'd have to change too much.*

212

Father was sitting in his chair reading a book when I came in. He must be feeling better, I thought. I explained to him that although he had fired me from the trial, meeting with Sam Shortridge might establish a good line of communication with the defense.

"You look like you are feeling better Father, so you can come with me. Frank Moody can drive us both up there. He will be here at five-thirty. Or, I said rather weakly, you can go alone."

"No, no, you go." He sighed and went back to reading his book. Mother smiled at me as I walked passed her hurrying up the stairs to freshen up a bit. Glancing in the mirror, I was shocked to see how dark my two shiners had become. I looked like a close cousin to a raccoon or had been in a bar brawl. The knot on my head was bruised and still swollen. *Nothing to do about it now.*

I sat down on my bed, took a deep breath, closing my eyes for a few minutes. *Was this dinner a mistake? Why didn't I ask Charlie to come with me?*

I stood up and patted cold water on my face from the pitcher and bowl on my dresser and tried to do something with my hair. It had gone rogue after I took off my hat. My black eyes and bruised face made things even worse. I corralled my hair in a clip, shrugged my shoulders in dismay, and avoiding the mirror, rushed downstairs. The carriage was waiting out in front.

"Call Moody's if you need a ride home," Father said as I passed him and headed for the door.

As went up the hill, the colors of the sunset changed from gold to pink, then to purple, and were reflected in the scalloped tin siding of the St. James. The towering hotel was visible everywhere below it; it was the tallest and finest hotel in the city. I had never been there; my parents hadn't either.

213

We reached the front of the hotel just after five-thirty. The uniformed doorman approached us and offered his hand to help me down. "Good evening Miss," he said.

"Fancy schmancy," Frank said with a grin as I stepped out of the carriage. "Need a ride home. Mary Kate? We don't want you getting into any more scrapes."

"No thanks, Frank, I have a ride. I'll drop off the fare on my way to the paper in the morning."

"No worries, you're good for it."

"Actually, put it on the *Union's* account. This is business."

"Will do," he said.

The hotel lobby was impressive, opulent, and, at least right now, very quiet. The front desk clerk directed me to The Savoy. The host, dressed in a black tuxedo-type uniform, was standing at a podium just inside the restaurant door.

"Miss Riley?"

"Yes, please... I mean, yes, I'm Miss Riley."

"Follow me, Miss."

I was immediately struck by the splendor of the room. It was almost empty, it was too early for the dinner crowd. I spotted Sam Shortridge right away. He was drinking what looked like whiskey in a crystal glass. It was so quiet in the room it was almost reverential. The only sound was the strumming of a gilded harp by a beautiful young woman in the back of the room dressed in a flowing white goddess-like garb.

I followed the host to the table across a stunning cream and sea green Persian carpet that matched the damask drapes and the table décor. The magnificent electric chandeliers bathed the room in soft light. *And less than a mile from Rabbitville.*

Mr. Shortridge stood while the host pulled out my chair. "Miss Riley, so glad you could make it," he said, looking at me rather flirtatiously. We sat down, and he regarded me across the table. "I've been dying to ask, what happened to you? Where did you get those shiners?"

"Just a wee bit of a tussle with a six-foot statue. It's a long story—let's skip it for tonight if you don't mind."

"Well, I am intrigued, but I don't mind." He signaled to the waiter. "Let's order some wine, shall we?" The waiter handed him the wine list, and Mr. Shortridge pointed to one of them. After the waiter left with the order, he turned to me, "Why don't you tell me a little about yourself, Miss Riley?"

Of course, asking me to talk about myself was like turning on a faucet; I immediately started blathering. Mr. Shortridge listened intently and laughed once or twice. This bothered me a bit as I didn't think anything I said was funny. Was he laughing at me, my inexperience, my newness? He often looked amused, smug even.

Did I find Sam Shortridge attractive? Not really. He was too old, and he wasn't very handsome either. But he did have something about him; hmm... I couldn't put my finger on just what it was.

He seemed very serious in the courtroom, but I soon learned he had a good sense of humor. By my second glass of wine, I found myself relaxed and laughing a bit. *Charming, that's what he is, charming.*

At one point, he urged me again to tell him more about myself, but I put up my hand to stop him. "I came here to learn about you, your client, and the defense side of the case. I will sing for my supper by giving you my take on the trial and the players in it."

"Fine," he said, "let's start with the judge. What do you think of that old curmudgeon?"

"He seems tough but fair," I replied. "He certainly is a bit rough around the edges, isn't he?"

"Yes, indeed," he chuckled.

That deep rich voice; it could melt butter.

"But he does have remarkable aim at that cuspidor he employs from time to time."

"Yes, he does, Mr. Shortridge, and sometimes I think he does it to emphasize a point," I said with a smile.

"Sam, please," he said.

"What about Mrs. Tingley's lawyer, Mr. McKinley, I really don't know much about him."

"My father, who is the courthouse reporter for the *Union,* says most people call him Judge McKinley or simply Judge. This is because he once sat as a judge in the Superior Court in Los Angeles. He got bored with the job and went back to trial work."

"Father says he's a great courtroom lawyer who is often underestimated. Despite his simple country-lawyer persona, he's Harvard-educated, smart as a whip, and wily as a fox."

"I have found that out already," Mr. Shortridge said dryly.

Taking a sip of wine, the heat seemed to run down my throat and warm my innards. Taking a gulp of water, I paused.

"My father knows Mr. McKinley very well, and he respects him. He does a great deal of work at the San Diego courthouse, and even though he is from Los Angeles, he is at the top of the legal community here. He socializes with all the judges who frequent the courthouse watering hole, the Harbor Bar at the Horton House. My father says the judges and the lawyers have their booths there pretty well worn in."

"So I'm likely to be home-towned?"

"I'm afraid so," I told him.

"Had you met the great Purple Mother before the trial?" he asked me.

"No," I said truthfully, but I know a great deal about her. Most everyone here knows about Mrs. Tingley and Lomaland. It is the most famous place in the area, except for the Hotel Del Coronado. The Del even runs weekly tours to Lomaland; it's just a short boat ride across the bay. Both places are the most visited attractions here, both for tourists and locals. Both have put San Diego on the map, not only in California but nationwide and around the world. They have contributed a great deal to the growth and prosperity of San Diego."

I took a sip of wine. "Katherine Tingley and her followers, along with the students at Lomaland, put on a great deal of plays and musical productions of very high quality, and they have contributed significantly to the cultural life of this city. The Theosophists even have a theater, The Isis, just a few blocks from here."

"Some top-notch artists and writers have taken up residence in Lomaland. They even have a weather station on the Point that provides our weather information to us in San Diego.

"The large, lighted temples of Lomaland are so striking at night that they guide the way for arriving ships far better than the lighthouse that sits right below Lomaland on the far tip of the peninsula. This has proved to be an important guidance system for ships coming into San Diego Bay because the lighthouse is often fogged in.

I interrupted my nervous babbling and picked up my wine glass for another sip, thought better of it, put the glass down, and switched to water. Looking up to see if Mr. Shortridge noticed— he did.

"And so, Mr. Shortridge, the regard our citizens have for Katherine Tingley and what she has brought to this city will certainly give her a leg-up in this case. People here think the whole thing is a curiosity, sure, but they know Mrs. Tingley and her followers are doing a great deal of good for San Diego."

Mr. Shortridge took a sip of wine, leaned back in his chair, and thought about this for a second or two." I've always known that this is the biggest obstacle I will face in this case. Katherine Tingley is not only a San Diego citizen, but she is a respected one, popular even. Harrison Otis, as you heard at the venue motion, is not revered here and is not at all popular."

"Have you been to Lomaland?" he asked.

"Charlie and I went to Lomaland to see *Midsummer Night's Dream* in the spring; we were both very impressed. We didn't meet Mrs. Tingley, but she introduced the production."

"I read the story after the lawsuit was filed, front page, right? Did you write it?"

"I did," I said, impressed that he had done his homework. "It was my first page-one story. I'm an apprentice to my father, and he must have edited the story a dozen times. He usually writes the stories. I just help with research and give him my take on things. The Lomaland story was an exception. My father is a wonderful writer, and he has taught me so much already."

"Why wasn't he in court today?" Mr. Shortridge asked.

"He hurt his back a few days ago and couldn't make it; he's doing much better and he should be at the trial on Monday."

218

"And you will be with him?"

"I hope so," I said, not wanting to tell him I had been fired from the trial. "Have *you* been to Lomaland?" I asked him.

"I haven't had the chance. I'm at a bit at loose ends here, being from out of town. Maybe I can get you to take me out there this Sunday; what do you say? I can rent a boat to take us, or I can hire a carriage if you like."

"No," I said a bit too abruptly, adding, "I . . . I'll probably be busy Sunday. I mean, I am busy Sunday."

He smiled. *Is he making a pass at me?* This, even I knew, was not something you would expect to be asked as a newspaper reporter. He took my rejection of his offer in stride. I quickly changed the subject and asked him another question.

"Have you met Katherine Tingley?"

"No, I haven't. I'm looking forward to meeting her at the trial. She is due to take the stand Tuesday. I wanted to take her testimony before the trial, but for one reason or another, McKinley was able to wiggle out of it. He outfoxed me on this, I'm afraid." He added, "That's not for publication, please."

"No trial lawyer worth his salt wants to take a witness on cross-examination unless he's darn sure what she is going to say on the stand. I'm going in blind. I don't know what to expect from her."

The waiter sat our dinners on the table. Mr. Shortridge smiled at me. "Mmm, smells good; I am hungry; I haven't eaten today."

We ate a wonderful roast beef dinner, followed by an orange soufflé. At one point, I turned the tables on him during dinner and asked him about his famous older sister, Clara Shortridge Foltz.

Henry mentioned a few weeks back that she was Sam Shortridge's older sister and that they used to work together at the Union. "Do some research about her, he said. She is a very accomplished woman; she's perfect for a story in your women's section."

I learned in my research that she was the first woman to be admitted to the University of California law school and licensed to practice law in California—actually on the entire West Coast. She originally opened her law practice in San Diego but now works in Los Angeles. She also was in the newspaper business, and she sold her paper, The *San Diego Bee,* to the *Union* some years back.

Mr. Shortridge seemed surprised that I knew who his sister was.

"It is so ironic that you are in a highly publicized trial trying to take down an accomplished, determined woman like Katherine Tingley, I said earnestly, "when you have such a woman in your own family. It's obvious you don't like Katherine Tingley."

"That is not true, Miss Riley; I don't like or dislike her. I am representing a client; I am simply his mouthpiece."

"I have nothing but respect for my sister and what she has achieved, and indeed, I became a lawyer because of her."

"Will she be at the trial?"

"I don't know. She practices in Los Angeles. She's very interested in the case but she won't be rooting for me. She's no fan of Harrison Otis; I can tell you that not many women are. She says she is going to try to make it down for closing arguments; I hope you will have a chance to meet her."

"What is Mrs. Otis like?" I asked.

He huffed and then smiled. "I have represented Harrison for a long time, and I've never met the lady. Why do you ask?" he said with a curious look.

"I am a writer, Mr. Shortridge, and someday I want to write novels. Mr. Otis is an interesting man. The woman he chooses for a wife tells me quite a bit about him."

After we finished dinner, Mr. Shortridge signed the bill, walked me to the front door, and ordered a hansom cab to take me home. He helped me in, and as he did, he slowly ran his hand up and down my back. It made me *very* uncomfortable. He surprised me by following me into the cab, sitting right *beside* me. *This situation made me very nervous.*

"It's only a few blocks down the hill, Mr. Shortridge; you don't have to see me home. I'll be fine." I said a little too rapidly.

"Of course, I will see you home, Miss Riley."

We arrived in front of the house without further incident. He helped me down and walked me to the door. I hoped this wouldn't get awkward. Fortunately, just before we got to the door, Father opened it and came onto the porch.

"Hello," Father said. The two men shook hands and introduced themselves.

"Thank you for your time tonight, Miss Riley, I hope you will give me another opportunity to meet with you to discuss the case before the trial is over."

I simply nodded, not knowing what to say. Father's looming presence didn't help, but I was sure glad he was there.

"Goodnight, then," he said, got into the carriage, and was gone. The clock chimed eight o'clock. *Best not to keep the General waiting.*

Chapter 28

My alarm went off at eight. It was Saturday, and I could sleep a little longer, take my time, and relax. I wanted to be there at breakfast when my father had his. I was anxious to get down to the table to see Jack's story in the paper about yesterday's trial proceedings and, of course, my contributions to the story. I had scored a good scoop regardless of the risky manner I got it. The morning paper was left on my plate with Jack's story on page one, above the fold.

"Good morning," I said glumly.

"Good morning," Father replied.

Mother poured my coffee and laid down a plate of biscuits and two fried eggs. I took a sip of coffee and began reading the story.

Father said nothing about it but commented that his back was much better. "I can't wait to get to the trial on Monday. I've looked forward to seeing this epic battle since Kate Tingley filed her lawsuit."

His words stung me and brought tears to my eyes, knowing I wouldn't be there to see this with him. Turning away so Father didn't see my tears, I finished reading the story. I was disappointed that the vital information I had overheard in court or got from Mr. McKinley wasn't in the story. It was all about the jury's makeup and Mr. McKinley's opening. Father had approved it; that's what hurt. He said nothing about it, and deciding to go about it another way, I finished my breakfast in silence and then turned to him.

"Father, since there is a lot of important information about the Tingley case that hasn't gone into the paper yet, including the things I got from Sam Shortridge last night, could we write a story together for Sunday's paper? It would be my last work on the trial. I've already lined up my materials for my women's section; I wrote it last Tuesday before the trial started."

"Hmm, that sounds like a good idea," he said, shooting a look at Mother for her two cents. Father often back-slid in doling out discipline in our house, but you could count on Mother to stay firm. She decided not to weigh in this time and continued fussing in the kitchen.

"Check with Jack; he will be at the paper today. See if he has any information to add to the story."

"But Father . . ." He ignored me.

"He has a few stories to catch up on today, and he's out on a story this morning, so I doubt he has anything to add. Ask him anyway. Write your draft of the story at the paper, bring it back, and I'll edit it. You can finalize it and give it to the printers. Tell the print fellas it will come in about six."

I rode my bicycle to the paper at about ten o'clock, my curls flying in the wind. The last person I wanted to consult about Sunday's story was Jack, so I escaped to the archives to write the story. He had not yet returned from his story when I got to the paper. Charlie was in his darkroom, and the "Do Not Disturb" sign was on his door.

I was afraid to confront Jack and let him know how angry and hurt I was that he told Father he wanted me fired without hearing my side of things. After finishing my story upstairs and not hearing any voices downstairs, I took a break. Leaning back in the chair, cracking my neck with some satisfaction, and bemoaning my firing from the *Tingley* trial, Old Betsy caught my eye, sitting by the bookcase.

Old Betsy looked like a strange sewing machine. Henry told me she was the first model of the new-fangled typewriting machine the *Union* bought thirty years before. It didn't have a shift button; it could only type in upper case, and its carriage was operated by foot. Henry said she still worked. Nobody used her now, but Old Betsy was a piece of the paper's history.

Woolgathering there for a few more minutes, thinking about how far I had come as a reporter, I wondered how to get Jack back in my corner. Right now, things look pretty grim.

He must have been frantic after looking for me at the Brewster Hotel and learning that nobody had seen me there. Father said that his anxiety shot through the roof when he was told that Mrs. Tingley had never checked in. I sat back and gave the whole mess some more thought.

Cracking my neck, moving my head in a circle; I was still stiff from my tumble on Horton Hill. After thinking for a minute or two about how everything had gone so wrong, it dawned on me. Jack knew I wasn't going to the Brewster and that I was going to the Hortons. It was in my note to Father that I gave him. He never read it. Jack forgot about it!

I'll bet the note was still stuffed in his vest pocket, I thought, that's it! Why else would Jack have spent so much time at the Brewster looking for me?

How did I forget about the note? I was filthy, injured, and exhausted when I got home that night and was just so shocked at how angry Father was and didn't have time to think about anything. Yes, he was going to be upset that I was so late and that it was dark, but that was all. I simply forgot about the note. The next day I was so busy that I just didn't think about it.

224

"Hmm…" The note also cleared me of any intention to lie to Jack. He had the truth right in his pocket. Standing at the top of the stairs, I could hear Jack and Charlie talking.

Taking a breath for courage, I thought, I will talk to him first thing. Nope, the story must come first. Grabbing the draft of our Sunday edition trial story, I came downstairs and headed over to Jack's desk. Charlie was showing him some photographs he had taken the day before.

"Hey, Mary Kate," Charlie said with a big smile. "How was your dinner with Sam Shortridge last night? He sure looked like he has eyes for you."

"Yes and no. Yes, I had a pleasant dinner with him, and no— no romance was involved. It was a business dinner… it was *all* business."

"Honestly, he was a real gentleman; he— Before I even got the words out of my mouth, a deliveryman came in the door carrying a large bouquet of flowers.

"Delivery for Mary Kate Riley," he called.

Jack pointed to me. "That would be her." Charlie scoffed.

I rushed over to the deliveryman who was standing near my office, took the flowers out of his hands, and plopped them down on my desk. No need to open the card. I was humiliated.

The messenger just stood there looking at me. What? I thought, irritated, staring back at him. Charlie came over and handed him a quarter. "You probably left your satchel upstairs."

"Uh . . . yes, thank you," I said with relief, not knowing that a tip was called for.

"No problem," Charlie said. "I've just got a few more pictures to prepare for tomorrow's edition. I'll see you tonight at your house for dinner and cards."

I smiled and nodded. He turned to go back into his inner sanctum, his darkroom. I was looking forward to spending some alone time with Charlie. My parents usually would go upstairs early when he came for dinner, leaving us alone in the front room.

The flowers on my desk just made me angry, I was certain that Sam Shortridge was trying to manipulate me. Would he have sent Jack flowers if he had been the reporter at dinner last night? Of course not, but then he wouldn't have been invited to dinner in the first place. Worse, the flowers only confirmed Jack's opinion that women did not belong in the newsroom.

Mr. Shortridge made me look like a fool. And this made me angry, but mostly at myself. I liked Sam Shortridge; He's as old as my father, but somehow I found him attractive, sophisticated, and oh-so-charming. Maybe it was the fancy dinner, the hotel, and a good bit of wine.

Jack wouldn't be happy that he wasn't writing the trial story for the Sunday edition and that I was involved. But, the only new things to put in the story about the trial, there being no court on Saturday, were the scoops I had to offer. Jack, who didn't know that Father had fired me off the trial, was sure to see my helping with the story as a reward for my misbehavior on Thursday night.

Father must have thought of that and he just didn't care. Jack knew that the information I got needed to go into the story. As it was, he didn't put in much of it in Saturday's edition just to spite me. He did it to punish me. I thought he was a better newspaperman than that; he obviously let his personal feelings get in the way.

Father was all about delivering a good story and didn't care if my feathers or Jack's got a bit ruffled for one reason or the other.

But I knew this was my mess to clean up. My behavior on Thursday night from Father's point of view, was both personally and professionally unacceptable. He was right.

Jack needed to give his additions to Sunday's trial story if he had any. Then it needed to go back to Father for approval and rewrites, then back to the printers. Nate, one of the printers, had been in the newsroom asking when the story would be ready. I told him to hold room on page one and that we'd have the story in before six.

I included in Sunday's story Mr. McKinley's intention to ask the judge on Monday morning for a jury viewing of Lomaland. I also added Sam Shortridge's remarkable admission last night that nobody on the defense team, including Harrison Otis, had ever been to Lomaland or even met Katherine Tingley.

Treating a bit gingerly the information from Sam Shortridge about his client and his trial strategy, I did mention his regret that he would face the formidable Katherine Tingley without the benefit of having taken her testimony before trial. I opted only to use one of his many quotes, this one: "I'll be flying blind."

He didn't say it was off the record, and he's smart enough to know that after all things are said and done, I'm a reporter. He's a lawyer accustomed to representing newspapers, so he knows the rules better than most.

Jack didn't mention the flowers when I came over to his desk; he was back to business, typing the story about a fishing boat accident the night before where two men were killed. He had been out that morning interviewing some of the witnesses. He looked up when I put Sunday's trial story in his box.

"Jack, Father, and I are writing the trial story for tomorrow morning's edition. He wanted me to run it by you for any suggestions or additions you might have. I'll include your contributions, run it home, get the corrected version from Father, make the changes, and then get the story to the printers. It's my last work on the trial; Father fired me off the case."

Jack said nothing and didn't look at me. He took his glasses out of his vest pocket, picked up my draft of the story, and began to read it. After a few minutes, he said coldly, "Looks good." and handed it to me, turning back to his typing.

Jack, may I speak to you upstairs, it's important. It will just take a few minutes," I assured him. He didn't hesitate or ask me why; he just followed me upstairs and sat at the table across from me.

"Jack, please, hear me out," I began. "I never meant to lie to you." He started to get up to leave. "Just give me a few minutes . . . please."

Looking at his face across the table, he had the belligerent expression of a two-year-old deprived of a cookie.

"Jack, did you clean out your vest pocket Thursday night after court?"

"What does that have to do with anything?" he said gruffly.

I stared at him and said nothing.

"No, I didn't." He looked down at his pocket, still stuffed with notes, a pencil, and other debris.

"Take out the notes, please. You'll find the one I gave you Thursday afternoon when I left to interview Mrs. Tingley...the one I asked you to be sure to give my father about where I was going."

Jack dragged everything out of his pocket, and there it was— the note. He read it out loud:

"Father, I might be home late, as I'm going to try to interview Katherine Tingley at the Hortons' house on the hill. I left court

early. Jack has my notes on this morning's trial doings for his story. M.K."

Jack sat quietly for a minute. "I'm sorry, I did read your trial notes and put them in my pants pocket. I put the small note to your dad in my vest pocket and forgot about it. I never read it." He thought for a minute.

"But still, you knew when you left that I thought you were going to the Brewster. This was at three o'clock, plenty of time for you to get home before dark. I figured you would go there; they would turn you away because Mrs. Tingley wasn't giving interviews, and you'd go home or to the paper while it was still light out."

"That's true, but you were so impatient and hurried away to talk to your buddies. You didn't want to listen. I didn't have a chance to tell you what the bailiff said about where Mrs. Tingley was actually recuperating; something no other reporters knew. You can be awfully short with me sometimes."

I added, "I admit that I was glad you didn't let me tell you where Mrs. Tingley was staying because I knew you would say no. For that, I'm sorry. But I didn't lie to you, Jack; I wouldn't do that."

He looked up at me and I could see in his face that admitting my role in the confusion that afternoon seemed to calm the waters a bit. The truth was that his dismissive behavior and his rushing away gave me a chance to avoid giving him any details or having to fib about my plans.

He sighed deeply and looked at me with disappointment in his eyes. "Damn right, I wouldn't have let you make that trip alone, probably coming home in the dark—hell no. You knew better than to go up that hill alone, but you did it anyway."

He thought for a minute, looking down at his hands clasped in front of him on the table. "But, I see I made a mistake. I'll clear

229

things with your father on the way home. Hang back here for a half-hour so I can have some time to set things straight."

"Thanks," I said, relieved. "One more thing, Jack. Everyone was upset when I didn't show up at home, especially after dark. Still, you really let me down by urging Father to fire me, not only from the trial but from the paper for gosh sake, without even talking to me first. I thought we were friends."

He nodded. "And right you are, and for that, I'm sorry. I was just so worried, frantic, really. Your mother was beside herself. I felt responsible. Your father told me what happened when I came over after you went to bed, and I was pretty hot. Now I see I was wrong, and I'm glad I was."

Waiting on pins and needles for a half hour, I practically flew home on my bicycle, exhilarated, knowing Jack would fix things with Father and I'd be back at the trial on Monday. At least, that was my hope.

After I got home, my father, Jack, and I had some discussion about the foolish choices I made that night and how dangerous they were, but in the end, after saying an act of contrition of sorts, and eating some humble pie, I was back on trial. I knew they were right and was sorry for worrying them so.

Mother surprised me by staying out of the matter; she remained in the kitchen making dinner. I have no doubt that she was involved in the discussion between Father and Jack before I got home. All said and done, they all wanted to see me back on the trial and were glad it worked out the way it did.

Father didn't apologize after learning what had happened on Thursday night because he said the plan was dangerous and foolish, and that I well knew it. He drove an arrow through my heart when he told me again how frantic he and Mother were and added, "You are so precious to us. We've lost our Tim, and you are all we have left."

Charlie came over for dinner after he finished at the paper that day. He was on an assignment all day Thursday and was out most of Friday and pretended not to know about my trip to the Hortons. I had a chance to explain the whole mess to him from my side of things. I was pretty sure though that Jack had told him all about it that morning.

All I knew was that I would be back on the trial, and that tomorrow was Sunday. I looked forward to reading the paper in the morning and taking some time to relax. Father's back was better, and he would go to court with me on Monday. That was such a relief. It would be easier for me to stay out of trouble with Father taking the lead.

Chapter 29

Father wasn't at breakfast that Sunday morning. He left early to help Hank Moody with some project he had. He left the paper face up with "Good work, M. R." printed in the space above the banner. The front page headline was "TINGLEY SEEKS LOMALAND JURY VISIT.

I was pleased that most of the story was written by me and included the information I got at the Horton's on Thursday night and from Sam Shortridge. I knew Mr. McKinley would be pleased.

After church, Mother and I had time to talk. We hadn't had any real time together since the trial started. She seemed to have let go of, at least for now, her hurt and anger over my trip up Horton Hill Thursday night. I think she didn't want to be the cause of my missing the exciting opportunity to be at the trial with Father, something I had worked so hard for.

She laughed when I told her about the showdown between Judge Torrance and me, his skirmish with the General, and most of all, my elegant dinner with Sam Shortridge. This especially got her attention. She wanted all the details.

"Hmm . . . did he make a pass at you? They always like the young ones, and you're a very pretty girl, so watch yourself."

She looked dubious when I insisted the dinner was all business. I thought it best not to tell her about his rubbing my back when he put me in the carriage or his offer to take me alone on a trip to Lomaland. I did tell her about the flowers.

She laughed. "Well, now, that settles it, doesn't it? That rascal, I bet he's married too. Is he?"

"I don't know." *He probably is.*

When Charlie arrived to take me out for the afternoon, he was driving the old buggy we had taken to Lomaland but with a different horse. "Taffy is no longer with us," he said solemnly.

We were going for a picnic with some of his friends at a park by the bay. Mother had prepared a nice picnic lunch for us. Handing me our picnic basket, her parting shot was, "Have a nice time, and Charlie, try to keep her out of trouble."

"Will do, Ma'am," he replied with a grin.

I played croquet for the first time. It was a new game and very popular. I didn't win but came very close to winning in the second match. After hanging around with Tim and his gang, all boys, I was always very competitive in any game.

Really tired, Charlie took me home right before dinner. My remarkable week had caught up with me. After we finished eating, I turned to Mother. "I forgot to tell you that Charlie asked me to go to his parents' New Year's Eve party. Jack will be there too. It will be in the ballroom of the St. James."

Father whistled. "The Saint James, is it?" My parents looked at each other. Mother was delighted but soon turned all-business. She had a look that said there was work to be done; details to manage.

"Oh, you'll need a new dress and some slippers too."

"No need, I can wear the dress you fixed for me for the Wednesday Ball, you know, your wedding dress. I have shoes for that already."

"No, no, no, that wouldn't suit for this party, dear."

"I'm sure Fiona Riggs would be pleased to give you one of her frocks," Mother said.

"Charlie told me that Fiona Riggs will be at the party with her husband John. He's a banker and he knows Mr. and Mrs. Wilson quite well."

"Well, that's even better," Mother enthusiastically replied. "I'm sure she would love to see you there in one of her dresses. We can get you a new pair of slippers to match. I will do your hair. Maybe a Gibson, hmm," she thought for a moment rubbing her chin.

"It's all settled, then," Father said impatiently. "What's for dessert, Maggie?"

Over the past year, I had often come for tea to pick up dresses from Mrs. Riggs for my use; she was my size, only more well-endowed. Mrs. Riggs also donated clothing to the women in the Children's Home. Mother had become very active in collecting and altering clothes for the women and girls there. She had all but taken over the donated-clothing effort. She loved the work.

Theodora also got involved. She often went with me when Mother sent me forth to pick up clothes from her wealthy dressmaking customers. Theodora was disappointed that she was not heir to any of Mrs. Riggs' lovely frocks because they were much too small.

Mrs. Riggs got great amusement out of the stories Theodora told her when we all got together. She even complimented our singing after we sang a few of our favorite songs for her. Liar! I pointed out to Theodora that she never requested a serenade and was never heard to say, "Please sing a few more."

Theodora laughed about this, imagining that Mrs. Riggs told her husband at dinner something like this: They are enthusiastic dear, but they can't carry a tune in a basket." We didn't care. We always serenaded her whenever we visited her.

Mother sent me up to Mrs. Riggs' house the very next Saturday. As usual, she had set out a lovely tea for me. She always had the most elegant little sandwiches and cakes. They were awfully small, though, so if you were hungry, this wasn't the place for you. I had missed lunch this particular Saturday, I *was* hungry, and gobbled the little buggers down, much to the amusement of my hostess. I told her stories about the trial, the paper, and my romantic adventures and she was delighted to hear them.

Mrs. Riggs had no children, her husband worked long hours, and she was lonely in that big house. She enjoyed the company; I enjoyed our visits too. We didn't have any relatives near San Diego like so many others my age, so we adopted aunts and uncles whenever we could. This is how I felt about Mrs. Riggs, a benevolent Aunt.

She was most interested in hearing about my elegant dinner with Samuel Shortridge. I described the dinner and insisted it was all business skipping the back-rubbing incident. I told her about his asking me to go with him alone to Lomaland and about the flowers. She huffed, "All business, was it? Funny business I'd say!"

After finishing our repast that day, Mrs. Riggs sat down to view the gowns she thought might work for the New Year's Eve *fete* at St. James. I sashayed out from behind the screen she had set up with different selections from the evening gowns she had hung there for our little fashion show. I recognized some of them as my mother's creations.

Mrs. Riggs was excited that I would go to the Wilson's New Year's Eve party in one of her gowns and "with that handsome Charlie Wilson." She insisted that I try on every one of the dresses she had selected for me.

Coming out from behind the screen in a gold velvet and satin creation with a plunging neckline, trimmed with gold beading on the short cap sleeves, she clapped her hands in delight. "This is the one, dear—you look lovely in it. Do you like it?"

Looking down at the bust line, it gaped like a bag waiting to be filled with fruit. "I don't have the goods to go into this one," I said wistfully.

"Well, as my husband says, you only need a handful!" I was shocked and blushed at her frankness. "Don't worry, dear; your mother can fix you up just fine. Do you like it?"

I looked at myself in the mirror and nodded. "I do, I really do." Mother could fix the bust line; she had altered other dresses Mrs. Riggs had given me.

"Take your hair down, dear; let me see those beautiful red curls flying wild. Men love to see women with that wild, untethered look. It's inappropriate for a formal event, but you 'll look wonderful that way. "

I took the clip out of my hair, shook out my curls, and looked in the mirror. Mrs. Riggs was all praise. She was right; somehow, it worked on me: wild, mysterious, pretty. It wasn't me; I wasn't wild or mysterious, but I sure wanted to be.

Mrs. Riggs had her maid wrap up the dress for me along with a matching gold-beaded purse which, for the first time, she said was just a loan. "I can't give it to you, dear, because I love it and wear it all the time. I'm wearing blue that night so you must borrow it. What about shoes?"

"Mother said we could go to Marston's and see if we can find some slippers to go with whatever dress we decide on." As I walked out the door to the carriage, Mrs. Riggs called to me from her porch: "Black velvet would work."

Chapter 30

First thing Monday morning, Mr. McKinley brought his bid for a jury inspection of Lomaland. Judge Torrance, before they got started, asked the bailiff to escort the jury out of the courtroom. Glaring at Mr. McKinley, it was apparent that the judge was not pleased. "It's your motion."

Mr. McKinley stood and cleared his throat. "I know I'm a bit tardy in bringing this to the court's attention, Your Honor, but my thought was that a site inspection could save a good deal of time in the trial if the jurors could see Lomaland. As we know from their responses during jury selection, none of them have been there."

Judge Torrance moved right to the double horse-eye over his bench at Mr. McKinley and then nodded to Sam Shortridge, inviting his response. When he took the podium he was angry.

"The fact that this brilliant, time-saving notion just occurred to Mr. McKinley over the weekend I suppose, doesn't give the defense any opportunity to respond."

"This could have been brought up before the trial even started. At least I should have been given some notice this was coming. Instead, my notice was reading about this plan in the Sunday edition of The *San Diego Union*. A jury site inspection would be too disruptive and time-consuming for the court to schedule now. It's just too late."

Sam Shortridge didn't even complete his trip to the counsel table before *crack!* Judge Torrance brought his gavel down hard. "Denied, now bring back the jury," he snarled.

He paused." On second thought, it's nine-forty; let's take our break early, we'll reconvene at ten."

He glared at Mr. McKinley, who was not the least bit surprised by the judge's ruling and not the least bit ruffled by his rebuke. He expected to get spanked. He simply wanted the jury to read about the request in the paper and wonder why the defense didn't want them to see Lomaland. Mr. McKinley looked pretty darn smug when he glanced at us walking out the door.

"Pretty sneaky," Father said.

After the break, when the jury was seated, the judge looked at Sam Shortridge.

"I believe you have the floor."

He stepped to the podium, moving it closer to the jury box. Sam Shortridge has a graceful yet still masculine way about him in his walk, how he uses his hands, and how he moves. This doesn't say power, but it does say control. Like a panther, I thought, and just as deadly.

He has the panther's sultry and, yes, dangerous green eyes, ready to strike, to attack. He's clean-shaven with the swarthy skin of a farmer, probably from s spending so much time on his sailboat sailing on San Francisco Bay. His brown sun-leathered skin seems entirely out of place with the rest of his oh-so-smooth presentation, which makes him even more interesting, and, I admit, attractive.

Mr. Shortridge from the start used his graceful movement, his elegant but understated clothing, and his rich, deep voice to quietly command the attention of this jury of farmers and ranchers. He would walk away from the jury box and then turn suddenly to make a point as if he'd forgotten to mention it. He didn't; he's mercurial, a chameleon.

The unspoken burden of his song throughout his opening statement was that these men should be afraid, very afraid, of what this woman, Katherine Tingley, and her ilk might do. Angry and outraged at one point, quickly changing to a sympathetic and caring man at another. He was deeply concerned, he told the jury, about the threat that Katherine Tingley posed to the sanctity of marriage and to the family. He raised his voice in moments of particular outrage and then lowered it to include in his parade of horribles at the hands of Katherine Tingley, the threat of the wreck and ruin of Christianity itself.

"All this at the hands of *this woman*," he said, referring to Katherine Tingley, his outstretched hand pointing like a weapon at her empty seat at her counsel table. I was sure he intended to point to her in making these references, but she was not there. Not yet.

The jury couldn't keep their eyes off him, and most leaned forward in their chairs during much of his opening statement, making sure they caught his every word. He had them spellbound.

"I'd say you need to button your pockets around that guy," Father joked when we left for the lunch break. "I'm sure these men never even met a man like Samuel Shortridge. Will they relate better to a rough-around-the-edges lawyer like Mr. McKinley? Maybe. It could be that Sam Shortridge is just too smooth by half. The jury could see this as the slick big-city lawyer against a country lawyer, a man more like themselves."

"On the other hand, they may listen to a man they perceive as their better. They might think that if Mrs. Tingley had a stronger case, she would have gotten a better lawyer, one more like Sam Shortridge."

"Silver-tongued Sam," as one San Francisco newspaper dubbed him, finished his impressive opening statement ten minutes into our lunch hour. He sure gave the jurors something to think about during the break.

After lunch, the judge turned to Mr. McKinley. "Call your first witness, sir."

"Plaintiff calls Harrison Gray Otis."

Hearing his name called gave Mr. Otis such a start that he jumped in his chair, the bald spot on the back of his head signaling red. A nervous twitter went through the courtroom; everyone seemed surprised that he would be called as the first witness. The General stood and stiffly marched directly to the witness stand only to be interrupted by Judge Torrance. "Please stop and be sworn by the clerk, sir."

The General took the oath and proceeded once again to the witness stand, sitting down with a loud "humph" as his rear abruptly hit the seat which was lower than he expected. This drew a gasp from the gallery and a look of displeasure from Judge Torrance.

Mr. Otis immediately let everyone know who was in charge, first giving a belligerent look at the judge and then at his longtime nemesis J.W. McKinley. He didn't seem to notice that neither took much notice that the General had laid down the gauntlet.

Mr. McKinley, without any preliminaries, immediately fired questions at the General, aiming to find out the income and net worth of Harrison Otis, his powerful paper, and the *Times Mirror Company,* which he owned. After the first question and all that came later, Mr. Otis glared at his lawyer, begging an objection It didn't come.

"Answer the question, sir," the judge ordered.

"Yes, sir. The *Los Angeles Times Mirror Company* is worth a million dollars, and its income for the last two years was $25,000."

Mr. McKinley began his next question about the financial wherewithal of Harrison Otis when Mr. Shortridge stood.

"Ob-ject-ion!" he cried, outraged. "This is highly improper, highly prejudicial, and irrelevant to the issues before this jury. The defendant's ability to respond to a judgment is out of bounds, and my opposing counsel well knows this."

"I move to strike, belatedly, Mr. Otis's response to the last question on those grounds. On second thought, I move for a mistrial."

"Mistrial denied," the judge responded tersely and turned to Mr. McKinley for his input on the objection.

"I agree, Your Honor, this line of inquiry is not normally permitted; Mr. Shortridge is quite correct. But in this case, punitive damages are claimed, and the issue of the income and net worth of the defendant is not about the ability to satisfy a judgment. It is evidence that goes to the issue of what amount would be sufficient to punish the wrongdoer and deter the misbehavior in the future. A hundred dollars might sting and deter a poor man but be of no consequence to a rich man."

Judge Torrance turned back to Mr. Shortridge. "Objection overruled."

The General shot a disapproving look at the judge. The next few questions posed in the same vein were objected to on the same grounds, each time overruled. You could see that this turn of events made the General most uncomfortable. He moved around in his seat like a June bug on a porch light.

At the break, Father stopped to talk to one of his cronies in the hallway. "I'm going to get some air, Father."

Sitting on the bench in front of the courthouse, I scribbled a few notes about the General's testimony and about some research I had done on Harrison Otis that Father might find useful in writing today's trial story.

241

Father,

My research tells me that Harrison Otis is a prominent player in all doings of significance in Los Angeles. A rival newspaper's description of him that I read just before the trial was fitting: "Otis thinks he owns the town in fee simple."

But even his harshest critics, and there are many, admit that this particular little devil has done a great deal of good for the City of Angels over the years.

Most important for our purposes here, is that Mr. Otis contributed substantially to the effort, dirty tricks and all, that brought Los Angeles the coveted prize of being the southern terminus of the transcontinental railroad. This, as you know, was a crushing defeat for San Diego. Of course, that accomplishment is unlikely to endear him to a San Diego jury.

M . K.

After the break, Mr. Otis returned to the stand. "You remain under oath," the judge warned him. Otis nodded and glared at Mr. McKinley, who resumed his questioning.

"You don't like Katherine Tingley, do you, General?"

"No, I can't say that I do," Mr. Otis replied.

"You've never met her?"

"No."

"Never been to Lomaland, is that right?"

"It is."

"None of your representatives have been there either, correct?"

"That *is* correct, sir," Otis answered, signaling that he was proud of his answer.

"Now, you have referred to Katherine Tingley over the past two years as Purple Person, Purple Mother, and The Portly Mistress of Purple; isn't that correct, sir?"

"Yes, all of them," Mr. Otis admitted with a defiant look.

"These names were designed to make fun, to make a fool out of her, isn't that true?"

"Yes, I guess you could say I was having a bit of fun at her expense. Her followers call her names with the color purple in them McKinley," he said contemptuously, deliberately leaving out the Mister. The judge shot him a disapproving look.

"You have described Katherine Tingley and her followers many times as a bunch of dangerous kooks, isn't that so?"

"Yes, and it's true," he said, fixing his jaw and glaring at his interrogator.

"And that was long before your paper printed the articles we are here about in this trial. Am I right about that, sir?"

"Yes."

"And you kept track of Mrs. Tingley and her followers largely from reading articles about her in news releases over the wires from the Associated Press?"

"For the most part, yes. I am the vice president of that organization," he said with pride, puffing out his chest.

Mr. McKinley looked at the judge. "I move to strike the last comment, Your Honor; it's non-responsive."

"Sustained. Mr. Otis, the General, or whatever you call yourself, just answer the questions asked—don't volunteer information you are not asked about. Are we clear?"

"Very clear," he said, pursing his thin lips and setting his jaw angrily, his face reddening yet again.

"He's no poker player," Father whispered.

"So you never actually investigated the truth of the articles you published about Mrs. Tingley before you printed them, did you?"

Otis didn't answer. Irritated, Mr. McKinley turned to the judge. "Judge, please instruct the witness to answer my question."

Judge Torrance nodded. "Mr. Otis, you are here to answer the lawyer's questions. I order you to do just that. Answer the question, sir." Mr. Otis paused and looked at his lawyer.

"Right now," the judge growled.

"We relied on the investigation which we knew must have been done by other papers; that's just responsible journalism." He said this glaring at Mr. Mc Kinley."

"Yes, indeed it is, General, and not doing such an investigation before sullying someone's good name in a newspaper for everyone to read is *irresponsible* journalism, isn't that a fact, sir?"

Once again, the General didn't answer, looking at his lawyer, begging for help. Going right to the kick, Judge Torrance told him, "Answer the question, Sir, and do it now."

"That's true," he said in a soft, barely audible voice.

Mr. McKinley returned to the podium in front of the jury box facing the witness. "You described Katherine Tingley at public events as just plain ugly?"

There was a twitter of laughter in the gallery.

"I did, and she is."

More laughter; the judge glared at the spectators.

"You find this funny, don't you, Mr. Otis?"

He didn't reply.

"You said a number of times to anyone who'd listen that Katherine Tingley is downright unpleasant to look at, sometimes adding that she has an excess of adipose tissue, didn't you, sir?"

Sam Shortridge rose. "Objection, this is irrelevant. What does this have to do with the issues in this case?"

"Sustained; move on, Mr. McKinley."

"May I address the objection, Your Honor?" The judge nodded. "It is relevant to the issue of malice, the personal malice that Mr. Otis has for Katherine Tingley, which *is* an element in this case."

Judge Torrance shook his head in agreement. "Objection overruled. Answer the question, sir."

Mr. Otis looked at the judge, "Can he repeat the question?"

The judge nodded at Mr. McKinley. "You said many times to anyone who'd listen that Katherine Tingley is downright unpleasant to look at, sometimes adding that she has an excess of adipose tissue, didn't you?"

Mr. Otis turned towards the jury. "Yes, I have said that a few times and it's true, yes it is," he declared. "If she was here, you'd see for yourself." He said this looking at the jury as if they were his confederates. There was another round of laughter in the courtroom.

This time the judge brought down his gavel. "Stop with the laughter; we are conducting serious business here. And you, sir, just answer the question; we don't want your personal views. Move on, Mr. McKinley."

"Of course, Your Honor, just one more question on this issue." Mr. Otis, in a speech addressing the Los Angeles Chamber of Commerce, you told the members that Mrs. Tingley was an eyesore, a gargoyle, whose likeness should be placed on the corners of the temples at Lomaland. Did you say that or words like it?"

"Not words like it; I said exactly that," he said, punctuating the truth of his opinion with a shake of his head up and down with a determined look at the jury."

"Okay then," I said to Father.. "I wish Kate Tingley were here."

Mr. McKinley continued, "Now, earlier this year, Mrs. Tingley asked you by this letter, Plaintiff's Exhibit A, to stop printing the articles about her and Lomaland in the *Times.* Mr. McKinley handed the letter to Mr. Otis. Did you receive this letter, sir?"

"I did."

"Your Honor, I ask that this be admitted into evidence."

"No objection," Mr. Shortridge said.

Mr. McKinley waited as Mr. Otis scrutinized the letter.

"And in this letter, she expressed her concern about the articles you were printing about her and her followers, didn't she?"

"She explained to you the damage she was suffering due to your printing those articles. Isn't that true?"

"That's what she claimed," he said with a cynical look at Mr. Shortridge.

"And you didn't make any effort to contact Mrs. Tingley to discuss the concerns found in the letter, Exhibit A, did you?"

"I object, Your Honor," the witness told the judge.

"Let's leave the objections to the lawyers, Mr. Otis, now just answer the question."

He nodded to the judge. "No, I didn't."

"Instead, you turned up the heat, printing articles even more frequently that were even more inflammatory than before; isn't that right, Mr. Otis?"

Mr. Shortridge began to rise, but the General answered before he could object. "Yes. and they were all true."

"You did this because we're making money on these articles, weren't you, sir?"

"Your readers were amused by them, isn't that true?"

"Yes."

"Now, I take it that you have read the lawsuit that Mrs. Tingley has brought against you and the *Times-Mirror Company*?"

"I've skimmed it. It's nonsense."

"So you are familiar with the articles you printed that she claims are libelous and untrue?"

"Generally, yes."

"Let me review with you what you printed about Katherine Tingley in your paper. I have provided copies of them for you. May I approach the witness, Your Honor?"

Judge Torrance nodded. Mr. McKinley handed Mr. Otis the stack of articles cut out of the *Times*. Mr. Otis started to look at them, peeling them back in front of him slowly, one by one. Mr. McKinley waited while he did so, increasing the tension in the room.

"Mr. Otis, General, in articles on November 12, 16, 22, and 25 and December 6, 1902, you referred to Mrs. Tingley as the 'Boss of the Spookery.' One article had the headline 'Mother Tingley: Head Spook Rules the Roost.' Did you—"

Mr. Otis interrupted him. "Yes, she is, and she does."

Judge Torrance interrupted, "Now, one minute, one minute, you will confine yourself to the questions put to you by the lawyer."

"She does what, sir?" Mr. McKinley pressed him.

"Tingley rules the roost out at Lomaland. She makes no bones about it. It's even in their constitution. She's the boss for life."

"Another article is headlined, 'Spook Gabfest at Lomaland'—do you see that?"

"I do."

This time, Sam Shortridge rose to object. "These articles are of like import and carry a similar sting. They are cumulative and time-consuming. The articles themselves are in evidence. They do not need to be read by Mr. McKinley who is doing so merely to humiliate, belittle, and injure the defendant."

The judge nodded at Mr. McKinley, who responded, "Mr. Shortridge is correct—it is cumulative, Your Honor. Every time these articles were printed, the damage to Katherine Tingley, he said slowly, emphasizing her name, *ac-cum-u-lated.*"

"He is also correct that the cumulative effect of reading these outlandish articles caused Katherine Tingley to feel, now how did Mr. Shortridge put it, belittled, humiliated, and, what was the last one?" he looked at Mr. Shortridge as if asking him to prompt him, "oh, I remember now, injured."

"Your Honor, the temerity of Mr. Shortridge complaining to this court about the injurious effects to *his client* of my reading to this jury the libelous materials about Katherine Tingley that the *Times* published about *her;* it's outrageous." After a long pause, he said, "Mr. Shortridge, I declare, has just made my case."

"Objection overruled," said Judge Torrance firmly. "Sit down, Mr. Shortridge. Mr. McKinley, next question."

"I think ol' Sam just put his foot in it," Father said quietly.

"The article, dated October 14, 1901, claims that Katherine Tingley inflicted 'Spook Theology' on her followers; do you recall that?"

"I do, and I approved it."

"By the way, General, do you know anything of the liturgy or, as you call it, the theology taught at Lomaland?"

"No, I don't."

"On October 22," Mr. McKinley continued, holding up a clipping, "Mr. Otis, "an article appeared in the *Times* in which Lomaland was referred to as The Center of Spookadora. Laughter erupted at this reference drawing a glare from the judge.

"Do you see it there?"

"Yes, and I approved it."

Mr. McKinley wound up the day getting Otis to admit that he had approved the publishing of a poem, called a "Pome," printed in the

Times on October 19, 1901. He finished his cross-examination by standing with both hands on the railing of the jury box and reciting it from memory in a most dramatic fashion, prompting laughter from the gallery and the jury.

Point Loma Pome

Tingle, Tingle, little star,
Oft I've wondered who you are.
What you do that isn't right,
Every blessed, spooky night.
Tingle, Tingle, little star,
What a rotten serf you are,
Better take a way back seat,
With all your brassy bold conceit.

After Mr. McKinley sat down, the judge nodded to Mr. Shortridge. "I have no questions for his witness at this time, Your Honor."

"Who is up for tomorrow morning Mr. McKinley?"

The plaintiff, Katherine Tingley will take the stand first thing, Your Honor."

"Fine." Judge Torrance replied. "This court is adjourned."

Chapter 31

First thing the following morning, after the jury was seated and the judge was on the bench, Mr. McKinley stood and announced in a loud voice, "Plaintiff calls Katherine Tingley to the stand."

Anyone who had expected Katherine Tingley to arrive that morning bedecked as she often was, in long, flowing purple dresses trimmed with flowers and jewels, was in for a shock. Instead, at five minutes past nine, the double doors in the back opened, and a very different Katherine Tingley entered the courtroom. Everyone turned around, craning their necks to see her. A hush, then a murmur among the spectators, could be heard as she passed them in the gallery.

Mrs. Tingley came to court dressed for the part she intended to play. She appeared in a plain black muslin dress with a white, lace-trimmed collar. She topped this off with a simple dark blue jacket that strained at the buttons that secured it around her ample figure. Her hair was pinned back in a bun at her neck. The dramatic white streaks in the thick black hair around her face I saw Thursday night were gone.

She topped this ensemble with a crumpled black hat that looked as though someone had sat on it before she put it on her head. The effort to make this powerful woman look like a benign, kindly, rather dowdy, grandmother was spot-on.

"She looks a bit like the recently departed Queen Victoria," Father whispered to me when he saw her.

Katherine Tingley's husband, Philo, assisted her and she took his left arm for support. Her left leg in a cast, Mrs. Tingley steadied herself with a cane.

Philo Tingley is a small, pleasant-appearing man with snow-white hair, bright blue eyes, and a clean-shaven face. He wore a simple, Sunday-go-to-meetin' suit with a blue paisley bow tie. Vulnerable and dependent on her man was undoubtedly the picture Mr. McKinley wanted to present to this jury. It worked.

Mr. Tingley ushered his wife to her specially padded witness chair in front of her lawyer's counsel table, right below the witness stand, facing the gallery and the jury. She hobbled there, wincing with every step. At one point, she stumbled, drawing a gasp from the spectators. She reached the witness chair and slowly lowered herself, then clasped her hands on her lap.

Mr. Tingley hurriedly picked up an upholstered stool for his wife's casted foot. Her mouth trembled slightly as she put her injured foot on the chair, chirping softly but audibly, "Thank you, Philo."

The General watched the performance from his seat at the defense table just a few feet away. He couldn't hide his scowl when Mrs. Tingley came to rest in her chair. He appreciated the impact of her performance on the jury and knew it did not redound to his benefit. He glared in her direction while she was sworn.

Mr. McKinley started his examination of Mrs. Tingley with a few background questions from the podium near the rear of the jury box. "Good morning, Madam, Mr. McKinley said with a smile. Let's start out by having you briefly describe your early life."

She looked at the jury and responded calmly. "I spent my early childhood in Massachusetts, where my father owned a saloon and hotel. I completed my formal education in elementary school and I was self-educated after that.

"It's often said that I was a loner, and that is true, but I was not a *lonely* girl. I had no friends except my maternal grandfather, who understood me when nobody else did. He knew that I was called to serve others at a very early age."

Mrs. Tingley consistently faced the jury when responding to questions from Mr. McKinley, speaking to them directly with her hands clasped in her lap. She was calm and firm in her responses, but not at all aggressive.

"When did you first start your humanitarian work, Mrs. Tingley?" Mr. McKinley asked her.

"I started my work serving others when I was a young girl, volunteering at a hospital near my home nursing the wounded from the Civil War. I never saw such misery and death. I vowed then to work for world peace and the elimination of man's perpetual quest for war."

"This is a real focus of the Universal Brotherhood. We recently had a very successful international peace conference at Lomaland; leaders came from all over the world."

"You are the worldwide leader of the Theosophists?"

"I am."

Mr. McKinley walked away from the podium and stood at the rear of the jury box, putting one hand on the railing facing Mrs. Tingley's witness chair.

"What experience did you have in a leadership role of an organization before you assumed that position with the Universal Brotherhood? "

"At fifteen, I lived for a couple of years in a Catholic convent in Canada. I learned a great deal from the experience. The Mother Superior there taught me so much about the management and supervision of others. A few years later, I returned to New York and worked for several years serving the poor in the slums of New York City. I was the leader of that effort."

"When did you first become interested in Theosophy?

"The worldwide leader of the Theosophists, William Quan Judge, approached me to discuss the work I was doing at the time in New York. It was called the Do-Good Outreach Mission. He admired the progress we were making helping the poor. We became acquainted, and we soon formed a strong bond. We worked closely together after that to promote the Theosophist movement."

"Were you a Theosophist at the time?

"No, and I knew very little about it. I soon discovered, by working with Mr. Judge, that the basic tenets of Theosophy mirrored my long-held beliefs. I was convinced, as was Mr. Judge, that the key to better living, world peace, and the improvement of humanity was education. This meant teaching children from a very young age how to live better, happier, and more peaceful lives."

Mrs. Tingley paused for a minute to gather her thoughts. The jury was paying strict attention. She looked at Mr. McKinley.

"How did it come to pass that you became the successor to Mr. Judge as the worldwide leader of the Theosophists?"

"Mr. Judge started to groom me for that role from our first acquaintance. When he died a few years later, and at his direction, I took his place as the leader of the Theosophists. I have remained in that position ever since."

"So you were relatively new to the Theosophy movement when you became its worldwide leader."

This time Mrs. Tingley looked at the jury when she answered his question. "That's true. Looking back on it now, I think Mr. Judge and I were meant to meet and work together. Mr. Judge said it was divine providence, and I can't disagree with that assessment."

Mr. McKinley turned and returned to the podium.

"Mrs. Tingley, will you explain to the jury the role of Christianity in the beliefs of the Theosophists?"

She responded, looking at the jury. "We believe in Christianity, yes. But Christians have much to learn from other faiths and philosophies. It is absurd to believe that the only religious dogma worth our consideration stopped at the shores of the Western world. God could not have intended that the word, *his* word, was to reach only a small fragment of the planet he made for us."

"The truth is, most religions have the same core beliefs, including Christianity. It is the mission of every true Theosophist to hold to the spirit of tolerance, to the belief in brotherly love, and that we are all of God's great family."

Mr. McKinley gently guided her through the rest of his examination. He reviewed with her each of the articles that the *Times* had printed about her and asked if anything in them was true.

"Of course not," she replied earnestly, again addressing the jury.

Mr. Shortridge repeatedly objected to Mrs. Tingley's long, self-serving answers to almost every question Mr. McKinley asked her. At first, the judge overruled these objections saying that she had a right to explain herself. It didn't take long before he regretted that view.

Mrs. Tingley soon became comfortable as a witness, giving long explanations even to the most straightforward questions. Even Mr. McKinley admonished her not to run long on every answer, and when he did, Mrs. Tingley asked the judge for help. "Would you have the objection of my lawyer withdrawn, Your Honor?"

Judge Torrance shot back, "No, Madam. If I did, we wouldn't have the trial over until the end of the new year. Let's leave the objections to the lawyers, shall we?"

Mrs. Tingley nodded; reverent, respectful, looking like a penitent child. Judge Torrance leaned over and scored another perfect shot of tobacco into his spittoon.

Mr. McKinley concluded his examination by having Mrs. Tingley describe the physical injury and emotional distress she suffered due to printing the articles in the *Times.*

"I couldn't sleep for weeks, and remember, this went on for well over a year, each article worse and worse," she said, summoning a tear or two. Then she said this, her voice cracking with emotion.

"But it was the claims that I would ever abuse children that caused me the most distress. It was all so horrible. If Mr. Otis had only visited Lomaland he would have seen all we have accomplished there."

"Why didn't you just ignore the articles, Mrs. Tingley?"

She looked at Mr. McKinley and explained in a soft, solemn tone.

"I tried to at first, but it went on for so long. The claims against me got even worse after I asked him to stop printing the lies about me. I knew that all I had accomplished or would accomplish could be compromised if the public believed that I was a fraud and a child abuser... ah, um..."

She seemed to lose her train of thought, but then she continued, "And that I took the money donated to our cause for my use. These lies could destroy everything we have worked for. After all, our mission is entirely supported by donations."

Mrs. Tingley then turned in her chair to face the jury. "Who would donate to such a woman? A joke, a fraud, a sorceress? It's painful for me even to think about it," she said, dabbing her eyes with her handkerchief. "Take money for my own use? Preposterous, I have donated my entire life to the service of others."

The jury was listening carefully; they looked like they believed her. A couple of the jurors nodded in agreement. She was convincing. The General's face reddened. He looked like he was about to raise the white flag of surrender.

"I also brought this lawsuit to serve San Diego, the community I love. It is a ..."

Mr. Shortridge popped up suddenly like an unexpected visit from a jack in the box. "I object, Your Honor. This has nothing to do with this case. It's irrelevant, not to mention highly prejudicial."

Judge Torrance thought for a moment. "Overruled. From what I heard in your opening Mr. Shortridge, you expect a bit of leeway from this court. I intend to give the same treatment to the plaintiff so long as it is not abused. Now sit down. You may answer, Madame."

"San Diego is a young city, yes, but I have built my dreams here along with my fellow Theosophists at the Point. We have done this not to serve ourselves but rather to serve humankind. The Universal Brethren have been leaders in this community, along with many others, at this most dynamic time in our city's history. We have made significant contributions which have helped this city though its rather difficult birth, to take its place on the world stage as a dynamic, modern metropolis."

The exception to Mrs. Tingley's composed presentation was her testimony about the effect of reading the articles in the *Times* about her purported abuse of children. Her lips trembled, and she appeared to be near tears as she told the jury,

"My whole life has been in the service of children. It upset me so much when I read those terrible lies in the *Times* I couldn't eat or sleep."

That afternoon there was a reverential silence in the courtroom when Mrs. Tingley took up the issue of her dog Spots. The *Times,* in one article, claimed that Mrs. Tingley channeled the spirit of William Quan Judge through the dog.

"Did you ever say anything to anyone that your dog Spots had special powers and that William Quan Judge, after his death, spoke to you through the dog?"

"Absolutely not. I never considered that Spots was a remarkable dog any more than any other dog would be that was treated as kindly as he was. We are all very fond of animals, and he was a special pet of my family."

"Thank you, Madam," Mr. McKinley told her. "I have no further questions at this time."

Judge Torrance nodded to Sam Shortridge: "Your witness."

Chapter 32

There was an air of nervous anticipation in the courtroom as Sam Shortridge stood to cross-examine Mrs. Tingley. The spectators were shuffling about and the sound of soft t murmuring came from the gallery. The clock ticked forward, two o'clock, just one hour left of the court day. It was Christmas Eve; the judge announced that morning that we would adjourn early.

Sam Shortridge moved downright leisurely into a position behind the counsel table, leaning against the gallery railing to make eye contact with Mrs. Tingley, and where the jury could watch his every move. He turned to the jury. His glasses were poised in his right hand, and before he began, he waved them with a certain flair, almost a salute in their direction as if to signal that the contest had begun. Then he paused, looking at them for another moment as if he were asking them to get on board the train he was planning on running over Katherine Tingley.

The courtroom was dead silent. The jury leaned slightly forward in anticipation. Tension was high. Mr. Shortridge shot Mrs. Tingley a baleful glare. She sat up in her seat and looked right back at him, unfazed. The swords were crossed—*en garde!*

"There is no heaven or hell in your world, is there, Mrs. Tingley?"

"That's true," she replied. "Theosophists believe that your sins are answered through karmic justice: you pay for them in a particular lifetime for the sins of the past and sometimes in the lifetime when they occurred. This is how we are made ready to meet our creator after we have been karmically cleansed."

Mr. Shortridge turned to the judge. "Move to strike the witnesses comments after. "That's true."

"Overruled, she is entitled to explain her answer."

Mr. Otis shot a disapproving look at the judge.

"And," Shortridge continued, "If there is no heaven and no hell, people are free to misbehave as much as they like, regardless of the consequences to society as a whole. Isn't that true, Madam?"

"No, sir, it is not," she retorted. "Karmic retribution is in play for all of us."

"You have gone around the world cherry-picking from different religions what you want to add to the Theosophist liturgy. Do I have that right?"

"No sir, you do not," she said, indignant.

"But you don't believe that Christianity is the true and only path?"

"No. My whole aim has always been to bring out the spiritual possibilities of the individual."

"Just answer the question yes or no, Madam," Mr. Shortridge demanded, looking at the judge for support but not making any objection. The judge ignored him.

He quickly moved on as it was obvious that Mrs. Tingley was doing a little too well for his liking. Next, he posed a long series of questions suggesting that Mrs. Tingley was a sexual libertine who promoted free love and other immoral activities at Lomaland. She successfully rebuffed this approach

Appreciating how persuasive she was on the issue, Mr. Shortridge once again moved away from this line of questioning. He next asked Mrs. Tingley about her views about marriage and about her own matrimonial history.

"Isn't it true that you do not believe in matrimony?"

"No, that is not true," she countered. "I do believe in matrimony. I will say…"

"Your Honor, please direct the witness to answer the question without elaborating."

"Mrs. Tingley, Mr. Shortridge asked only if you believe in matrimony, not *what* you believed on the subject. Please confine your answers to the questions asked."

"You were married three times. Did I get that right, Madam?"

"That is correct," she replied. "I make no apologies. I have always been wedded first to my work…"

"Your Honor, please direct the witness to answer the question."

"Again, Mrs. Tingley, Mr. Shortridge did not ask you to explain but to tell us only if you had been married three times. Confine your answers to the questions asked, nothing more."

"Marriage hasn't worked out too well for you, has it?" Mr. Shortridge asked, his question dripping with sarcasm.

"No, not until I married Philo." The judge sighed.

"So he knows his place, does he?" Mr. Shortridge snarled. She didn't answer; she just glared at him pursing her lips.

Mr. McKinley jumped to his feet. "Ob-ject-ion!"

"Sustained," Judge Torrance barked.

Mr. Shortridge walked across the room to the open window, and then, as graceful as a ballerina, slowly pivoted and faced the jury and the witness.

"Isn't it true that your followers are sun worshippers, Madam?"

"Of course not," she replied, indignant.

"Do they not rise in the morning and go out upon the hill to worship the sun, after the fashion of idolaters?" Just getting warmed up, Mr. Shortridge's voice rose when Mrs. Tingley paused before answering his question.

"Answer me, Madam, answer my question," he demanded, drawing a glare of disapproval from the judge.

"No," Mrs. Tingley calmly replied. "They do not. They may get up in the morning—I presume they do; all people at the Point get up in the morning, and some of them do get up very early. I don't doubt that they see the sun. It's there, and they can see it, but they do not worship the sun. They are intelligent people."

Mr. Shortridge ended the day by questioning Mrs. Tingley about the nature of the late-night ceremonies at Lomaland and in particular, the flimsiness of the Greek robes worn by her followers.

The *Times* had charged that immoral activities took place at Lomaland late at night, the participants wearing indecent, flimsy costumes to secret initiations and ceremonies. This line of questioning provided an occasion for some humor in the cross-examination by Mr. Shortridge.

"The togas are not flimsy or suggestive," Mrs. Tingley responded; I have brought one here to show you if you wish." She pointed to a box on the counsel table in front of Mr. McKinley.

Always the actor, Mr. Shortridge jumped on the suggestion. "That's an excellent idea—perhaps my esteemed opposing counsel could model the robe for us."

Mr. McKinley smiled broadly, stood, removed the toga from the box, showed it to the jury, and made an alternative suggestion. "Since Mr. Shortridge has aspirations of being in the United States Senate, this garment, which is the classic garb of Greek politicians, would more appropriately be modeled by one who aspires to the toga."

This last sally drew laughter from the judge, the jurors, and the gallery. The clock ticked loudly, drawing the attention of the judge.

"It's three o'clock. We will adjourn early. Mr. Shortridge will continue his cross-examination of Mrs. Tingley on Friday morning. Have a wonderful Christmas."

Chapter 33

We had a pretty dismal Christmas Eve. We went to bed early; we missed our Tim so much. The heavy rain on Christmas Day further dampened our spirits. I donned my festive red and green plaid jumper that I usually wore for Christmas, which somehow lifted my spirits. Babe and Henry were there as always. After dinner, we opened presents with the fire blazing, the Christmas tree festooned with lighted candles, and the sound of rain pounding on the roof.

Charlie had dinner with his parents and was due to come over for a while, but he hadn't arrived. He wanted me to spend Christmas with him at his house. This was a tough Christmas for the Riley family, so I said no.

As we sat by the fire, Henry read to us about Christmas at the March household out of *Little Women.* He knew that book was one of my favorites. He was interrupted by what sounded like Christmas carolers singing silent night. I recognized Jack's voice leading the carol. I hopped up and opened the front door.

Charlie, Jack, and Theodora stood there, still singing. They were all bundled up; their faces flushed from the cold, puffs of warm breath coming from their mouths as they sang.

"We thought you could do with a little extra cheer this year," Charlie said.

"Well, that's for sure. Come in," I said with a smile.

We all sat by the fire while Henry finished the chapter he had been reading. We all drank Mother's famous eggnog and sampled some of the many Christmas treats she had baked. Her white

264

divinity fudge is sweet but delicious and was the star of her candy plate. Babe brought candy from the best chocolatier in town, and it went fast.

Pretty soon, Mother took to the piano and we all sang carols together. This was accompanied by the sound of the pounding rain, unusual for San Diego any time of the year. The rain let up for a while, and as the night wore on, Charlie looked at his watch. "Ben is outside, he said, we've gotta' go."

Jack and Theodora bid us good night and Merry Christmas as they left and got into the carriage. Charlie and I followed them but we stayed on the porch. " Be down in a minute," Charlie called to Jack.

I knew he was going to kiss me, and he did. The surprise was that after he did, he handed me a black velvet box. "Merry Christmas."

I opened the box and found a lovely strand of pearls.

"Do you like them?" he asked.

"Like them, I love them," I said, kissing him again.

"But I don't have a present for you."

"Being with you is present enough for me." I put my arms around his neck and kissed him again.

"Hey, it's cold out here, Jack called from the carriage, "save the smoochin' for tomorrow."

We both smiled, "I'll see you in court tomorrow," Charlie said, releasing his embrace. He rushed down the steps and hopped into the carriage. As I watched it pull away I thought about how wonderful it was that these three good friends shared Christmas with us; it made it so much easier to bear.

Chapter 34

First thing Friday morning, the day after Christmas, Mrs. Tingley resumed the witness chair with the help of her husband. She was, no doubt, prepared for the incoming fire she certainly expected. Everyone knew Sam Shortridge would be locked and loaded, ready to take her down. She wore the same costume that day as in her prior stint as a witness.

"You remain under oath," Judge Torrance advised her.

The judge nodded to Mr. Shortridge, who wasted no time going after Mrs. Tingley for her policy of underfeeding babies at Lomaland as claimed by the *Times*.

"You deliberately endangered the health of babies under your care at Lomaland, didn't you, Madame?"

"Absolutely not," she said, outraged.

"You thought you knew better how to care for them than the trained medical doctors at Lomaland? "

"That is not true either, sir. I made suggestions, and the doctor usually followed them."

"After all, Madam, you are *she* who must be obeyed out on the Point, isn't that so? "

She didn't respond.

"You made a diet list for the babies, correct?"

"No, but I made suggestions to the doctors."

"And after that, you ordered them to follow your suggestions, didn't you?

"Not at all, but they did follow some of them. I advised them to put the cream into what they were feeding the children, making the food more nutritious. I also suggested feeding them more frequently, every half-hour."

"You became actively involved in dietary issues for the children at Lomaland, although you have no training or experience in such matters, isn't that true?"

"No formal training, that is true, but I have worked with feeding poor children for many years. It has been my experience that children who eat less are more receptive to spiritual growth, not to mention general education."

"And that is just something you came up with on your own—it isn't a tenet of Theosophy, is it?"

"No, that is true."

And even Doctor Anderson, himself a Theosophist who sat on your Cabinet, strongly disapproved of your involvement in medical issues and, in particular, to the underfeeding of babies at Lomaland. Isn't that true?

"That is true," she said quietly.

"And underfeeding a baby is a form of child abuse, isn't that true, Madame?"

She put her head down and began her response with her voice breaking at times. When she looked up and faced the jury, she had tears in her eyes." Certainly not; I would never abuse any child. I have devoted my entire life to serving children."

If this was acting, she did a great job. She was very convincing. I looked at the clock, and it was eleven thirty, just before the lunch break. Mr. Shortridge walked to a position near the rear of the jury box. He questioned Mrs. Tingley about her past activities as a spiritualist.

Spiritualism, Father told me at the morning break, is the use of mediums who claim to have special powers to do such things as telling fortunes and calling up the dead to communicate with them.

"This was very popular all across the country in the latter part of the nineteenth century but not so much anymore. There was too much fraud and chicanery. Many people still believe in spiritualism, which takes many forms, and spend a great deal of money on such things as contacting their dead loved ones."

"We all took our places after the break, and Judge Torrance nodded to Mr. Shortridge. You may continue your cross-examination, Sir."

Mr. Shortridge stood and took his previous position leaning his rear end on the gallery rail near the jury box facing Mrs. Tingley and took somewhat of an extended, even uncomfortable pause before he began questioning her. He had done this once before apparently to increase the interest of the jury as to what he planned to do next. It was effective. I looked at the jurors, who were rapt with attention.

"You are a spiritualist, are not Mrs. Tingley?" Mr. Shortridge asked her in a decidedly disapproving tone.

"I have never denied being a spiritualist, Mr. Shortridge, during 1893, 1894, and 1895. I only did these readings for charity. Spiritualism is not part of the program at Lomaland."

"And you used to take money to tell fortunes and communicate with the dead."

"Yes, I had those gifts."

But you don't have them now, Madam. Is that your claim? What, did they just disappear? Or did you just find another way of taking people's money?" Mr. Shortridge looked at the jury with skepticism.

Mr. McKinley rose. "Objection, this is argumentative, and Your Honor, this is three questions; which one does Mr. Shortridge want the witness to respond to?"

"He's got a good point, Mr. Shortridge," Judge Torrance told him.

"I'll withdraw the question, Your Honor."

"And besides holding yourself out as a woman who can summon the dead and communicate with them, you offer your services for money as a hypnotist, isn't that right, Madam?"

"No, it is not right."

"And it became part of the show Katherine Tingley offered to people who wanted to pay her money for her services as a medium, a fortune teller, and a hypnotist. Isn't that so, Madam?"

"Absolutely not."

"But part of the program at Lomaland involves hypnosis, does it not?"

"No, I have opposed hypnotism there, opposed it on every occasion."

Sam Shortridge then brought the issue of thought waves into the discussion.

"Mrs. Tingley, you claimed to be able to send thought waves to your followers and to the world population at large?"

"I have no recollection of sending out thought waves, sir, only kind thoughts, possibly. I have not reached a point where I can control the human mind. But I will say that having pure thoughts and doing

269

good deeds, setting a good example, can change people's thinking and can make for a better world. If I had a pure thought, by way of illustration, I might influence you," she told him.

Mr. Shortridge fired back: "That is Madam if you ever had a pure thought."

Changing course once again, Mr. Shortridge asked, "Mrs. George F. Mohn, a former resident at Lomaland, claims that you separated her from her seven-year-old daughter. Is that true?"

She looked at the jury. "It is. We promote this separation as early on as possible at the Raja School. Most of the parents live in Lomaland and see their children on the weekends. The children live with a teacher in the Lotus Pod children's residences during the week. We call our children Lotus Buds, you see." She smiled at the jury. The jurors were listening, but their faces revealed nothing.

"This separation allows the child to learn the principles of better living, the teachings of the Universal Brotherhood, from an early age. They are not limited by the experiences of their mother or father that often hold the child back from spiritual development," she explained.

"Our parents are happy to have their children at Lomaland, which is a wonderful school. They agree to this separation policy so that their children have the privilege of going to school there."

"Did you tell Mrs. Mohn that you intended to make all the children at Lomaland workers for humanity?"

"I did. It is the intention of the Raja School to prepare the children when they are grown to go out in the world to spread the teachings of the Universal Brotherhood. They are apostles in the making of the tenets of Theosophy. We are very proud of our school and our students."

Mr. Shortridge seemed to take great exception to Katherine Tingley declaring herself the final word on any subject concerning the

Universal Brotherhood. Mrs. Tingley surprised him when she took no issue with this.

She explained to the jury, "When it comes to forging a path for a better way of living, a better path for humanity, you must have an ultimate authority. I am that authority at Lomaland, and I'm not ashamed to say it. This is even in our constitution, which our Cabinet has wholly endorsed, unanimously, mind you."

"Madam, you consider yourself like Jesus Christ, a Buddha, Muhammad, and other religious avatars. Isn't that true?"

"No, it is not, but I am a teacher of the Principles of the Universal Brotherhood at Lomaland, as are many others there."

"But you have publicly declared yourself to be in the company of such religious teachers as Christ, Buddha, and Muhammad, have you not?"

"I have not, sir, absolutely not. I don't know where you get such information," she said in a huff, crossing her arms defensively.

"But you, and only you, can overrule the beliefs of those *many others* you refer to if they don't follow your version of things?"

This time, Mrs. Tingley faltered. "Yes, that's true; I have the final say."

"So again, you are indeed 'she who must be obeyed' out there on the Point, aren't you, Madam?" Mr. Shortridge asked her this using a phrase attributed to Harrison Otis, which appeared in one of the *Times'* articles. Mrs. Tingley snapped back, glaring at her inquisitor.

"We have a constitution and a Cabinet, which is our board of directors; there is much consultation, and we work together. But if we can't reach an agreement, I will make the final call.

271

"This arrangement of my having the final say allows me to put the theoretical into the practical reality in the Raja School experiment. I learned this living with the Mother Superior system in a convent. I lived in a convent for three years, you know."

"And Mrs. Tingley," Mr. Shortridge pressed on, "you cannot give me one occasion your Cabinet even attempted to overrule your decision, isn't that true?"

She didn't answer.

"Mrs. Tingley, may I have your answer?" Shortridge drilled down.

"I can't think of one right now, sir." She said softly.

"I don't imagine you can, Madam," Mr. Shortridge remarked derisively.

"And indeed, Madam, you can take any money from the Brotherhood and spend it as you see fit, isn't that true?"

"I have the ultimate say, but I make decisions in consultation with the Cabinet. We trust each other."

"You have singular control over the Brotherhood's bank accounts, don't you, Madam?"

"No sir. Three members of the Cabinet have access to the accounts as well."

Looking at the clock, Judge Torrance announced: "It's time for our morning break. See you all at 10:15."

As soon as the judge left the bench, the General rushed out of the courtroom before the crowd. Mrs. Tingley, assisted by her husband, left the witness chair and was allowed to leave before the spectators and the press. As she reached the courtroom door, it opened, and she suddenly found herself face-to-face with Harrison Otis, who towered over her.

There was a brief standoff. They stared at each other, taking each other's measure. The General said in a loud voice, "Since I'm a gentleman, I suppose I have to open the door for you, Madam."

He started to open the door farther to let her pass. Instead, Mrs. Tingley pushed the door open with her casted foot and replied, "You are no gentlemen, sir; why would you suppose you need to start acting like one now?"

"Ouch," I said to Father.

The General, after Mrs. Tingley passed through the door, roughly pushed his way through the outgoing crowd of spectators carrying a large envelope. He headed back to the counsel table where Sam Shortridge was gathering his notes.

He handed the envelope to him, he opened it and pulled out a sheaf of papers. Otis stood sentry beside his lawyer when he looked at the materials. Mr. Shortridge paged through them, and as he turned to leave, a look of interest crossed his face, or was that concern?

We left the courtroom for lunch without finding out what was in the mysterious envelope. I made a note to check with Mr. McKinley to see if I could find out what he knew about this.

After we all settled in after lunch, the judge took the bench and looked at Mr. Shortridge. "You may continue your cross-examination, sir."

He nodded, walked over to his counsel table, and again rested his behind on the end, facing the jury. He then turned his attention back to Mrs. Tingley.

"Mrs. Tingley, we were talking before lunch about your access to all the funds collected on behalf of the Brotherhood. Isn't that so,

Ma'am? And this is without the need to obtain approval before the funds are withdrawn. Am I right about that?"

"You are. But I clear all large expenditures with the Cabinet before the money is withdrawn."

"Mrs. Tingley, isn't it true that other newspapers have printed materials about Lomaland that you claimed were libelous?"

"Yes, that is true."

"And some of them were about your mistreatment of children, isn't that true?"

"Yes," she said softly.

"And these articles involved damage to your reputation too, isn't that right?"

"Yes."

"So we don't know if your damages, be they physical distress or damages to your reputation, were related to the *Times'* articles or to these other articles, do we now Madam?"

Mr. McKinley rose to his feet. "Objection, whether other newspapers published libelous materials does not absolve or even mitigate the damage done by the *Times*."

"Sustained," the judge ruled.

Sam Shortridge looked at the judge. "May I be heard, Your Honor?"

"You may."

"Your Honor, if the actions of other newspapers contributed to Mrs. Tingley's damages, we are entitled to discuss them."

"No sir, you are not," the judge said gruffly.

Mr. Shortridge sometimes treated Judge Torrance as if he were some backwater judge and that only he, Sam Shortridge, knew the law or how things should be handled in Courtroom One of the San Diego Superior Court.

It was not so much what he said but the way he said it. Every time he slipped into this high-handed attitude, the judge didn't wait to give him the horse-eye treatment; he just smacked him down hard. On these occasions, Mr. Shortridge always acted like he didn't notice the rebuke. Judge Torrance often seemed amused by the antics of this high-priced San Francisco lawyer. Still, he wasn't going to put up with them either.

"Objection sustained. Mrs. Tingley's damages, if any, are discrete as to each publication of libelous materials. If she has chosen to seek damages only against the *Times* for their misconduct, this is her prerogative. Ask your next question, Mr. Shortridge."

"I have no further questions for Mrs. Tingley at this time."

After Mr. Shortridge took his seat, Judge Torrance looked at Mr. McKinley. "Anything further, Counsel?"

It was 3:45, and nobody, including the judge, expected Mr. McKinley to question his client further, but he surprised us.

He stood. "Just a few questions, Your Honor."

Mr. McKinley stayed in his place behind his counsel table, which was in front of Mrs. Tingley, and looked at her straight on. This time it was he who paused to increase the anticipation of what he was going to ask her. "Mrs. Tingley, do you believe in the equality of the sexes?"

She bowed her head and thought for a minute.

"Yes, I do, but I believe that men and women have separate roles and that they should remain in those roles. Voting, politics, and the role of a civic leader are a man's role, and women have no place assuming that role or any aspect of it. This is because it would take her away from her fundamental and most important task of child-rearing and maintaining the family home."

"What do you see as a woman's role, Mrs. Tingley?"

"The greatest work a woman can do is to become so sweetly feminine, so sweetly spiritual and strong, yet so grandly compliant and helpful, that she will hold the whole human family in her keeping. She will make her home her kingdom."

I was stunned when I heard these words come from this woman's mouth. She was so far from the woman she described. She was hardly sweetly feminine, let alone compliant. She was the autocratic leader, for life, of the Theosophist community at Point Loma and, of the entire country and the world.

She did not deny this or excuse it. There were no other women in the Cabinet, and women did not play a significant role in any of the organization's leadership. Only one woman did, and that was Katherine Tingley.

Insofar as her personal life, Katherine Tingley was far from the queen of her domestic domain. She had no children and had been married three times. She had no real domestic life with any of her husbands. Her mission dominated her life; there was little room for anything else. She did not live the role she prescribed for other women, *all o*ther women.

It was obvious to me that her responses to these questions were carefully planned by Mr. McKinley. He wanted to show the jury that this woman was not, as Mr. Shortridge had claimed from the get-go, a threat to traditional roles of men and women or any threat to the family for that matter.

276

This remarkable testimony confirmed what I had known for some time: Katherine Tingley was a mass of contradictions. She wasn't lying, nor was she a hypocrite. I don't think Mrs. Tingley saw the irony of her taking this remarkable position in terms of a woman's role in the world.

Katherine Tingley stood astride the new century with all her progressive ideas, but in terms of the relationship between the sexes, and in her views on sexual mores and behavior, she remained in the Victorian era she came from.

After Mr. McKinley sat down, another surprise came when the court asked Mr. Shortridge if he had any further questions. He nodded yes and stood up, but after giving it some thought, he looked at Judge Torrance, "No, Your Honor," he said simply.

Mrs. Tingley had clearly won the day, and he didn't want to give her any further opportunities to gain favor with the jury. This last bit of questioning by Mr. McKinley did create a fly in the ointment in terms of the defense strategy of turning off this conservative, all-male jury to a woman who was a threat to their masculine roles, both in their own homes and in society.

"Very well, the judge said. You are excused, Madam."

Mr. McKinley stood and faced the judge. "Your Honor, Plaintiff rests."

There was a twittering heard from the gallery, the spectators were surprised no doubt, that the plaintiff only called two witnesses. The clock ticked loudly forward as if to punctuate this dramatic moment in the trial. Judge Torrance glanced at the clock; it was 4:00. He raised his gavel as he looked into the gallery, "This court is adjourned."

Chapter 35

I didn't walk to the courthouse with Father that morning; he left early. Father was talking to Mr. McKinley when I got to the hallway outside Department One. He told me that he wanted to see if he could snag a moment with to ask him about the package delivered by Mr. Otis to Mr. Shortridge at the counsel table the day before.

The bailiff opened the door to the courtroom at about 8:50 to let the parties and their lawyers in. Mr. McKinley went in, but Mr. Shortridge and Mr. Otis had not yet arrived. Mrs. Tingley was probably already in the courtroom; she usually came in a back way through the doors leading to the judge's chambers. She was given this privilege because of her injury. It was an easier route than through the front door of the courtroom, and there were no crowds to get in her way. Mr. Shortridge and Mr. Otis were given the same access, but they always came in through the front door.

Before the proceedings started, Father solved the mystery of the mysterious package. "You won't believe it. McKinley told me that his client had sued Otis a second time for his attempt to blackmail Katherine Tingley over what Otis claimed was some scandalous material he had on her and her doings at Point Loma. The price for keeping this material secret was her dropping the lawsuit in this case before it got to the jury."

"The package delivered by Otis yesterday was the lawsuit McKinley filed late yesterday. It involves the attempt to blackmail her into withdrawing the libel case. He served him that morning when he came to court."

"McKinley said he saw the front page of the lawsuit when Shortridge pulled it out of the envelope. He said that he was sure

278

Shortridge had not been told about Otis' activities as a blackmailer. He apparently learned of it when Otis told him in court that morning that he had been served. Shortridge told him to go get it and he did. "Just in time to confront Mrs. Tingley in the doorway," Father said.

"McKinley said it won't have anything to do with this case. The best part, Mary Kate, is that I don't think any other papers have this story, at least not yet, so we probably will have the scoop on this for tomorrow's edition."

"The General, that horrible man, will do anything to win, won't he?" I replied.

"Ya--up," Father drew the word out slowly for effect," that's pretty accurate. I bet Shortridge will be glad when the case is over. Otis is a difficult client."

A few minutes later we heard the clerk call out in a clear voice as he did every morning: "All rise, Department One of the San Diego Superior Court is now in session. The Honorable E.S. Torrance presiding."

It was a chilly morning, and the judge had an especially ruddy face as he took the bench. The jury was seated and the lawyers and Mr. Otis were at their counsel tables. Mrs. Tingley was not in the courtroom. Judge Torrance bid everyone a good morning and looked at Mr. Shortridge.

"Your first witness, Sir.."

"The defense calls Alfred Andrews to the stand."

Mr. Andrews was a middle-aged, bookish man, mostly bald, wearing a dark brown, very bad toupee plopped too far forward on his head. He wore thick tortoise-shell glasses. He sported a wrinkled plaid jacket, a white shirt, and a bright green, rather hideous tie.

Mr. Andrews appeared uncomfortable and tentative on the stand, constantly looking to Harrison Otis for approval but mostly not getting it. He testified that he was the longtime senior editor at the *Los Angeles Times.* "I've worked there for over twenty years. I started as a cub reporter," he added.

He said that he approved for publication the series of articles printed about Mrs. Tingley written by one of the reporters under his supervision, Charlie Bartlett.

He told the jury that before he did so, he read previous articles about Katherine Tingley, Lomaland, and the Universal Brotherhood that had been published in *The San Diego Union*, the *Los Angeles Herald*, the *Pasadena Daily News*, and the *San Francisco Chronicle.* "I assumed those papers looked into the matter," he said.

Mr. Shortridge then asked him a series of questions about the source of information used in the articles about Mrs. Tingley. Mr. Andrews testified that apart from what was obtained from other publications, the rest of the information in the *Times'* articles came from one source: Mrs. George Leavitt.

"Did you know anything about the reliability of Mrs. Leavitt before you approved the articles?" Mr. Shortridge asked him.

"Not personally, no, but the reporter that wrote the story, Johnny Bartlett, told me that he felt she looked trustworthy and that the articles about Mrs. Tingley in the other papers aligned with what Mrs. Leavitt told our reporter."

Mr. Shortridge left it at that, gingerly stepping away from the witness and taking his seat. "I have nothing further for this witness."

Mr. McKinley stood up and got right to it. "Mr. Bartlett told you that he didn't ask Mrs. Leavitt why he should believe the information she gave him or why it was reliable enough to print, did he sir?"

"No sir, he didn't. He only said that she looked reliable to him. He said she was a good-appearing woman who seemed like she was telling the truth."

"And that was good enough for you?"

"Yes, sir," he mumbled, barely audible.

"To paint with such a broad brush tarnishing this good woman's reputation because your reporter thought the source *'looked* reliable, is that what you are telling this jury?"

"Yes," he croaked. He paused, his face in a hard-set grimace. "I could have used the more inflammatory material Mrs. Leavitt gave us to put in the articles, but I didn't," he sputtered, clearly wounded.

He paused again and calmed down a tad. "I *was* a bit suspicious of her motives what with her being from a rival Theosophist sect and all, and especially because Johnny told me she didn't want her name in the paper as the source I…"

Mr. McKinley interrupted him. "So you're the hero now, your excuse being that it could have been even worse. Really sir, have you no shame?"

Bang went the gavel before Mr. Shortridge could even get the word "Objection" out of his mouth. "Enough of that kind of stuff, Mr. McKinley, move on."

"Neither your reporter nor anyone else at the *Times* thought of calling Mrs. Tingley to check the information from the person whose reputation you intended to smear?"

"I told Johnny to do that, but it got late, and he didn't get it done before it went to print." He glanced nervously at Mr. Otis.

"It got late *each* time you printed this material in the *Times*?"

Mr. Andrews didn't answer.

"Harrison Otis told you to run the articles each time, didn't he?"

No answer. "Your Honor, will you instruct the witness to answer the question?" Mr. McKinley urged the judge.

"I will. Mr. Andrews, you must answer."

He cleared his throat. "Mr. Otis told me to run the articles."

There was a quiet rumble in the courtroom.

"You never checked with Mrs. Tingley about the claims Mrs. Leavitt made?"

"No."

"And checking with both sides would be your normal practice, am I right?"

"Yes," he said softly, looking again at Mr. Otis.

"Speak up, sir!" the judge barked.

"Yes," he said, a little too loud.

"Do you have a policy at the *Times* of printing stories without investigation into their truth?"

"No sir it is not. It is the policy at the *Times* to use great care in the investigation of facts before articles go in the paper."

"You didn't follow this policy in this case, did you?"

"No."

"And that is because your boss-man, Harrison Otis—the General, as he likes to call himself, told you to print the articles regardless of the truth or the damage they might cause, isn't that true?"

"He didn't say that. He just said to go ahead and print them; he wanted them in."

Mr. McKinley looked over at Harrison Otis, who was squirming in his seat at the counsel table.

"And Harrison Otis here," giving a wave in his direction, "never told you that Katherine Tingley had contacted him and told him that what the *Times* were printing about her was untrue and that it should be stopped, did he?"

"No Sir, he did not."

Mr. McKinley walked away from the witness, pausing as he reached the counsel table. He turned and looked up at the judge. "I have nothing further, Your Honor."

"Anything further, Mr. Shortridge?"

"Just one question, Your Honor," Mr. Shortridge replied. "Was there anything in the *Times* articles not found in one or more of the other newspapers you consulted about Katherine Tingley?"

"No, sir."

Mr. McKinley rose. "I move to strike the witness's last answer. Mr. Andrews telling of what he read in other publications is hearsay, and it's irrelevant. We've been over this. Just because one paper prints libelous materials doesn't absolve another for printing them, whether or not the other newspapers are called into account."

"Motion granted. The jury is not to consider this evidence."

"Your Honor…" Mr. Shortridge stood and again began to dispute the court's dismissal of this approach. Judge Torrance ignored him.

"Next witness," he said gruffly.

"Your Honor, my witness has not arrived. It is four-twenty; could we adjourn until tomorrow morning?"

"Of course, I lost track of the time," Judge Torrance told him.

"This court is adjourned," he said and brought his gavel down.

As my father and I left the courthouse, I turned to him, "Sam Shortridge probably expected a little more help from Mr. Andrews, being his first witness and all," I think he hurt his client's case rather than helped it."

As we walked down Broadway, Father explained to me why Mr. Shortridge called Mr. Andrews as his first witness.

"Don't shortchange Ol' Sam. He got what he wanted from Andrews. He called him for a key element in his defense: maybe the *Times* libeled Mrs. Tingley, but other papers did too, and she didn't sue them."

"The idea is she wasn't damaged by these statements in the *Times* or the other papers, so don't give her any money. Or, if the *Times* did damage her, the other papers did too, and they should pay for some of her damages."

"Shortridge knows he has no case on the issue of libel; that's a clear loser. If he can bring in evidence that makes Katherine Tingley look bad, that makes her not likable by this jury, someone who is a threat to them, or convince them that she wasn't damaged, he might just win this. And by a win, I mean the jury will award her nothing."

"But Father, the judge said the jury couldn't consider that other papers had published the same type of statements. He said it was irrelevant."

"That's right, he did, but the jury heard it. They will remember it too. That's all Shortridge needed."

284

Chapter 36

The next morning, before the judge arrived to start things off for the day, Katherine Tingley came through the back door of the courtroom. She nodded to Mr. McKinley and then sat down quietly her aide sat behind her in a chair near the gallery. Her husband was not with her. A few minutes later, the judge took the bench and the jury was seated. He nodded to Sam Shortridge.

He stood, and in a tone taken when announcing someone of great significance, he proclaimed, "The defense calls Henry Ruethling to the stand."

Everyone turned around to see who would be coming through the courtroom door. Henry Ruethling did not impress when he did. He was a diminutive man, five-foot-three or four, slight in build. He wore a new suit for the occasion that was too big and pooled around his well-polished shoes. His thinning dark hair was carefully arranged and pomaded to his head; it wasn't going anywhere.

He smiled at the folks in the gallery as he walked by, his demeanor one of a person excited about the prospect of being a witness in this important trial. He had bright blue eyes that were set off by his rosy cheeks. He stopped on his way to the witness stand to face the clerk and raise his right hand. "Henry H. Ruethling," he stated proudly and then took the oath. His deep voice surprised me; it was outsized for such a little fellow.

Sam Shortridge gently walked him through the first part of his direct examination. He testified that he was brought to the trial by representatives of the *Los Angeles Times* who he said, had met with him three or four times in the past month in his home state of New

York. At first, he looked to his left at Mr. Shortridge when he testified.

"I live just outside the city of New York; I don't know how they found me," he said pleasantly. They paid for my trip out here, and they said I could bring my wife Clara with me, so I did. "We are staying over at the Brewster Hotel; it's a real nice place."

"She's sitting in the back," he added looking in her direction and smiling. Sitting in the front row of the gallery, Mrs. Ruethling proudly smiled back at her husband.

He testified that "the *Times* people," as he called them, contacted him about three weeks before the trial to get the information he had about Katherine Tingley. They took notes of what they discussed about Mrs. Tingley, typed them, and a week later gave them back to him, telling him to review them before he testified at the trial.

Mr. Ruethling then turned and spoke directly to the jury. "I only met her once, mind you, but I do know a great deal about her shenanigans." he huffed. Indignant, he continued his indictment of Katherine Tingley "She was purporting to act on behalf of the worldwide Theosophy movement, which I can tell you, she does not."

This drew an objection from Mr. McKinley.

"Sustained. Mr. Ruethling, we want facts from you, not your opinions," Judge Torrance warned him.

His face colored, but he was undeterred. He admitted to being a member of a rival group of Theosophists who, he said, "do not believe that the Point Loma Brethren are true Theosophists."

He admitted what was by then obvious, that he did not like Katherine Tingley. He said that he only had a brief meeting with her about eight months before the trial at a Theosophy conference she held in New York City.

"I met with her and some of her aides after the conference."

"What did you observe about Mrs. Tingley on that occasion?" Mr. Shortridge asked.

"I tell you, gentlemen, that woman is too bossy. She was bossing around everyone in the room. Worse, they were following her orders, way too bossy by half, I'd say," he told the jury.

Mr. McKinley began to rise to object, but his instincts as an experienced trial lawyer took over. He slid back into his chair.

"What else did you observe about Mrs. Tingley that day?"

Well, sir, I could see that her assistants were taking donations of money from people who attended the conference. She apparently convinced them to contribute to her cause."

"I will say this, Mr. Shortridge, the woman is a magnetic, dynamic speaker. Why people were mesmerized by what she was spouting off at that conference. I've heard that she hypnotizes people when she speaks to groups; that's how she makes people give her money." Pausing, he looked at the jury. "She lives off other people's money."

Mr. McKinley began to rise from his seat to object, but again he thought better of it. His instincts told him that he should let Mr. Ruethling march on with his opinions about Katherine Tingley which were getting more outlandish by the minute. And then it came.

"And another thing," he said, becoming increasingly indignant and looking at the jury, who were paying strict attention, "I sat in that room after the conference, and I could tell that Katherine Tingley wanted to have sexual intercourse with me."

This caused the entire jury and the gallery to break into raucous laughter. The jury seemed to lean forward in a wave to see Mrs.

Tingley's reaction to this testimony. She kept her composure; she had no expression on her face, her hands were folded on her lap. Harrison Otis on the other hand, did plenty of moving about nervously in his seat, and frantically whispering in his lawyer's ear.

Judge Torrance, who had been resting his head on his palm, close to falling asleep, snapped to attention and brought down his gavel."Order!"

The laughter didn't faze Mr. Ruethling a bit. He didn't recognize that he was being laughed _at_ by almost everyone there, including the jurors.

"Yes, gentlemen, as you know, a man can tell such things, yes indeed, and that is what she wanted from me, sexual intercourse."

Another twittering of laughter, and down went the gavel a second time. "Order!"

The room fell silent. Everyone was waiting for another question from the often-verbose Sam Shortridge, but nothing came. He had no words. Finally, after what seemed like a very long minute, the judge looked at him and asked, I swear with a bit of mischief in his eyes, "Anything further, Mr. Shortridge?"

"No, Your Honor," he said softly and sat down.

Mr. Ruethling got up and began to leave the witness stand.

"Not so fast, Sir," the judge told him, "I expect Mr. McKinley might have a few questions for you."

Unperturbed, the little man sat back down. With that, Judge Torrance, who had taken a chaw of tobacco, spit into his spittoon—another perfect shot, a fitting editorial on the outrageous testimony he had just heard. Mr. McKinley rose and slowly meandered over to the rear of the jury box, put his right hand on the railing, and faced the witness.

"Good afternoon, sir; I'd like to go over with you a couple of things you raised in your testimony."

"I'll just bet you do," Father whispered to me, drawing a warning glare from the bailiff.

First Mr. McKinley asked him about his interactions with the *Times* people and their lawyers and how they had pretty much molded what he told the jury. He got him to admit that he did not know if what the *Times* people had told him was true.

"So, as you sit here before us on the witness stand today, under oath, you can't tell us if anything the *Times* people told you about Mrs. Tingley was true?"

"I thought it was true."

"Or why the information they gave you about Mrs. Tingley should be viewed as reliable, isn't that right?"

"I didn't really know. I assumed it was reliable; after all, they represented the *Los Angeles Times* newspaper. It's their job to report the truth."

"Indeed it is," Mr. McKinley replied sarcastically.

Appearing to be winding down, he asked Mr. Ruethling, "So as you sit here today, sir, would be fair to say that you knew nothing about Katherine Tingley other than what the *Times* people shared with you, the information you got from talking to people at the Theosophist group you are affiliated with, and the one time she was seducing you from across the room at a conference in New York City?"

"Yes, that's true," he replied, seemingly oblivious to the fact that he was being mocked.

"And you don't know whether what you were told by the *Times* people was made up, gossip, or simply not true, do you?"

"I thought it was true. I had no reason to believe it wasn't true. These people are *not* liars, sir." He was getting flustered.

"Hmm," Mr. McKinley replied, rubbing his chin in thought.

"Now, you told us that you thought Mrs. Tingley was too bossy—too bossy by half, you said. Did I get that right?"

"Yes, sir."

"And you base that on the one meeting you had with her, looking at her across the room after the conference she held about eight months ago."

"Correct."

"And she was bossing around people that worked for her?"

"Yes."

"She was their *boss*?"

"Yes. I guess so."

"And you couldn't observe where the money went that was collected that day?"

"How could I know that?"

"Well, you seem to be willing to tell us a great deal of information you have no real knowledge of."

"That is not true, sir."

Sam Shortridge rose. "Objection; Mr. McKinley is badgering the witness."

"Mr. McKinley, knock it off," the judge growled.

He took a few steps over to his counsel table; all eyes were on him. Before he got there, he turned, backed up a foot or so, and faced the witness as if he had forgotten to ask him something. He was just a couple of feet from the rear of the jury box. He was in the perfect position to be seen by the jury for the performance that came next.

"So, Mr. Ruethling, we were speaking of your testifying about facts. Let's talk about the claim you made that Mrs. Tingley signaled to you that she wanted to have sexual intercourse with you. Do you recall that testimony?"

"I certainly do," he said, pursing his lips.

"Now, she didn't do this communicating her sexual desire for you in front of all the people in the room after the conference, did she?" Mr. McKinley asked, sounding skeptical.

"Well, yes, it was in that room."

"I see. Is that where you said you saw her bossing everyone around?"

"Not everybody, just the people that worked for her."

"Hmm… And many people were in that room at the time; I think you said employees taking money and donations, right?"

"Well, I don't know if they were employees; I just saw people taking money from quite a few people."

"By the way, you never actually spoke to Mrs. Tingley that day, did you?"

"No, I didn't."

"You didn't meet her one-on-one?"

"That's right."

"Again, you never actually spoke to her?"

"That's true; I was part of a group that attended the conference, and we came into the large room after the conference. We were introduced to her as a group. I think the group was brought in there so she could fleece them out of their money. She called it "facilitating donations," those were her exact words. He looked at the jury and then at Mr. Shortridge. "She got no money from me, not from me, no sir."

"So let me get this straight: she was attempting to mesmerize you into sexual relations with her by looking at you across the room. Is that your testimony, sir?"

"Yes," he said, adamant, looking at the jury, who were all ears.

"So if she didn't talk to you, did Mrs. Tingley signal that she wanted you sexually by a wink, sir, from across the room?"

He turned slightly around to face the jury, and I believe, from their laughter, that he winked after he asked the question. This was met with laughter from the gallery and the jury.

"No, sir, it was not a wink."

Mr. McKinley took a couple of steps back and again and stood even closer to the jury box. Hugging himself, he began to shimmy slowly from side to side, facing the witness.

"So, did she shimmy back and forth to you with a seductive come-hither look reserved for you alone?"

"No, no, no!" This time he raised his voice; this time, he knew he had been wounded.

"Watch it, Mr. McKinley," Judge Torrance warned, giving him the solo horse eye over his bench.

"No pursing of the lips in a kiss to you, sending it across the room, promising greater things to come?" Mr. McKinley pursed his lips in a mock kiss when he finished the question, turning partially toward the jury so they could see him do this.

Sam Shortridge began to rise to object but sat back down when the judge banged the gavel. "Enough!" Judge Torrance shouted angrily, glaring at Mr. McKinley.

Unfazed, Mr. McKinley responded. "I'll withdraw the question, Your Honor." The damage had been done.

"He's is enjoying this way too much," Father whispered.

One person who was decidedly not pleased with Mr. Ruethling's performance was Harrison Otis. Once again, the back of his head was a rosy red as he huffed and puffed and squirmed through much of the s testimony. At one point I could hear the muffled boom, boom, boom, of his fingers drumming on the arm of his chair. This was soon silenced by a glare from the Judge. Otis knew, as did everyone else, that the star witness for the defense was being made a laughingstock before the jury.

Mr. McKinley returned to the podium that was near the jury box and lobbed the last of his artillery at the witness.

"So what you are claiming, Sir, is that somehow the lascivious Katherine Tingley, this lady who sits before you here, signaled to you in some private, secret manner, in front of all her employees and donors, that she wanted to have sexual intercourse with you, a man she had never met. Is that what you are telling us, sir?"

"Yes!" he barked, looking at the jury. "If you saw how the woman looked at me, it was unmistakable. She wanted me, no doubt about it!"

This brought the house down. There was another round of hearty laughter from the audience and the jury. Crack! Judge Torrance slammed down his gavel for the third time.

"That's it! The laughter and merriment will stop, or I will clear this courtroom. This is a court of law, not a circus."

Mrs. Tingley had restrained herself and sat quietly during the whole of Mr. Rustling's testimony up to this point, but his last comment proved to be too much for her. "Outrageous, ridiculous—I don't even know the man."

"Silence, Mrs. Tingley, you are out of order. I assure you that you will have your chance to respond," Judge Torrance told her in a firm but rather gentle manner. He probably thought Mrs. Tingley had behaved admirably, considering the outrageous testimony about her coming out of Mr. Rustling's mouth.

After hearing the judge's gavel come down for the third time, I looked at the jurors, who suddenly looked stone-faced at the witness. The air had gone out of their hilarity balloons present just a moment before.

"I have nothing further for this witness, Your Honor," Mr. McKinley said.

"Mr. Shortridge?"

"Nothing further, Your Honor." He said this with a tiny but telling hint of exasperation in his tone.

"Fine, you are excused, sir." The judge brought down his gavel. "This court is adjourned." I looked at the clock above the back door. It was 4:45.

Chapter 37

I hurried out of the courtroom—I had an early dinner engagement with Mrs. Tingley and Mr. McKinley at the New Town, the restaurant at the Brewster Hotel. Father said he was sure Mr. McKinley was just itching for a rehash of the afternoons' proceedings. It was one for the books, that's for sure.

Mrs. Tingley was now staying at the Brewster. It was far more convenient to the courthouse than the Hortons. Mr. McKinley had invited Father to dinner too, but he declined; it was too long a day for him. His back usually acted up by the end of the day from sitting on the hard benches in the courtroom.

"You go, Mary Kate. I'll write today's story and wait for you until six-thirty. Call me at the paper with quotes from both McKinley and Tingley. I'll add them to the story, give it to the printers and head home to have dinner with your mother. She loves to hear about the trial, and today's doings will make a good tale. George Ruethling put on quite a show. And Mary Kate, have Mr. McKinley see you home; he's coming this way."

I left the courthouse late after stopping to pick up my real estate statistics so I took the trolley up the hill to the Brewster. The fresh air and the breeze in the open trolley were cool but invigorating. When I arrived at the restaurant, Mrs. Tingley and Mr. McKinley were already at the table. Mrs. Tingley had her casted foot up on a small stool. It was a beautiful pale-green room lighted with simple electric light fixtures, with the tables dressed in cream-colored linens with green-striped seats on the wicker chairs. Potted plants in Chinese pots were placed in the corners of the room.

Mr. McKinley stood up and pulled out my chair. "Hello, Miss Riley, I'm glad you could join us."

We chatted for a few minutes about the trial that day, quickly moving to the remarkable testimony of George Ruethling. "You've got to think that if this is Sam Shortridge's best witness, he doesn't have much of a case. I expect Sam will step up the defense on Monday." Mr. McKinley remarked.

"His testimony was absurd, that silly little man. I think the repeated bursts of laughter from the spectators and the jury made for a bad start for the *Times*. I never even met the man—sexual intercourse, indeed," Mrs. Tingley commented.

"I have never known Sam Shortridge to be at a loss for words, but after that debacle, he was downright speechless." Obviously delighted, Mr. McKinley chuckled, "You can quote me on that."

Nodding, I took my notepad from my satchel and wrote down his comment verbatim, along with the statement Mrs. Tingley had made in court on the subject.

"I guess Sam didn't take the time to interview the witness himself, or maybe *nobody* got around to interviewing him. He's a very busy lawyer, and now he's got his Senate campaign too, so I'm sure he delegates some of the witness preparation to an underling. That's sometimes the case with a high-profile lawyer like he is. This can be dangerous as you saw today."

"Sammy-boy was blindsided, and you don't see that often from him. He had no idea something like what happened was coming. Once it came out, he was stuck. He was afraid to try to unring the bell and question Ruethling further; he just wanted him gone, off the stand as fast as possible before things got worse."

"He knew I was going to go after him. I couldn't wait.! As for me, this was one of the most enjoyable cross-examinations I have ever conducted, and I've been at this a long time."

"It was obvious how much you were enjoying yourself, Judge," Mrs. Tingley told him dryly.

Mr. McKinley turned to me. "So what was your take on the testimony of George *H.* Ruethling, Miss Riley?"

"Well Mr. McKinley, the courtroom was hot and stuffy this afternoon. After a long day in there, people could use a good laugh, and laugh they did, repeatedly. I must say, you outdid yourself on your cross-examination."

I shook my head in mock disapproval. "You were very close to getting a spanking from Judge Torrance."

"I noticed that," he cut in with a broad smile, "but I couldn't resist. It wasn't a good day for the defense."

Nodding, "The General was clearly in defeat. He slumped in his chair after you finished with Mr. Ruethling. He obviously fully appreciated the disaster that had just unfolded before his eyes."

"And it is this remarkable performance that our jury will be taking home with them for the weekend." He paused and took a sip of water."

"I enjoyed the afternoon's proceedings as almost everyone else did," I said. It was quite a show. The General was not amused. He was frantically whispering in his lawyer's ear even before you started your cross-examination. He was probably trying to get Mr. Shortridge to clean things up with Mr. Ruethling before you came after him. Mr. Shortridge nodded as if in agreement, but he thought better of it."

"I would have done the same thing," Mr. McKinley said. He needed to get this disastrous witness off the stand. He could only have done more damage to the defense. Judge Torrance, I think it's safe to say, will be sharing the story of Mr. Rustling's sexual magnetism with his wife over dinner tonight.

"I don't think he was lying," I said. He was talked into his ridiculous position by the *Times* representatives. He practiced the written script they made up for him so many times that he came to believe what he testified to. It took him quite a while to recognize that he had been made to look mighty foolish. I felt a bit sorry for that little man when he left the stand with his head bowed and his tail between his legs."

"Well, I did *not* feel sorry for the man," Mrs. Tingley said; she was quite indignant. "He was totally irresponsible. Let's order. I'm hungry," she said gruffly.

OK, then, I thought, surprised at her tone.

The rotund Mrs. Tingley, who could afford to skip a meal or two, obviously got grumpy when she was tired and hungry.

Unperturbed, Mr. McKinley replied, "I'm hungry too," as he waved the waiter over.

Mrs. Tingley was a teetotaler; she drank tea with her dinner. We all had local fish of different varieties. Mr. McKinley did not order wine or dessert or ask us if we wanted any. I stuck with water.

After we ordered, I excused myself and used the telephone at the front desk to call Father at the paper with my two quotes for the next day's story. Jack picked up the telephone.

"*San Diego Union.*"

"Oh, hello, Jack. May I speak to my father?"

"He left about an hour ago. He gave me the story and told me you would call with two quotes from your dinner at the Brewster. Let me grab a pencil so I can write them down. I'll add them and give the printers the story and then head up there to pick you up."

I gave him the quotes.

"Okay, 'got it. What time do you think you'll be ready?"

"Mr. McKinley said he will see me home."

"No need. I'll come to get you. It's not far. It'll feel good to get out a bit."

Hmm… a short walk would be nice after being cooped up all day in the courtroom.

"Can you be here around seven?"

"Perfect, Jack replied, "that will give me a little time to finish my work. Wait for me in the lobby."

"Great," I said and hung up.

Charlie had left that morning on a train trip to San Francisco with his father for some sort of business meeting the following Monday. He told me that his Grandfather, Thomas Wilson Sr., was considering opening a bank there. The San Diego branch had been so successful he thought they might expand to have branches in San Francisco *and* Los Angeles.

His grandfather planned to meet them in the city and then take the train with Charlie and his father back to San Diego and stay for a week or two. I missed Charlie and couldn't wait to go to the St. James for his parent's New Year's Eve party.

"Can I get you a lift home, Miss Riley?" Mr. McKinley asked.

"No, thank you. A friend from the paper is coming to walk me home. It's not far."

Jack was in the lobby when we came in; I heard him before I saw him. "Mary Kate, I'm over here," he called with a big friendly smile, his too-long hair escaping from his cap and pencils popping out of his vest pocket along with his reading glasses. He came over to us and stuck out his hand to Mr. McKinley.

"Jack Flatly, sir."

The two men shook hands. Jack turned to Mrs. Tingley and gave her a rather flirtatious smile. "Mrs. Tingley, so nice to finally meet you. How is your trial going?"

"We'll soon find out; we expect the verdict next week," she replied. Are you a reporter too, young man?"

"Sure am, Ma'am—I'm kind of Miss Riley's assistant."

"He is *not*. He's one of our top reporters at the paper."

She smiled, looked at Jack, and shook her head. She turned her gaze back to me and gave me a funny smile. I suspected that she thought Jack was my beau.

Mr. McKinley looked at his pocket watch. "I've got to get going; I have trial work to do," he said. We all walked out together. The carriage was waiting out front.

"Good night," I replied. "Thank you for dinner. I hope you can find some time for me after the verdict."

"Sure thing, I enjoyed it." Mr. McKinley said and looked up at the clear night sky. "It looks like a nice night for a walk."

"Good night Kate," he said to Mrs. Tingley "I'm heading off to bed; I have had a very long day. I'm exhausted."

"Good night, Mr. McKinley, Mrs. Tingley," Jack said.

Mrs. Tingley smiled and nodded in response, looking pretty tired herself. Jack and I turned and walked a bit out of our way down Broadway as it was lighted, and then down my street, where it was pretty dark, just a few porch lights on to light our way. It was chilly, so we walked quickly to warm up.

I refused Jack's coat offer, but I took his arm when he offered it. It was an especially dark night with no moon, and our street had quite a few holes to trip an unwary pedestrian. Jack stumbled into one of them and almost took me down with him, but he was able to make a last-minute recovery. "Whoops, we best slow down a bit, or we're going to wind up on the ground," he said pleasantly.

He told me that he had heard all about George Ruethling's stint on the witness stand from Father. "He spent a bit more time on his story because it made such a good yarn."

Jack went over the comedy performance that was George Rustling's performance, but when he retold it, it sounded like he was there in the courtroom. He had already made it his tale and even added a couple of embellishments as an excellent Irish storyteller would wont to do. He had me laughing until tears came to my eyes. My parents were sitting in the living room when I came through the door with Jack following behind me.

"Oh my goodness, who is this stranger?" Mother said, standing up and reaching out to give Jack a hug.

He hugged her back and picked her up off her feet. "And lucky I am to get a squeeze from the prettiest girl in town."

"Oh, Jack," she said, it's so good to see you."

"Come have a sit-down," Father said with a big smile.

"Can I get you some lemon pie? I made it today." Mother asked.

"Well, I guess you could twist my arm," Jack replied.

"Let's sit at the table."

Mother led the way, put the teapot on the stove, and sliced large pieces of pie for Jack; one for Father, who was happy to have a second slice, and one for me.

301

As I took a bite of pie my mouth watered when its mild tartness hit my tongue. I spent a few minutes talking about my dinner with Mrs. Tingley and Mr. McKinley and, of course, about Mr. Ruethling.

After finishing his pie, Jack stood up. "That was delicious, and I thank you, but I must get home. I need to get in early tomorrow and get some stories finished for the Sunday edition.

"Thanks for fetching me, Jack," I said.

He nodded.

Mother stood on her tiptoes to give him a peck on the cheek.

"We'll see you tomorrow at the paper, Jack," Father said.

"Fine. Good night to ya."

Father shut the door, and I headed right up to my room. My day had caught up with me too.

Chapter 38

The first witness Monday morning was Mrs. George F. Mohn who is an attractive, pleasant woman of about forty. She testified in a very meek, yet straightforward manner in response to Mr. Shortridge's questioning. She claimed that Mrs. Tingley had separated her from her daughter at Lomaland.

"Mrs. Tingley told me that a mother's love was powerful, but it was not good for the child's education. Her plan at Lomaland was entirely independent of a mother's love," she told the jury.

"Katherine Tingley believes that mothers hold their children back because they can only go as far as their mothers went. She told me that she is going to make the children at Lomaland into workers, apostles for humanity, so they can go into the world and spread the word of Universal Brotherhood when they are grown."

Mrs. Mohn admitted that she knew before she moved to Lomaland that her child would live separately from her and that she would only see her on weekends. Most of the parents lived in another section of the property. "I didn't like that, so I left."

Mrs. Mohn's demeanor changed when she was questioned by Mr. McKinley. She looked at the jury when she testified with a look of anger, or was it fear on her face?

Mr. McKinley finished his cross-examination of this witness with this question, "What kind of education did your daughter receive at Lomaland, Ma'am?"

"My daughter got a good education there; she was far ahead of the students in her new school, and honestly, she misses the place."

"I have no further questions for this witness."

After Mrs. Mohn left the stand, the judge nodded to Mr. Shortridge. The defense calls Mrs. E. August Nereshiemer to the stand."

Mrs. Nereshiemer was a horse-faced woman who testified with what looked like a permanent grimace on her face. "Mrs. N. looks like she has serious elimination issues," my father whispered.

She testified in response to Mr. Shortridge's brief set of questions that she had been held as a prisoner at Lomaland and separated from her husband by Katherine Tingley. This claim, unlike so many of the others brought forth in the trial, *was* something that was printed in the articles published by the *Times*.

"I was treated like a convict, practically starved to death, worked like a slave in the fields, then forced out," she cried, "made to leave!" Her demeanor under Mr. Shortridge's questioning was dramatic but short.

Mr. McKinley stood up to cross-examine her. She squirmed in her chair, rubbed her neck, folded her arms, set her chin, and leveled an ominous stare in his direction. She was ready for incoming fire.

She testified in response to Mr. Shortridge's questioning that Katherine Tingley was ruining her marriage by keeping her husband from her, even suggesting that Mrs. Tingley had some kind of mysterious hold on him.

Mr. McKinley quickly disposed of this claim. "Mrs. Nereshiemer, isn't it true that you left Lomaland by choice?"

"Not really, no," she said, eyes narrowing, her tone angry and defensive.

"It was, in fact, at the insistence of your husband, Ma'am. Isn't that true?" She squirmed in her seat and simply stared defiantly at Mr. McKinley without answering.

"Ma'am?" he said.

"Mrs. Nereshiemer," the judge said, looking at her from his perch on his bench, "You are here to answer the lawyer's questions; you must answer Mr. McKinley's question."

At first, she paused, shot the same defiant look at the judge that she had directed at Mr. McKinley moments before, and then said meekly, "All right, but I know he is going to twist things... Yes, my husband insisted that I leave Lomaland and go live with my sister. So, I had no choice."

"Mrs. Tingley never spoke to you about leaving, did she?"

Mrs. Nereshiemer thought about the question for a moment and then replied "Well, no, but Katherine Tingley must have bewitched or hypnotized my husband to make him follow the Lomaland Theosophists with such ardor."

Ultimately she admitted that the request to leave Lomaland and separate from her husband was entirely at her husband's request.

"He made me leave and live with my sister. She must have hypnotized him or something."

Mr. McKinley asked her, "You don't have any information that Mrs. Tingley knows how to hypnotize anyone, do you, Madam?"

"No, but I bet she does," the witness sputtered, her face red in anger. Before she left the stand, she stood and directed her parting shot to the judge. "My brother is a lawyer. I assure you that I know how lawyers twist things and, and... I've been stipulated to," she told him then she turned and left the witness stand. Judge Torrance shook his head back and forth in dismay but said nothing.

The next witness called by the defense was Lena Morris. She testified that she was a former maid at Mrs. Tingley's home in New York City. She was a plain, angry, gimlet-eyed woman who clearly didn't want to be there.

She testified that she had worked for Mrs. Tingley for several years and that in her opinion, Mrs. Tingley's reputation was not good. "The woman's a fraud," she huffed to punctuate her statement, looking to the jurors for their concurrence.

Mrs. Morris said that she knew Mrs. Tingley was a spiritualist and had heard that she had given séances at the house "for money," she added. She admitted that she never saw Mrs. Tingley give a séance, "but I heard she did."

On Mr. Shortridge's questioning, she also suggested that Mrs. Tingley was abusive to her adopted daughter Flossie by making her do jobs in the house that "no child should be made to do." Mr. Shortridge left it at that and sat down.

This sounded pretty ominous to be sure. But, on cross-examination by Mr. McKinley, she admitted that those jobs included dusting the furniture, doing the dishes, and sweeping the floor. These jobs were nothing the hardworking farmers on the jury would object to a daughter doing in the house.

She ended her testimony by admitting that she considered Mrs. Tingley a fraud because of a dispute over money she was owed when she left her employ.

"She never paid me. I don't recall what it was all about or how much money was involved. After all, this was nearly a decade ago."

"Yes, indeed," Mr. McKinley replied. He then moved to have her testimony stricken as irrelevant. Judge Torrance agreed.

After lunch, the defense called Emile Nereshliner, a member of Mrs. Tingley's Cabinet at Lomaland. He seemed like a pleasant enough fellow who spoke with a strong German accent. His testimony was short and simply confirmed Mr. Shortridge's claim, which Mrs. Tingley never denied, that all the property at Lomaland as well as the Isis Theater downtown, were in Mrs. Tingley's name. "Her name is on all the deeds. We voted on this; it was unanimous."

Next, we heard the reading of the out-of-state deposition testimony of Thomas Johnson by a young attorney from Mr. Shortridge's firm. Mr. Johnson claimed that Mrs. Tingley was of low morals and once resided in a house of ill repute in Tennessee. He admitted that he didn't know who told him this and he admitted that he didn't know if Mrs. Tingley had ever even been to Tennessee.

After Mr. Shortridge's cohort finished reading this testimony, Mr. McKinley stood and faced the judge. "I move the court to strike all of Mr. Johnson's testimony. It's hearsay and irrelevant."

"Motion granted. Next witness, Mr. Shortridge," Judge Torrance said, clearly annoyed.

I followed the *Times'* coverage all through the trial. Harrison Otis described in his paper and press releases to the Associated Press what he called Judge Torrance's "improper striking key defense witnesses' testimony." This was the outcome of all the testimony by out-of-state witnesses whose depositions were read to the jury.

After the three o'clock break, Mr. Shortridge stood and announced, "The defense calls Louis Fitch to the stand."

Mr. Fitch, a pleasant-looking man of about forty-five, testified that he was a bookkeeper employed by the Universal Brotherhood for nine months. He was told he was being let go because he never balanced the books. He admitted that this was true but claimed he didn't have the time to do so because of Mrs. Tingley's constant demands.

He told the jury that besides being the bookkeeper, he also performed as Mrs. Tingley's assistant. In that role, he said he had many other duties that would change almost daily, "pretty much at her whim." He said that this was the real reason that he was fired. "And she never spoke up for me," he told the jury.

Mr. Fitch testified that Mrs. Tingley saw her role at Lomaland as a prophetess, a successor to Jesus Christ, Buddha, and Muhammad. "*The Tingleyites*" bought this hook, line, and sinker."

"What areas of life at Lomaland did Mrs. Tingley supervise?" Mr. Shortridge inquired.

"Mrs. Tingley managed every aspect of life at Lomaland: where people could live, who they could talk to, when they could talk, and what they should eat. She even interfered with relations between members of the same family."

"She is a hypocrite. She told her devotees that they should get up in the morning to greet the sunrise and eat a light breakfast, but she slept late and ate breakfast in her room… and a large breakfast it was. I was the one who brought the tray. There was no starving for her to help in her spiritual growth. She practically starved everyone else, but she was well-fed, I'll tell you that."

There was snickering in the gallery at this response.

"Did she impose a rule of silence on the devotees?"

"Not for herself, she didn't, Mr. Shortridge," he replied. "She wanted everyone there to be silent all the time. But as her assistant, I assure you that women rarely shut her trap. She preached living simply but dressed flamboyantly, spent money she didn't have, took extravagant trips, and put on lavish theatrical productions. This was all on other people's money."

He turned in his seat and looked directly at the jury. "She is a basket of contradiction, of hypocrisy. She preaches to us to eat less

308

for spiritual growth, yet she is overweight and eats her meals in her quarters away from prying eyes. She always had plenty to eat. The woman is a good fifty pounds overweight."

Mrs. Tingley remained stoic throughout Mr. Fitch's testimony, but she huffed when Mr. Fitch talked about her weight. This drew a warning glance from the judge, but he said nothing.

"What were Mrs. Tingley's views about marriage?" Mr. Shortridge asked him.

"She disapproved of marriage. She said we didn't need it. She felt that if the principles of Universal Brotherhood were lived by all, no marriage would be necessary."

The next subject broached by Mr. Shortridge was Mrs. Tingley's dog Spots. Again, this brought an air of silent anticipation to the courtroom. This might be some spooky stuff.

"Mrs. Tingley told me that her dog Spots was much more than a pet," Mr. Fitch recalled. He was referred to by her and many of her followers as *The Purple Inspiration.* She told me that the former leader of the Theosophists, William Quan Judge, entered into the dog when Judge died and she assumed leadership of the Universal Brotherhood. Mrs. Tingley claims that he inhabits the dog and still directs the activities of the Brotherhood."

Did Mrs. Tingley claim she could send thought waves?

"She did and she taught us to do so as well."

"Did you ever spread any thought waves?" Mr. Shortridge inquired in a sarcastic tone.

"Not to my knowledge, but I joined the others, and since they were all told they were spreading thought waves, I did what the rest did, 'stood there like a dummy."

Mr. Shortridge walked back to the counsel table and changed the subject. He then posed a series of questions suggesting Mrs. Tingley was a sexual libertine. She employed the practices of a loose woman at Lomaland, Mr. Fitch told the jury.

"Mrs. Tingley allowed some licentious practices at the Point. Isn't that true, sir?"

"It certainly is. "

"People were running around with flimsy, sexually suggestive attire. Is that your recollection of the situation, sir?"

"It is."

"And Mrs. Tingley's followers traipsed around in all manner of undress, isn't that true, sir?"

"That *is* true."

"Mr. Fitch, would you describe the immodest costumes worn at Lomaland?"

"I've seen them low-necked, sometimes as low as an evening gown, adding, "and then there were always togas, crossed in the front with a rope, open partially at the sides. I think that was indecent in effect."

"Did Mrs. Tingley wear skimpy, suggestive attire?"

"At her weight, how could she?" This response was greeted with laughter from the gallery and a warning glare from Judge Torrance.

Mr. McKinley stood, "Move to strike, Your Honor, non-responsive, opinion. "

"Sustained, just answer the question asked, sir," Judge Torrance ordered gruffly.

"Did Mrs. Tingley tell you she believed in free love?"

"Well, she didn't say that in so many words, Mr. Shortridge, but you could tell that was what she was getting at. I heard she once took a group of girls to New York City, and we all know what happens there."

Judge Torrance shook his head in frustration but said nothing.

"What about the craftsmen's outfits? What did those young men wear?" Mr. Shortridge asked.

"They wore plain brown outfits with most of their arms and legs exposed. Short pants; my wife didn't approve. She didn't like the bareness of the arms and legs, the way the muscles stuck out and things like that, or at least that's what she said."

Father leaned over and said, "Sounds like she appreciated the view."

"Did Katherine Tingley treat her followers as slaves or convicts?" Mr. Shortridge inquired as he tacked in yet another direction.

"Well, I wouldn't say convicts," Mr. Fitch told the jury, "She didn't lock them up or anything, but the devotees at Lomaland did the work of servants . . . slaves, I guess you could say."

"Everyone worked, even Mrs. Tingley—yes, she worked too, I'll give that to her; she's a hard worker. But, she's a slovenly, messy woman about her appearance. She'd do some work in the gardens and then she'd walk all over Lomaland with mud on her dress. She had no pride in her appearance, and yet she considers herself the grand leader of Lomaland."

Mr. Shortridge left it at that and moved on to Mrs. Tingley's practices in what he called the "spirit world." Mr. Fitch testified that

Mrs. Tingley told him many times that she liked to stay in the spirit world and that she only came back to serve humanity.

"She was often under the influence of liquor on these occasions," Mr. Fitch added.

"I was not," Mrs. Tingley said out loud. "I don't even drink."

Judge Torrance pointed at her with a stern warning in his eyes, "Silence, Madam, or I will ask you to leave the courtroom."

She nodded and then bowed her head in submission.

Mr. McKinley dismissed Mr. Fitch's testimony with a disgusted dismissal. "No questions."

Father told me at the break that Mr. McKinley got good testimony from Fitch and didn't want to give Mr. Shortridge a chance to unring the bell. He said that without cross-examination, the opposing lawyer may not ask any further questions.

Sam Shortridge next called several other witnesses who confirmed that Mrs. Tingley liked to reside in the spirit world whenever possible. Mr. McKinley moved to strike this testimony as irrelevant because this was not the subject of any of the libelous statements that were the subject of the trial. This time the judge let the testimony stand.

Mr. Fitch and the other witnesses that day did little to support the defense in connection with the statements made in the *Times* articles. Still, Father told me that the cumulative effect of their testimony might convince the jury that Mrs. Tingley was someone they didn't like and wouldn't want to give money to. I agreed. Mr. Shortridge scored some points that afternoon.

The next day, two young women testified that Mrs. Tingley worked everyone at Lomaland very hard, "almost like slaves." They admitted that "Mother Purple" worked in the fields herself. "Everyone works hard at Lomaland," one of them told the jury.

After these witnesses concluded, Mr. Shortridge had his young associate attorney once again read the deposition testimony of several out-of-state witnesses. After this dull-as-dirt performance, which consisted of the witnesses reporting all manner of unfounded gossip and accusations, none of it related to the case but which did, if believed, cast shade on the character of Katherine Tingley. This even included the testimony of another witness who claimed Mrs. Tingley as a young woman, once lived in a house of ill repute in Tennessee.

Mr. McKinley successfully had the testimony stricken from the record. "You may _not_ consider this evidence," the judge told the jury.

After these witnesses concluded, the day ended with Mr. Edward Parker called by the defense.

Mr. Parker is a nondescript, fastidious gentleman with white hair and a neatly trimmed mustache. He wore a brown plaid jacket with a spiffy string tie and shiny new brown cowboy boots which he apparently bought for the occasion. He must have figured he should dress as they do in the West, thinking it would give him an extra shot of credibility. Let's just say this effort didn't work for him.

Mr. Parker testified that he had been commissioned by a group of New York Theosophists to go out and dig up dirt; he called it "negative information, about Kathrine Tingley. He admitted that he learned this from talking to other Theosophists who didn't like Mrs. Tingley either. He turned and looked at the jury.

"They knew, as I do, that she's a flim-flam. She should be prosecuted for fraud."

"I have no further questions of this witness, Your Honor," Mr. Shortridge told the judge and returned to his seat.

Mr. McKinley stood at the counsel table for his cross-examination. "You claim sir, that Mrs. Tingley should be prosecuted as a criminal for fraud. Did I get that right?"

"Yes, sir."

"Really, Mr. Parker, what crimes did Mrs. Tingley commit?"

"Well, no crimes, but I think she did something funny to take over the Theosophists."

Mr. McKinley got the witness to squirm when he drilled down in a series of questions about his claim that a *number* of people told him that Katherine Tingley once lived in a house of ill repute, as he called it.

"I can't really recall any of them by name. I can try to get them for you," he added.

"That won't be necessary. Your Honor, I move to strike all of the testimony about the house of ill repute. It is irrelevant and, like so much of this witness's testimony, has nothing to do with the issues in this case."

"Any response Mr. Shortridge?"

"No, Your Honor."

Judge Torrance looked at the jury. "Motion to strike granted. The testimony on this subject is stricken. You may not consider it."

Mr. Parker admitted, in response to one of Mr. McKinley's questions, that he had contacted Harrison Otis to volunteer to give the information he had found about Mrs. Tingley as a witness in this trial. "I contacted him after learning about the case by reading the *New York Times.*"

"I read it every morning," he added. "I sent a wire to Mr. Otis and at first received no reply. Later, about three weeks before the

314

trial, I was contacted by investigators sent by the *Times*. They came to the house. Nice fellas, they were. They knew quite a bit about Mrs. Tingley that I didn't know."

He said that they discussed his potential testimony with him and made arrangements for him to come to California. "They typed up what I was going to testify to and sent it to me. I was told to review this before the trial, and I did."

"Did you bring it with you today, in case you needed to study a bit more?" Mr. McKinley said sarcastically.

Mr. Parker didn't notice. "No, sir, I left it at home. I can tell you what was in it, though."

"You already have," Mr. McKinley replied.

He crossed the room to the open window as if to get a breath of air; when he got there, he turned to the witness.

"Mr. Parker, I assume you met with Mr. Shortridge here before the trial?"

"Never met the man," he said indignantly.

"But you did meet with other lawyers in his firm, also representing the *Times,* who prepared you for your testimony here today?"

"Yes, sir, I did *that*. We met twice last week."

Mr. Parker went on to tell the jury that his Theosophist friends back in New York were excited about the prospect of his testifying against Mrs. Tingley in this famous case.

"They can't wait for me to get home to tell them all about it," he said excitedly. He wound up his testimony by saying that he had met Mrs. Tingley only once after a conference she had given in New York.

"Did you meet her one-on-one, face-to-face?" Mr. McKinley asked him. Ever talk to her?"

"No, I was part of a group. She had such a powerful ability to mesmerize people that I could feel her glare at me across the room even when my back was turned to her. The force of that glance was so strong that she made me turn around and look at her."

This got everyone's attention, anticipating a possible repeat of Mr. Ruethling's testimony of the Friday before.

"What happened after Katherine Tingley mesmerized you and made you turn to look at her?"

Mr. Parker considered this for a few seconds and said simply, "Why, nothing, sir."

"No further questions," Mr. McKinley said and turned, walked to his counsel table, and sat down, shaking his head in disgust.

"Mr. Shortridge?" Judge Torrance sighed and looked at the clock. It was four-thirty-five.

Sam Shortridge remained seated. "No questions, Your Honor."

"I have a few things to take up with the lawyers, the judge said, looking toward the gallery, but everyone else may go home."

"This court is adjourned."

As Father and I walked back to the paper, he turned to me. "If this is all Sam Shortridge has, he's in trouble. These witnesses reminded me of *The Horribles*."

"Pretty close," I replied.

"Shortridge dressed them up nice, but they were still clowns. Somehow I can't see that plump, grandmotherly Queen Victoria look-alike as a resident of a house of ill repute," He chuckled.

"Come to think of it; there wouldn't be many sales made if she was."

"I suspect that Judge Torrance's pow-wow with the lawyers after the court today will halt this nonsense testimony or strictly limit it. My experience with this judge is that he gives the lawyers a wide berth to put on their cases. But so far, Shortridge has offered very little evidence pertinent to the case. This is why the judge struck most of the testimony."

"Evidence about claimed facts drawn from a bunch of people who got their information third or fourth-hand is not evidence any jury should consider. Not to mention that the claimed misdeeds of Mrs. Tingley, even if they are true, are mostly over a decade old and have nothing to do with what she is doing at Lomaland."

"That's true, Father, but the jurors heard this nonsense. I think some damage was done, and there were so many witnesses saying pretty much the same thing, that she's a fraud."

As we turned the corner on Fourth Street, heading towards the paper, Father continued his take on the day's proceedings.

"Sam Shortridge is simply putting shiny objects before the jury to distract them from the real issues. The *Times* admits to printing the materials; the only issue is whether they're true. Not one of these witnesses spoke to that critical issue."

"A bunch of smoke and mirrors is the eminent Mr. Shortridge's only path to victory, even a partial victory, denying her damages or limiting the amount of money she gets. You never know with a jury."

"I expect, that Shortridge will come to court tomorrow with his wings clipped and that the type of evidence we saw today will be seriously curtailed." Father opened the front door for me once we reached the paper and followed me in.

"Shortridge is simply playing the hand he's been given, Mary Kate. I'm sure that Otis refused to settle the matter. He's a stubborn old varmint. He isn't about to back down to a woman. He doesn't care how much money he has to spend to beat up Katherine Tingley even more, to punish her to dare to oppose him and in battle no less."

He stopped when he got to my little office. I squeezed behind my desk. Father paused, put his hands on the door jam, and finished his assessment of the day's performance.

"And to top it off, Otis makes money on the fight. He knows the battle itself makes good copy and sells papers. Either way, he wins. He wants to let his victims know that if they fight the General, they are in for quite a battle. Lawsuits are expensive. Otis wants to discourage others from taking him on, even if his conduct warrants it."

Father gets pretty wound up about the case. He loves to dissect it with me, not only what happened but why and what impact one event or another might have on the outcome. He thinks a lot about how he would present issues to a jury if he were the lawyer. He would have been a great lawyer. After all, lawyers and newspapermen are both wordsmiths and storytellers, both skills my father has in spades.

I worked late that night, and after Father gave me his story notes, he went home early. Jack and I finalized it for the next morning's addition. Charlie had taken a great picture of Mrs. Tingley and Mr. McKinley, which went on the front page with the story. Ben was going to pick Charlie up at my house, so we all walked home together, sharing our day and having a laugh or two.

We were a team now, I thought, the Three Musketeers, although more and more, I felt that two of the musketeers, Charlie and I, were becoming much closer.

318

This time, when we got to our house, Jack didn't come in. He knew Charlie and I wanted some alone time which we had these days almost every night. My parents often went to bed before we got home to give us some time together.

"Good night, you two. Now you behave yourself, Charlie," Jack called as he turned and walked towards his house.

Chapter 39

The next morning when the trial resumed, one of Mr. Shortridge's underling attorneys again read the deposition testimony from the written transcript of several out-of-state witnesses; all were all members of a rival sect of Theosophists.

These witnesses all told the same sorry tale: Mrs. Tingley was a fraud, a grifter, and a pretender to the throne as the leader of the Theosophists. Like many of the live witnesses called by the defense, the testimony was based upon second or third-hand reports they had *heard* about Mrs. Tingley.

The defense then called John F. Price of New York. He testified that he had known Mrs. Tingley seven years before the trial. "She was a spiritualist in belief and is given to going into trances like a spirit medium. I have seen her in a trance giving forth prophesies that never came true and all that sort of thing."

He admitted to being a devotee of spiritualism himself and said he had good results with other mediums. He told the jury that he consulted astrologers and believed in automatic writing but had little faith in Mrs. Tingley's ability as a spiritualist.

"She pretended to be able to see the future and talk to the dead, but I believe she was a fraud trying to bilk people who came to her out of their money," he told the jury.

Mr. McKinley objected to all the testimony and asked the judge to strike it. "Whether Mrs. Tingley is or was a spiritualist years ago has nothing to do with this case."

Judge Torrance obliged and struck the testimony of these witnesses, telling the jury, "You may not consider any of this testimony." He turned to Mr. Shortridge, irritated. "Now, let's move on."

Mr. Shortridge began to rise and argue this ruling, but the judge put up his hand to silence him. "None of this testimony is relevant to the issues in this trial. It was a colossal waste of time, Mr. Shortridge, now sit down," he ordered; he was angry this time. He remained standing and began to argue, but the judge shot him down with an ominous glare.

Mr. Shortridge next called Mr. Frances Pierce to the stand. Things didn't go as planned. Mr. Pierce is a tall, thin, pleasant-looking man who wore an expensive-looking gray suit, a starched white shirt, and a gray silk tie. He testified in a straightforward, business-like manner. He told the jury that about ten years before, he left a successful business career to follow Katherine Tingley and the Universal Brotherhood.

"I was with her at Point Loma from the beginning. I wear many hats in the organization. I am the General Secretary and a member of its governing Cabinet. I am also in charge of the discipline of the boys at the Raja School."

He said that he considered his most important role with the Universal Brotherhood to be that of chief adviser to Mrs. Tingley. He said that he had been in that role since the founding of what he called the Point Loma experiment. He had high praise for Mrs. Tingley's management skills and her vision.

You could tell from the start of his brief testimony that he was totally in support of what the Universal Brotherhood and its leader, Katherine Tingley, aimed to achieve—not only at Lomaland but also in their efforts throughout the country and worldwide.

"Our mission has always been the betterment of the lives of everyday men and women," he told the jury.

He seemed sincere, and his conservative demeanor, as well as his history as a successful businessman who gave up that life to serve humanity, ended up hurting the defense. This was a successful, intelligent, reasonable man whose testimony was at odds with Mr. Shortridge's efforts to portray the activities of the Universal Brotherhood as something kooky, immoral, sinister, and dangerous.

Mr. Shortridge asked him a series of questions about the management and control of the Universal Brotherhood. Father called this his no-man-likes-a-bossy-woman issue. "It might just work with these farmers and ranchers."

Mr. Pierce answered each of Sam Shortridge's questions in a thoughtful, straightforward manner.

"Mrs. Tingley had been given, by a vote of the Cabinet, the last word on the Universal Brotherhood's operations, financial and otherwise, isn't that true?"

"Yes, it was a unanimous vote."

"So, Mr. Pierce, Katherine Tingley has autocratic control of the whole operation of the Universal Brotherhood, isn't that true?

"Yes, that's true," he admitted.

"And that's for her entire life. Am I right about that, sir?"

"Yes, that's true, but the Cabinet has input," he added. Mr. Shortridge paused, it looked like he considered objecting, but then he proceeded.

"So when Mr. Otis says that Mrs. Tingley is the boss at Lomaland, that's true, isn't it?"

"Yes, I supposed so."

"And it is true that Mrs. Tingley is: "she who must be obeyed" out there to use Mr. Otis' words?"

He smiled. "I guess that would be true."

"And if the Cabinet doesn't agree with one of Mrs. Tingley's decisions, they don't have the power to overrule it, do they?"

"It is true that if we do not agree with her decision, according to our constitution, the Cabinet has no power to second-guess Mrs. Tingley; but we do have the option to change the constitution that gives her that final say-so."

"I move to strike, Mr. Shortridge said to the judge. The witness should be instructed to simply answer yes or no."

"Overruled."

"And the Cabinet has never made any efforts to overrule Mrs. Tingley's edicts, have they, sir?"

"No. "

"I have no further questions of this witness, Your Honor."

"Cross, Mr. McKinley?" the judge asked.

He rose and stood at his counsel table. "And the Cabinet voted unanimously to give Mrs. Tingley the final say, isn't that the case, sir?"

"That's true."

"What would happen if the Cabinet disagreed with one of Mrs. Tingley's decisions?"

"We would discuss the issue among ourselves, then with her, and in all instances, we worked things out. We all agreed that there has to be someone who has the final say."

"And that was considered so important the Cabinet voted to give that final say to Katherine Tingley in the organization's constitution. Isn't that true?

"Yes."

I have no further questions of this witness."

The last witness that afternoon called by the defense was Dr. Gerome Anderson. He came to court dressed in an attractive gray pin-striped suit, a high-collared white shirt, and a plain grey tie that went nicely with his thick head of white hair. He is a handsome, distinguished-looking man who reminded me of Dr. Haskell, our family doctor.

Dr. Anderson told the jury he was a medical doctor and a long-time Theosophist. As he testified, he looked at the jury often, probably to avoid Mrs. Tingley's glare; she sat at the counsel table where she faced the witness. Most of the jury and the spectators could only see her expression from the side of her face.

This time, she could not keep the stoic, poker face she wore for the most part with all of the other witnesses. Her expression reflected a sense that Dr. Anderson was a threat to her, and to some extent, she was right.

The good doctor testified under Mr. Shortridge's examination that he had spent considerable time at Lomaland but kept his home and medical practice in San Francisco. He appeared on the stand as an honest and amiable witness.

It soon became apparent that if Sam Shortridge had saved him as the most powerful witness for the defense, to deliver the *coup de grâce* against Mrs. Tingley, he was in for a disappointment. But, more than any other witness, Dr. Anderson managed to leave some mud on her skirts at the end of the case. His responses to Mr. Shortridge's questions about his experiences at Lomaland were straightforward and believable.

324

He testified that he had been a long-time member of the Cabinet for the Universal Brotherhood but was no longer affiliated with the operations at the Point.

"I still am a Theosophist, just not the Tingley version of it."

"Everything at Point Loma is show and pretense, but she hasn't accomplished much. She is a megalomaniac and suffers under the delusion that she is some exalted personality. The worst is that her followers have suffered as a result."

"She chose purple as her royal color, wore gowns in that color, and called herself the name of it, The Purple Lady, The Purple Mother, The Purple Queen, sometimes just Purple."

"What was your role at Lomaland, Doctor Anderson?" Mr. Shortridge asked him.

"I was designated by Katherine Tingley, along with about ten other men, to be what she called Scribes. As I understood it, Scribes were tasked with expounding on what she called the Lost Mysteries of the Lost Antiquities, but we never did. She never found them, the Lost Antiquities, I mean."

This triggered soft laughter in the courtroom. Even the ordinarily stoic Judge Torrance smiled at this statement.

Doctor Anderson told Mr. Shortridge that he had observed when he visited Lomaland, many absurd and wasteful ceremonies. "I am embarrassed that I participated in them for so long."

"Did you participate in immoral midnight ceremonies at Lomaland, Doctor?" Mr. Shortridge asked him with a decidedly self-righteous tone.

"Well, they were not immoral; they might have been more interesting if they were," he quipped. This again drew laughter from the jury and the gallery and another smile from Judge Torrance.

"What they were was just plain silly and had nothing to do with Theosophy. Katherine Tingley came up with all these ceremonies and costumes to go with them. She has a flair for the dramatic, that's for sure."

"One ceremony and there were many; we wore silly-looking Greek-like costumes of lightweight muslin; togas, she called them. I put mine on along with the rest of the Scribes. I don't know why we were called Scribes; we never wrote anything," he added.

Mr. Shortridge interrupted him. "And those flimsy togas were indecent, isn't that true, sir?" his voice raised in heated outrage.

"No, the costumes were worn over our nightclothes. It was midnight. I remember it because it was cold that night with the wind blowing up the cliffs from the ocean where we stood, freezing our rear ends off. These flimsy costumes were open on the side with no protection from the wind and cold."

"But these flimsy togas were worn sometimes without underclothes beneath them, the bare naked body visible. Isn't that true, sir?" Mr. Shortridge sounded shocked, outraged.

"Not that I ever observed," he said dryly.

"What did you do that night, Doctor, in the ceremony you referred to?" Mr. Shortridge asked.

"We were going to the site of what was to be a new school at Lomaland. It was to be called The School for the Lost Mysteries of Antiquity. The building had not been started. I guess they had to find the Lost Mysteries first."

"We sat on the cold ground in this vacant lot and waited for Mrs. Tingley for quite a long time. She finally arrived with her dog Spots. She spent some time, at first, talking about how wonderful a pet he was."

Dr. Anderson turned and looked directly at the jurors who seemed very interested in what he had to say on this topic.

"And Mrs. Tingley told you that night that Spots acted as a medium through which the previous leader of the Theosophists, William Quan Judge, spoke to her. Isn't that true, sir?"

"I don't remember that. I guess it could have happened, but it was late at night by that time, and I wasn't that interested in the Spots stories Mrs. Tingley was telling us. I was tired and cold and wanted to go home and go to bed."

"I do remember that a fellow Scribe told me when we were walking home that night when we got to the subject of Spots, that Mrs. Tingley pinched the dog's tail to make him yelp at appropriate moments in her narrative as if he were talking to her."

"Do you recall anything else that happened at that ceremony Doctor?" Mr. Shortridge asked in a low voice, laced with suspicion, hinting in his question that we were about to hear something ominous.

"Not really, not at all ominous." At one point in the proceedings, she passed around some fruit that she claimed had mystical properties. It was served on a beautiful gold tray. I ate it along with the rest of the Scribes. Mrs. Tingley ate it too. It tasted like plain old fruit to me." The good doctor smiled and shook his head from side to side. He seemed to be thinking back on that night.

"Was anything happening that night of an immoral or secular nature, any gross immoralities?" Once again, there was outrage in his voice when Mr. Shortridge asked this question; he sounded a bit like the Reverend Dimsdale of *Scarlet Letter* fame.

Dr. Anderson laughed and shook his head. "No, absolutely not. I wish there had been. It would have been considerably more diverting than listening to Katherine Tingley ramble on about things personal and philosophical. This nonsense, which I willingly

327

participated in, was all created by Mrs. Tingley. It had nothing to do with Theosophy, or anything else, for that matter."

"Any other ceremonies you can tell us about, Dr. Anderson?"

The witness shook his head in disgust, embarrassed that he had gone along with these silly routines.

"Yes, I can recall another ceremony. It was at sunrise, at about six. This time I just watched, sitting on the staircase of one of the temples. I was up anyway; I'm an early riser."

"Most of the participants wore costumes with sunflowers sewn on the front. Some took off their shoes and marched around barefoot singing songs. It was in the summer, so it was pretty warm."

"There wasn't anything untoward or salacious about this ceremony either. Mrs. Tingley wasn't there. She never held forth until about the crack of noon." This drew a snicker from the gallery.

"Were these people worshiping the sun?" Mr. Shortridge said somberly.

"No. It was just a goofy, welcome-the-day ceremony, another Tingley creation. There were many of this type on the Point. They seemed to make people feel part of something good, so I guess they were all right."

"Did Mrs. Tingley ever wear these costumes?"

"No. Mostly she would wear flowing wrappers. She would cover these with special embroidered robes if visitors were coming; to appear more queenly, I suppose. I believe they were in purple, as she favored that color, but the color of a woman's attire is a question a man is very seldom able to answer."

"Any other ceremonies you can recall?"

328

"I participated in one that was billed as a welcoming ceremony for a newly-married couple. It was late at night. We carried torches to their home, sang songs, and chanted from the *Gita*. Most people didn't know the chants and were just kind of moving their lips, mumbling along with the rest of the group. The married couple never came out of their house. They probably had more interesting things to do. They couldn't hear us, so it didn't matter."

Sam Shortridge, hoping to end the day on a high note, asked Dr. Anderson about the issue of underfeeding children.

He told the jury that he disagreed with Mrs. Tingley's policy of reducing the food given to babies and children. His testimony fell far short of the defense claim that the children were kept on the verge of starvation, as claimed in the *Times* articles.

"The resident physician at Lomaland wanted the children to be fed more; Mrs. Tingley wanted them fed less. She believed eating less would help kill the lower impulses in favor of their higher, more spiritual selves. What she based this idea on, I don't know. I never saw any starving children, I can tell you that. I'm a doctor, so I supported the doctor's view on this issue."

Mr. Shortridge paused for a second, maybe two. It seemed like a long pause which increased the tension in the room, everyone wondering what he would do next.

Then he pulled out his bow and a shiny arrow and aimed it at Katherine Tingley's heart.

"Do you consider Mrs. Tingley a fraud, Dr. Anderson?"

His arrow went awry. "Was she a fraud? No, not that I could see," he replied. "She seemed to believe in what she was doing and was a very hard worker for the cause."

Mr. Shortridge fired back in a cynical tone. "And that cause was to serve herself, was it, not sir?"

He looked rather sad and answered softly. "No, that's *not* true. It was to serve humanity, to make things better in this world."

"She did appropriate money for her own use, didn't she?"

"Technically, no, but I will say she was extravagant in funding the many ceremonies and theatrical productions at Lomaland and the Isis Theater in town. The issue was brought up often in the Cabinet meetings, but it never went anywhere."

"I personally felt that the money should have been spent elsewhere to promote Theosophist ideals rather than to satisfy Mrs. Tingley's need to be involved in stage productions. She is a disappointed, foiled actress."

Doctor Anderson turned in his seat again and faced the jury. "She told us that she used to be in a theater company as a young woman. She would often talk to us longingly about those days. She loved it and greatly romanticized her experiences in a traveling dramatic troupe. I don't fault her for that; we all pretty- up the experiences of our past, of our youth."

"I will say that her skills as an actress do come in handy as a spiritual leader. She is a dynamic and compelling speaker when she wants to be. When she got into personal issues, such as the incredible dog Spots, hmm… not really."

Doctor Anderson paused, and for the first time, he looked directly at Mrs. Tingley, who was seated below him; it was a rather kindly look. He turned back to the jury.

"There is no question that she is an excellent fundraiser and often went on speaking tours to collect money. They were always very successful. Mrs. Tingley was without question, our number one rainmaker for the cause of Universal Brotherhood as practiced at the Point when I was there. So, I guess you could say she wasted a good deal of money on extravagant theatrical productions and crazy ceremonies. Still, she was the principal breadwinner, so I guess she earned the right to spend at least some of the money as she thought best."

"But really, Dr. Anderson, her extravagance wouldn't be best for her followers, would it?" Mr. Shortridge asked him.

"Her claim was that the theatrical presentations she staged were good publicity, good public relations for our cause. The ceremonies increased the fervor of the faithful, she told us. And, as I observed, to some extent, she was right on both counts.

"Many of us feared, and I was one of them, that with this kind of spending, the money might run out, the donations might dry up, and we needed to be prepared for that. We expressed this concern, and it went nowhere."

"But for me, after a while, I became disenchanted with what we were achieving. I started visiting less and less, and my stays grew shorter as time went on. The bloom was off the rose. I just didn't like the changes in Theosophy that Lomaland represented, so I left. I'm still a Theosophist but not a Tingley Theosophist.

Changing course, Mr. Shortridge asked, "Do you have any criticism of the way Mrs. Tingley treated the children at the school?"

"I do," Dr. Anderson replied. I considered it degrading to train the children to worship her, to have them believe her to be a divine being. This would have an injurious effect on any child."

"So she wanted them to treat her as a Christ, a Buddha or Mohamad, some divine figure?"

"Yes, that was my impression."

"And the children at Point Loma treated her as a saint, some as a great avatar, an incarnation of the almighty, isn't that true?"

"That is true, Mr. Shortridge."

Mrs. Tingley jumped at this, leaned over, and whispered something in Mr. McKinley's ear. She had been wounded.

Mr. Shortridge appeared to have lost his steam and stood for a minute gathering his thoughts when Judge Torrance abruptly asked him,

"Any further questions, Mr. Shortridge?"

"No, Your Honor." He sat down.

Mr. McKinley, any cross-examination?

He stood, "Yes, Your Honor. He unbuttoned his jacket and tucked his thumbs in his suspenders before he started his questioning. This move worked well with his good old-boy persona.

"Now, Dr. Anderson, you don't know if the children at Lomaland were told to treat Mrs. Tingley as you have described, do you?"

"No, I don't."

"And you don't know if they treated her this way simply out of their respect or admiration, even love for Katherine Tingley, do you?"

"No, I do not. I do know she let it go on, and she didn't put a stop to it."

Mr. McKinley responded by asking Judge Torrance to strike the last part of his answer as nonresponsive to the question.

"Denied," the judge said simply.

"May I address that ruling, Your Honor?"

"No, you may not. Now move on," he said, obviously irritated. Judge Torrance often got short-tempered at the end of the court day and gave the lawyers less leeway.

Mr. McKinley turned back to Dr. Anderson. "You aware that the children at Lomaland often referred to Katherine Tingley as Mother Purple or simply Mother? Isn't that true?"

"It is."

"But Mrs. Tingley didn't tell them to call her that, did she?"

"I don't know."

"In fact, she asked them to stop calling her that. Isn't that true?"

"Yes," he said softly, his response barely audible.

"Now, let me change horses for a minute. Since we were talking about the garb Mrs. Tingley wears at Lomaland, Mr. Fitch testified here about that. Do you know Mr. Fitch, Doctor?"

"Yes, not well, but I am acquainted with him. He was supposedly an accountant for us at the Point. He never did balance the books, so we had to let him go."

"He told us in his testimony a few days ago that he considered Mrs. Tingley a slovenly woman because he often saw her in work clothes, soiled with mud or dirt on them after working outside. Did you ever see her dressed like that at Lomaland?"

Dr. Anderson looked chagrined. "Yes, I did… I guess so, but that's a bit unfair. Mrs. Tingley often wore clothes she could work in outside in the gardens. Most of us worked in the gardens; it was part of life there. Naturally, our clothes got dirty; hers did too."

"Most people that came to the Point, including Katherine Tingley, worked hard. We were there for what we could give, and most of us did give: our money, time, and talent, and not for our

333

own benefit, but to create a better world, to serve humanity. We all felt we were part of a worthy cause, something better than ourselves."

Mr. McKinley walked back to his counsel table. "I have no further questions of this witness, Your Honor."

Mr. Shortridge, anything further? May this witness be excused, Mr. Shortridge?"

"He may be excused, Your Honor."

Dr. Anderson didn't look at Mrs. Tingley when he left the stand. He mostly avoided looking at her when he testified and instead directed his comments either to the lawyer that was questioning him or to the jury.

Mrs. Tingley leveled her powerful gaze at him throughout his testimony. But other than that, she did not betray her feelings by her demeanor and had no visible reaction to what was mostly derogatory testimony by this witness about her version of Theosophy as practiced at the Point.

She sat expressionless, face forward when Dr. Anderson left the stand and walked in front of her. She hadn't attended the trial most days, but she wanted to be present for what was expected to be the testimony of the key witness for the defense. Indeed, Dr. Anderson was the most powerful witness Mr. Shortridge put in the witness box and did the most damage to Mr. Tingley.

He made an excellent witness who gave a fair and reasonable opinion as to the practices at Lomaland as he saw them firsthand. None supported the claims made in the *Times'* articles. Still, he painted Katherine Tingley as a disappointed actress and an autocratic, sometimes silly leader.

Judge Torrance looked at the clock and then at Mr. Shortridge. "Do you have another witness?"

Sam Shortridge stood. "No, Your Honor, the Defense rests."

This statement was punctuated by the sound of the clock ticking forward. It was ten minutes past three.

"This court is adjourned," Judge Torrance announced. "Happy New Year to you all. Closing arguments will start first thing Friday morning."

The judge hadn't planned to close down early, but that was how it turned out.

Yahoo! I needed time to prepare for the big doings at the St. James that night. Charlie was going to pick me up at eight.

Chapter 40

Charlie looked elegant in his black tuxedo with tails, no less, when he picked me up to take me to the party. He looked at me with approval when I came down the stairs in my gold gown, my hair untethered around my face. Mother had inserted a gold silk panel in the dress at the bust line and created a matching high collar at my throat. This covered up my deficiencies in the bust area quite well. Mother was so skillful as a seamstress that nobody could have ever dreamed that this was not part of the original design of this spectacular gown. I couldn't wait to see Fiona Riggs in Mother's version of her lovely dress. I wore the pearls that Charlie gave me.

Predictably Mother frowned upon my hairstyle. We compromised. She left my hair down and placed a couple of pearl hairpins on each side to keep my hair from falling in my face. My wild red curls still tumbled around my face and down my back.

I could tell by the way he looked at me when I came down the stairs that Charlie approved—at first. He hurt my feelings, though, when he asked Mother if she could put my hair up like she had when he had taken me to the anniversary party.

"You look beautiful, Mary Kate, but wearing your hair up is more appropriate for this formal event."

Mother agreed with Charlie. He meant well, but still, it hurt. We went upstairs, and she quickly put my hair under control on top of my head.

"I seriously doubt that anyone at the party would care if I had my hair up or down, Mother," I told her, irritated.

Charlie is the conservative son of a banker and not a man to go against the grain. This annoyed me sometimes. When we arrived at St. James, I soon forgot about my hair.

The ballroom was decorated for New Year's Eve. A giant 1903 in silver and black hung over the bandstand. Jack wasn't there. Charlie said that he told him that he had made other plans. I was pretty sure he didn't have the clothes or the interest in an elegant occasion like this one.

Charlie said he had offered Jack a tuxedo, but he said no, explaining that it was not his kind of party. He was right—I just couldn't picture Jack Flatly in a tuxedo and tails kicking up his heels at the St. James.

"You look stunning," Fiona Riggs said when she saw me, very much wearing the proud look of a mother hen. She was standing with her husband near the bar.

"John, this is my young friend Mary Kate Riley, and you already know her handsome escort, Charlie Wilson." I nodded, and the two men shook hands. He turned to me, "I have heard so many nice things about you from my wife Miss Riley."

Charlie waltzed me around the dance floor all evening. It seemed fitting in this elegant ballroom; it was so romantic. Some of Charlie's friends were there, including Pamela Spaulding. She and her beau, Edward, Eddie she called him, sat with us at our table. We had a great time together and often changed partners when it was time to dance. Eddie is quite shy, but he's an excellent dancer.

There were very few young people there; the crowd consisted mainly of friends and business associates of Charlie's parents. At midnight the band played "Auld Lang Syne," and Charlie kissed me. It was a passionate kiss. I kissed him right back, and he bent me way back and kissed me again. We both laughed. I looked around; everyone on the dance floor seemed to be kissing.

337

"Happy New Year, Mary Kate Riley," he said.

"Happy New Year, Charlie Wilson."

I got a fourth kiss at my door. Charlie started courting me in earnest after that including walking me home from the paper most nights which involved kisses goodnight too. Charlie was often invited to stay for a late dinner and he and Mother got to know each other better.

We all worked late every trial day as we had to finalize and edit the stories of the proceedings. Father left a bit earlier than the rest of us after finishing his trial story for the day. Charlie had to prepare the pictures taken that day and get the photographs to the printers, who stayed late too. Jack handled the rest of the news and got down to the courthouse as much as time allowed. He was there for most of the important parts of the trial, but only after he covered the rest of the day's news, and he worked nights too. The *Tingley* trial was a big moment in San Diego's brief history, and we all were excited about witnessing it. *And recording it too, I thought.*

My parents knew that Charlie and I were getting serious as time passed. I could tell that Jack could see this, too, but he didn't say anything, at least to me. Charlie and I got together often with Jack and Mary, going to various events with them around town.

Were they getting serious?

I hadn't seen Jack with anyone else in a while. Sometimes Charlie and I would go out with Pamela and Eddie or Theodora and Johnny, her current flame. Johnny was a bit of a smart-aleck, and Charlie didn't care much for him. We shared this assessment. It wasn't long before Theodora moved to a new swain, and the problem solved itself.

Charlie and I always had a great deal of fun together, and we had a lot in common. He loved books. We now shared a love of photography. Henry and Babe bought me a Brownie camera for

338

Christmas. Charlie was teaching me how to take good photographs with it.

We had picture-taking outings on the weekends and we often took pictures of our family and friends. He would develop them at the paper in his dark room, but he said there were now places around town where anyone could pay to develop their photographs. We loved to surprise our friends with the pictures we had taken of them.

"This type of home photography, Charlie told me, was simply not available to everyday people before the invention of the Brownie."

I was falling in love with him; at least, that's how it felt. What I like best about him is his thoughtfulness and kindness, even to strangers. He is solid and reliable; he's just a very good man. Charlie is a person who takes the time to think of the needs of others; he doesn't wait to be asked for help.

Chapter 41

Father, Jack, and I walked to the courthouse even earlier than usual Friday morning, dodging raindrops from a freak thunderstorm that had come up from Mexico. The atmosphere in the crowded hall outside the courtroom was crackling with electricity in anticipation of closing arguments in the case which were starting first thing.

He was standing with the press pack. I waved to him, smiled, and got in line. Father and I took our usual seats in the front row. Jack arrived late and found a seat in the back row behind us.

Judge Torrance took the bench; the bailiff brought the jury in. "Good morning, everyone."

He nodded to Mr. McKinley. "Are you ready to give your closing, sir?"

Mr. McKinley nodded and walked up to the jury box. He unbuttoned his coat, leaving it open, hanging like curtains on each side of his ample belly, and hooked his thumbs in his suspenders. The podium was near the jury box, but the lawyers had enough space to get closer to the jurors in their closing arguments which they both did. This created more intimacy with them without the physical barrier of the podium.

Mr. McKinley was talking to the jurors as if he was a fellow San Diegan—he was one of *them*. This was something the oh-so-smooth Sam Shortridge, whom Mr. McKinley was fond of painting as the slick, big-city lawyer, could never pull off.

"Good morning, gentlemen," he began. "First, I want to thank you for your attention and patience. It has been a long trial. I know that for most of you serving in this case, involved some sacrifice. On behalf of my client, I thank you for your service." He paused and took the time to look at each juror.

"You will recall when I spoke to you at the beginning of this trial that I promised you what the evidence would show in this case. I asked you to hold me to that promise at the end of the trial. And gentlemen, I've kept that promise."

"We had a few surprises, but let's go over what we know for sure: Harrison Otis admitted on the stand that he published the libelous articles that Mrs. Tingley has brought to this court, and he offered no evidence that they were true."

"You will recall that The General thought he was quite the comedian in the things he said to anyone who would listen about Mrs. Tingley and the fine work she has done at Lomaland. He freely admitted that he was trying to make her a laughingstock. He called her every name in the book. This is all a big joke to him."

"You heard them, gentlemen, right here on the witness stand, admit that he and his troops trashed Katherine Tingley's life's work without ever talking to her or even bothering to visit Lomaland to see what was actually being done out there. There was no evidence to the contrary."

He paused and looked at the jury. "Ab-so-lutely none," he drawled, "It's just that simple."

"The General here," waving his hand in his direction, told us that he owns a mighty sword, a newspaper with a large circulation in Los Angeles and here in San Diego. He told us that the *Times* even sends stories nationwide through the Associated Press wire service.

"*The Times* is a powerful voice—nobody disputes this. The General, as you saw, is very proud of that power. And you know what Mark Twain said about the power of newspapers: "Never pick a fight with people who buy ink by the barrel. " There was soft laughter in the courtroom.

"The General figured Mrs. Tingley couldn't or wouldn't do anything about his outrageous actions, the reign of terror he conducted against her for almost two years. She asked him to stop; he ignored her. The fact is, he gave her no choice; she had to preserve her good reputation."

"Why? He asked, making eye contact with each of the jurors before him, because a good reputation is important to all of us, of course, but it is essential to Katherine Tingley. This is because a good reputation is critical to funding her life's work and that of her followers, which is entirely supported by donations."

He walked back to the podium and paused for a moment. "Common sense and the testimony of Mrs. Tingley support her claim that her reputation *was* tarnished, as well as that of the good work she and her followers have done at Lomaland and all over the world." And how much money was lost to the cause of the Universal Brotherhood in donations because of these articles is hard to say. But it certainly occurred.

And that's the thing about libel, gentlemen, no one can ever know for certain who read these terrible lies about Mrs. Tingley and who those folks may have told about them. It is impossible to unring the bell of libel. And as you heard from a number of witnesses in this trial, many people believe that if it's in the newspaper, it must be true.

"Mrs. Tingley testified here about how much she suffered in terms of stress, worry, and sleeplessness as a result of reading what the *Times* had written about her and all that she has accomplished. And I submit to you, gentlemen, anyone would have had this reaction."

Mr. McKinley paused for a few seconds, letting this sink in.

"Harrison Otis knew when he printed these articles that it would likely cause this fine woman harm and distress...he just didn't care. This was about money, pure and simple. These outrageous lies made good copy, increased circulation, and made the General money. Greed is what we're talking about here, gentlemen, greed."

He took a step or two back from the podium and once again put his thumbs in his suspenders, leaning back a bit. "The evidence brought by the defense was about everything but the issues in this case. And gentlemen, even that evidence was about claimed events occurring a decade ago. Much of it was put in the trash can, where it belongs, by this good judge."

"Mr. Shortridge simply dangled before you any distraction he could think of, hoping you would miss your duty here: to address the actual issues in this case: the behavior of Harrison Otis and his minions at the *Los Angeles Times.*"

"I know you weren't fooled. Not one witness confirmed that Mrs. Tingley was a fraud, took money for her own use, starved children in her care, carried on sexual outrages in midnight ceremonies at Lomaland, or was a spook, a fraud, or anything else found in those *Times'* articles."

"Mr. Shortridge," he said, waving his reading glasses in his opposing counsel's direction, is a pretty slick customer to be sure. He puts on a good show, but he isn't fooling anybody." He turned around and looked down as if he was looking for something on the floor behind him. Turning back to the jury, he shrugged his shoulders and asked them, "Where *is* the evidence he said he would bring that would prove what the *Times* printed was true?"

"Mrs. Tingley is a San Diegan like all of you gentlemen. She has contributed a great deal to this town. Harrison Otis, the General, thinks he is free to tear down San Diego and its citizens—and, as you know, he has a habit of doing so."

343

Mr. McKinley paused and then exhorted the jury, "You need to send a message to him: "No, you can't," he told them, he repeated even louder, "No…you …can't."

This brought Sam Shortridge to his feet. "I object, Your Honor. There was no evidence of any habit on the part of Mr. Otis to tear down San Diego and its citizens. This is a highly improper argument, designed simply to inflame the jury."

Judge Torrance looked to Mr. McKinley.

"Your Honor, there was plenty of evidence of Harrison Otis downing San Diego and a San Diegan, Katherine Tingley. I read to Mr. Otis when he was on the stand eighteen such references to Mrs. Tingley, her followers, and Lomaland, the second biggest tourist destination in San Diego."

"And so, Your Honor, when the General shoots his cannon at Mrs. Tingley and Lomaland, he shoots it at San Diego too. Indeed for so many reasons, Mrs. Tingley and her followers have made significant contributions to this city's moving forward into the new century."

Mr. Shortridge shot out of his seat. "Ob-jection, this is not only irrelevant, but it is highly prejudicial."

Judge Torrance responded with a disapproving look. "Overruled, Mr. Shortridge, now sit down. You may continue, Mr. McKinley."

Harrison Otis leaned over and whispered a comment to Mr. Shortridge. It was obvious that he was pushing his lawyer to object. Mr. Shortridge was expressionless in response to his client's prompting and did not interrupt again. Mr. McKinley stepped around the podium and returned to the jury box, putting his hands on the brass rail.

"And so, by your verdict, gentlemen, I ask you to send this message to the General: that the things printed by the *Times* were false, that they were printed maliciously without regard to the truth, and that he pay substantial damages to Katherine Tingley for the damage she suffered."

"How much? I am going to leave that to you. I ask you to keep this in mind: a substantial verdict would be most fitting in this case, gentlemen. I ask you to take away the money Mr. Otis made on his calumny. "

"Harrison Otis, in his influential newspaper, libeled Mrs. Tingley recklessly and maliciously, disregarding the truth and violating the paper's own policies. He did this simply to make money—and money, gentlemen, is an appropriate remedy for his greed."

He concluded with these powerful words: "May I remind you that you walked every day of this trial through the arched doorway of this fine courthouse where it's etched in stone: Hall of Justice. Katherine Tingley comes to you, her fellow citizens, for just that, justice. I am confident, based on the evidence, that by your verdict, you will bring that to her in this case."

"I thank you."

He returned to his seat, a bit flushed from his performance. The judge glanced at the clock. It was eleven o'clock.

"Mr. Shortridge, are you ready to give your closing?"

He stood and faced the judge. "I am, Your Honor. It's rather lengthy; this has been a long trial. Could I impose on the court to dismiss early for lunch? I could start right after lunch."

"No, you may not. It's eleven o'clock. Let's get started. You can finish after lunch."

And so Sam Shortridge began his dramatic, over-the-top performance. It was highly entertaining; he kept everybody on the edge of their seats, even the judge. Early in his presentation, he leaned against the edge of his counsel table and looked at the jury, talking to them as if it were a casual chat on a park bench.

Always characterizing Mrs. Tingley's work as a perversion of the natural, he called her activities at Lomaland immoral, pagan, and foreign. There was no limit to the bile he shoveled upon her, telling the jurors, "The witnesses have been clear: this woman is dangerous, a fraud even." He paused, put his hands on the jury rail, and looked at them intently. "I tell you, gentlemen, she is both."

Mr. Shortridge spent most of his time making the case not about the conduct of Harrison Otis, but rather about Katherine Tingley, painting her as sinister, mysterious, "The Other," someone to be feared.

"Who is Katherine Tingley?" he asked the jurors. "What do you think of a woman who cloaks herself in mystery while she takes other people's money to fund her empire?"

Lowering his voice to a loud conspiratorial whisper, leaning forward with his hands on the jury box railing once again, he was their confidante and as such, he asked them, "Who is she really? This woman of uncertain past. We don't know. What I can tell you is that Katherine Tingley is the enemy of all that is good and noble in our lives."

"It is Mrs. Tingley's claim that the long parade of witnesses called by the defense are all liars and perjurers and that only she is telling the truth. These included her former followers, employees, and even a former Cabinet member. That simply is not believable, gentlemen, not believable at all."

At one point, he veered off of his personal attack on Mrs. Tingley, pointing his bow and poisoned-tipped arrows directly at Lomaland itself.

"What do we know about this school at Lomaland? Is it not hidden by a fog or a cloud on the mountain's brow? Does it not breathe of mystery? Of insanity? Is it a religion? Of what sort? Is it Christianity? Of what kind?"

Sam Shortridge was all about sowing fear and doubt in the jury about nothing that was before them in the case. He put on a good show. He had a beautiful command of the language that he delivered in that deep, melodious voice. I'd even describe him as poetic. It was impressive. You could see in his father's influence as a fiery Methodist preacher, spewing out from the pulpit warnings of retribution and damnation.

Nothing was too bold or too outrageous for Sam Shortridge. He even told the jury that the articles in the *Times* helped rather than hurt Katherine Tingley, claiming that she suffered no actual loss. "After all," he said, "they gave her what she wanted most: notoriety and publicity."

"Fifty thousand dollars is what she wants you to give her gentlemen, *fifty thousand dollars*, he said slowly, in almost a whisper, "and for what? The *Times* printing what other papers already printed about her. How would you like to make fifty thousand dollars the same way?"

After four hours, Sam Shortridge wound up his lengthy parade of horribles about Katherine Tingley without ever going to the actual issues in the case, a place he very much wanted to avoid. It was hot in the courtroom, and at one point, even the normally cool Sam Shortridge took out his silk handkerchief and wiped the sweat from his forehead.

He concluded his closing by standing in front of the jury, his outstretched hands facing toward heaven. It was a Christ-like pose as if he was delivering the sermon on the mount. His tone was somber, and he had a demeanor consistent with the seriousness of his message when he made these remarkable claims:

"If, gentlemen, you believe in the Christian religion, your duty is clear."

"If you believe in the family circle and the hearth and fireside, your duty is plain."

"If you believe in the institution of marriage, the marriage of one man and one woman, your duty is clear."

"In the name of society and civilization, and in the name of the Savior of Nazareth upon Calvary, where he shed his blood that we might live, I ask you for justice here, an American justice. Society is involved in this matter, and Christian civilization is at stake."

It was this message that the jury would take home with them that day. It was so spellbinding and effective. Father commented, "I think Kate Tingley is in trouble."

He was right. I watched the jurors during Mrs. Shortridge's performance. They were riveted by what he was telling them. They seemed convinced.

The clock clicked forward. It was five minutes passed four. Mr. Shortridge's behind hadn't even hit the chair at his counsel table when Judge Torrance shocked us all. The colorful balloon Sam Shortridge had so carefully blown up, and with a considerable amount of hot air mind you, was entirely deflated by what the judge did next.

Judge Torrance, with a sheaf of papers in his hand, leaned toward the jury and explained that he was taking the most important decision they had to make in the case from them: whether the *Times* had libeled Katherine Tingley. Yes, it did, he concluded, delivering his ruling with these words:

"You, as jurors, are here to decide disputed facts. There are simply no disputed facts for you to decide here, no evidence to weigh. The decision then, is a matter of law, which is my purview, my job, he said with determination. "I have made that decision," he said, looking down at his notes.

The jurors, almost in unison, leaned forward, staring at the judge, clearly not understanding what was happening.

Judge Torrance continued, "I find that the publications at issue in this case, as set forth in plaintiff's complaint, are libelous in all respects."

He then went through each of the articles published by the *Times* and ruled, using the same language as to each one. "This is libel, plain and simple; there was no evidence whatsoever that this claim is true."

He leaned back in his chair and paused. He looked at the jury again and told them solemnly, "I direct you to find a verdict that determines that all the statements published by the *Times* were libelous."

The jurors looked perplexed. As if this were not bad enough, Judge Torrance went further, giving a withering takedown of the claims made by Sam Shortridge in the closing argument he had concluded just moments before. Before he did, the good judge gave a double horse-eye look of disapproval to Sam Shortridge and then came the kick.

"Nor is it the opinion of the court that either the progress of Christian civilization or the principles of the Christian religion are involved in the issues of this case unless it is said that God's command 'Thou shalt not bear false witness against thy neighbor' is the underlying principle that justifies the enactment and enforcement of the law of libel."

The courtroom was at first as quiet as a tomb. The jurors looked gob-smacked. Then the sound of whispering and the spectators shuffling around could be heard from the gallery. Judge Torrance glared at them, which immediately silenced them; then he turned his attention back to the jury,

"The only issue left for you to decide, gentlemen, is the damages, if any, that should be awarded to Katherine Tingley. I will instruct you Monday morning on that issue, and after that, you will be sent out to deliberate. This court is adjourned." Down came his gavel, hard—*crack!*

Harrison Otis jumped in his seat.

"Ouch," Father whispered. "I'd say the eminent Sam Shortridge may have difficulty sitting down for a while."

I looked at the clock. It was late, 4:45. The jury filed out of the courtroom. Mr. Otis, whose bald spot signaled red after the first few minutes of the judge's comments, leaned over to his lawyer and said something I couldn't hear. The General's expression could only be described as stunned. They both just sat there, neither one saying a word.

After the jurors filed out, Mrs. Tingley slowly left the courtroom leaning on her cane, her lawyer beside her. Mr. McKinley looked pretty self-satisfied; a large smile covered his round, flushed face. Mr. Shortridge and Mr. Otis remained at the counsel table.

Father and I walked behind Mr. McKinley when he left with Mrs. Tingley. She was stoic and exhibited no reaction. Both nodded to me and smiled as they walked by us. Mr. McKinley was ebullient about the judge's dramatic turn in his client's favor. He smiled and nodded to people in the gallery; Mrs. Tingley just looked tired. Father noticed this too.

"Ya know, Mary Kate, it's stressful sitting in a courtroom in your case, even if you are not doing anything on that particular day. It's exhausting."

We walked into the hallway and saw Charlie rushing down the hall after Mrs. Tingley and Mr. McKinley—hoping, no doubt, to get a shot of them outside of the courthouse for tomorrow's edition. Jack wasn't there; he must have left as soon as the gavel went down.

Chapter 42

Charlie rushed up behind us as we walked back to the paper. "Got a great shot of both Kate and McKinley."

"That's fine, Charlie," Father said.

It started to rain and hard. It was as if the heavens had opened. I squealed. None of us had brought an umbrella. We laughed and rushed back to the paper.

Charlie went directly into his darkroom to develop his photographs. Jack was already at his desk, head down, working, when we came in. We were drenched.

"You guys look like drowned rats," he said. He had his green tweed jacket hanging on the back of his chair and brought it over to me. "Here ya go, Mary Kate," he said, putting it around my shoulders. It smelled like a musty wool tent.

"Hey, Mary Kate, it's Friday night, and the trial's all but over— let's get our work done here, grab Charlie, and go for a beer at Patrick's, maybe play some darts."

"Like this? I'm soaked."

"You'll dry; stand over by the heater. Find out when Charlie will be done with his photographs. I'm almost done here."

Father was already seated before his typewriter, wiping the rain from his face and hair with his handkerchief. "I'll finish the story, Mary Kate; you go. He shouted to Jack," Not too late, and make sure you boys walk her home."

"Will do," Jack said, putting his head down to finish typing his work.

I checked in with Charlie, took off Jack's coat, and stood over the floor heater. Pretty soon I was wrinkled but dry. After a horrifying look at the state of my hair in my hand mirror, and a brief struggle to bring my errant mass of curls into some sort of order, I decided to just forget it. Damp weather and rain made my hair simply out of control. Jack came over and placed a newsie hat on my head. "Somebody left it here."

We walked to Patrick's trying to avoid puddles in what was now a very light rain. It was only a few blocks down the hill. Charlie and Jack seemed to know everyone in the place and were pleased to introduce me. After our first beer, Charlie offered to teach me to play darts. "I'm pretty good," he confided.

So, the World Champion Dart Player of Rabbitville, as I called myself, listened intently to his instructions; Jack was drinking his beer and listening too. After I played a game with Charlie and one with Charlie and Jack, beating them handily, Jack shook his head. "I think we 've been had Charlie, this is no beginner at the game."

Tim and I played darts often at home with my parents. Tim could seldom beat me. I took my time; which was my secret weapon. He had no patience. I would just wait out my opponents, always boys; they just can't be patient and take the time to take careful aim. Darts is a game of concentration.

"You bore your opponent to death," Tim would say.

Charlie said Ben was going to pick us up at Patrick's at nine. We stood outside waiting for him. The rain had stopped about an hour before. The night sky was clear and it was cool, but not cold.

"I think I am going to hoof it," Jack said. It's a nice night. It has cleared up. We've been cooped up all day in that stuffy courtroom, and a good walk down the hill is just what I need."

Charlie agreed. "That does sound pretty good."

"You know, I think I'd like to walk too," I said. "This way, you don't have to have Ben drive me in the opposite direction and then have to double back to go up to Banker's Hill. It's only a few blocks home."

"Are you sure? He'll be here soon."

"Yes, a walk sounds grand. I'm pretty keyed up from my big win in the dart tournament."

Charlie shook his head. "OK, I'll pick you up at about six tomorrow for dinner at my parents. I can't wait for you to meet Grandfather Hal."

"I'm looking forward to it," I replied.

Grandfather Hal had come for a two-week visit. I was anxious to meet him. Charlie followed Jack and me out the door. Knowing Charlie would want to kiss me goodnight, Jack left us on the sidewalk, walked down the street, and waited for me. Ben drove up in the carriage.

"Are you sure you don't want a lift?"

"No, I said; a brisk walk sounds good."

"Well then, good night, my sweet girl, he said, putting his arms around me and kissing me. It was such a sweet, lovely kiss and one I returned with some enthusiasm."

"Okay, enough of that, let's get going, Mary Kate," the ever-impatient Jack called to me.

My house was right on Jack's way home. He insisted I wear his coat and take his arm. It was a bit chilly, and the coat was warm but cumbersome. This time there was a pretty good light from the moon which was nearly full.

"Oh my, I said as we got to my very dark street, "look at those stars. There are thousands of them. It's really something, isn't it?" He looked up but didn't reply

We don't see a display of stars that often in San Diego on the coast. There is usually a blanket of cloud cover masking them from view. But we sometimes have a clear night, especially after a rain. As we approached the house, we could see that Father had left the porch light on.

"See ya tomorrow," Jack said as I hopped up the steps. He turned and walked a few feet down the street.

"Thanks for walking me, … and Jack, I called to him, here's your coat."

He walked back and jumped up on the bottom of the stairs and put his hand out to take his coat. Instead, he took my hand and held it for a second, looking into my eyes with what sure looked like longing. He quickly looked away, removed his hand, took the coat, and walked towards home saying nothing, not even goodnight.

Whatever it was, it made me feel uncomfortable, *very* uncomfortable. Stunned and upset, I didn't want to hurt Jack, but it is Charlie I loved; I was sure of that.

The house was dark. Walking up the stairs I thought about Jack's look, then pushed it out of my mind. I got into bed and soon felt the thump of Lucy hopping on the foot of the bed. My head had barely hit the pillow when sleep overcame me.

Chapter 43

I enjoyed the dinner at Charlie's parents on Saturday night with Grandfather Hal. He was just as Charlie had described him; an *interested* human being. He's very charming and is interested in so many things.

Charlie talked with enthusiasm about his work as a photojournalist and reminded his grandfather about his role in training him for that work. Grandfather Hal's response shocked me, "I was surprised when you told me that you planned to leave your job at the paper and go to work with your father at the bank. You are such a natural as a news photographer."

"The photographs you showed me that have taken here in San Diego are spectacular. You have a real talent for this."

Charlie assured his grandfather that he still was planning to pursue his love of photography, but more as a hobby. "I'm going to be a family man before long, and I need to make more money to support a wife and children. Besides Grandfather, I will take to banking just fine."

Grandfather Hal smiled but said nothing. He clearly wasn't convinced. Was he disappointed? I thought so. On the way home I asked Charlie why he didn't tell me about this. He said simply," I really hadn't made up my mind until today."

On Monday morning at nine o'clock, I went to the courtroom alone to hear Judge Torrance instruct the jury and send them out to make a decision. The instructions were short; the jury was to decide whether Mrs. Tingley was damaged by the *Times'* having published the libelous articles and, if so, how much money should be awarded to her. This was a snoozer for the jurors, who didn't seem to be listening. The press gang was present, but there were only a few spectators. The jury was sent out to deliberate at ten o'clock.

I went back to the paper and thought about how strange it was to be back doing routine work. Three hours later, Father got a call from the clerk in Department One.

"Jury's back!" he yelled across the newsroom.

Father, Charlie, Jack, and I hurried down Broadway to the courthouse. It was raining hard. We laughed at our unsuccessful attempt to use our umbrellas in the strong wind blowing off the bay in our direction. Sopping wet and flushed from the run when we got to the hallway outside of the courtroom, we were as excited as the rest of the swarm of bees buzzing around there waiting to hear the verdict.

Sam Shortridge and Harrison Otis arrived a few minutes after we did and somehow they were dry as a bone. They didn't look at anyone as they passed. The bailiff, who was minding the door, let them into the courtroom. Mrs. Tingley, I learned from the bailiff, was already inside with Mr. McKinley. A few minutes later, the spectators and the press were let in.

Mrs. Tingley was nervous. The sphinx-like demeanor she had had throughout most of the trial had been replaced by restlessness; her hands were fluttering in her lap.

She had taken a great risk bringing the lawsuit; the result would be news all over the country. She had much to lose, far more than Harrison Otis. If the jury, by its verdict, gave no credibility to her claims of loss or damage by giving her no damages, her good reputation would still be affected. This was despite the judge's finding that the charges published in the *Times* were both untrue and libelous. It would also be of little deterrent to Harrison Otis and his ilk to engage in this type of conduct in the future.

San Diego too would suffer as Harrison Otis would have a victory under his belt against one of San Diego's leading citizens. He would be vindicated despite the judge's ruling in the present case. Even a partial victory would give him some credibility, despite the falsehoods he had published about San Diego for years.

Most people in San Diego knew that it was primarily Otis and his paper that sowed the seeds of doubt as to whether our city would be superior to Los Angeles as the sight for the terminus of the transcontinental railroad.

Anyone looking at the matter objectively would have to conclude that San Diego was a far better location. After all, Los Angeles had its center of commerce and its train station some thirty miles away from its port in San Pedro; not in the least favorable to commerce on the railroad. San Diego should have gotten the nod. It had its center of commerce and its train station right next to its far superior harbor. Instead, the choice of Los Angeles was birthed out of corruption and graft; much of it was engineered by none other than Harrison Otis.

The loss of this competition was a tremendous economic setback for San Diego. A large percentage of the population had to move out of town when the jobs the national railroad connection would deliver, evaporated.

Harrison Otis sat at the counsel table still and confident. After all, on the surface, the only thing he had to lose was money, and he had made a great deal of money on Katherine Tingley. He did risk a loss of face, a severe rebuke, a humiliation if taken down by a woman, especially this particular woman.

Judge Torrance took the bench and told the bailiff to bring in the jury. A few minutes later, they filed in, stone-faced, giving no clue as to their decision. You could cut the tension in the courtroom with a knife. Harrison Otis sat face forward. Katherine Tingley stared at the jurors, hoping for a hint at their decision. The jurors all avoided looking at her. Father noticed.

"Uh-oh, they're not looking at her. Most trial watchers think that signals an unfavorable verdict," Father said.

After the jury was seated, still not looking at Katherine Tingley, the judge said to the foreman, "Have you reached a verdict?"

"We have, Your Honor."

"Hand it to the bailiff, please." The bailiff took the verdict and gave it to Judge Torrance who held it for a minute without opening it. The suspense built during that minute—it seemed longer, but then he turned to the spectators in the gallery.

"This is a courtroom. I expect decorum after the verdict is read. Keep that in mind. I ask that you wait for the parties and the jury to leave before exiting the courtroom."

He looked down, read the verdict to himself, and then, his face expressionless, gave it to the clerk, who read it out loud.

"We, the jury, in the case now pending before this court, entitled *Tingley v. Times-Mirror Company*, find in favor of the plaintiff, Katherine Tingley, in the amount of seven thousand- five hundred dollars."

The gallery erupted in cheers. The jurors smiled but did not applaud. The judge expected this response, ignored it, and turned to the jury.

"Gentlemen, I thank you for your service in this case. You are free to go. This court is adjourned." He brought down his gavel and left the bench.

Harrison Otis sat in stunned silence at the unexpected defeat. He had suffered a reckoning, a rebuke as sharp as a hard slap in the face. He stood up to leave, then paused to wait for Sam Shortridge. Watching him after the verdict, Mr. Otis pretended to be unaffected by his loss, his take-down. His demeanor was defiant, but not for long.

Father was right—Mr. Otis is no poker player. He wasn't fooling anybody. It was clear he felt humbled by the verdict. His demeanor was one of a deflated man, a General in total defeat. His shoulders slumped, his chest was no longer puffed out, and his face held none of the determination or confidence he had throughout the trial. This time he was not flushed; he was white as a sheet, the blood had drained from his face. Clearly, he was a man that was not used to losing.

He knew he would have no choice but to report the verdict in his paper and over the wires of the Associated Press. I expected that he would claim there had been some mistake by the judge or the jury. He did whine all through the trial in the stories in his paper about the proceedings, mostly claiming that substantial evidence from defense witnesses was unfairly excluded by Judge Torrance. Father said that the opposite was the case: the judge let the jury hear too much irrelevant evidence only to strike it after they had heard it.

Sam Shortridge led his client out of the courtroom, both men stone-faced, looking straight ahead. Before he left the counsel table, Mr. Otis turned to face Katherine Tingley, giving her his parting shot: a belligerent, defiant look. Mrs. Tingley returned the General's baleful look by staring back at the old bird. She was not cowed by Harrison Otis or ebullient at her success; determined is all.

Mr. McKinley took her left arm she limped toward the door, smiling when she passed me. Smiling back at her, I gave her a thumbs-up. Father gave me a look of disapproval. We didn't see Jack or Charlie in the busy hallway. They had left after Mr. Otis and probably were going after him to try to get a photo and a quote. We planned to snag Mrs. Tingley for a short interview but we soon discovered we would have to set that up later. This is because we were the last spectators to leave the courtroom and she was probably surrounded by other reporters.

As we headed out the front door of the courthouse, we saw Mr. McKinley and Katherine Tingley on the courthouse steps; the press gang was peppering them with questions. We stopped just as she gave her prepared comments. She took no questions.

"I'm pleased to see that the jury recognized that the good work done by the Universal Brotherhood at Lomaland and throughout the world, should not be sullied by irresponsible journalists like Harrison-Gray-Otis she said, emphasizing each part of his name."

"We have been vindicated, yes, but hopefully, this verdict will discourage Mr. Otis and others so inclined, from engaging in this type of reprehensible journalism in the future."

Scribbling this into my tablet, I turned to Father and pulled on his sleeve to get his attention. "There's Jack," I said.

He had caught up with Otis, who had dodged the press corps and stood by the bench near the sidewalk alone. As we approached, he remained defiant in responding to Jack's questions, taking a this-isn't-over attitude, promising to appeal to the Supreme Court.

"That woman will never see a single Simoleon from me, never, not a single one." Otis repeatedly threaded a call for a rematch throughout his remarks.

I was distracted by the press commotion around Sam Shortridge, who was getting into a carriage nearby, leaving his obstreperous client behind. At first, I thought this was petty of him. Otis needed his lawyer beside him right about then. But to be fair, Otis probably had dismissed his lawyer, preferring, as usual, to handle things himself. We talked about this as Father, and I headed back to the paper. The rain had stopped.

"I have thought all along Father, that Harrison Otis is at his core, a lonely, isolated man. He is an audience and a support team of one: that's lonely. Was that just fine with him as he claimed? Methinks the man protests too much. I've always thought that any bully gets to be that way from an underlying insecurity about their own self-worth."

"I never thought of it that way, but I expect you're right," Father replied.

"Come to think of it, Harrison and Katherine Tingley are both rather solitary people. They have this in common, too: Mrs. Tingley is very progressive in many ways, but in terms of social mores, both she and Harrison Otis, for the most part, are very much a part of the Victorian era that they both came from."

Father wrote the story and even wove a subtle version of what I had said about Harrison Otis as a lonely, isolated man. When we returned to the paper, the "Do Not Disturb" sign was on Charlie's darkroom door. I stopped at the Hot Box and looked through it to see if there were any announcements. It was hard to believe it was all over and that soon we'd be getting back to normal. We all had to work very long hours as we all juggled our regular duties at the paper with our reporting of the twenty days of this historic trial.

I was standing near Father's desk looking at the photographs that Charlie took after the verdict. He looked at them with me waiting for my reaction. As I thumbed through the stack, they seemed pretty ordinary until I got to the bottom of the pile.

Charlie had taken one very perceptive shot of the General, standing alone and looking a bit forlorn, next to the bench near the sidewalk in front of the courthouse. He had captured Harrison Otis perfectly as the solitary man that he is. He had lost the bluster, the bravado which returned just minutes later when he was talking to Jack. Instead, he looked wounded, deserted. He probably thought

362

nobody was looking; Charlie was, and click, click, click, he caught this important moment on film.

Father handed me his story to review. Charlie looked over my shoulder and read it too. The headline was:

"TINGLEY TAKES DOWN *THE TIMES.*"

His instruction to the printers was scribbled beside it: *Page 1 - Two inches- above the fold. M.R.*

After we finished reading the story, Charlie, Father, and I looked at each other and cheered.

Jack was at his desk. "What's going on over there? How can a fella get some work done?" He laughed and came over with a suggestion that we all have a little celebration at the Horton House. "Most of the reporters on the trial will be there; it's where most of the out-of-towners are staying."

"Sounds good, Jack. Father said. "Let me get Henry."

Things were normal after my little incident with Jack after Patrick's the other night. I may have read too much into it. It wasn't an issue between us. I did tell Theodora about the little flirtation if that was what it was. She told me it was probably nothing." He's a lady's man, a flirt; it didn't mean anything. That's just Jack."

Still, I couldn't get that look out of my head. No, it was not a silly flirtation, I was pretty sure of that. But, Jack didn't act any different with me the next time I saw him, so I decided to forget it...

We had an early dinner at the restaurant at the Horton House that Henry was pleased to pay for. He even ordered a bottle of champagne for a toast to his crew. He was all praise about what a great job we did. He singled me out for special mention for my early scoops. Father noticeably didn't chime in. I wasn't surprised; he hadn't gotten over my little "venture" up Horton Hill.

Father and Henry left right after dinner. Father put two dollars on the table in front of me. I pushed them away, saying indignantly, "I have my own money." Jack huffed and laughed a little too loudly for my taste. "Let's move the party to the bar," he suggested.

There were several reporters from the trial already there. Two were local. Jack and Charlie knew them well. We pulled the tables together and sat around trading war stories, the men taking turns paying for rounds of beer. I offered to pay for a round; the suggestion met with dead silence.

Pretty soon, a few more out-of-town reporters joined us and had their own tales about the trial. I had gotten to know all of the reporters covering the trial; we were comrades in arms. We often talked about the battle unfolding before us during the breaks in the hallway outside the courtroom, and sometimes after court.

Theodora, always on the hunt for fresh male prey, asked me during the first week of the trial if any of the reporters were attractive. "Not to me," I told her. I wasn't interested; I was seeing Charlie, and things were getting serious. "You aren't missing anything Theodora, most of them are old, and not a one is good-looking."

I kept up with the coverage of the other papers during the trial, as Father had asked me to do by reading the Associated Press bulletins; all papers that sent reporters to the trial were members. Of course, I read *the Times* every day. It was interesting to see how the evidence was viewed by different reporters watching the same trial. Father was right; reading what other reporters had to say about an important story was a great learning experience.

"You can learn from the good and the bad, and they have their scoops, too," he said.

We all enjoyed chewing over those differences in the viewpoint that night at the Harbor Bar, sloshing down our discussions with beer and for some, copious quantities of whiskey. I hated the smell of whiskey. It was for me the smell of my father's grief during those dark weeks after Tim's death.

We didn't discuss how we got scoops or the sources we had in reporting one story or another. Father and I often talked at dinner during the trial about the coverage in other papers, both local and across the country. We talked about how the slanted facts, as found in the coverage in the *Times,* often appeared in articles written about the case in out-of-town papers where the reporters were not at the trial. These papers were all members of the Associated Press. Harrison Otis was diligent about sending regular dispatches over the wires, giving *his* version of what was happening at the trial.

At home, Mother was fascinated by all the goings-on in the courtroom and outside the hall. Father loved to give his own particular spin, great storyteller that he is, to describe to her the performances of the witnesses in the box that day. She especially liked to hear about the actions between the two combatants, Katherine Tingley and Harrison Otis. She laughed heartily when I told her about their confrontation in the doorway several days before the verdict. "He's quite a character," she said.

"So is she," Father replied. "From what I saw, the General was outgunned in that little skirmish. Kate Tingley doesn't take any guff from anyone."

It was hard to believe it was nearly three weeks ago that the trial began and demanded so much of our attention. It went so fast—so much had happened.

Most of the reporters at the Harbor Bar that night felt, as we did, that both by the verdict and otherwise, no San Diegans, even a jury of all very conservative men, would be inclined towards the *Los Angeles Times.* It was easy for these jurors to see Harrison Otis as Mr. Los Angeles. Ironically, all who knew him would tell you he felt this way about himself.

I got to know Dan Harris pretty well during the trial; he's a reporter from the San Francisco Chronicle. He summed up the consensus of the reporters who covered it: "This was a verdict for San Diego against its archrival Los Angeles, plain and simple."

As it turned out, what Sam Shortridge told me that night at the Savoy was right; the rivalry between San Diego and Los Angeles would likely carry the day for Mrs. Tingley in the trial.

Gus, a reporter from the New York Times, offered the opinion that Mrs. Tingley got short-changed in the amount awarded in the verdict. Jack disagreed. "Those farmers probably thought this was a great deal of money for just saying things about her that other papers had already said."

Charlie walked me home after the celebration broke up and we kissed on the porch. It was cold out there, but my parents were sitting in the front room. Pretty soon, I got warmed up. Over the past few weeks, he had awakened something I had never felt before; the feelings of a grown woman.

After that night, Charlie usually walked me home from the paper after work. We spent time together on weekends; he usually stayed for dinner. My parents liked him very much. He invited me to his parent's house quite a bit, and they seemed to feel the same way about me.

Was I falling in love with Charlie? It sure felt like it. These were feelings I didn't have for Izzy. I certainly hadn't seen love coming my way so soon, let alone being ready to settle down. Things were changing; I was changing.

Charlie was comfortable at our home in Rabbitville and at the paper, both a far cry from Banker's Hill. It's the world where we met and where we fell in love. He worked there, and his best friends lived there. But was he just visiting?

"You're a snob, my dear," he said gently one night when we talked about the differences in our worlds, how we grew up, our education, and things like that.

Am I just visiting Banker's Hill?

Chapter 44

A couple of weeks later, Charlie was over for an early Sunday dinner and some cards. He surprised me by asking Father to take him down to the old wharf after dinner so he could see the *Serenity*. This was an odd request. Charlie hated the water and would never go sailing.

"I haven't seen it restored—Jack says it looks great. The girls are busy here, so let's take a walk."

"I'd be pleased to show you, Charlie. She's a real beauty."

He and Father were gone about an hour. When they came back we played cards until nine when my parents went to bed. Charlie and I were glad to have a bit of alone time. He had arranged for Ben to bring the carriage to get him at ten o'clock. At about nine-thirty, Charlie stood up and took something out of his pocket. He turned to me, reached down, and took my left hand.

"Mary Kate Riley, will you be my wife? I got your father's blessing, so if you'll have me, you will make me a very happy man."

Flustered but not surprised, I said, "Why yes… yes I will marry you, Charlie Wilson," I said, and kissed him.

He put the ring on my finger; it was way too big. "It's beautiful," I said, putting up my hand and looking at the ring in the lamplight. It was a filigreed gold ring with a spectacular solitaire diamond.

"It was my grandmother's. She had fat fingers. I can get it sized," he added.

We sat on the couch holding hands, saying very little; we both were somewhat stunned by the road we were embarking on together. Pretty soon we heard Ben pull up in the carriage outside. "Ben's here," he said, and we kissed again. "I love you," he said as he headed for the door.

"I love you too."

Running up the stairs I saw that my parents' light was on with the door closed. I couldn't wait until the morning to show them my ring, so I knocked.

"Come in," Mother called innocently. Of course, they were waiting for me.

Sashaying over to her side of the bed, putting up my left hand, and showing off my ring, I said proudly. "Mrs. Charles Wilson—how does that sound to you?"

They were not in the least surprised. The trip to the *Serenity* was obviously to clear things with Father. "It sounds fine dear; congratulations. I know you two will be happy," Mother said, all smiles. "He's so handsome; my grandchildren will be some of the most handsome in town."

"Or, we could have a carrot head or two, Maggie," Father said, looking at me with a wide grin."

"Oh, for gosh sake, we aren't married yet, and you are already planning for grandchildren. Looking at my ring again, I turned to my happy parents, "I'll say goodnight then."

Lying in bed that night, I was excited, happy, and a bit scared about getting married, something that would have been unthinkable a year ago when Tim died and my life changed forever. It seems like ten years have passed in terms of all that has happened since then.

Monday morning at the paper, Jack offered his congratulations to us both.

"So, you're gonna let her slip the halter on ya?"

Charlie nodded and grinned. Jack put his arm around Charlie and roughly pulled him towards him, and gave him an affectionate squeeze. "OK, then, he said chuckling, if that's what you want, I'm happy for the both of ya."

Chapter 45

Our engagement announcement appeared the following Sunday in the women's section of the paper, along with my picture. Charlie used a nice shot he had taken of me at the Spreckles' wedding. We had chosen the date of September 29$^{th.}$

Mrs. Wilson said it would take several months to plan "a wedding of this size," as she put it. Charlie and I wanted a smaller wedding, but I could see that it wasn't going to happen.

"My parents have a lot of business associates that will expect to be invited," Charlie told me. It was apparent that we would have no say in this decision. It bothered me that Charlie didn't question this or even want to discuss it. I brought it up, and he just brushed me off, saying simply, "It's business, Mary Kate."

The following Saturday night, Charlie took me to an early dinner at Fresh Catch, a popular fish house on the bay. Nothing fancy, but the fish served was cooked over an open fire in a pit near the docks. He had taken me there before and we both loved the place; the fish was delicious, and the view of the bay was even better.

After we finished dessert, we sat quietly watching the boats on the bay. Charlie reached across the table and took my hand. " I am leaving the paper to go work with my father as the Assistant Manager of the bank. It's a real opportunity and much more money."

I wasn't too surprised. Charlie had obviously thought of our future together when he decided he needed to make more money to support a family. He had talked about this a few weeks ago with

Grandfather Hal, but he never said anything further about it. What happened in between is that we became engaged.

"But Charlie, photography is your passion; it's what you love to do."

"Yes," he said, "but I can't keep a wife and children on what I make at the *Union*."

"My father does," I said defensively.

There was a moment of uncomfortable silence. I knew what Charlie was thinking: I'd like to be able to do more for my family than your father can do.

"I'd like to travel with my family, to be able to send our children to the East Coast for college, San Francisco even, give them some of the opportunities I had growing up. Is that so wrong, Mary Kate? I can still be a photographer, but just not as my profession. It just doesn't pay enough; there's no future in it. I've gone as far as I can already."

"So when will you be leaving the paper?"

"I've already told Henry. I will stay until he can find a replacement. I've lined up a friend of mine, Thomas Greenwood, who works for the *Sun*. He is an outstanding photographer. Henry is meeting with him tomorrow.

"I can't believe you have taken all these steps and made all these plans without discussing it with me. I *am* going to be your wife, Charlie," I said petulantly. Angry and hurt, I felt pretty low on the totem pole about this important issue that affected *both* of our lives.

Charlie dismissed my concerns as if it was something I should have expected. "This is the right thing for me to do, for us, for our children."

I was unhappy about this and worried that someday Charlie would blame me for his decision to give up his dream. But, Mother gave up her dream of being a singer in the San Francisco Opera, maybe even an opera star, her chance for a life much like Charlie was offering me, to marry Father. She was happy with that decision.

The following Saturday night, the Wilsons hosted a lovely engagement *soiree* for Charlie and me in the ballroom of the Brewster Hotel. I sensed that they chose that hotel to make my side of the wedding equation more comfortable. The Brewster is a fine hotel but not in the least bit elegant. The engagement parties of the upper class that I had covered over the past year were never at the Brewster. Mother and I agreed that the choice was a good compromise.

Mother picked out a new suit for Father at Marston's, which she tailored to fit him. He looked so handsome. Mother wore her sea-green silk and looked spectacular. Jack got a dark suit from Charlie; they're about the same size. Charlie is a bit taller, so Mother hemmed the pants. He even got a haircut.

"Why Jack, I never knew you were so handsome," Mother said, giving him a peck on the cheek when he arrived at the party.

"Yeah," Father said sarcastically, "who knew?"

Jack came to the party alone. He had stopped seeing Mary, who naturally expected a commitment after seeing each other for almost nine months. The way he explained it to Charlie was that he was just not ready to go down that road. This was a surprise; she and Jack made such a good pair.

The party was not black tie as Mrs. Wilson suggested it should be. Charlie and I wanted to make it more informal. My parents were asked to dinner at the Wilsons' to plan the party. Father offered to pay for it or split the cost with Mr. Wilson, but he wouldn't even consider it.

Father didn't seem to mind and didn't say anything about it, at least in front of me. Mr. Wilson wasn't being high-handed; it was something he could afford, and he wanted to relieve my family of the expense. We appreciated the consideration,

Theodora came to the party late. She looked stunning in her dark blue velvet frock with her long blond hair, which she wore piled on her head. She didn't have an escort; she wasn't planning to go because she needed to stay home to watch over her mother, who was now quite ill. At the last minute, a neighbor agreed to take on the duty that night, so she had Frank Moody drive her to the party.

I noticed as the evening went on that "our Jack" let no grass grow under his feet and took an immediate shine to Theodora. They'd known each other for a long time but never had any romantic connection until now. They laughed, danced, and spent pretty much the whole evening together.

"Hmm . . . now what do you make of that?" Charlie asked.

"Looks like they make a really nice pair," I replied.

At one point, Jack took to the stage and announced that as the Best Man, he had a song he'd liked to sing "for these young lovers."

It was a poignant Irish ballad that I recognized. It was a love song that he and Mother often harmonized to in our after-dinner song fests. Mother teared up a bit when he was singing. She told me later that Jack had told her he had made arrangements with the musical ensemble the week before to play the song.

Later in the evening, I danced with Jack, a waltz, no less. He must have been practicing; he wasn't too bad. Charlie told me that his mother had given Jack a few lessons." It was pretty rough going at first." he said.

Theodora danced with Charlie several times. She is a wonderful dancer. On one occasion, Jack, Theodora, Charlie, and I swirled around the dance floor to my favorite waltz, the only couples on the floor. I was so happy.

Ben took Mother, Father, and me home, with Charlie joining us of course. As I lay in bed that night, I thought of the prospect of Jack and Theodora getting together, marrying even. Theodora was the sister I never had, and Jack, after a few rough edges were sanded off, was the brother I had lost… well, almost. We would all be one big happy family.

Theodora and Jack started seeing each other after the party. It didn't last long enough to get serious, at least for Jack. One day a week or so later, Jack suggested Charlie and I head to the Waterfront with him for lunch. We went early because Jack said he wanted to sit at a table rather than the counter where we usually sat. After we finished our cheese sandwiches and drank our cups of tomato soup, Jack shocked us with some news.

"I've taken a job at the *Los Angeles Times* working for Harrison Otis if you can believe it. I've lived in San Diego most of my life; trying out someplace new has always appealed to me, and Los Angeles is just a hop and a jump away." He was excited to be sharing his big news with us.

I was stunned. What about the wedding?

Jack leaned back in his chair, picked up his cup, and took the last gulp of his soup. "This has been in the works for a while," he said. "I have a buddy up there who works for the *Times;* he told me there was a job open as a senior editor so I went up for an interview."

"You remember, just before the trial started, I went to San Pedro to visit my Aunt Mary and Uncle Jack? He works on the docks there. I had the interview at the *Times* that Monday. Mr. Andrews, who later testified at the Tingley trial, interviewed me. I showed him some of my stories; he liked them. He offered me the job the very next week."

"I didn't tell anybody because I wanted to get things firmed- up first and let your dad and Henry know. I'll be the editor and lead reporter there—your dad's job. Only I'll have *three* reporters working for me. Oh, and I'm getting a big raise to boot."

"I've always wanted to try someplace else. I've lived in San Diego since I was a boy. This is my chance," he said earnestly, turning towards me, no doubt noticing my downcast expression.

"Don't worry, it's not far away,—and I'll visit too. I'll be will back for the wedding, and I will be the best-Best Man that ever was. I'm already working on the toast."

"When will you be leaving," I asked sadly.

"Two weeks. Henry knows, and your father is already looking for a replacement. They didn't tell you because I wanted to be the one to break the news."

Two weeks?

"My aunt and uncle live near the harbor in San Pedro and will put me up until I get my own place. Uncle Jack said I could pick up some extra cash working with him on Saturdays if that suits me."

He leaned back in his chair. "I'll take the train downtown to the *Times* to get to work, at least for a while. My buddy does that, and he said that you have to catch the train really early but that it's not a bad ride. I'm sure I can find a place near the paper. I may even buy an automobile once I get settled."

"My uncle is good with engines and he said that we can find a broken-down automobile pretty cheap. You might see me one day when I visit, putting down Broadway. I can bring it on the ferry," he said with a smile, looking into my eyes.

"Gosh, we'll miss you so much," I told him softly, with hurt in my voice, trying to hold back tears.

376

"We'll sure miss you, Jack, but it sounds like a good opportunity," Charlie told him. He didn't seem surprised at all. I was sure that Jack told him about the opportunity he had to get a great job at the *Times* before he went for the interview. And as his best friend, Charlie was probably the first to know when Jack got the job.

After lunch, as we walked back to the paper, Jack continued with the details of leaving for a new life in Los Angeles. Charlie seemed to take the news in stride, his usual easy-going self. Speechless for once, this news lit a fire of emotions in me; confusion, sadness, and even a bit of resentment.

What about the wedding? He's our best man, I thought as we walked along. He seemed to have forgotten that as he just babbled on excitedly about *his* plans.

Theodora was heartbroken when I told her. Jack didn't share the news with her. I knew she had fallen for Jack, and now he was leaving. Theodora falls in love quickly and often. Still, she thought Jack was what she called her "true love," adding that she was sure of it *this time*.

"I'm not sure Jack is the marrying kind, I said, at least not for a while; he courted Mary for nine months.".

Writing in my journal that night, I surprised myself by pouring out my grief and disappointment about Jack leaving us…leaving me. What about the three musketeers? Feeling pretty sorry for myself, I thought about losing one brother at about the same time last year, and now I was losing another.

Jack could be pretty irritating, but he was always there for me He's family. He felt the loss of Tim nearly as much as we did. He had lost a brother and his adopted family too. Jack mentored Tim at work and even personal matters in the romance department.

It was Jack that stepped in and helped Father heal. I thought of that night when he took me to the *Serenity* and told me of the plan to get Father back on track by getting him back to the paper and working on the boat together. Father got a son back that way and Jack got his family.

They spent a good deal of time fixing up the boat last June, and they often went sailing together after that. Jack always stayed for dinner when he and Father got together, and we sang and told tales. It seemed like old times. Jack enjoyed these visits too

That night after pouring out my feelings in my journal. I sighed, and sat back in my chair,. and looked at the last pages; my tears had blurred the ink. *Why now when everything was going so well? I just couldn't let him go... out of our lives forever. He'd be back for the wedding, but after that, we'd lose him; l just knew it.*

Putting down my pen and closing my journal, I was determined that for all the world to see, that I would be happy for Jack, to wish him well. But I would miss him so much and wished he would change his mind.

Father already knew about Jack's leaving; he thought it was an excellent opportunity for him. "He'll probably make more money than I do, he said. "Besides, Los Angeles is a lively town for a single young man; he'll enjoy it there."

"I guess so," I said sadly, wondering how our world would change without *our Jack.*

Chapter 46

Predictably, there was still news in the Tingley case after the verdict. Father sent me down to the courthouse alone to a hearing brought by Hugh Hannon, an attractive, young, and very earnest attorney from Sam Shortridge's law firm, who asked for a new trial for the *Times*.

Granting a new trial would be in the interest of justice, he told Judge Torrance. The basis for his request was hidden somewhere in his blustery, dramatic, and very lengthy argument. The young man was a poor imitation of his mentor, the silver-tongued Sam Shortridge.

Judge Torrance was very patient, and after about five minutes of what the judge calls attorney bloviating, he only pretended to be listening. He raised his head from the papers before him to glance at Mr. Hannon occasionally and nod his head about nothing in particular. Mr. Hannon didn't notice one way or the other; he was entirely absorbed in his own performance.

The gist of his presentation was that the judge should not have struck the irrelevant, nonsense-evidence brought into the trial by the defense. Of course, he didn't characterize it that way. He also claimed that it was an error for the judge to deny Mr. Otis his request for a change in the trial's location. He concluded his remarks by saying, "Harrison Otis, in the interest of justice, deserves a new trial to set things right."

Judge Torrance, looking unimpressed, bored even by then, nodded to Mr. McKinley for his response. He responded with what amounted to a "no comment."

"Defendants Motion for a new trial is denied."

Harrison Otis was later rebuffed on the same issues in the California Supreme Court. The General had no choice but to go into full retreat and pay the judgment. The word was that he added a bit of money to settle the blackmail case as well.

Otis knew that if he didn't pay her, Kate Tingley would start attachment proceedings, and the fact that she got a judgment against him, a humiliating defeat, would be brought to the public eye once again.

I never saw Sam Shortridge after the trial, but I did call him at his office in San Francisco and spoke with him. He was very amiable and seemed pleased to hear from me. We exchanged pleasantries for a few minutes and then he asked me the purpose of my call.

"You remember my telling you at our dinner that I wanted to interview your sister after the trial for my Sunday women's section? Would you mind giving me her contact information?"

"I'd be delighted," he said. "You'll like Clara, I am sure of that."

"He gave me the information and then asked if he could take me to lunch when he was in San Diego next month to attend a campaign event. He said his campaign for a seat in the United States Senate was in full swing.

I don't think so, Mr. Shortridge."

"Sam, call me Sam."

"Do you remember Charlie Wilson?" I replied.

"Of course; how is Charlie?"

"He's just fine; we're engaged to be married."

He didn't miss a beat. "I guess that congratulations are in order, Miss Riley."

"Thank you," I said. We chatted for a little while longer and he closed with this, "I hope you'll ask your father and your friends to vote for me , Miss Riley."

There was a pause on my side of the telephone, "I'll sure consider it, Mr. Shortridge." I said, and we ended the call with his remarkable comment, "I'll call you when I'm in town; maybe I can change your mind about that lunch."

I ran into Judge McKinley in the hall of the courthouse the next day. He was very cordial. "What's the latest on Katherine Tingley? I haven't heard from her," he asked.

"My mother and I had tea with her after a performance at the Isis Theater last month. "She told me that she was planning a trip out of the country, was leaving in a month or so, and was busy getting things together. She said it was a world tour to promote the Universal Brotherhood."

"I heard that. She's a fascinating woman," Mr. McKinley replied. "What most people don't know about her is that she's a lot of fun; she has a great sense of humor. I like her, and that is not always the case with my clients."

"The best thing about her winning the case against the *Times* is that the other newspapers that have taken her on in a similar vein have since backed down and printed retractions. And Otis hasn't crossed the line again, at least not yet."

"Katherine Tingley is a formidable woman, and those in the newspaper game have come to respect her and know that if they push her, she will push back. Besides that," he said with a smile, she has a darn good lawyer."

"Indeed she does," I said.

Later that day, I contacted Clara Shortridge Foltz. She told me that she was going to be in San Diego for a conference on criminal justice reform at the end of the month and that she would be pleased to meet with me. We met at the lobby of the St. James. As I walked into the hotel, I thought about my dinner with her brother at the hotel's restaurant. It was just a month or so ago but it seemed much longer.

All of my previous articles about prominent women leaders had been about San Diego women. Mrs. Foltz was the exception. But, she did have a significant connection to the city well beyond her filial relationship with the lawyer for Harrison Otis. She is now a very successful lawyer in Los Angles, but she had her first law office in San Diego.

She stood when I approached her and extended my hand to her. "Mrs. Foltz, Mary Kate Riley from the *San Diego Union.*"

"Oh, for heaven's sake, call me Clara," she said, shaking my hand. "Sit, she said, motioning to the seat across from hers. I've ordered tea; please have some."

She is a plain, pleasant-looking woman of about sixty. She was well-dressed but a bit out of fashion. She's a no-nonsense, I've-got-things-to-do kind of woman. I liked her right away.

We sat down and she poured the tea. She surprised me by asking me first thing about Henry Seymour. She said she worked with Henry after she sold her paper, the *San Diego Bee,* to the *Union.* I knew from my research that she worked in the newspaper business for a while before she became interested in the law.

"Of course, that was twenty-five years ago. As part of the merger, I agreed to stay on for a while to ensure everything went smoothly. Henry was our lead reporter then. He's a real kick in the pants," she said with fondness. "Give him my best. Sam tells me that your father is the lead reporter now."

I nodded and smiled. She had done her homework about me too. Our interview started with my asking her for some personal background information.

She said that at the age of fifteen, she had eloped with Jeremiah Foltz, a handsome soldier who had just returned from the Civil War. She had five children with him and they made their home on a farm in the Midwest. Her young husband deserted her after their fifth child was born.

"He liked making the babies; he just didn't like supporting them," she said sadly. "I was desperate. I was left the sole support of our children." Mrs. Foltz sat back in her chair, thought for a moment, and then continued.

"I had little formal education. The jobs open to women were very poor-paying positions. I couldn't get remarried because none of the men I came in contact with wanted to take on five young children. She huffed and smiled. "Who could blame them?"

Mrs. Foltz told me she had acquired some legal experience working in her father's law practice so she thought she could work in a law-related field. He had since left law practice to become a Methodist minister. She said that it was her father who encouraged her to start at the top, to go to law school.

"I wouldn't have thought of it, but he urged me on. 'You can do it, Clara; I know you can, " he told me.

She took a sip of tea and paused for a moment. "This was an extraordinary suggestion at the time, Miss Riley; women were *not* lawyers. But with my father's support, I quietly pursued it."

She said that she applied to Hastings law school, the only law school in the state. "The Regents of the University of California unanimously voted to deny me admittance after only one interview."

383

"It was obvious after a few questions from the panel that they had already made up their minds. One Regent told me it would be too distracting to have women in the courtroom, the swishing of skirts and all. One suggested that a woman attorney might seduce jurors into acquitting the guilty; after all, there were no women on juries.

Another said that if women became lawyers, they might become what he called de-sexed. She shook her head in disgust and sighed. The rest of them remained mute, which based on the comments that were made, was probably best." She sighed.

"But, this outrageous rejection by men who should have known better, only hardened my resolve. And so, Miss Riley, I just swished my skirts right out of there and got to work on taking the matter to court. I lost the first round in the Superior Court; the judge agreed with the Regents. I took the case to the Supreme Court and won after writing my own briefs and arguing the case myself."

"There wasn't much need for argument; this was a public school for heaven's sake. I knew I had the right to be admitted and all the justices did too, so they ordered the Regents to admit me."

She leaned back in her chair and sipped some of her tea. She picked up the teapot, "How about a warm-up, Miss Riley?" Not waiting for a reply, she filled up my cup.

"The irony was that even after I successfully gained admittance to the law school, I discovered that only white males were eligible to be licensed as attorneys under existing California law. The law needed to be changed, and with a good deal of help, it was."

"The new law was not called *The Women Lawyer Bill,* as some of my colleagues suggested, it simply changed the words in the existing law from white males to persons. It now didn't apply just to women but to people of color who could not be admitted under the old law either."

"So, how did you manage to get the law changed?" I asked her.

"It wasn't easy, but I had a good deal of help from many women and some men. It finally got to the governor's desk and can you believe it, he refused to sign it."

"Why? It seems so straightforward."

"You don't want to even hear his excuses the governor gave us: they were even sillier than the ones I heard from the Regents. But we weren't taking no for an answer. He took some persuading and he knew we aimed to stay in his office until he signed the bill.

"You'll have to drag us out of here," we told him, she said with a chuckle. Late that night, and a little worse for wear, the governor signed the law and it went into immediate effect.

"And do you know what?" she said, shaking her head in disgust, "Just a few months later, that scoundrel had the gall to tell audiences that that bill was one of his proudest achievements."

"Tell me a little about starting your legal career in San Diego, I asked her.

"After I was licensed as a lawyer, I opened my office right around the corner from here. I would do any kind of work then, but most men didn't like having a woman lawyer. "And so, I took almost anything to support my children for very low fees. I often represented people who had to pay me over time or with offerings of produce they had grown or chickens they had raised."

"I took a great many criminal matters and soon learned about the inequities in our courts in terms of the poor obtaining justice there. Criminal justice reform, and in particular, protecting the rights of the poor when life or liberty is at stake, became my passion. Since that time, I have worked tirelessly for the funding of what I called Public Defenders."

"I first presented the idea as a speaker at the Chicago World's Fair. I spoke to the Congress on Law Reform some twenty years ago now. The idea met with considerable success there."

"What of your many accomplishments Mrs. Foltz, are you most proud of?"

"Without question, that would be that I have led the way for the appointment of publicly-funded lawyers to balance out the power of the publicly-financed prosecutors. After years of working on the issue, I am pleased to tell you that it has gained acceptance in many of the courts of this state. Los Angeles County already has a system in place."

"That was me," she said proudly. "I wouldn't let the subject rest until our county leaders did something. It got so they would groan when they saw me coming."

After we sat quietly for a minute or two, sipping our tea, I continued the interview.

"Dr. Charlotte Baker told me that you were the leader in Los Angeles in the fight for women's suffrage. Can you tell me a little about that effort?"

"Oh my, Doctor Baker, hmm… what a powerhouse for change that woman is. Please give her my regards when you see her. We have worked together many times. I'll say this, it is a new century and people are changing their minds about the role of women in our society. I argue before male jurors every day, and yet I'm not considered qualified to be a juror. It's ridiculous."

Concluding the interview, we briefly discussed her brother, Sam. "He told me that you were the reason he went to law school. He's very proud of you," I said.

"Sam's a fine lawyer, but I still think I can beat him in a courtroom. I've never had the chance; he doesn't do criminal work—he might get those carefully manicured hands dirty."

"I told him I wished I had been Mrs. Tingley's lawyer. That would have been quite a match. You know Sam is running for the United States Senate, and none other than Harrison Otis is his biggest supporter; that horse's rump," she added. "I'm supporting Sam, he's my baby brother, although politically, we're opposites."

Does he have a wife and children?

She shot me a curious look. "Yes, he's married and has four children. Why do you ask, did he make a pass at you?"

'No, of course not," I said unable to look her in the eye.

I finished my tea and posed this question to her. "I just have to ask you, what is Mrs. Otis like? This is not for the article."

"I've thought a good deal about the character of Harrison Otis in those long trial days; who the man really is behind all the bluster? I wondered what kind of woman he would choose to marry. I intend to become a novelist one day, Mrs. Foltz, and I want to keep track of interesting characters I meet along the way to prepare me for that."

"Well, he's an interesting man to be sure," she said.

"Hmm…Mrs. Otis, there isn't much to tell. We sometimes wonder in Los Angeles if Mrs. Harrison Otis even exists. He seems to be wed to his one true love, the City of Los Angeles, and he has done a great deal of good for her.

Otis rarely takes his wife anywhere; he usually shows up in all his uniformed glory alone. I met her once at a funeral of a former mayor. She never said a word to anyone. Let's just say that she does nothing to take any attention away from The General."

We concluded our discussion with Mrs. Foltz asking me questions about *my* life and *my* work. We had a short chat about that and I concluded by asking her if I could contact her again.

"I'd like to do a follow-up interview with you focused on women's suffrage in California; perhaps we could discuss this over the telephone?" She readily agreed, looked at her watch, and abruptly stood up to leave.

"I have to run, she said. It's been a pleasure dear… and Miss Riley, don't forget to say hello to Doctor Baker for me, and Henry too." I watched as she scurried out the door.

Father and Henry were all praise about the article I wrote about this remarkable woman. It was my best work to date: *Clara Shortridge Foltz: The Portia of the Pacific*. She had been given this moniker many years ago by a San Francisco newspaper. It certainly fits. Letters from women in response to the piece flooded into the paper. I had never received this many about my previous stories.

Father told me he had talked to Henry months ago that I wanted to have a letters column in my women's section; a place for the women of San Diego to have their say. They finally agreed. *Letters,* as it was titled, went in as a regular Sunday feature. This column proved to be an excellent forum for the women of our community to have a public say about issues that affected them. It had only been part of the paper for two weeks, and the letters were pouring in.

Chapter 47

There was a wonderful going-away dinner at our house for Jack on his last night in town. We had the chow-chow Charlie picked up for dinner from Li Wang on his way over. Father had ordered a couple of spicy dishes for Henry and Babe. As it turned out, Jack loved spicy food as well. We all squeezed in around the table and talked about all the fun times we'd had together. Henry and Babe gave Jack a hundred dollars to start his new life.

The dinner broke up at about eight-thirty. Henry planned to give Charlie a ride home as they lived in that direction. Babe and Henry got into their carriage after saying good night and wishing Jack well. Charlie followed them out and shook Jack's hand before he left. He responded by pulling him in for a big hug. Charlie kissed me on the cheek and rushed down the stairs and got into Henry's carriage.

We all stood on the porch and waved goodbye. Jack said he preferred to walk home, so he didn't take the carriage with them. "It isn't far, and a brisk walk is good for clearin' the head. I'm a little jittery this evening, what with me leaving for my new life in the morning."

Mother and Father said their goodbyes making Jack promise to write often and let them know how he was doing. Mother had knitted him a dark green and brown tweed scarf to wear on the ferry. Jack took it and put it around his neck.

"How do I look? He said with a grin. It will be like getting a hug from you every time I put it on."

Mother packed him some food and a jar of lemonade and included four Snickerdoodles. He took the food and lifted Mother, gave her a big hug and a kiss on the cheek, swinging her around as he usually did.

"Now I have something for you," he said. He pulled a little suede pouch from his vest pocket and handed it to her. She opened it and found a small gold locket. She opened it, but there was no picture in it. "It's for those grandchildren you'll be having soon. It was my mother's. You've always been so good to me; you remind me of her. I wanted you to have it."

"Thank you, dear," she said with tears in her eyes. "I will treasure it. Please come visit us soon. And write and let us know how you are doing. Of course, we'll see you at the wedding, which will be here before you know it."

He turned and shook hands with Father. "Thanks for everything, Mike. You have done so much for me and have taught me so much."

"We'll miss ya, Jack. Come visit soon and we'll take the *Serenity* for a sail."

Jack sold the boat to Father when he decided to take the job in Los Angeles. He knew how much Father loved sailing. He wanted to give it to him, but Father wouldn't hear of it. "It's a great sail all right; I miss her already. But I'll soon be living near the *Times* plant downtown, so I'll have nowhere to put a boat there. "

He looked at me; it was my turn to say goodbye. "Let me walk with you a ways, Jack."

It was getting dark. We s we reached the street at the end of the steps, Father called to me, "I'll put the porch light on for you Mary Kate. Don't go too far."

We had only gone as far as the Sweeney's, just three houses down when Jack stopped and looked at me. "Ya don't need to walk me, Mary Kate; then I will have to walk *you* home, and where will that leave us?"

Suddenly it hit me how much I was going to miss him. He is such an important part of my life, our lives, Charlie's and mine, and my parents' lives too.

Reaching up and putting my hands on his shoulders to steady myself on my tiptoes, I gave him a soft kiss on the cheek. "Goodbye Jack, we'll miss you so much."

I felt tears come to my eyes. Jack looked down at me, put his arm around my waist, and pulled me close. Surprised, I looked up as he drew me to him and kissed my lips. It was a slow, passionate kiss. A shudder raced down my spine, heat pulsing through me like I'd never felt. Not thinking even for a second, I sighed, "Oh, Jack," and I kissed him back.

He returned my kiss gently but then surprised me again by roughly pushing me away. "Goodbye, Mary Kate," he said. Then he turned and walked down the street towards the bay and home. He was taking the ferry to Los Angeles in the morning.

Come back, look at me; please Jack, just turn around.

I was lying in bed that night, and the thought of Jack's kiss consumed me. It triggered feelings in my body that I didn't know I had. It was like being awakened from a long sleep. Confused and upset, one thing was sure: I wanted more. It was hard for me to go to sleep that night.

How long had I had feelings for Jack? We cared for each other; he was my impatient, often exasperating big brother, but romantic inclinations? No. But the physical longing I felt for him since that kiss was entirely foreign *and* unwelcome. It upset my life and knocked me "arse over teakettle," to use my father's expression.

What was Jack feeling for me? That was not the kiss of a friend—that much was certain.

Charlie and I were shocked that Jack took a job at the *Los Angeles Times,* working for Harrison Otis no less, and before our wedding; after all, he was our best man. Now I suspected he did this because he did not want his feelings for me to interfere with our happiness.

That longing look on the porch that night a few weeks ago came back to me. I wondered if Jack held back and didn't pursue his feelings for me then, because Charlie was his best friend *and* the life he could give me was far superior to what he could afford.

Did I love Charlie? I thought I did. No... I was sure I did. He would make me happy. The fact is, Charlie kissing me never made me feel like Jack just did. This felt different, a lot different. I was on fire when he kissed me. The problem was, I didn't know if I should put out the fire or fan the flames.

I already felt a terrible longing to kiss him again and sure didn't want him to move away. But at the same time, the weight of guilt, a sense we had betrayed Charlie, hovered over me like a dark cloud. I didn't ask Jack for that kiss, but I went back for seconds without hesitation. Things would never be nor could ever be the same again between Jack and me. Between Charlie and me?

It was clear that it was too early for me to commit to a life with Charlie as his wife, at least until these feelings were sorted. Everything was different now; I was different. That kiss had turned me inside out. I couldn't stop thinking about how it made me feel to have Jack's arms around me, kissing me, loving me. What I couldn't sort is how I felt about him now.

After that day, we didn't hear from Jack at all. "He must be busy with his new job," Mother said one night at dinner. "He needs to settle in. He'll write soon, I'm sure, or maybe call at the paper." I said nothing.

Chapter 48

Hattie died just after Jack left for Los Angeles. Hattie and I had become close over the past year, and we got together often at The Children's Home when I went there with Mother. We both knew that when we spent time together last Sunday it would be our last visit. She was weak, her complexion was yellow, and it was clear that she had accepted her impending death. She wasn't fearful; she seemed happy to be going to her rest, as she put it.

She gave me two presents that day. One was her most treasured possession: her picture with her young siblings that she kept by her bed. It reminded her every day of where she came from, the people she loved, and better times. She looked so young, so happy.

"I was fifteen," she told me. The picture was taken before she was forced into prostitution by her parents' untimely death. She had to support her family.

Hattie also gave me a well-worn leather change purse. It had four green marbles in it. "I don't know why I kept them," she said, "but I want you to have them."

She must have kept these to remind her of where she'd been, her life as a green girl in one of the brothels she worked in— green dress, green door.

Babe knew Hattie well from her work at the Children's Home. They were friends. She didn't want her buried in a potter's field, so we split the cost of her grave and headstone. I insisted on contributing. Hattie loved Yeats, but his verses were too long for the headstone. So, we settled on this: Here lies a good woman, Hattie Daniels, 1883–1903.

Hattie's early death had a profound impact on me. I resolved not only to publicize the issue of prostitution and drug use as a significant part of what San Diego is, but to work with Babe, Dr. Baker, and Mother to end it, or at least curtail it in our city. As it was now, it was a dirty little secret that respectable San Diegans chose to ignore.

Most city leaders realized that if San Diego was going to take its rightful place on the world stage, that this issue must be addressed, but apparently not yet. My feature article about the Stingaree being the biggest prostitution and drug center in the southwest, included the personal story of one young prostitute I called Clare.

It was a good story and I worked very hard on it but didn't know if Father and Henry would run it. They wouldn't. Having earned my chops as a reporter over the past year, this was a slap in the face.

This was the second time I had written an article about prostitution that was rejected. Disappointed, angry, but not surprised, I was sure Babe would talk to Henry about it. I didn't ask her to, but she loved the story when I showed it to her, so I knew she would work on her husband to print it.

The weeks after Jack left flew by. Charlie was still working two days a week at the paper while the new photographer was broken in. This proved to be a difficult task. He was working at the bank the other days and seemed to enjoy it, but working in two such different jobs wasn't easy for him.

Father had to take over Jack's duties until a replacement could be found and he gave some of that work to me. We had already gone through one reporter who seemed promising until he returned from lunch drunk after only four days of work. The next one wasn't a very good writer and Father wanted to keep looking. So, just over a year as an apprentice, I was given at least temporarily, the assignment of writing most of the page-one news stories that my father couldn't get to. It was Jack's beat.

This was a problem because I was not allowed to go out on most of the stories alone as Jack did. Father, and sometimes even Cheesy, went with me to fire scenes, accidents, and crime scenes. Father just didn't like the idea of my going by myself; the work could be dangerous.

Father approved the stories after I wrote them. He did the interviews at first. He soon found that I was a quick study and pretty soon he let me do them. We made a good team. Replacing Jack at the paper was a tall order. He is an excellent reporter who required very little supervision; after all, he took what would be Father's job at the *Los Angeles Times*.

Father was surprised that I could hold my own as a hard news reporter that didn't need much supervision anymore. It was a hectic time. Looking in the mirror in my bedroom as I left for work one morning, I wondered who that grown-up woman was looking back at me.

During this time, my workload doubled, and so did Father's. Juggling my old duties, including my women's pages, and my new duties, was difficult. Snowed under with work at the paper and with the wedding planning, I didn't think much about Jack's kiss. I just tried to forget about it, hoping it would not change things between Jack and me before the wedding. After the wedding, he'd be back to his new life in Los Angeles, and I would be in my new life as Charlie's wife.

It did change things a bit between Charlie and me. After our engagement, our physical relationship progressed. There was a good deal more kissing and touching between us. We both enjoyed it, but it was clear we had to be cautious until the wedding. Mother warned me about this when Charlie and I started seeing each other almost every night. I admit that part of this was my effort to duplicate the passion I felt with Jack on the night we said goodbye.

Working with Father brought us closer together and in a new way: less parent and child and more adult father and daughter who were friends. Getting to know him, really knowing him, made me love him even more. He got to know me too and saw that his "Little Bit" had grown into much more than that little red-headed tom-boy who used to run through his house.

He seemed surprised, or so it seemed, at how good a reporter I turned out to be. He was proud of me. Looking back, I think his idea of having me as his apprentice was meant to be only temporary. It was important to be at Father's side during that awful time of grieving. I wanted to do anything I could to help him and the rest of the Riley family heal. As it turned out, we helped each other.

Father was a good teacher during this time although sometimes he was cantankerous and impatient. There were no more tear-filled exits as I had early on at the paper, but now, like everyone else, I took a snarl or two from Father in stride.

I had gotten used to his prickly manner of supervision which lessened considerably after the first six months as he weaned himself off the need to drink. He had that one serious relapse in October, around Tim's birthday, but he has had no problems since.

Chapter 49

Theodora came over almost every day after I got home from the paper. I filled her in on the plans for the wedding and my future life with Charlie up on Banker's Hill. I decided not to tell her about Jack's kiss. Things were pretty rocky in her life; her mother was dying, and I didn't want to make it worse. Still, the guilt was getting to me; we always told each other everything.

She wasn't at Jack's going-away party. Her mother was pretty low that night, and she made plans with Jack to walk him to the boat early the next day to say goodbye. Did he kiss her goodbye the way he kissed me the night before? I didn't ask. She didn't say.

She told me several times that Jack had broken her heart when he took the job with the *Times*. After seeing him for only a couple of weeks, she said that she thought that this time she was really in love. I wondered at the time if my getting married made her want to get married too, and Jack just happened to be her current beau. I liked the idea of Jack and Theodora as our couple friends after Charlie and I were married. We liked them both so much.

Theodora was a girl who was pretty fickle when it came to romance, and so was Jack. She knew that he fell in and out of "like" with many women and that he was very popular with the ladies. He had broken things off with Mary only a month before he started seeing her.

I asked Charlie why Jack broke things off with Mary. "She was moving him too fast toward the altar. That's probably one of the reasons he decided to move out of town. She was jingling wedding bells in his ears every chance she got."

Theodora was stunned that Jack didn't feel the same about her as she did about him. She wasn't used to being rejected. She was the one who usually ended the relationships she had, and there were many. Maybe that was what caused her to want so badly to get Jack back on her line; he was the one that got away.

Not one to give up on a conquest, she told me that she intended to keep in touch with Jack and, if he was amenable, possibly take me, and we could visit him. If not, she said that she hoped they would renew their relationship at the wedding in September when he returned to be our best man. Taking a wait-and-see attitude about Jack and Theodora, and putting Jack's kiss out of my mind, my attention was focused on my wedding and my work.

Father called me to his desk one Monday morning first thing: "Let's go, Mary Kate—there was a double murder, a shooting, in the Stingaree. I just got a call from Sargent Sanders at the police department. I've called Moody's, and a driver is probably out front now. I'd like to get over there before the other papers get the tip."

Grabbing my satchel and my notepad, we rushed out the door. Sean Moody, the youngest of the Moody sons, was already waiting in a carriage outside the front door. Moody's had purchased two used automobiles, but their regular livery service was still by horse-drawn carriage. Father helped me into the buggy. I called to Sean "Will you drive us up Fourth to Island Street to get to the wharf?"

"Sure thing," he replied.

"I want to see what Hattie told me was one of the fanciest brothels in town, the Canary Cottage."

"I know where it is, Sean said; you can't miss it."

We headed up the hill on Market and turned down Fourth. When we got to Island and turned left, there it was: The Canary Cottage—a pretty yellow house in the middle of the block where the swells and fat cats went for service. Freshly painted, it stood out like a big yellow sun amid the shabby gambling halls on the same block.

Hattie said she worked there for a couple of years for Ida Baily, the most notorious madam in the Stingaree. She was working for Madam Ida when she lost her virginity. "I got a bonus that night," she told me in a matter-of-fact tone.

Miss Ida, a former prostitute herself, was renowned all over the city, not only because she ran the fanciest, most expensive brothel in the Stingaree, but because her girls were known to be the most beautiful and were often very young. Ida dressed her girls as if they were going to the opera. Only high-class gents were admitted to the Canary Cottage.

She was well known for "plying her wares," as she described it. She did this by having her most beautiful girls ride in her white barouche carriage with its heavy gilt trim, driven out of the Stingaree on Sunday afternoons through respectable neighborhoods all over the city.

They took the same route every week at the same time. Hattie told me that the gents would sit on their porches whistling, waving, and hollering while these beautiful girls passed by. This was a source of amusement for the girls, too, as the wives would try to put a stop to this practice by their menfolk. They did this by expressing their disapproval in no uncertain terms and often unceremoniously hauling the men inside.

"I've never heard such cussin.' The men didn't pay it any mind; usually, they would be out there the next Sunday," Hattie told me. "We didn't do any business on the rides, and we couldn't get out of the carriage. We took turns going; it was great fun. It got us out of the Stingaree and allowed Miss Ida to stick her thumb in the eye of respectable people."

Sean soon turned on Fifth Street heading towards the wharf. Father pointed to the Railroad Coffee House, which he said was very popular because they served after-hours coffee spiked with whiskey. "They did this to sidestep the law against serving alcohol after midnight."

Hattie had told me about the place, she said that she and many of the gals went there often on their breaks. She said that Wyatt Earp used to frequent the place. "He kept to himself, he's a quiet sort of man. He was always real respectful to all the girls," she said. Mighty handsome too," she added. Hattie told me that Wyatt Earp dealt cards at his gambling hall until late at night, and went to " The Railroad" to get out of the place for a while and for a little company.

As Sean brought us closer to the wharf, we saw prostitutes walking the sidewalks outside the gambling halls. Even in daylight, they were flirting and calling to men passing by. Father noticed me looking at the girls.

"The gambling goes on all night; the girls are out front waiting for them twenty-four hours a day. Did you know there are over two hundred girls working in the Sting? "

As we passed, I noticed the different colored dresses the girls wore and thought about what Hattie had told me about the green marbles she gave me. The girls wear dresses to match the room in the brothel with a door the same color. This is where the sexual liaison would take place. The customers chose a girl on the street. She gave them a marble in her color, and the business end, the payment, would be conducted at the brothel. Hattie was a green girl. She had a partner, Nan, who shared the green room on the half hour. She had the first half hour and Nan had the second.

The prostitutes working for Miss Ida did not sleep in their place of business. They slept on old mattresses in a smelly, unheated, and unventilated horse barn behind the brothel. Hattie said it was stifling in hot weather.

Sean dropped us off in the seediest part of the Stingaree near the wharf: the cribs. It made me sick to look at them. They were tiny run-down shacks. There was a white sign nailed on one of them with *Girls-25* cents scrawled on it in red.

The cribs were Hattie's last stop as a prostitute before she got hepatitis and had to move to the Children's Home. She was addicted to cocaine and opium by then.

The cribs were filthy, disgusting, and degrading for the women and their customers. There was no privacy. There were no issues of race there like there were in the other brothels in the Stingaree; crib prostitutes were of all colors and nationalities. After all, this was the end of the line, the bottom of the barrel.

Father seemed to know where we were going; he had gotten the details from Sargent Sanders. He was at the scene of the murders when we arrived. He told Father that the victims were drug dealers picking up product: cocaine and opium mostly. There were two dead bodies laid out a few feet away; both had been shot in the chest. Nobody bothered to cover them. It was a shocking sight.

"This was a drug deal gone wrong, Mike," he said.

"A great deal of money changes hands down here—local distributors selling drugs to locals, but also to dealers from Los Angeles and even as far away as Arizona. The drugs come off the ships and over the Mexican border."

"Believe it or not, he said, looking at me, "San Diego is a drug mecca. Los Angeles is too far from the Mexican border, and there is no harbor near the city. San Diego has it all when it comes to the drug trade. I can tell you this: big money is made here on drug sales."

"These buyers, both from Los Angeles, were killed in some sort of dispute over money. Self-defense, the shooter told me. There were no witnesses. I suspect that there were witnesses, but mum's the word down here."

Father interviewed the man who admitted to doing the shooting—Jake Jolson. He was a short, stocky man with greasy hair and the reddened face and bulbous nose of an alcoholic. Jolson didn't have much to say besides what Sargent Sanders had already told us. Pointing to the first body, Mr. Jolson turned and looked our way, "He pulled a gun on me so I shot him; his partner then pulled his gun and I had to plug him too."

He said this in the most matter-of-fact way, as if he was describing what he had for breakfast. Predictably, he gave us few details and didn't mention that it involved a drug transaction. The sale of cocaine and opium, like prostitution, was illegal in San Diego, but these laws were not enforced. On the ride back to the paper, I asked Father why.

"It's sort of an unwritten agreement with the business owners in the Stingaree. They agreed to keep the prostitutes and the drug dealing confined to the Stingaree, and the police and civic leaders agreed there would be no actual enforcement of drug and prostitution laws. In other words, they would look the other way. It's called containment.

"Civic leaders and upstanding citizens don't like the arrangement, but they like the idea of prostitutes and drug dealers in their neighborhoods, businesses, and churches even less. And, of course, many of our finest citizens own the buildings in the Sting' and make a tidy profit off the rents without having to do much maintenance."

Containment, Father told me, means that prostitutes are never allowed to go into businesses outside the Stingaree. Messenger boys are sent out of the district to buy needed items. Doctors and dentists sometimes came to the district, although most of the girls rarely sought professional help for their ailments. Mostly they self-medicated with a ready supply of painkillers right in the neighborhood.

Abortions were frequent and were mostly performed by untrained midwives or even more frequently by other prostitutes. Many women died in these procedures, and they often resulted in sterility. Hattie said she was sterile from one of these operations, which was performed by her madam at the time.

Members of the religious community in San Diego claimed they prayed for the prostitutes and dance hall girls in The Stingaree but they were not welcomed in their churches. There was no church in the Stingaree, although many women who lived there were quite religious.

Hattie said many of the rooms where the sex acts were performed had pictures of Jesus or Mother Mary looking down on the couple from above the bed. Local clergy avoided the district like the plague. They claimed empathy for the women, but they offered nothing by way of help.

She told me there was an occasional police raid of the brothels to keep up the appearance of enforcement. These were done after reasonable notice to the madams, handlers, and their customers. A few girls were brought in, jailed for a few hours, and given a minimal fine. Their customers always seemed to escape these raids.

We returned to the paper, and I wrote the story of the murders for the front page. Father told me that murders were infrequent in the city and that this was big news.

I decided to weave in materials from some of my unpublished articles about prostitution in the city. This time I got a hearty agreement from Father when he reviewed the story before it went to press. "Mary Kate, your prostitution background material really added depth to the story."

The following week, I wrote a new article about prostitution and its victims, "The Soiled Doves," as some men call prostitutes. Father and Henry gave me the go-ahead to print it in the women's section. I added some additional information I had gotten from some local leaders who were working on the issue but so far, with little success.

Nearly a week after the article was published in the Sunday women's section, to my shock, Henry made a point to compliment me on the piece. "Mary Kate, I received no negative response, at least not yet. Very well done, yes indeed, very well done."

Babe took me to lunch the next day. She loved the article. "Everyone knows we need to take care of this problem sooner rather than later, but nobody has wanted to take leadership on the issue until now… including my husband."

"*The San Diego Sun* has been doing some work on drugs and prostitution in the Stingaree in a series of articles, and I think that got Henry to look at doing some work on the subject at the *Union*."

"Mary Kate, newspapers and their reporters and publishers are leaders in their communities, and what they print, what they expose and inform the public about, molds public opinion."

"The mess at the Stingaree, starting with the Cribs, is the first thing to greet anyone arriving in the city by sea: men, women, and children, rich and poor," Babe said with chagrin. "Is this the way we want to welcome new arrivals? It's like taking a guest in your home through an outhouse to get to the parlor. Thousands of visitors a year get their first glance at San Diego when they get off the boat at the wharf in the Stingaree. It's disgraceful."

"Everyone knows that most visitors arriving at the wharf are likely coming into the city with money. Henry says that just walking through the Stingaree from the wharf to get to the decent side of town, or even waiting at the wharf for a ride, can get you mugged. "

"We have finally realized that San Diego is first and foremost a tourist destination because of our mild year-round climate and natural beauty. San Diego can never really take its rightful place on the world stage until this shameful remnant of our Wild West days is eliminated or at least controlled."

Chapter 50

The weeks seemed to fly by. I kept busy both with the paper and making preparations for the wedding. It was an exciting time with a few big surprises and more than a few bumps in the road.

Charlie was already doing well at the bank, and he seemed to like it. He often commented on the good work done by the Union's new photographer. He was better than the photographers from the other local papers. Still, we both knew that his work product was far below Charlie's; to his credit, he never said so.

Henry paid for a celebration with the folks at the paper at the Harbor Bar, where we all bid Charlie good luck on his new job as a banker. His stint working both at the bank *and t*he paper had come to an end. The Union without Jack and Charlie just didn't seem possible. But, I was so busy I didn't think much about it.

He took me to dinner last Saturday night at the home of one of his wealthy bank customers. It was at a huge house not far from his parent's place. Mrs. Riggs gave me a lovely gown to wear.

At the party, I found that Charlie was quite skilled at what Jack called shmoozin' and boozin'. I never saw that side of him. He's a natural salesman. His parents were there, and Mrs. Wilson took me under her wing. After dinner, she introduced me to the wives who congregated in the parlor while the men smoked cigars and discussed business in the wood-paneled library.

Maisie Wilson was perfectly charming. I could see after meeting her over a year ago, that she is very much like her father, Grandfather Hal. She has many interests and seemed to have something in common with everyone she spoke with. Her particular skill is making everyone feel they are the most interesting person in the room. Unlike me, she is a good listener, a skill I determined that night I was going to acquire.

"It's a learned skill, dear, she told me; it just takes practice." It is challenging for us bossy women," she added with a chuckle, taking my hand.

Mother and I met with Mrs. Wilson frequently to discuss the wedding details. Sometimes we would meet at the Wilsons and sometimes she would come to our house. Mother always got completely twitter-pated on those occasions, cleaning every inch of the place, even getting fresh flowers for the front room. She always made special cookies to have with our tea; Snickerdoodles would simply not do.

"She's not royalty Maggie," Father told her at breakfast one morning. Mother paid him no mind.

Mrs. Wilson resigned from the start that Charlie and I would get married in a Catholic church. She didn't even bring it up. The Wilsons are what Charlie calls "lukewarm Episcopalians. We don't go to church unless someone gets married or dies."

Mother already knew Mrs. Wilson. The two women worked together at the Children's home before I got engaged to Charlie. Both women were on the board and they had become friends.

The first issue to come up was the location of the wedding. I didn't want a large wedding, but with the business associates and friends the Wilsons "needed to invite," as Mrs. Wilson put it, we would have to move the ceremony from our parish church to the Catholic cathedral on the hill. Mother and I agreed.

"St. Paul's is a beautiful church," Mother chimed in. "Maybe our parish priest would do the ceremony there. I'll check with him."

The very next week, a serious bump in the road presented itself. Charlie and I went to see Father Hackett, the pastor at St. Pat's, about our marriage plans. He is a nasty, mean old Irishman. He is no charmer on his best day. Nobody likes him.

As soon as we sat down in his office in the rectory, and without any pleasantries to get in his way, he told me flat out, "If you want to be married in the Church, with a Mass, your husband must convert to Catholicism."

He directed his comments only to me as if Charlie wasn't there. He treated him all through the meeting like the infidel he clearly considered him to be. The good father made it clear to me that marrying outside the faith was, to say the least, frowned upon by the Church. With that introduction, Charlie refused to convert. He told Father Hackett this before we left that day.

I found a way around this with Mother's help. If we didn't have a Mass, we could be married in the Church if Charlie agreed to raise our children Catholic. At first, Charlie and his parents balked at that too. Apparently, all Protestants looked at Catholics as infidels.

Father, who is my expert on all things Irish, explained that Maisie Wilson, formerly Maisie O'Flaherty, was as Irish as could be, but that she was from a Protestant family that hailed from Belfast, Northern Ireland. "The last thing her people want to see is an Irish Catholic in the family."

After a bit of time passed, Charlie agreed that our children would be raised Catholic. He reminded me of the advice he got from Jack right after we got engaged. Jack was no church-goin' man himself, but he was raised by a mother that was. He hadn't seen much of the inside of a church since his mother died.

Jack told Charlie some time ago when we were sitting on the porch after dinner one night, that he would have to agree to raise our children in the Church if he wanted to marry me. "It has to be that way—her mother will never allow Mary Kate to be married outside the church. And it's the mother that has the say when it comes to matters concerning the children. Women pretend the husband decides, but that's pure fiction."

The very next Sunday afternoon, Charlie asked me to dinner at his parent's house. He asked me if I wanted to take a walk with him before we ate. He took me by the hand, and we walked up the hill. He stopped in front of a beautiful house, much smaller than his parents' house, far less grand, but still beautiful. It was two stories, gray with black trim and white around the window sashes.

"Come, darling," he said, leading me up the front steps by the hand. "Let's go see our new house. My grandfather Wilson is giving it to us as a wedding present."

We went into the large front room. It was already fully furnished. "Do you l like it?"

"Of course, I do," I replied, but I didn't say much for a minute or two. "I'm just a little disappointed that nobody asked me what kind of house I wanted or where I wanted to live."

"I know, I know, but Grandfather already had this house, and he was getting ready to sell it. He thought it would be a nice wedding present. And, when we have children, they will have their grandparents around the corner. Don't worry; you can run this house, redecorate it, and make it your own." He went on, making things even worse.

"You'll be quitting your job soon to prepare for the wedding; you can redecorate then. Mother will help you; she loves that type of thing. She says you two should start ordering wallpaper, fabric, and things like that now because it takes some time to get things."

"Charlie," I said, irritated, "you have this all worked out, don't you? Do I have a say in any of this?"

He looked shocked at my response, wounded even. "Of course you do."

"I love my work and I have every intention of keeping my job at the paper, both before and after we're married."

"Be realistic Mary Kate, he countered, "you'll have a house to run, you'll be involved in charitable work, and there will be parties you need to host for my clients at the bank. And pretty soon, there will be children to mind."

"Hold your horses, Charlie; we need to think about this, where we're heading, where *I'm* heading. There have been all these plans made without me. It's just too much to think about all at once."

We walked back to his parent's house in silence. He took me home a little while later. In the carriage on the ride home, he told me that I was right, that we needed to think about our lives and make plans together.

The next time I saw Charlie was for dinner at my house. The subject of our making plans came up again as we sat on the porch waiting for Ben.

"It will all work out, Mary Kate. I talked to my mother about it, and she says all brides get the jitters and that this is to be expected. I'm sure she's right, so don't get your dander up; just try to simmer down."

He took my hand and rubbed it. It didn't soothe. I was furious that he talked to his mother about my concerns, but I said nothing. When Ben pulled up, Charlie said that it was getting late and that he had early meetings at the bank. He pulled me to him and gave me a very passionate kiss. Our physical desire for each other increased as time went on. He never pushed things but we both were anxious to be married. Charlie kissed me again and hopped down the porch and into the carriage. He leaned out the window. "Don't worry, Mary Kate, you'll be fine."

410

Later that night, I spoke to Mother about my concerns, and she agreed with Mrs. Wilson. This infuriated me even more. I felt abandoned. She simply dismissed my concerns as *my* problem, pre-wedding nerves.

"Every bride goes through this— doubts, wondering if you are making the right choice."

Charlie and I were spending a great deal of time in his world with his friends. We often went out with Pamela Spaulding and Eddie to various events around town. One Sunday, we all went by train to the bathhouse in La Jolla. Charlie agreed to go but warned me he didn't want to swim. I convinced him by telling him that La Jolla Cove was a great place for us to spend time alone while Eddie and Pamela were in the bathhouse.

Our train arrived at lunchtime, just after the sun burst through the usual morning clouds. It was a beautiful sunny day. Before we went our separate ways, we all sat at a table outside the bathhouse which overlooked the cove, laughing and joking, eating the picnic lunch Pamela had prepared.

After the La Jolla trip, Pamela asked Theodora and me to help her install wallpaper in her new house. It seemed like an odd request at the time, but we agreed. She said her father had bought her a small but charming cottage on Union Street near the courthouse.

Theodora and I surprised her the following Sunday by riding on our women's bicycles to her house. It was a short ride. It was a bit of a challenge to bring our contribution to dinner, one of mothers lemon pies, but Theodora balanced the pie box on her handlebars.

Pamela told us when we got there that she didn't have a women's bicycle. "I don't need one. I have one without the skirt guard. I just borrowed some short pants from Eddie's brother."

Theodora and I were impressed with this idea and vowed to try it. Pamela knew how to ride a bicycle, could swim, sail a boat, play

411

golf and tennis, and even, like her famous father, play baseball. What did I expect? Her father was a world-class athlete, a former baseball star, and he owned a successful athletic equipment company.

Pamela, Theodora, and I all wallpapered her front room together. I was surprised she asked us to help; she certainly could afford a professional, but I think she wanted to spend the day with us. She put some music on the gramophone, and we had a great day.

The wallpaper hanging didn't work out too well. We forgot to match the flowers on the seams of the wallpaper and hung a few panels upside down. The whole thing looked a bit disconnected and goofy. After we finished the last section, we stood back and looked at our work.

"It looks great." Pamela fibbed. We looked at each other and laughed. "We can fix it," she said.

We got together often after that day, especially Pamela and Theodora. They both loved horses and spent a lot of time riding at a ranch a few miles up the hill, where Pamela boarded several horses. Theodora soon moved her horse there, and they rode even more often. She picked up some extra money teaching wealthy young women how to ride and how to compete in equestrian matches which were very popular with the upper class in San Diego.

Chapter 51

I was getting more and more nervous about getting married—cold feet, my mother said. I wasn't sure that marrying Charlie was what I wanted or what would make either of us happy. I talked to my mother often about this, but she seemed so hell-bent on my marrying *anyone* that she didn't have an objective view of things. So, I decided to talk to Babe Seymour.

Babe came from a well-off family of college professors and writers. We arranged a date for lunch at the Horton Hotel. I left that lunch with this thought: Love does not overcome all obstacles; there can be compromises, but those must be worked out, at least on the major issues, before the wedding.

"Henry was not considered a prize by my family," she told me. He had little formal education, didn't have much money, and, as they saw it, he didn't have much ambition. They couldn't understand what the attraction was.

"He isn't even good-looking," my mother told me one day. She laughed softly. "I knew these criticisms were unfair. I think our love for each other and my willingness to leave the more sophisticated life I came from made our marriage work. And, of course, moving far away from my family."

She took my hands in hers and asked me: "Can you leave Rabbitville behind, be content to just come back for a visit from time to time—is Banker's Hill where you want to be?"

"Your father will never want to be a part of your life on Banker's Hill. He'd be like a fish out of water. But my dear, a compromise might be made. Both parties need to bend. This is a hard one, Mary Kate."

Henry and Babe had recently bought an automobile—a fancy red Cadillac Model A. Babe let me try it out that day. She took me out on a country road in the valley. It was thrilling to drive, feeling out of control at times, squealing with delight while careening down the road, loving the excitement of the ride. Tim would have loved this, I thought, driving that new red Cadillac. This time it wasn't a sad thought.

Babe took over to drive me home. "Don't share with your parents just how wild the ride was, Mary Kate," she told me when she dropped me off at home.

She honked the horn when we got to the house. Mother and father came out on the porch to see what was happening. Father insisted on taking a spin in the Cadillac. Babe agreed.

"Take Maggie with you, she said. I will wait for you on the porch." Father helped Mother into the passenger seat and pulled away.

They weren't gone long, but when they returned, Father was besotted with owning his own automobile. "Hank Moody has restored two already, and he'll help me get my own in shape. Maggie looked mighty good in this shiny red Cadillac; maybe I will try to find a red one too," he said, breathless with excitement. Mother's face was flushed; was that fear or excitement?

Charlie had already ordered a black 1902 Mercedes 40HP, one of the fastest cars made. He pointed one out downtown one day. It wasn't as pretty a car as Henry and Babe's Cadillac, but he told me that it was much faster. I couldn't wait for him to get it.

A few days later, I had tea with Fiona Riggs and talked to her about my concerns about marrying Charlie. She told me she had come from a middle-class farm family outside Kansas City. She met her husband at the Methodist church they both attended when they were both involved in fundraising for the poor. They fell in love. "My husband is a banker, as was his father," she said.

"John is from a wealthy, well-respected Kansas City family. His parents disapproved of the match and discouraged him from marrying me. We loved each other, and so we got married."

"But his involvement in his banking business has never included me, except as a hostess or a wife on his arm or to socialize with the other wives while the men discuss business. I knew that would be my role before we married, but I told myself I would have children to fill the space. And then we couldn't have children."

"John and I still love each other; he's wonderful. But I have been quite lonely in this big house. I miss my family and the friends that I had growing up, who have a history with me; they can never be replaced. I especially miss my older sister, Bess. She writes, which keeps us in touch, at least a little."

"John says I can visit them when I want to, but he doesn't like me traveling alone, and we rarely return to Kansas. My family has never come out here, and neither have my friends. They think this is the Wild West, with Indians, cowboys, and all that. They're afraid. They have never gone anywhere outside of Kansas. "Wyatt Earp lives there, for gosh sake," my mother wrote me when we first moved here."

"Would they be comfortable in my world out here in San Diego? Probably not, but I do miss them. John's family is still in Kansas, too; we don't have any real family here. Except you, dear," she said wistfully."

"You have become like a daughter to me, or at least a favored niece," she responded warmly. "I've so enjoyed hearing about your adventures at the paper, your romances, getting to know you."

I felt the same way about Mrs. Riggs, that she was family, a dear aunt. San Diego was a city of transplants. Most of the people here came from somewhere else. This is except for the leftovers from Mexican rule that were born here and chose to remain here after San Diego became part of California.

Tim and I were unusual; we were born in San Diego when it was still a dusty western town. Few of our friends or even natives had extended family in San Diego. So most of us here adopted family: parents, grandparents, cousins, as well as aunts and uncles. People in Rabbitville treat each other as one big family.

Mrs. Riggs and I spoke for a long time about how well I had adjusted to Charlie's world. "I do fine on Banker's Hill; I like his parents and friends. Still…"

"I know you're in love, and Charlie is a fine young man, and so handsome too, but you're moving up the hill will not be without difficulties. The good news is that Rabbitville to Banker's Hill is not moving across the country. There is a divide there, though."

"You are blinded by love right now, so checking things out with people who love you and who you respect as you are doing now is a good way to sort things out. She stopped talking and laughed. "Oh, how I blather on."

She warmed up the tea in my cup, sat back in her chair, gave me a Cheshire cat smile, and said, "Now, tell me every detail of the wedding dress your mother will make for you. And if you're not sworn to secrecy, tell me about the wedding plans so far—I won't tell a soul."

"Oh, one minute," she said, jumping up. She came back with a large box. She set it on the table and opened it. "It's from Paris. It's not a wedding dress, but your mother can alter it for the occasion. I haven't worn it; it is my present if you want it. You might favor a more traditional style, but I think you might like this modern gown."

416

She opened the box and took out a simple silk-satin, cream-colored dress. It had a deep V-neck, and I had nothing to put in the crevasse, but its simple lines were exquisite. Only a very slim-figured girl could wear it. I loved it. She looked at me in anticipation of my response. "I love it, Mrs. Riggs, but it's too much; you haven't even worn it." She interrupted me.

"Of course, you should have it. I would be thrilled to see you walk down the aisle in it."

"May I take it home and see what Mother says? She will know if she can tailor it so it works for me. You are so good; thank you."

"You have changed so much in the last year; you have matured— you are so sophisticated, so beautiful. I think you have even grown a bust line," she said with a smile. I looked down; there wasn't much change. "You look like a woman now; you're not a little girl as you were when we first met."

As her driver took me home, I thought about what she had told me. Would Charlie's family and friends feel comfortable in Rabbitville? Charlie and I met and fell in love in my world, working at the paper and going places with Jack. Now Charlie was suddenly planning a life for me, for us, in a different world, leaving that old world and the people in it behind.

I'd see my family, yes, but somehow I would be just visiting. Even more troubling was that I would be expected to leave a good part of myself behind to take on a role that I just wasn't interested in or suited for. *Me, a society matron?*

Did I really want to spend my days as a hostess and companion to my banker husband? I didn't like the separation of the sexes in our former library arrangement when I was a girl, I sure didn't like the after-dinner segregation of wives and their husbands so that the men could discuss matters of business, of importance really while smoking their cigars in the library. That's s just not me. I had important things to say too.

I didn't envy Fiona Riggs's life *or* Masie Wilson's for that matter. This is the role Charlie clearly intended for me. It was the role he *needed* his wife to play, I was sure of that. It felt more and more that I would be moving not just my life to Banker's Hill, but changing the woman I am. Is this what I wanted?

Charlie gave up his passion, photojournalism, which he loves so much, to get married to me and provide a better life for our family. Was his asking me to give up my work and take on a new role any different?

Chapter 52

I was so confused about what had happened between Jack and me the day we said goodbye, and at first, I couldn't get it out of my mind. But as the weeks passed, there was wedding planning and the extra work Father and I had to do to make up for Jack's absence. This took up so much of my time that putting Jack's kiss aside, putting it away really, was easy.

Ironically, the decisions Charlie and his parents had made for *our* lives, *my* life, sowed the seeds of doubt that I was marrying the right man. It wasn't intentional. Charlie loved me, and I loved him. Still, the more things went along, the less sure I was that we belonged together.

It was clear that his parents would likely call the shots about Charlie's future *and mine.* If I couldn't accept this, we shouldn't marry. They already told him where he would work and where we would live—on Banker's Hill, right around the corner from them. It became obvious that Charlie Wilson, an only son, would act at the direction of his parents, as he was groomed to do.

Was he a mama's boy? More and more, I thought so. He consulted her about everything, it seemed, even before he discussed it with me. I knew that this was not going to change. Theodora assured me that things would be different when I became "the woman of the house."

I had grown this past year into not only being comfortable in the world of the upper class, after all, that was my beat at the paper, but I started to picture myself there, wanting to be there. Izzy came from a wealthy family too. His father is very successful in real estate. Izzy, like Charlie, followed his father in his profession. Izzy's mother was dead, so I knew I would be the woman in his life if we were married. Charlie? I was beginning to doubt it.

All summer as Izzy took me on his arm to various parties and events I became comfortable with his friends, his family, and their world. I fit in just fine, and I loved it. I just didn't love him and didn't have to make any decisions about living in that world as a married woman.

Now, Charlie's parents have plucked him out of Rabbitville and brought him back to the world he came from. He seems comfortable with that. I see now that there was a certain inevitability about his returning to life on Banker's Hill. I didn't consider then that my family and friends had no real place where Charlie and I would make our lives together. It wasn't that they wouldn't be welcome; it was a question of whether they would want to be there.

And what about our children and their grandchildren? I thought about talking to my mother about this—she came from a reasonably well-to-do family. But, she married a handsome newspaperman with an Irish brogue, a beautiful voice, and a wicked sense of humor— and could he dance! She did this out of love, giving up her dream of singing in the San Francisco Opera and the many wealthy suitors who wanted to marry her. Could I give up my world for the man I loved?

"Well, she told me, we moved far away from my family, didn't we? This was what Babe and Fiona Riggs had told me. "After we moved here and my mother came to visit and help me with Tim when he was born, she came to love your father, and everything worked out fine. But I don't know how well your father would have blended into my family's life had we stayed."

Chapter 53

Jack's kiss was stored in my memory and in my journal. Still, despite my efforts to forget it, I found myself reading over the entry on the night of his kiss and writing some new pages, weighing the pros and cons of my life with Charlie. I would review those pages often before going to bed.

Jack would be coming here the weekend of the wedding at the end of September, but we probably wouldn't be seeing him before that. He had a new life now. He called Charlie a few times and he told me that Jack said that he was working hard and settling into his new job. He was spending his days off on the docks with his uncle to earn some money to buy a disabled Ford he had seen for sale parked near the waterfront.

"Taking the train every day doesn't suit him at all," Charlie said. "If he has to work late, which he often does, he has to bunk with a friend or get a cheap hotel downtown. There are no late trains to San Pedro. He's looking to find a place downtown."

"He likes his new job and the excitement of Los Angeles. He has already made some friends at the paper. They have their own reporter's watering hole near the *Times* plant."

Charlie didn't say so, but he probably already had a new lass on his arm. This was for the best, although I missed him a great deal. Trying not to think about Jack had the opposite effect. As things became uncertain about my future with Charlie, I began to think about finding out if Jack was in love with me as I suspected he was, and sorting out my feelings for him. I decided after not hearing from him, that I would tell my mother about his kiss. She wasn't surprised.

"Your father could see this coming; you must have at least wondered about it?"

"I would sometimes catch Jack looking at me a certain way, but I just ignored it, dismissed it, thinking that it didn't mean anything. He is such a flirt. Besides, he has taken on the role of a cantankerous big brother since Time died. Most of the time, he was teasing me and acting as big brothers do; that their younger siblings are simply annoying."

"He seemed happy with Mary and had been seeing her for eight months, an eternity for Jack. I like Mary and thought she had a leveling, calming influence on him. Charlie and I were shocked when Jack took the job in Los Angeles. After his kiss, I understood why. He didn't like it that he had fallen for his best friend's gal."

"He didn't enjoy seeing you two lovebirds every day. It hurt him," Mother said. "I know Jack pretty well. I think he kissed you that night to tell you how he felt. He didn't plan it. He can be very impetuous. He pushed you away because he knew the kiss was way out of line, a betrayal of his best friend. This is why he hasn't contacted you since he left."

Nodding, I told her, "He hasn't even contacted Theodora. She told me that she has sent him several letters."

"Jack's a bit rough around the edges, but he is very sensitive in matters of the heart, just like your father." Mother paused for a moment. "So, are you going to do anything about it?"

"I've thought about that a great deal. Charlie is out of town with his father until next Tuesday. I want to take a trip to Los Angeles on Saturday with Father to see Jack; to work this out. I have to know; to find out how I feel about him and to see if I'm right about how he feels about me."

"But Mother, what if I am wrong? It could be very embarrassing."

"If he loves you, Mary Kate, you need to find out. If he doesn't, he'll come for the wedding and return to his life in Los Angeles, and you can go back to your life. But if you seriously think you have feelings for Jack, you must see him."

"And if you are even asking about this now, you shouldn't marry Charlie, at least not until you're sure he is who you want, Jack or no Jack. I can tell you this: if you aren't sure about him before the wedding, it does not bode well for your life together after you are married."

"Father and I could take the ferry which docks in San Pedro. Jack works on the docks there with his uncle, and I can see him there. Would that be wrong of me?"

She sighed, "No, A woman knows a great deal from a man's kiss. You just will have to see Jack to find out. You are dealing with the rest of your life dear; you need to make the right choice."

"Will you tell Father? I don't think I can face him. It seems like I'm doing something behind Charlie's back. And I guess I am. But I have to know."

"Your father will not be surprised, dear, kiss or no kiss. He told me months ago that he thought Jack had feelings for you. I didn't see it, but he didn't come over that often, and usually, Charlie was around."

The following day was a Thursday, Mother and I talked it over with Father after dinner. Mother was right; Father didn't act surprised.

"Well, my girl, I guess I need to take you to fetch your man out of the clutches of Harrison Otis and the *Los Angeles Times.* We can catch the early morning ferry on Saturday to San Pedro. He left me his uncle's address if we can't find him working on the docks."

"But Father, what if I have this wrong? He hasn't written, not even to you."

"Well, that's just the chance you'll have to take. If you think you love the lad, you must go after him and find out if he feels the same. If he doesn't, we'll jump back on the ferry and come home. I'll get the ferry tickets tomorrow."

We left at eight-thirty on a foggy San Diego morning on a ferry headed for Los Angeles, docking in San Pedro. It's steam-powered with large smokestacks and a paddlewheel, with a pilothouse on each end. This allows the ferry to come into the dock with a pilot in front and leave the dock with a pilot on the other end. There were two ferries a day each way between Los Angeles and San Diego, one in the early morning and one in the mid-afternoon. I had never been out of San Diego and never had been on a ferry, but that was the last thing on my mind.

Father and I took seats on the second level with the rest of the passengers. About twenty minutes later, we heard the shrill whistle announcing our departure. The ferry was full; there were two hundred passengers. Soon we felt a trembling of the boat and heard the sound of the engines firing up. I looked at my father, worry on my face. "Is this the right thing to do, Father?"

He put his arm around me and gave me a squeeze. "Don't worry."

I *was* worried, as well as scared. Tired from a fretful night, I slept on Father's shoulder while he read his book. After I woke up, we ate some of the food Mother had packed. She didn't want to go with us; she doesn't swim and doesn't like being out in the ocean.

We were still a ways out, so Father and I walked on the promenade on the upper deck. It was windy and chilly up there, so we didn't stay too long. It felt nice to clear my head in the salty air.

424

We saw a school of dolphins swimming beside the boat, traveling with us, jumping with delight, and enjoying the trip.

We pulled into San Pedro Harbor around noon. It was cloudy and cool when we got off the ferry. Father and I walked down the docks for about a quarter of a mile. We were about to give up when I saw him—Jack. He was loading a big box onto the dock about a hundred feet in front of us. He was wearing his newsie cap. Father saw him too. "I think I will wait over there," he said, turning to walk to a bench about fifty feet behind us.

I stopped suddenly, panicked, and grabbed his arm. He turned to me. "Father, what if Jack doesn't feel the way I think he does? Maybe he's moved on. Things could get embarrassing."

"If that's the case, we'll get a bite to eat and take the afternoon ferry back home. Now just get over there and put your heart on the line. And Mary Kate, the man would be a fool not to want you." He smiled. I hugged him, then turned to do what I came for.

So nervous my mouth was dry; I wanted to turn around. As I approached the area where Jack was working, I could see that the man he was working with looked like a younger version of his father. This must be his Uncle Jack. I was about ten feet away; he looked up at me and gave me a smile and a nod like he'd give any pretty woman passing by. Jack still hadn't seen me.

I stood still, frozen in fear, feeling sick to my stomach. His uncle looked at Jack and nodded his head toward me. Jack turned around and looked at me. At first, he didn't react. He slowly put down the box, and stood still just looking at me for just a second or two more; it seemed so much longer. He didn't look happy or surprised. I looked back at him; this time, I was the one with longing in my eyes. We looked at each other for what seemed like an eternity. At that moment, I knew I was in love with him, that he was the man I wanted.

425

Suddenly he jumped up on the dock and put his arms around me, lifting me up to kiss me, and what a kiss it was. "So, ya think you have me wrapped around your little finger and I'm just going to give up my job and move back to San Diego with you—is that what you're thinking, Missy?"

I looked into his eyes. "Of course I am," I said softly, kissing him. He picked me up off my feet again and twirled me around, and kissed me; this time it was a much longer kiss. I felt the same charge run through me as the first time he kissed me.

"I love you, Jack," I whispered, and he kissed me again.

"Do ya now?" he said.

"How did you get here?" he asked, putting me down. I turned to where Father was seated on the bench.

"Well, let's go say hello to him then. . . Oh, wait, just a second." He introduced me to his Uncle Jack and told him he needed to take the rest of the day off. "I have an unexpected visitor."

"Go ahead," his uncle said with a wide smile. "I don't blame ya none—she's mighty pretty."

Father stood up when Jack and I walked towards him hand in hand. "So good to see you, Jack."

He looked at me. "So, are you sure this big lug is who you'll be wantin' Mary Kate?" He said, his brogue especially thick.

Jack took us to a wonderful fish dinner at a place called Maggie's Café, just a short walk down the dock. "I think of your beautiful Ma when I come to this place."

After our meal, he told Father where we could get inexpensive but clean lodging for the night. "The Graham Hotel, just a few blocks away, right on this street, left going out the door."

"OK, then, I'm off to find a room, Father said. You two need to work a few things out. 'Don't be too late—the ferry home leaves early in the morning."

Father left, and Jack looked across the table at me and took both of my hands in his. What I saw in his eyes was unmistakable; he did love me.

Chapter 54

As we finished our coffee, Jack explained that he had taken the job at the *Times* because he couldn't stand his longing for me and his guilt for falling for his best friend's bride-to-be. "I tried, but I just couldn't get you off my mind."

"The job came up, the money was good, and I felt I could make some good progress in my life. It's a big outfit and, believe it or not, Otis gives you a lot of freedom to do your job. You just have to put up with the old blowhard once in a while, but that's no problem—he isn't at the paper very much. Once I got to know him a bit, I got to like the old coot."

"I don't know how long I've felt this way about you. You were so cantankerous with me, and I was with you when you started at the paper." He paused and looked into my eyes. "It must have been those freckles on your nose that bewitched me."

"I didn't like it that you were your father's apprentice. I saw it as replacing me as his heir apparent, and yes, I was jealous, or maybe threatened is a better word. He seemed to go easy on you and give you special treatment, and you took advantage of it."

"I don't know why I wasn't threatened by Tim. I lost so much when he died," he said sadly. "I guess I blamed you for that, too. Tim was gone, and with him went the only real family life I had. There was a strong bond there with your father, mother, and of course, Tim. I didn't know you, Mary Kate, not really—you were just the pesky kid sister."

"I could see what a great pair you and Charlie made, and he could give you a life I never could. I resented that too. You seemed very happy together. It was so much fun going out with you two."

"Over time, I grew to respect you as a reporter, as a writer, and I came to like you as a person, a friend. When I started seeing Mary, she liked you too, and I even thought of settling down myself. She wanted that and I couldn't blame her; we were spending a lot of time together. I like her very much—she is a pretty girl and fun too, but I knew I didn't love her."

"Hmm, you never did have any trouble attracting the prettiest girls in town, Jack Flatly."

He smiled broadly. "That's a fact, Missy, and do ya know why? They like me because they think I'm a challenge, a black sheep in need of fixing, and each gal thinks they are the ones to do it."

Nodding, I replied, "That's what my mother told me long ago. I have no such illusions; I know you too well. So, what are we going to do about all this, Jack?" He didn't answer for a minute or two.

"Well, Mary Kate Riley," he began, then paused, taking my hand and holding it for a moment, "will you be my wife?"

I looked up at him; "Yes— adding, I didn't come all this way for nothing."

"Huh," he laughed. "Now don't give me any of your sauce; and to think I'm willing to take you even if you can't sing or whistle much either."

He paused and looked into my eyes. "I can't believe this has happened …you… here." He smiled, then knitted his eyebrows and thought for a moment.

"I have made a commitment to the *Times*. I 'll ask them whether they want me to work there while they find a replacement. If they do, I will do the time. A promise is a promise. In the meantime, we'll need to work things out with Charlie."

"The wedding is only five months away, and the preparations need to be called off just as soon as possible. I can come there next weekend. There is simply not going to be an easy way to do this. We'll do it together. I'll have to go back to wind things up at the *Times.* I will need to stay until they find somebody; I don't want to leave them in the lurch."

"No, Jack, I 'll tell him on Tuesday; he's out of town until then. I love Charlie; he's a wonderful man. But I see now that the security and the glamour of the life he was offering me blinded me. I couldn't see that the love I feel for him is nothing like the feelings I have for you. I knew when you first kissed me, that it was *you* who I wanted to spend the rest of my life with, it was *you* I wanted to marry. I didn't want to believe it then, but now I know it's true."

"When I didn't hear from you, I thought I was reading too much into your kiss. I was busy at the paper and with the wedding planning, so I just pushed those feelings deep inside me and tried to forget them."

"Mother said that my father told her that he had seen this coming for a while. He said he knew you had feelings for me. They didn't say anything to me because I seemed so happy with Charlie. Do you think Charlie suspected that you had feelings for me?"

Jack took a sip of coffee and sat back in his chair. "No, and that made it all the harder. I think he knew I liked you a great deal, in a sisterly, third-musketeer kind of way. And at first, that is what I thought myself. You were annoying sometimes, like a kid sister. But along the way, that changed."

"Did you ever think that I might have feelings for you?" I asked him.

430

"No, I never did. I knew you cared about me, but I never thought I had a chance with you. Charlie offered you a life I could never give you, and he's a darn good man to boot. Better looking, too."

I leaned forward, took his hand, and looked into his eyes. "When I started having reservations about Charlie, I dismissed those feelings as just having jitters about the whole getting-married thing. I loved all the glamour and glitter of what would be my life with him and thought I wanted that life."

"Last summer, I saw Charlie squiring a beautiful young woman around the dance floor of the Del, the most charming young couple at the Wednesday ball. I watched them and wondered then if that could ever be me. I *wanted* it to be me."

"But there were times after I got engaged to Charlie that I questioned if I could fit into that life. Would I be happy leaving my friends and family behind? They just wouldn't fit, nor would they want to fit, into my new life. Would I be happy in the life of a society matron on Banker's Hill? Charlie loves his job at the bank and fits in there just fine. I think he always knew that is where he would end up."

"Until we got engaged, I never considered whether the life I would have with Charlie would make me happier than the one I had living in Rabbitville. "

"Even you, Jack, didn't want to come to the New Year's Eve party because you didn't fit in— didn't want to fit in. I understood that, and so did Charlie. We started to plan the wedding to accommodate the differences between our families and our friends. Still, we could see as time went on, that this would only be temporary." I sighed.

"We didn't talk about it, but I could feel it. Charlie went to work for his father at the bank because he knew he must so that he could give his children and me the life he had growing up. It was fun for him to live in your world, Jack, our world, but he would never feel comfortable staying there. He was shocked to learn that I had doubts about whether what he saw as the far superior life he was offering me was something I wanted."

"It bothered me too that he was willing to give up his calling, his passion, to become a banker, so that he could make more money and give me and his children that life. I appreciated that he wanted his family to have a better life than he could give us on a news photographer's pay, but I feared he would always regret this decision. It surprised me that he took to banking so easily. He seems to really like it."

"He will find a way to continue as an extremely talented photographer but not as a photojournalist. He's a true artist. He told me once that he could see photography in the new century as evolving into an art form. I hope he pursues this, as it means so much to him. I think he will." I took a sip of coffee and paused to think for a minute.

"After developing a relationship with Mrs. Wilson, I put my reservations about living in her world aside— at first. She's wonderful. I like her very much and identified with her too. She came from a middle-class background, much like mine. Well, maybe a couple of notches up the social ladder."

"She told me that pedigree is much less important in the emerging city of San Diego than it is in other large cities because, for so long, there have not been sufficient marriageable women here. Many society matrons here were either plucked from the upper middle class as she was or imported from the East."

"Charlie always loved living the rough-and-tumble life he had working at the paper and running around with you. Who but you would take him ostrich riding? Charlie saw his life with you as his best friend as much more fun than the world he comes from. But he sees it now as the world of a boy; that he is a man now with responsibilities, a man soon to be married and have a family."

Jack listened quietly, finishing his apple pie.

"I never thought Charlie would be happy being a banker, but he seems to like it just fine," Jack said. He knows he would miss that Banker's Hill life if he had to give it up permanently to work as a poorly- paid photojournalist. As a young single man, he could have a foot in both camps; but permanently, no, I don't think so. 'Just as you don't want to be in his world, he will soon no longer want to be in yours."

"It's like all the swells that come down to Tent City from the Del. Sure, they love to mix and mingle with the poorer folks on a Sunday afternoon—it is where the fun is. But at the end of the day, they are glad to stay at the hotel with all its amenities and people around them like themselves."

We didn't talk for a few minutes; we just sat quietly, sipping our coffee.

"What about your mother, was she disappointed that you would turn in a handsome, rich man who loves you for Jack Flatly, who loves ya too but offers you a life as the wife of a newspaperman?"

"Oh, Jack, you already have my mother's heart. She has always had a soft spot for you, and you have been such a terrible flirt, making sure to keep that flame going. But before this past week, she was thrilled that I would marry the son of one of the most prominent bankers in San Diego. I would be one of those women she makes dresses for. But she was all for it once I told her I might be in love with you and needed to find out how you felt about me."

I reached for an errant curl that dropped over Jack's forehead and gently smoothed it to the side of his face. He smiled.

"She gave up the possibility of a glamorous life as a singer in the San Francisco Opera to marry my father. She was pretty enough and attracted many of San Francisco's high-society suitors. Still, she found happiness with her own poorly paid newspaperman."

"She has always said she doesn't regret it, and I don't think she does. When I hear her singing Puccini while playing her gramophone, I know she has thoughts of what might have been if she became an opera star. Still, I know she wouldn't make a different choice if she had it to do over again. My father has made her happy."

I looked at Jack across the table. He looked up at me with sadness in his eyes and took my hands in his. "I'd need to come with you when you tell Charlie—we'll do it together next weekend. It's the right thing to do. I'll call Henry tomorrow to see if he can give me my job back at the paper. If not, there are other outfits there that I can try. I have a lot of connections in town."

We walked to the hotel in silence, thinking about what lay ahead. When we got there, he kissed me goodnight. It was a sweet kiss but a wistful one. "I guess there will be no more Three Musketeers," he said sadly.

"No, Jack, but they were already broken up when you and Charlie left the paper. I hope we can all be friends again someday. But if it happens, it won't be until Charlie moves on with someone else. And, it may never happen.."

"I guess so," he said softly.

Jack returned to the hotel early in the morning and walked us to the ferry. He kissed me goodbye and shook Father's hand. "I have to get to work—see you next Saturday."

He turned and rushed down to meet his uncle at the loading area where he had worked the day before.

Chapter 55

Tired and happy that everything with Jack had turned out so right, Father and I had plenty of time on our return trip home to talk about the mess I'd found myself in.

"Jack wants to be with me when I tell Charlie, but he can't get away until next weekend."

"Daughter, finding the right man to spend the rest of your life with, someone you love, sometimes gets messy. You're going to get this sorted, Charlie will get hurt, and there is no avoiding it. But waiting another week for you and Jack to tell him together is a bad idea. He can't get away until then, so you'll have to do this alone. Charlie will be back from his trip on Tuesday."

"Do you think you can pretend for almost a week, making plans with him, kissing him? No, you'll have to do it Tuesday— the sooner, the better. You didn't plan this. Charlie won't see that now, but maybe someday he will. He is a good man, rich too. He will find someone else and move on."

Father was right. All the pressure and emotional turmoil of the past two days poured out of me. I started to cry. He hugged me and held me against his chest saying nothing, just comforting me. After a minute or so, I pulled away. "Father, I'll tell Charlie when he comes over Tuesday night for dinner. It will be so hard. He means so much to me."

"OK, Tuesday it is. I'll ask Hank Moody to take your mother and me to pick up the chow-chow so that you and Charlie can talk."

We talked a bit about Jack returning to work at the paper. "Well, his timing is right. Henry wanted to hire another reporter anyway. Frank is a good man and an excellent reporter, but he's still pretty green. Besides, Henry considers Jack family."

"He'll have to take a pay cut because the *Union* cannot compete with his *Times'* salary. But then the two of you will have two salaries to live on once you're married." He paused a moment. "Are you sure you want to work in the same place as your husband?"

"I'm sure, Father," I replied. "Jack and I have had our work conflicts, and I'm sure we'll still have them, but Jack has come to respect my work at the paper. We are both pretty bull-headed and hot-tempered, but that is just what makes it work between us. Charlie keeps his feelings and most everything else he has in mind to himself."

"Jack supports me in my wanting to work after we're married and not just because of my salary. He knows I have my own ideas, my own dreams, and how much my job means to me. Charlie never saw that. I don't think he knows me at all. He is very traditional, and I never have been that. He made all these plans for my life but never asked me what I wanted. Worse, he didn't even feel that he should have to ask me."

Monday morning when I got to the paper, I went upstairs to call Jack to let him know I would break the news to Charlie the next day. I woke up filled with dread on Tuesday morning. Charlie was all smiles when I answered the door that night.

"Pick me up at seven," he turned and called to Ben. He met Charlie, his father, and grandfather Wilson at the train station at six o'clock. He dropped Charlie off at my house on their way home. He was pleased to find that my parents had gone out to pick up the chow-chow for dinner. We sat on the couch, and he kissed me first thing. "I missed you."

436

He was excited about his trip and how much promise there was in his new position at his grandfather's bank. "Grandfather has big plans for me. He's going to open branches in San Francisco and Los Angeles and when he does my responsibilities here will be greater. I can't wait or you to meet him."

He kissed me again, and this time I gently pushed him away. Father was right; acting as if nothing had changed, making small talk, planning for our future, and kissing him with this hanging over my head, was unbearable.

He was stunned when I told him I couldn't marry him, that we didn't want the same things. I don't remember exactly what I said; it all came tumbling out. I didn't mention Jack, he didn't give me a chance to. Truthfully, I just couldn't.

Charlie sat in silence for a while; then he stood, turned, and just walked out the door, saying nothing at all.

Filled with sadness and guilt, I was glad he didn't want to discuss it further. Maybe he had reservations of his own, or he *had* listened to mine over the past weeks. He will want to know when all this happened and when it all changed, but not now. It was Jack's kiss, but so many things had come up in planning our lives together that I knew Charlie and I shouldn't marry. After he left, I wrote my parents a note and put it on the table. "Gone to bed—we'll talk in the morning. M. K."

Exhausted and miserable, I fell right to sleep. Lucy had taken her usual spot right next to me on the bed, and we were lying face-to-face the next morning. Her snoring and chronic doggie bad breath woke me up. Laughing, it was a welcome bit of humor.

I missed Jack so much and called him from the paper as soon as I arrived the next morning. "*Times- Mirror*," he said. My heart jumped when I heard his voice.

"Hello, Jack," I said softly. After telling him what happened with Charlie he was quiet for a while. Sadness and regret hung in the air between us.

"I love you, Mary Kate," he said finally. "I'm sorry you had to do this alone. I understand why you felt you needed to do it right away. I'll talk to Charlie when I get there next week."

Chapter 56

It was the Saturday after I had broken my engagement with Charlie. Father was at the paper, and Mother was working on her sewing machine in the front room. I was finishing up my women's section story at the kitchen table. After it was done I intended to ride my bicycle down to the paper to get my father's approval, then get it in for printing. I had just gotten home and I was in the kitchen grabbing something to eat when there was a knock at the door. Theodora?

Mother called, "I'll get it, Mary Kate."

"Why hello, Charlie, please, come in." I got up and went to greet him.

She turned to me, "I'm going upstairs to do a bit of reading."

Charlie was dressed in a suit; he was probably going to the bank for a few hours. He did this on Saturday so he and his father could work together without anyone at the bank there to bother them. He said he had so much to learn, and his father had no time to do much teaching during the week.

"Sit down, please," I said, nodding toward Father's chair which faced the fireplace, with its embers still glowing orange. "No thanks, he said, I don't plan to stay."

He thought better of it and walked over to Father's chair and sat down. I pulled a chair over so I could face him.

"Charlie…" he interrupted me.

"Let me talk, Mary Kate, please."

439

"I've been such a fool. I have really messed things up between us. I'm here to ask you for another chance. I love you and want to make this right.

He took my hand. "This marriage business is so new to me. I know I've handled this all wrong; not letting you be involved in most of the major decisions we should have made together as a couple. I've let my mother do the decision-making; I thought you'd be happy. That was just plain stupid."

I started to reply but he stopped me by putting up his hand. "Let me finish please," he said.

"We can make this work; I know it. Please, think about it for a few days, and let's go out for dinner on Friday to discuss this. Don't say anything now… please. 'Just promise me you'll think about it."

I started to respond, and he put his hand up again to stop me. He stood and headed towards the door. He turned and walked back to where I was sitting, leaned down, and gave me a sweet kiss on the cheek."I love you, and I want you to be my wife more than anything. Please, just give us a chance."

"I love you too, Charlie. I *will* think about what you've said. We can talk Friday."

"I'll pick you up at six. Does that work for you?"

"That will be fine."

I watched his carriage pull away and felt so tired all of a sudden and really, really sad. I called Jack on Monday morning. He had eight more days to finish his assignments and prepare for his replacement.

He listened and didn't say much when I told him about what had happened with Charlie. "I will have to tell him about us, I feel so bad. It kills me to have to hurt him."

There was a long pause on Jack's end. "You aren't regretting this are you?"

"No, I just don't know how I can explain to him how this happened, how *we* happened That there was no treachery on your part or mine? Father says there is no way to put this kindly or in any way that won't hurt him."

"I wish I could be with you, but actually, this is something that you need to talk about with Charlie alone."

Pausing to think about it, "You're right Jack. You're being there would only make it harder on him."

Charlie took me to the Brewster for dinner Friday night. We agreed to eat first and then talk about our future. I wasn't hungry and only picked at my food. He ate his dinner and ordered dessert. After the waiter left his dessert in front of him, I swallowed hard and took the lead.

"I thought long and hard about what you said on Saturday. I want you to know that maybe you were clumsy in how some things were handled, but you can't change *why* you made those decisions for me. This was and is the life you envisioned for us. It's the way things are done in your world. It's the kind of wife you want, the kind of wife you need... I just don't fit the bill."

He shook his head no and started to interrupt me.

"No, it's true, I said putting up my hand, let me finish. I don't fit into your world any more than you fit in mine. You were just visiting mine when you worked at the paper. You are a part of the upper class that I write about in the paper, but I never was. I'm a writer, a newspaper woman and I love my job. Even if you agreed to let me stay at the paper, it's not what you want, not what you need." He started to argue with me.

"Please… let me finish. There is something else, Charlie, and please hear me out." I paused and took a breath for courage, feeling nauseous.

"*After* I decided that even though we loved each other, it wasn't a good match, that we were not right for each other, I went to see Jack in Los Angeles. He kissed me goodbye the night he left in a way I couldn't forget. He did this on the spur of the moment, and after he did, he pushed me away. He didn't plan it."

"Jack? It can't be…" He was stunned.

"I didn't see this coming; it came out of the blue. Jack always treated me as a friend, a pesky kid sister at times, but it never occurred to me that he had feelings for me. He wanted to let me know that he did before leaving town. He never called me or contacted me after that."

"Charlie, we were both surprised when he took the job in Los Angeles. We didn't realize that the reason he did is that he didn't want to be anything but happy for us preparing for our wedding. He knew then that he was in love with me. What I didn't realize is that I was in love with him too."

"When we didn't hear from Jack, I figured I read too much into that kiss. But Charlie, when I knew we could never work as husband and wife, I wondered about my feelings for him. Mother told me I must see him, sort things out, find out what my feelings were… to be sure. She said I had to do that before marrying anyone."

He looked at me across the table and interrupted me. "You and Jack?" he said again, clearly angry.

"Nobody planned this, I didn't want to hurt you, and neither did he. It just happened. I do love him, Charlie, of that I'm sure," I sputtered. This was not what he wanted to hear.

"And here I'm thinking this was all my fault," he said bitterly. "Let's get out of here. There is nothing more to say."

Charlie had arranged for Ben to wait outside an hour while we had our dinner. He was smoking a cigarette leaning against the door of the carriage when we came out the front door of the hotel. "Let's go, Ben," he said gruffly; he was furious.

Ben shot a glance at me but said nothing. He just jumped up on his perch at the front of the carriage and pulled away. Neither of us said anything during the short ride to my house. As much as I tried to stop them, tears flowed down my cheeks as I sat in the dark carriage. Ben pulled up in front of the house. The porch light was on. Charlie, saying nothing, opened the carriage door, jumped out, reached to help me down, and then started towards the porch steps leaving me behind.

"No, let's just say good night here. Saying I'm sorry I hurt you doesn't mean much. But I am *so* sorry. I do love you."

He didn't reply. He simply turned and jumped into the carriage and yelled to Ben. "Take me home."

Mother and Father were reading in the front room when I got home and both looked up when I walked in the door. "Let's talk in the morning, I said with a sigh; it didn't go well."

Father and I met Jack at the ferry the following Monday after work. Father borrowed a carriage from Hank Moody to help with the few belongings Jack brought with him in his move to Los Angeles. He looked tired. Mother had lamb stew and biscuits waiting for us at the house. Jack ate heartily and filled us in on his last days at the *Times*.

"They are a great bunch of people. I liked it there. Even The General called me to his office the day I left and wished me well. He told me that he would be sorry to lose me. I never saw that side of him; he was downright amiable."

443

It was a short night. Father was going to take Jack home and help him take his things into the house. Before he left, we sat on the porch together. I had missed him so much. He missed me too. We talked about our future together and how easy it would be for him to join the Riley clan. After all, he had been pretty much a member of the family for several years now. My parents loved him, and he felt the same way about them.

The following Saturday, I went to the paper to finish my work for Sunday's edition. It was about noon. Jack had returned to his old job and was already there. I went to his desk; he had his head down typing a story. I could hear Father's voice; he was upstairs with Henry. Jack looked up when I approached. Ouch, I thought when I saw his black eye, it was a beauty.

Before I could say anything, he explained. "I ran into Charlie at Patrick's after I left your house last night. He was sitting at the bar near the dart boards waiting for his turn. I didn't know what to say to him, but I never got the chance. He saw me, turned my way, and punched me."

"He knocked me down, but for once, I didn't fight back. I could take him, but figured I deserved it. I left and felt pretty blue walking home. After all, Charlie is my best friend…*was* my best friend," he added sadly.

I reached down and gently touched his swollen eye. He winced.

"Let's get our work done and walk down to the bay. We can spend a little time on the *Serenity* and watch the sunset."

He smiled. "That sounds good."

Theodora was surprised but supportive when she found out about Jack and me. "Why didn't you tell me? We share everything."

"I didn't tell you to tell you about my feelings for Jack after the kiss; I wanted to pretend I didn't have any. I didn't want to hurt you. I thought that maybe I had read too much into it."

She was a bit icy at first, but she soon thawed. She had already found someone new. Although she thought Jack was the one and only man for her, she quickly found a replacement who she described the same way. I wondered if my little palomino would ever settle down.

An unexpected ally in all this was Pamela Spaulding. She knew and cared for Charlie, and her encouragement meant a great deal to me. She was very understanding. Theodora and I had become good friends with her since the engagement party. We rode our bicycles to her little cottage for lunch almost every Sunday.

We even went to Lomaland one Saturday to see a play at the Greek Theater. I told her we thought it would be fun to see the place with her—she could be our special nymph- guide. "You were such an outrageous flirt with Charlie that day last spring," I chided her.

She smiled. "We didn't have much of an opportunity to flirt out there where romance is not only frowned upon but forbidden."

"Katherine Tingley a sexual libertine? Hogwash! She may be forward-thinking in many ways, but when it comes to matters of romance, she is strictly Victorian."

"And Charlie Wilson is one handsome and charming man," she continued. "I wanted to marry him myself. My parents loved him, and so did Mrs. Tingley."

"We courted all summer and when I went away to school we wrote for a while, but we never got together again, except as friends. Love can be fickle, Mary Kate. It's nobody's fault; nobody planned this. Charlie is a great guy. He'll find someone new; men always do."

That night on the *Serenity*, Jack told me the *Times* people were very good about his untimely departure. Right after my visit, he gave his notice to his editor, Mr. Andrews, and explained why he had changed his mind. He said he would stay until they found a replacement.

"You remember him from the trial, Shortridge's first witness." I nodded.

"He was great about it. He told me they could limp along just fine if I wanted to leave right away. "I wouldn't want to stand in the way of true love."

That next week Jack and I started making wedding plans of our own. He was living at home but was at our house for dinner every night. We decided to marry on the Fourth of July weekend so that friends and family could make it from out of town. This would also give us a three-day weekend to have a short honeymoon. The wedding would be at St. Patrick's, with the reception in the parish hall and in the garden courtyard.

Our honeymoon would be in Coronado. We planned to spend a day or two on the *Serenity* docked in Glorietta Bay, which was in the shadow of the Hotel Del. They would have big doings that weekend at Tent City, and spectacular fireworks would be shot over the hotel on the evening of the Fourth.

Henry and Father were pleased to have Jack back on the job. He is an excellent reporter and writer, and besides, it just didn't feel right in the newsroom without him. Jack walked me home from the paper every night after work. We had dinner with my parents and then headed down to the *Serenity* for some alone time alone; maybe a sunset sail. That boat hardly ever left the dock.

Chapter 57

Pamela cooked for Jack and me once a week, to give my parents a break and gave us a chance to get out of the house. Pamela's Eddie was usually there, and we got to know him well.

He is not only a wonderful guy but he is a brilliant and very progressive architect. He, like so many young people, wanted to march into the new century with some new ideas in his pocket, not completely tethered to the ideas of the past. Like Pamela, he wanted to forge his own path in the world, to do something new with the buildings he designed.

Pamela was certainly of like mind. She's a talented painter. She emulated the French Impressionists who were causing such a stir in the art world and added her own flair. She painted the varied landscapes in San Diego with thick smears of paint and bold colors. She captured, as did the Impressionists, the light and movement in the spectacular natural environment she lived in. I imagine her experience growing up at Lomaland contributed to her free-spirit approach to her life as well as her art.

I don't know where Eddie got his Wild West individualism. He hailed from Boston and grew up in a traditional, conservative family. He and Pamela met at college. He loved to talk about architecture. He told us at dinner one night that he wanted to build houses that fit into the environment, built with materials consistent with that environment, both inside and out.

"The design of a house here in San Diego should be in harmony with the land it sits on rather than at odds with it. It should be positioned to maximize the view, the light, and the cooling of the sea air coming up from the bay."

"Here in San Diego, we need landscaping that reflects the shortage of water in the region and our warm climate. The fact is, if you pick the right plants, they will thrive."

"Kate Sessions has done a great deal of work here. She is the best and most forward-thinking horticulturist in this area; she wholeheartedly embraces these ideas. She landscaped the Del, you know, the courthouse too. And now she is tasked to implement the plans for the City Park project."

"She *is* a fascinating woman. I interviewed her for my Sunday Women's section just last week. It was a *long* interview. She was so excited to tell me all about her work and the work of so many others to make the City Park project a reality."

"She told me that Samuel Parsons Jr, who planned Central Park in New York City, did the plans for City Park. Our own George Marston put up his own money to hire this visionary planner. Parsons then tasked Kate Sessions to implement his design. She is totally in support of his vision of a large urban park, making use of native plants if possible, keeping the contours of the existing land and in harmony with the environment around it."

"That sounds like *your* vision too Eddie," I added.

"It certainly is. A twelve-hundred-acre urban park seems too large now to many. Developers are heard railing against it to everyone that will listen—too big, too much money. Many of them have their eye on the land for development, after all, it's prime real estate, and they are pushing back hard against the size."

"This is ironic because one of the two men who first set the park idea in motion was a developer, Alonso Horton. At least part of the reason for his support at the time was that he wanted a park to enhance the value of his own downtown development."

"City Park is big, it's even bigger than Central Park. But there is no doubt in my mind that the city will grow into it and soon. It will

448

be the crown jewel of San Diego, just like Central Park is in New York. And, it will draw visitors and stimulate business. This revolutionary park will bring the country into the hectic urban environment of what will be in the not-too-distant future, a large bustling metropolis.

"You know, we had excellent horticulture and forestry departments at Lomaland," Pamela told us. "We were very innovative in the growing of unusual vegetables and fruits that were brought in from all over the world. They were picked not only for their flavor and nutritional value but because they were well suited for this warm, arid place." Did you know it was the Theosophists from Lomaland that first brought avocados to this area?"

"The trees and orchards were those varieties that thrive in the heat without much water. We planted palm trees down the road leading to Lomaland and all over the site. They are getting pretty big now, and they look spectacular."

"The flowers were also chosen to work with the environment here, not in spite of it. A great deal of the planting was experimental. Some did not survive, but for the most part, they did. Many local horticulturists and foresters have learned a great deal from the Lomaland people, and it has made a mark on our city far beyond the Point."

Pamela, as I got to know her better, did have some criticism of her Lomaland experience, but she was still a Theosophist and overall she supported what Katherine Tingley and her followers had accomplished, and what they stood for. She said her mother still was an ardent supporter while her father mainly just goes along for the ride.

Pamela said that she knew early on that she didn't want to be an apostle for the cause. But, she still supported the principles that the cause represented: world peace, prison reform, abolishing capital punishment, and the fair treatment of women. I support them too.

We often ate dinner in the garden at Pamela's house where there was an unusual table that Eddie had designed. It was the trunk of a redwood tree cut lengthwise so you could see the interior imperfections, knot holes, and other distinctions that gave the piece interest. It was sanded down and rested on four small weathered segments of pilings from an old pier. We sat on tall, ornately-carved wooden chairs. Pamela had painted them turquoise blue with matching seat cushions. It was usual, but somehow it worked.

Jack and I loved eating dinner in Pamela's garden. It was a treat not only because it was so lovely outside at that time of day, but because Pamela had made her garden into a fairyland of colorful plants and flowers which she lighted in a truly magical way.

At one Sunday dinner before our wedding, Eddie and Pamela announced their engagement. She said they would be married on the exquisite grounds of Lomaland, at the Greek Theater, no less. Theodora would be her maid of honor.

"No worries about space there," Jack quipped.

"We plan to put up a large tent on the fifth hole of my father's golf course. It's a circus tent kind of thing, only all white. We'll have the wedding supper there. Outside the tent, there will be a bandstand, a dance floor, and a bar. It's in October, so we can count on a warm, cloudless night. I can get dressed at my parent's house, which is very close to the Greek Theater. It will be perfect."

"Sounds wonderful," I said. "I'm so happy for you."

"Is Mrs. Tingley going to let you have booze out there?" Jack asked.

"Normally, it wouldn't be permitted. But my father and mother are her biggest donors and supporters, so Mrs. T. can't really say no. She will be on her world tour and won't be at the wedding. We aren't going to try and hide it from her, but it will be nice that she won't be there to register her disapproval."

450

"It all sounds just great, Pamela," I said. "If I can help in any way, just tell me."

"Let's get your wedding done first, and then I'll let you know. I am helping Theodora with your reception."

Pamela went to get the peach cobbler we brought from the kitchen. Mother and I made it together. After she put it on the table, she stood facing us, her hands gripping the back of Eddie's chair.

"Eddie and I have an idea that might interest the two of you. He has been working on a home near the Horton house on the hill. It's all but done; it just needs a few finishing touches. He designed it for himself, to live in and with an office in the rear to work in. Now that we are getting married, his plans for the house have changed.

"It's small, cozy, and perfect for just the two of us. It will be our home when we get married, at least until we have children. It should be finished this month. This will give us time to furnish it and prepare it for us to live in as a couple in October.

"I know you and Jack plan to live with your parents until you can get a place of your own. How about moving in here after our wedding? I talked to my father about it, and he's fine with the idea. It's yours if you want it."

"My father is a very generous man. I'm his darling girl, and I can get him to give it to you at no rent or very low rent. He didn't say anything about renting it to you, so at least for a time, you can expect that he won't charge you rent. Father is a real softy—I'll just tell him you are a nice couple in love, without much money, and are friends of mine. That should do it."

She touched Eddie's arm, "I'll keep most of the furniture here, except for a few pieces, and of course, the wallpaper stays," she chuckled and added, "When Eddie first saw it, he asked me, "Who installed this, three blind mice?"

451

"So what do you think?" Pamela asked us.

Jack smiled, "Well, I think that sounds like a mighty good wedding present."

"Pamela gave me that sweet smile I first saw last spring at Lomaland. I reached for her and gave her a hug. "It's wonderful, my sweet nymph-guide. Thank you."

A press release came into the paper a few weeks back that said Mrs. Tingley had left for the world tour she had told us about. Her first stop on her current tour was meeting with the Queen of Sweden. After that, she would head to the Far East to meet with leaders there. I wrote a small front-page article about her trip.

We invited Mrs. Tingley to our wedding even though we knew she couldn't attend. I wanted to let her know of my high regard for her. She sent her regrets along with a lovely purple vase and a book she had written about Theosophy. Although I didn't know her well, I really felt that there was a bond between Katherine Tingley and me; we were kindred spirits. I sensed that she felt it too.

She seemed to look at me and my life with a bit of regret, of loss really, for the things she gave up in pursuit of her life's work, her mission: family, children, friends, romance, and fun. Hers was serious work, and for the most part, it was with great earnestness that she pursued it. I smiled, thinking about our first meeting at the Horton's home on the first day of her trial. I was so green, so young, but, like Mrs. Tingley herself, so very determined.

Pamela had a great fondness for Katherine Tingley—after all, she was once a *Tingleyite* who grew up at Lomaland. Just before she left on her world tour, Eddie, Pamela, Jack, and I, attended a lovely dinner at her parents' house in Lomaland. Kathrine Tingley and her husband Philo were there as well. We had a lively discussion and a wonderful time.

I liked Pamela's parents very much. Jack enjoyed talking to her father about his illustrious baseball career and about his golf course at Lomaland. "I love the game," Jack told him.

"Come out and play here anytime," Mr. Spaulding replied, delighted at the prospect.

Jack was also fascinated by Katherine Tingley and all that she had accomplished at the Point. He also asked her about the world tour she was embarking on. He argued with her on some of her ideas "strictly off the record," he told her with a wink and a grin. Like most women, after he turned on the charm, Madame Tingley seemed smitten with Jack and enjoyed every minute of their repartee.

Chapter 58

Mother and I planned a typical Rabbitville wedding, but really it was a team effort. The planning for the food for the reception was handled by Molly Moody. It involved most of our neighbors pitching in, offering their favorite specialties. Mother insisted on making our wedding cake. It was a simple square, two-layer cream-colored, marzipan-covered cake with white fondant dots like dotted Swiss fabric. It was elegant, lovely, and stylish-so very Mother.

Theodora was my maid of honor, and Jack's brother-in-law Jim was his best man. Theodora and Jack's sister Franny took charge of the reception details besides the food. It was to be in the church hall and outside on the patio. Babe, Fiona Riggs, and Pamela were their crew. Their plans were kept top secret.

Jack and I were married with our new pastor, Father Paul performing the ceremony. He took over for Father Hackett who died last month. He is a rotund Irishman from Dublin with a thick Irish brogue and a wicked sense of humor. He has an infectious smile with a twinkle in his eyes most of the time.

Franny helped Mother with the flowers that they arranged on the altar and at the end of every pew. Frank Moody picked us up at home and drove us to the church in a carriage that he and his brother Sean decorated with green garlands of ivy.

I walked down the aisle on Father's arm in the stunning cream-colored silk gown Fiona Riggs gave me, which Mother made truly mine. Babe gave me a beautiful brooch with an amber stone, which I wore near my right shoulder. Mother wanted to pin my hair up with her pearl-encrusted combs. Still, I was determined to let my red curls fly, wild, unrestrained, except for my bridal veil, which I tossed aside as soon as we left the church.

Jack told me I was the prettiest bride he ever saw. He got a new suit for the wedding, dispensing with his uniform newsie hat and tattered vest for at least one day. Mother altered the store-bought suit to fit him perfectly. He even got his hair cut for the occasion. He looked very handsome. Mother looked stunning in her blue silk dress.

As I walked down the aisle, all our friends and family stood and leaned towards us, wearing expressions of excitement and loving welcome. Mother's beautiful voice singing *Ave Maria* rang through the church. I could see Jack standing at the altar to the right of Father Paul, with his best man, his brother-in-law Jim, at his side.

We got to know Father Paul during the three weeks of marriage preparation, which included announcing the marriage banns every Sunday at Mass. We liked him very much. He told us that he wanted us to meet with him very briefly after the ceremony so that he could give us some parting advice about "the most sacred sacrament of matrimony."

My father, always the sentimental Irishman, was brought to tears when he watched the two young people he loved most in the world about to take their wedding vows. After he delivered me to Jack at the altar, he took out his handkerchief and patted his eyes.

Jack lifted my wedding veil; I said my vows first. Jim handed him the ring, a simple gold band, which he put on my finger. Looking into my eyes, he said softly, "I love you so." Then he quietly, reverently, took his vows. This brought tears to my eyes. I was so happy.

After we finished our vows, Father Paul looked out at the congregation and, in his strong Irish brogue, announced, "I now pronounce you man and wife."

Reverent no more, Jack being Jack, picked me up and pulled me to him for what was a lovely, if overlong, kiss. This triggered laughter from our guests and Father Paul. Jack turned me around to the sound of applause, welcoming us as a married couple. As we began our walk out of the church, a violinist struck up with a lively version of the wedding march.

I noticed that Mother and Gran were sitting together, dabbing the tears from their eyes. Jack's father was there, along with two of his brothers and his sister, Franny. Pamela and Eddie sat near the back with broad smiles on their faces. All of our friends, including everyone from the paper, were in the church, as well as most of Mother's dressmaking customers. I was so pleased to see, sitting next to Henry and Babe, Lydia Horton, and Dr. Charlotte Baker, who nodded to me as Jack and I walked by.

Mother had gotten to know these women very well in her work at the Children's Home. Fiona Riggs and her husband sat in the next row. She smiled and nodded with approval at how beautiful I looked in her dress, with my wild red curls framing my face.

We left the church under a hail of rice and headed over to the rectory to meet with Father Paul, but he didn't keep us too long. The gist of his message was simply this: "The sacrament of marriage is a serious undertaking, and it takes effort to make it work."

We both listened respectfully but were fidgeting, anxious to get to our reception. Father Paul could tell. "Well, if you want me to spend a bit more time with you, I have some wonderful scriptures on the sacrament of marriage…" He looked up with devilment in his eyes and smiled broadly. "Go, he said, be happy, the two of ya."

My friends, led by Theodora, and with help from Father, who climbed the ladder when needed, decorated the hall for the reception. Jack and I were forbidden to see it before the wedding. When we walked into the hall after the ceremony, we saw that it had been transformed into a tropical island with wild birds and all things exotic.

Theodora, with Pamela's help, had turned the drab room into a colorful beach at sunset. I knew she used my description of the decorations at the Wednesday Ball as her inspiration. She made two nine-foot palm trees from colored paper, broomsticks, and wire. They were backlit at their trunks by yellow-shaded lamps on the floor, giving it the look of a sunset behind the palms. Pamela had painted a beach scene near the palms.

The buffet table was set with yellow chrysanthemums from the backyard of one of our neighbors, Bess Murphy. Theodora and her crew placed these in large tin cans covered with tropical birds made of tissue paper. These displays were placed at each end of the table, which was stacked with homemade food, and a large crystal bowl mother borrowed from Mrs. Riggs was filled with lemonade. Bottles of beer were placed in large buckets.

A large, exotically-plumed parrot hung from the ceiling, greeting arrivals when they passed through the front door. Jack said later, "The parrot probably asks when people come in, 'Who the heck invited you?'"

We were among the last to get to the reception hall, and when we did arrive, nobody seemed to notice. Our family and friends sat drinking beer and lemonade at picnic tables covered with bright green tablecloths made from dyed old sheets with paper flower centerpieces. Kids were running around the room. We could hear the band tuning up and a cacophony of raucous folks talking and laughing, already celebrating our special day.

"Looks like they have got a good start on the party, wife," Jack said as he led me toward the bridal table at the front of the room. Before we knew it, the band welcomed us to the hall with a lively Irish tune played by the fiddlers. All eyes were on us as we took our place of honor at the head table, which was placed in the front of the room facing the other tables.

Jack ate his dinner, but I was too excited to eat. We could hear the musicians tuning up on the patio. Father and Hank Moody had made a wooden dance floor just for the wedding. There were long tables and a scattering of chairs surrounding it. The colorful paper lanterns Theodora had strung over the patio swaying in the slight breeze reminded me of the lanterns at the Wednesday Ball. I wondered that night if I could ever be part of a crowd like that. Now I knew it was a crowd like this, right here, where I felt at home.

I had great fun dancing with Jack's father that day. My father danced with every woman in the place but saved the first waltz for Mother. No one else was dancing—the floor was all theirs.

Later in the day, as the Father of the bride, he whirled me around the floor and told me for the first time how proud he was of me. I'd always known this, I guess, but it was nice to hear it.

Jack danced with Mother to a sweet Irish ballad played by the violin soloist. She wore the locket he had given her around her neck. Soon she would have a picture of her grandchild to put in it.

Jack danced with Gran, with Babe, and with Fiona Riggs. He was delighted when Fiona Riggs asked him to dance the jig, and they sure went to town. Of course, brother and sister, Franny and Jack, danced the jig to the delight of the crowd.

Father and Gran took to the floor and danced the waltz. She enjoyed it so much that just a few minutes later, he danced with her again. Later, Jack took his turn, waltzing her around the floor.

I had a great time sitting at the table with Jack's uncle, who reminded me of that day on the San Pedro wharf just a few months before. "It took a lot of moxie for you to come all the way to Los Angeles to fetch your man. I saw the look on Jack's face when he saw you, and I knew right away that he was all yours."

458

We had a few sad moments that day thinking of how much we missed Charlie being there and, of course, Tim. Izzy, who was one of Jack's best friends, was there with his wife Sally, who was already pregnant with their first child.

Izzy and I danced two waltzes together. There weren't any hard feelings between Izzy and me after our breakup. We remained friends. He was happy for Jack and for me too.

We stayed at my parent's house in my bedroom the night of our wedding. Gran slept next door in Tim's room which Mother had . quietly redecorated a few months after his death. She kept the door closed after that saying she did not want Lucy to sleep on the bed that she had shared with Tim since she was a pup.

I knew the real reason was that seeing the room without Tim was too painful for us all. Gran would be staying there now, celebrating with my new husband and me the happiest day of my life. She spent some time with Jack in the week before the wedding and he really turned on the charm. They got along well." He reminds me of your father at that age," she told me.

Chapter 59

Jack and I slept late the following day. It was quiet when we came down the stairs; nobody was home except Lucy, who followed us down the stairs and then padded over for some love. Mother had left us some fruit, some scones she and Gran had made, and a pot of coffee on the stove. She had left a note on the table with a large picnic basket next to it:

Gone to Sunday Mass, then we're having lunch with Henry and Babe. Have a great trip.
Love, Mother."

Jack lifted the lid of the basket and removed the red-and-white-checked napkin covering the food. He pulled out a chicken leg and started to gobble it down. "I'm hungry," he said, taking another bite.

"That's for the trip, Jack. I'm sure there are plenty of leftovers in the icebox."

He opened the icebox door and took out a plate of fried chicken, some ham, and a bowl of potato salad, and put it on the table. He took out plates and forks while I lit the burner under the coffee.

Jack went to the porch to retrieve the morning paper. We both ate heartily. Jack helped me clean up the dishes, whistling while he did so. We were acting like an old married couple already. After breakfast, we drank some more coffee and rocked in the chairs on the porch while reliving our wedding day. We had been too excited and nervous to think much about it at the time. I was anxious to see the pictures of the wedding taken by Theodora and thought wistfully that Charlie should have been there doing his magic for his two best friends on their special day.

It was already warm, and a soft wind came in from the bay. Before long, Jack put music on the gramophone. It was an instrumental version, violins mostly, of a poignant Irish ballad that he and my mother would often sing. Today, out on the porch, my husband sang a solo just for me, bringing tears to my eyes once again. I was so happy that as part of our family now, Jack would always be there at song fests as he had been when Tim was alive.

After an hour or so, we went back to bed, slept some more, and did what newlyweds do. At about two-thirty, we again woke up hungry. We ate some more leftovers from the reception. Jack said that he thought the food tasted even better the second day.

"Come to think of it, Jack, I can't even remember eating yesterday; I was too nervous. But I'm really hungry now."

After we ate, we went upstairs to get dressed. Jack took the small suitcase I had packed, and I grabbed the picnic basket off the table. We walked to the old wharf, where Jack helped me board the *Serenity* for the trip to Coronado Island.

I wore a purple muslin frock mother had made for me and carried a wool shawl in case it got cold on the water. I tied my hat on with a ribbon under my chin. I checked the amethyst brooch at my throat that Mother gave me, to make sure it was fastened securely. She surprised me with it the day before our wedding to commemorate my special day. Gran had given it to Mother when Tim was born, and I sure didn't want to lose it.

Jack wore the collarless white shirt with brown stripes and brown pants that Mother had made for him. He looked particularly devilish in his wide-brimmed straw hat. He took it off, though, when it almost blew away once we got on the bay.

We planned to spend the next two nights on the boat. Father and Jack had come on Friday, the day before our wedding, to make sure

461

Serenity was ready for the trip. They stocked some provisions in the hold along with some bedding.

It was a short sail, thirty minutes or so. As we sailed away from shore, I looked back and marveled at the skyline of San Diego. It grew by leaps and bounds after its tough path through the birth canal, with three major expansions and contractions, the economic booms and busts over the past twenty years.

I thought about growing up during those years as one of its few natives. San Diego and I are now both reaching our stride; there is no stopping us now. I'm a married woman, about to be a mother, and am a full-fledged newspaper reporter for the most important newspaper in the city.

San Diego is no longer a dusty, chaparral-covered western town where gunslingers like Wyatt Earp walk the streets and where the dominant population is rabbits. The dusty western town I grew up in is rapidly receding into the past.

We are sailing over to Coronado Island, home of the Hotel Del, one of the grandest tourist destinations in the world, which is getting more popular every year. San Diego had been discovered. We finally understood here in San Diego that it's the climate, the coast, and the bay that we need to market here— this is what makes our town unique in all the world. It was the success of the Del that made us realize that.

My thoughts were interrupted when Jack yelled, "Coming about!" as the boom swung my way, spraying water over my face. "Ah-hhh!" I squealed and ducked my head, both of us laughing. I watched him as he skillfully handled the boat. Once in a while, he would turn the boat in such a way as to spray me with a little water. He did this on purpose. Jack was like that, he had a bit of a prickly side, and he loves to tease. Today the cool, salty spray felt good.

Jack had promised to give me some more sailing lessons. I knew a little bit about it from sailing with Izzy and was looking forward to learning more from my new husband. Right now, just sitting here enjoying the scenery, lost in my thoughts, was wonderful too. It was a perfect summer day. The sun was shining; it was warm, clear, and just windy enough. The *Serenity* was a shiny red and white, gleaming in the sun as the wind sped her through the dark blue water of the bay toward Coronado. We were halfway there.

I thought of how hard we worked to restore this now-beautiful sailboat in the terrible months after Tim's death, and about the day Jack first brought me to see her. He was right. The restoration of the *Serenity* helped restore us all. Sunday after Sunday, Jack and Father worked on her, forgetting their grief for a few hours a week.

Mother and I had our own part in the restoration. We spruced up the hold with new curtains and pillows and now it was just so cozy. None of us could have guessed then that our first night spent on the boat would be on our honeymoon.

We arrived at Coronado just before sunset. Jack found a space to dock in Glorietta Bay just below the Hotel Del near its boathouse where a line of small rental sailboats had been retired for the evening. Tomorrow night, the grand white wedding cake of a hotel with its signature red roof would be the backdrop for the fireworks that would light up the sky behind it.

After securing the boat, Jack sat down next to me. "I'm 'zausted," he said, using the expression his four-year-old nephew, Billie, said often.

"Me too," I said, taking his hand.

We sat in silence for a while. boats from the mainland were beginning to fill up the small bay. Jack disappeared into the hold and returned with a blanket tucked under his arm, a bottle of champagne, and two glasses. "From Henry," he said.

He sat next to me, popped the cork, and poured the champagne into the glasses to overflowing. "Whoops," he said, wiping it up with one hand and raising his glass for a toast with the other.

"To you, my lovely bride."

I shook my head no, smiled at him, and raised my glass to meet his. "To us," I said, grabbing his neck and pulling him to me, delivering my most passionate kiss.

"Hmm…tonight we can make our own fireworks," he said.

We sipped the champagne and watched the sun slip slowly behind the hotel, first turning the sky orange, then pink, then almost purple. We sat for a while in silence as the sun finished its performance for the day, the bubbles of the champagne tickling my nose, a river of relief and relaxation flowing through me. Before I said anything, Jack took my hand. "What do you say, Mrs. Flatly, how 'bout we get us some sleep."

We walked to Tent City the next day, the Fourth of July. It was all dressed up for the holiday: hundreds of American flags were festooned on posts up and down the quarter-mile-long strip of red and white striped tents starting at the Hotel Del. It was crowded with merrymakers and was more festive and fun than ever. Everyone was in high spirits, ready to celebrate our country's 127th birthday.

"Another beautiful day in paradise," the man who sold us hot dogs and lemonade said with a smile. At six o'clock, we went to the gazebo at the hotel end of the boardwalk to watch a special holiday concert. The musical ensemble played popular music and some traditional patriotic songs. The hotel paid for the entertainment; it was free to anyone who wanted to come. We had to stand as almost all the seats were reserved for hotel guests, and the rest were filled by early arrivals, but we still had a good view of the show.

We laughed when the small musical ensemble opened the show with "Bicycle Built for Two. "Please, no whistling," Jack said with a stern look, putting his arm around my waist and pulling me close.

Next, there was a barbershop quartet and a soloist from Lomaland who sang "America, the Beautiful." She was especially talented, and she did Mrs. Tingley proud. Before long, the master of ceremonies led the crowd in singing patriotic songs. Everyone there enthusiastically joined in.

We left the concert early and returned to the boat; both of us were pretty worn out. We hitched a ride aboard a dinghy from another boat owner who was anchored close to ours. When we got back on board the *Serenity*, we set ourselves up on deck with a blanket between us in case it got cold. The warm night was filled with stars and a sliver of a moon.

The small bay was now at capacity; many people had sailed from the mainland to see the fireworks. We could hear the raucous sounds of revelers on the boats around us. Before long, we heard a loud pop that sounded like a cannon shot.

"That's the signal for the start of the fireworks," Jack said. He put a blanket around us, putting his arm around me. I snuggled closer to him, resting his head on his shoulder.

The show began with a burst of fireworks. The effect of the bright bursts of color lighting up the dark sky, with the grand hotel below seen only in silhouette, was magical. There were the usual oohs and ahhs as one firework display outdid the other. Sometimes you heard the sharp cracking of fireworks which drew our attention to fireworks that were set up on the lawn of the hotel. They were interspersed with the ones fired into the sky. Each had different colors and forms, some were displays with star-like bursts, others were like streaming waterfalls of color, and a few were candles shooting off beams of colored light. The first last one fired up right before the finale, was an American flag,

After the last explosion faded, it was very dark—only little white puffs of smoke were left in the sky from the grand finale display—it was so still, like the quiet you might expect after a noisy battle. For a few minutes, everyone sat silently, just listening to the distant strains of the *Star-Spangled Banner* from the orchestra playing in the gazebo in Tent City.

The End

Acknowledgment

I couldn't possibly list all the people who have helped me with this, my first novel, but I will mention a few here.

First of all, I want to acknowledge the help and encouragement I got from my former neighbor Emmet Small, now deceased, who was a lifelong Theosophist, and who was a student at Lomaland as a boy and grew up there during Katherine Tingley's tenure. He was the first one who told me the story of this fascinating social experiment that was once on the Point Loma property where we both lived. He encouraged me to write this book.

Special thanks go to my brother Mike, my nephew Nathan, my friend and coach David Dilworth, my "virgin" readers Marlene Anderson., Theo Jones, Diane Sedlock, and Neil Ledford, my editor Elissa Rabelino, and my tech-coaches Nori, and David.

I'd also like to give a shout-out to those folks who helped me with the historical aspects of this story at the San Diego Historical Society, The Gaslamp Historical Foundation (Sandy Wilhoit), The San Diego Main Public Library, the History and Archives department, the older court records department of the San Diego Superior Court, and the Point Loma Nazarene College Library.

Lomaland

Printed in the USA
CPSIA information can be obtained
at www.ICGtesting.com
LVHW061630131123
763724LV00012B/690